EMERGENCIES AND THE LIMITS OF LEGALITY

Most modern states turn swiftly to law in an emergency. The global response to the 11 September 2001 attacks on the United States was no exception, and the wave of legislative responses is well-documented. Yet there is an ever-present danger, borne out by historical and contemporary events, that even the most well-meaning executive, armed with extraordinary powers, will abuse them. This inevitably leads to another common tendency in an emergency, to invoke law not only to empower the state but also in a bid to constrain it. Can law constrain the emergency state or must the state at times act outside the law when its existence is threatened? If it must act outside the law, is such conduct necessarily fatal to aspirations of legality? This collection of essays – at the intersection of legal, political and social theory and practice – explores law's capacity to constrain state power in times of crisis.

Victor V. Ramraj is an Associate Professor in the Faculty of Law at the National University of Singapore, where he also serves as Vice-Dean for Academic Affairs.

'Combining a subtle appreciation of the complexities with brilliant insights into their resolution, together these essays form an important contribution and an intellectual feast.'

Lucia Zedner, Professor of Criminal Justice, University of Oxford

'This is an unusually fine collection of essays on one of the most important questions in legal and constitutional theory – the propriety of violating legal norms in times of emergency. What makes it especially illuminating is the way that the various essays are very much in dialogue – and sometimes in tension – with one another, as well as the ability of the international cast of essayists to draw from a very broad range of examples.'

Sanford Levinson, Professor of Government,
University of Texas at Austin

EMERGENCIES AND THE LIMITS OF LEGALITY

Edited by

VICTOR V. RAMRAJ

CAMBRIDGE
UNIVERSITY PRESS

CAMBRIDGE UNIVERSITY PRESS
Cambridge, New York, Melbourne, Madrid, Cape Town,
Singapore, São Paulo, Delhi, Tokyo, Mexico City

Cambridge University Press
The Edinburgh Building, Cambridge CB2 8RU, UK

Published in the United States of America by Cambridge University Press, New York

www.cambridge.org
Information on this title: www.cambridge.org/9781107403901

First published 2008
First paperback edition 2011

A catalogue record for this publication is available from the British Library

Library of Congress Cataloguing in Publication Data
Emergencies and the limits of legality / edited by Victor Ramraj.
p. cm.
Includes index.
Includes bibliographical references and index.
ISBN 978-0-521-89599-6
1. War and emergency powers. I. Ramraj, Victor Vridar, 1968– II. Title.
K4700.E42 2008
342′.062 – dc22 2008033577

ISBN 978-0-521-89599-6 Hardback
ISBN 978-1-107-40390-1 Paperback

For Eli and Satchel

CONTENTS

CONTRIBUTORS

R. RUEBAN BALASUBRAMANIAM,
Assistant Professor, Department of Law, Carleton University

COLM CAMPBELL,
Professor of Law, University of Ulster

TOM CAMPBELL,
Professor, Centre for Applied Philosophy and Public Ethics (CAPPE), Charles Sturt University

SIMON CHESTERMAN,
Associate Professor, Faculty of Law, National University of Singapore and Global Professor, New York University School of Law

DAVID DYZENHAUS,
Professor of Law and Philosophy, University of Toronto

OREN GROSS,
Irving Younger Professor of Law, University of Minnesota Law School

JOHAN GEERTSEMA,
Assistant Professor, University Scholars Programme, National University of Singapore

KANISHKA JAYASURIYA,
Principal Senior Research Fellow, Asia Research Centre, Murdoch University

NOMI CLAIRE LAZAR,
Canadian Bicentennial Visiting Assistant Professor, Department of Political Science, Yale University

C.L. LIM,
Professor of Law, University of Hong Kong

TERRY NARDIN,
Professor of Political Science, National University of Singapore

VICTOR V. RAMRAJ,
Associate Professor, Faculty of Law, National University of Singapore

KENT ROACH,
Professor of Law, Prichard and Wilson Chair in Law and Public Policy, University of Toronto

WILLIAM E. SCHEUERMAN,
Professor of Political Science and West European Studies, Indiana University, Bloomington

A.P. SIMESTER,
Professor of Law, National University of Singapore and Fellow, Wolfson College, Cambridge

MARK TUSHNET,
William Nelson Cromwell Professor of Law, Harvard Law School

PREFACE

This volume was inspired by a debate at a symposium in Singapore in 2004 between David Dyzenhaus, who attended the symposium in person, and Oren Gross, who spoke by teleconference. Their debate was later published in a volume I had the privilege of co-editing with Michael Hor and Kent Roach, *Global Anti-Terrorism Law and Policy*, published by Cambridge University Press in 2005. Reflecting on their debate, I became more and more convinced that the legal-theoretical issues they were confronting were likely to become the defining theoretical issues of our generation, and would preoccupy legal theorists for years, and probably decades, to come – in much the same way that the atrocities of World War II were the backdrop against which much of the subsequent twentieth-century jurisprudence developed. The more I reflected on the Gross–Dyzenhaus debate, the more determined I was to provide a forum in which the parameters of this debate could be fully examined, critiqued and challenged by a group of eminent legal, political and social theorists. And so the idea for this project was conceived.

I am especially grateful to David Dyzenhaus and Oren Gross for their enthusiasm from the very start, when I first broached the idea with them in late 2005. Their continued support for this project has been crucial to its completion. Convening an international symposium requires significant financial support, and the funding for this project came from a generous grant from the Ministry of Education, administered by the National University of Singapore (NUS). Thanks are due to NUS, the members of the Faculty Research Committee in the Faculty of Law and to my Dean, Tan Cheng Han, for their support of, and confidence in, this project.

I am also grateful for excellent research and editorial help from a superb team of students – Liu Huijun, Nishan Muthukrishnan, Li Daming, Dennis Tan Chuin Wei, Zhang Rui – and especially Cheryl Fung Shuyin, Teo Jin Huang and Crystal Tan Yan Shi, who provided invaluable assistance at critical stages in the project. I am indebted to my NUS colleagues Michael Hor, Arun Thiruvengadam, C.L. Ten and Alan Khee-Jin Tan for chairing sessions and for their thoughtful interventions at the symposium. Michael also kindly provided a guiding editorial hand on one of the chapters. I also owe Elizabeth Chua and Connie Yew an enormous debt of gratitude for their tireless logistical and administrative support, and their attention to detail.

My parents, Ruby and Victor, and my sister, Sharon (and her then-fiancé, now-husband Rob), graciously agreed to move our family holiday celebrations forward a month so that I could return to Singapore in time for the symposium. I am thankful for this small act of kindness – and deeply appreciative of their love and steadfast support over the years. My wife Sandy was especially understanding and encouraging when this project was at its most demanding. But my gratitude to her also extends much further back. Sandy's probing questions have prompted me to refine my thinking and the beauty of her prose has inspired me – since the day thirteen years ago when our respective interests in legal theory and the printed word brought us together. As E.B. White once wrote, it 'is not often that someone comes along who is a true friend and a good writer'. Like Wilbur, I am lucky to have found someone who is both.

Above all, the flying, no-holds-barred, bowl-me-over hugs that I get from my sons, Eli and Satchel, when I return home from the office – and the hours of uninhibited play, belly-splitting laughter and wondrous conversation that follow – remind me daily of what is most important in life, and help me to keep everything else in perspective.

Victor V. Ramraj
Singapore
December 2007

Introduction

1

No doctrine more pernicious? Emergencies and the limits of legality

VICTOR V. RAMRAJ

I. Introduction

Most modern states turn swiftly to law in times of emergency. The global response to the 11 September 2001 attacks on the United States was no exception and the wave of legislative responses, encouraged by the United Nations Security Council through its Counter-Terrorism Committee, is well-documented.[1] Yet there is an ever-present danger, borne out by historical and contemporary events, that even the most well-meaning executive, armed with emergency powers, will abuse them. And this inevitably leads to another common tendency in an emergency: to invoke law not only to empower the state, but also in a bid to constrain it. This volume explores law's capacity to do so.

Those who are interested in the use of law solely as an instrument of counter-terrorism policy might be inclined at this stage to put this volume promptly back on the shelf. But there are good reasons not to. For one, even in appropriating law as an instrument of counter-terrorism power, states commit to governing through law – and thus commit, in some fashion, to the principle of legality. Understanding the implications of this commitment is one of the primary objectives of this volume. Of course,

I am most grateful to all who made the time to comment on drafts of this introduction, especially Tom Campbell, Simon Chesterman, David Dyzehaus, Johan Geertsema, Sandy Meadow, Terry Nardin, Ruby Ramraj, Victor J. Ramraj, Sharon Ramraj-Thompson, Kent Roach, William E. Scheuerman, A.P. Simester, François Tanguay-Renaud and Arun K. Thiruvengadam.

[1] The Counter-Terrorism Committee, which was set up in the wake of the 9/11 attacks to monitor implementation of Security Council Resolution 1373, requires states to implement a range of legislative counter-terrorism measures. Its country reports, available through its website, provide a useful overview of the range of counter-terrorism legislation enacted after 11 September 2001 (9/11). See www.un.org/sc/ctc/. For a survey of counter-terrorism law and policy post-9/11, see V.V. Ramraj, M. Hor and K. Roach (eds.), *Global Anti-Terrorism Law and Policy* (Cambridge: Cambridge University Press, 2005).

the concept of legality (which is used in this volume interchangeably with the 'rule of law') is itself contentious. For some, it means formal legality, the idea that law implies clear, consistent, stable, prospective rules that are capable of being obeyed and are faithfully applied by public officials; others see legality as encompassing the minimum requirements of the formal account, but also substantive requirements of justice, whether in relation to the economic or political structure of the state or in relation to human rights.[2] Central to both of these conceptions of legality, however, is the notion that any power exercised by the state must be authorised by law.[3] This is the essence of modern, constitutional government.

Emergencies, especially violent emergencies, challenge the state's commitment to govern through law. Can a state confronted with a violent emergency take steps necessary to suppress the emergency while remaining faithful to the demands of legality? Nazi philosopher Carl Schmitt argued, notoriously, that it cannot. In times of crisis, Schmitt insisted, 'the state remains, whereas law recedes'.[4] At most, law could spell out *who* was to exercise emergency powers; it could not, however, set out in advance what would be a necessary or permissible response.[5] Even John Locke's theory of constitutional government, Schmitt observed, perhaps with some justification, could not escape the conclusion that the state, faced with an emergency, required the prerogative to act even 'against the direct Letter of the Law, for the publick good'.[6] Yet others, also sceptical of maintaining legality in a crisis, have looked further back, to the Ancient Roman institution of dictatorship, to find inspiration for a constitutional mechanism that temporarily transfers expansive emergency powers to the executive,

[2] See, for instance, P. Craig, 'Formal and Substantive Conceptions of the Rule of Law: An Analytical Framework' (1997) *Public Law* 467–87. The variations on these two basic models are extensive, and my brief descriptions here are not intended to be exhaustive.

[3] A.V. Dicey, in *Introduction to the Study of the Law of the Constitution*, 8th edn (London: Macmillan, 1920) at 179–201.

[4] G. Schwab (trans.), *Political Theology: Four Chapters on the Concept of Sovereignty* (Chicago: University of Chicago Press, 2005), p. 12.

[5] According to Schmitt, 'The precise details of an emergency cannot be anticipated, nor can one spell out what may take place in such a case, especially when it is truly a matter of extreme emergency and of how it is to be eliminated. The precondition as well as the content of jurisdictional competence in such a case must necessarily be unlimited. From the liberal constitutional point of view, there would be no jurisdictional competence at all. The most guidance the constitution can provide is to indicate who can act in such a case' (*ibid.* at 6–7). See also W.E. Scheuerman, 'Emergency Powers and the Rule of Law After 9/11' (2006) 14 *Journal of Political Philosophy* 61 at 65.

[6] J. Locke, *Two Treatises of Government*, Peter Laslett (ed.) (Cambridge: Cambridge University Press, 1988), p. 377.

which is entrusted with the task of ending the emergency and restoring constitutional order.[7] Even in the absence of a formal constitutional mechanism, many wartime courts have produced the same result, deferring to the executive's determination of what is necessary in an emergency.[8]

All the same, the importance of upholding legality in times of crisis has been eloquently defended by judges around the globe, sometimes in lone dissent,[9] at other times in unanimous resistance to a determined executive. 'In our view', the judges of the Singapore Court of Appeal once held, in reviewing the power of executive detention without trial under the Internal Security Act in *Chng Suan Tze*, 'the notion of a subjective or unfettered discretion is contrary to the rule of law. All power has legal limits and the rule of law demands that the courts should be able to examine the exercise of discretionary power'.[10] Such acts of judicial resistance resonate with the now-famous decision of the US Supreme Court in the Civil War case, *ex parte Milligan*:

> The Constitution of the United States is a law for rulers and people, equally in war and in peace, and covers with the shield of its protection all classes of men, at all times, and under all circumstances. No doctrine, involving more pernicious consequences, was ever invented by the wit of man than that any of its provisions can be suspended during any of the great exigencies of government. Such a doctrine leads directly to anarchy or despotism, but the theory of necessity on which it is based is false; for the government, within the Constitution, has all the powers granted to it, which are necessary to preserve its existence; as has been happily proved by the result of the great effort to throw off its just authority.[11]

But such eloquence is not always successful in checking emergency powers. It is often met with a swift executive or legislative response restoring those powers (as in *Chng Suan Tze*)[12] or comes well after the height of the conflict,

[7] C.L. Rossiter, *Constitutional Dictatorship: Crisis Government in Modern Democracies* (New Brunswick: Transaction Publishers, 2002). See also B. Ackerman, 'The Emergency Constitution' (2004) 113 *Yale Law Journal* 1029; *Before the Next Attack* (New Haven: Yale University Press, 2006).

[8] See, for example, *Liversidge* v. *Anderson*, [1942] AC 206 (HL); *Korematsu* v. *United States*, 323 US 214 (1944), esp. at 223–4.

[9] *Per* Lord Atkin in *Liversidge*, at 225–47, dissenting.

[10] *Chng Suan Tze* v. *Minister of Home Affairs*, [1988] SLR 132 (Singapore CA).

[11] *Ex parte Milligan*, 71 US 2 (1866), at 120–1.

[12] M. Hor, 'Law and Terror: Singapore Stories and Malaysian Dilemmas' in Ramraj, Hor and Roach (eds.), *Global Anti-Terrorism Law and Policy*, pp. 273–94; V.V. Ramraj, 'The *Teh Cheng Poh* Case' in A. Harding and H.P. Lee (eds.), *Constitutional Landmarks in Malaysia* (Kuala Lumpur: LexisNexis 2007), pp. 145–55.

when a measure of normalcy has returned (as was the case in *Milligan*).[13] Even the least controversial legal principles, which are regarded in international law as *jus cogens*, such as the prohibition on torture, can begin to unravel in the face of an emergency.

Many questions have been asked about a state's legal response to an emergency. Are new laws strictly necessary to address the emergency? Do the state's counter-terrorism measures strike the right balance between national security and human rights? What specific legal limits should be placed on the state's response and which rights, if any, are non-derogable even in times of emergency? These are important and contentious questions about which much has been and will continue to be said. But there is good reason to step back and ask a prior question, whether and to what extent *legality* can be preserved[14] when the state responds to an emergency. This is a prior question because, unless legality remains intact, those other important questions – about the need for new laws, the proportionality of the laws to their objectives, and the limitations on those laws – all become moot. It is perhaps for this reason that Schmitt has attracted such close attention in recent years – not because many sympathise with his views on political power, but rather because of the challenge he poses for liberalism, particularly in times of crisis. Can law constrain the state in an emergency or must the state at times act outside the law when its existence is threatened? If it must act outside the law, is such conduct necessarily fatal to aspirations of legality? In short, can liberalism survive an emergency?[15]

The essays in this volume confront these difficult questions and explore a range of theoretical and practical responses to them. They take their inspiration from two attempts to answer these questions by contemporary legal theorists who have studied and written extensively on emergencies

13 Arguably, the belated interventions of the United States Supreme Court in *Hamdi* v. *Rumsfeld*, 124 SCt 2633 (2004), the House of Lords in *A.* v. *Secretary of State for the Home Department* [2004] UKHL 56, [2005] 2 AC 68, and the Supreme Court of Canada in *Charkaoui* v. *Canada (Citizenship and Immigration)* [2007] 1 SCR 350, 2007 SCC 9, all post-9/11, fall into the same category. On the historical record of the courts, see: G.J. Alexander, 'The Illusory Protection of Human Rights by National Courts during Periods of Emergency' (1984), 5 *Human Rights Law Journal* 1; O. Gross and F. Ní Aoláin, 'From Discretion to Scrutiny: Revisiting the Application of the Margin of Appreciation Doctrine in the Context of Article 15 of the European Convention on Human Rights' (2001) 23 *Human Rights Quarterly* 625–49.

14 Framing the issue as one of preservation is itself problematic, for it assumes that the state and its legal and political institutions are largely established. This, however, is not always the case.

15 Scheuerman, 'Emergency Powers'.

and the limits of legality well before 9/11: David Dyzenhaus and Oren Gross. These authors have attempted, both independently and by engaging with one another's work, to articulate in a theoretical and practical way competing models for preserving legality in times of emergency.

In a provocative article in the *Yale Law Journal*,[16] Gross articulates his extra-legal measures model, arguing that it may occasionally be necessary for public officials to step outside the constitutional order to deal with grave dangers and threats, but that doing so need not undermine, and may in fact strengthen, the legal order. Gross explains: 'The model is premised on three essential components: official disobedience, disclosure, and *ex post* ratification. The model calls upon public officials having to deal with catastrophic cases to consider the possibility of acting outside the legal order while openly acknowledging their actions and the extralegal nature of such actions. If a public official determines that a particular case necessitates her deviation from a relevant legal rule, she may choose to depart from the rule'.[17] But Gross insists, and this is crucial to the model, that the rule prohibiting the conduct continues to apply in general, so 'rule departure constitutes, under all circumstances and all conditions, a violation of the relevant legal rule.[18] The consequences of the rule departure, however, are a different question. It is up to 'the people' to decide *ex post* whether to punish the disobedient official for the illegal conduct or to ratify her conduct retrospectively.[19] The uncertainty that public ratification will be forthcoming and the uncertainty of the personal consequences for the official in question even if the conduct were ratified, are together sufficient to deter public officials from abusing their power.

Dyzenhaus challenges the extra-legal measures model arguing that it would permit egregious departures from the principle of legality.[20] He proposes instead that we not give up 'on the idea that law provides moral resources sufficient to maintain the rule-of-law project even when legal and political order is under great stress'.[21] Judges, he insists, have a duty

[16] 'Chaos and Rules: Should Responses to Violent Crises Always be Constitutional?' (2003) 112 *Yale Law Journal* 1011; for further development of his ideas, see 'Stability and flexibility: A Dicey business' in Ramraj, Hor, and Roach (eds.), *Global Anti-Terrorism Law and Policy*, 90–106; O. Gross and F. Ní Aoláin, *Law in Times of Crisis: Emergency Powers in Theory and Practice* (Cambridge: Cambridge University Press, 2006), especially ch. 3.

[17] Gross, 'Stability and Flexibility', at 92. [18] *Ibid.* [19] *Ibid.*

[20] D. Dyzenhaus, 'The State of Emergency in Legal Theory' in Ramraj, Hor, and Roach, (eds), *Global Anti-Terrorism Law and Policy*, 65–89. See also *The Constitution of Legality: Law in a Time of Emergency* (Cambridge: Cambridge University Press, 2006).

[21] Dyzenhaus, *The Constitution of Legality*, p. 19.

to 'uphold a substantive conception of the rule of law'[22] in an emergency. Even when considerations of national security and confidentiality of intelligence sources require a departure from ordinary trial procedures, modern administrative law shows how, through 'imaginative experiments in institutional design',[23] we can deal with emergencies in a way that is consistent with the rule-of-law project and which transcends a rigid separation of powers by developing solutions that include the legislature and the executive. But, maintains Dyzenhaus, 'judges always have some role in ensuring that the rule of law is maintained even when the legislature and the executive are in fact cooperating in the project, and they have an important role when such cooperation wanes or ceases in calling attention to that fact'.[24]

The Gross–Dyzenhaus debate provides a useful starting point for a collection of essays on emergencies and the limits of legality because it sets out, in a compelling and theoretically sophisticated way, two competing approaches to the issue. One approach attempts to subordinate the state's emergency response to principles of legality while attempting to ensure, through the careful and sophisticated redesign of institutions, that the legal regime remains relevant and responsive to the exigencies of the emergency; the other aims to preserve the rule of law in the long-term by subjecting extra-legal measures to democratic and political, not judicial, checks on executive power to ensure that the inevitable exercise of such powers is not legally affirmed and thereby normalised.

This introduction seeks to unpack and clarify the central issues that emerge from the challenge posed to legality in times of emergency. Specifically, and with reference to the essays in this volume, it identifies three sets of issues that arise from this challenge. First, it explores the tension between normative theories that see law as providing a comprehensive and autonomous response to emergency powers and legal realist accounts that point to the limits of the law and the need for other, non-legal constraints. Second, in respect of those theories that affirm law's capacity to constrain emergency powers, it considers the divergence between those theories that emphasise *ex ante* constraints, typically in the form of framework emergency statutes, and those that stress *ex post* constraints, usually through judicial review. Third, it examines the lessons to be learnt from expanding our perspective beyond a contemporary and largely domestic perspective on legality, to include historical approaches to the role of law under

[22] *Ibid.*, at 64. [23] Dyzenhaus, 'The State of Emergency', at 67.
[24] *The Constitution of Legality*, at 201.

colonialism, and the international dimensions of the politics of law. The final section considers how our methodological and theoretical assumptions affect our response to the problem of legality, examining how the assumptions we make about the nature of theoretical inquiry and the intended audience affect our substantive conclusions on the scope and limits of legality in times of emergency.

II. Normative, political and sociological theories

Accounts of legality in times of crisis range from normative theories that defend law's capacity to constrain emergency powers, where legality serves as a 'regulative assumption' that informs and influences practice,[25] to those theories that, wary of law's ability to do so and mindful of the fine line between law and politics, emphasise instead the importance of alternative, non-legal or informal means of constraining the state. As will become clear in the discussion that follows, we can usefully approach these theories by inquiring into the scope and autonomy of law in a state of emergency. How comprehensive is the law's response to the exercise of emergency powers (does law, to paraphrase Mark Tushnet, fill the entire institutional space for evaluating emergency powers[26]) and how independent is law's control over these powers from social and political pressures?

A. Conceptual and normative theories

Consider, for example, normative theories of the rule of law. These theories might begin, as do several of the essays in this collection, with the assumption that a state is committed to governing through law, and then explore the conceptual and normative implications of that commitment. Dyzenhaus argues, for instance, that unless we commit to governing through law in an emergency, we are forced into either an internal or external realist position, neither of which is satisfactory, even for legal positivists.[27] An internal realist position undermines law's claim to authority by creating a veneer of legality over what is really the exercise of power by the political elite; an external realist position holds that the sovereign's power is not ultimately constrained by law. For the external legal realist, the state's

[25] Dyzenhaus, 'The Compulsion of Legality', Chapter 2, this volume, pp. 50–1.
[26] 'The Political Constitution of Emergency Powers: Some Conceptual Issues' (Chapter 6), this volume, p. 146.
[27] Dyzenhaus, Chapter 2.

authority comes from a political, not a legal constitution. But this position is problematic, because it undermines the assumption shared by positivists and non-positivists alike that the state is 'completely constituted by law'.[28]

In his contribution to this volume, Terry Nardin advances a similarly non-instrumental conception of the rule of law, according to which the rule of law 'implies a moral standard, one derived not from an arbitrary notion of the good but from the idea of human beings as autonomous persons who articulate their own conceptions of the good'.[29] Distinguishing this conception of morality 'from theories like political realism or utilitarianism, which understand rules in instrumental terms as expedients for bringing about desired states of affairs',[30] Nardin argues that an 'escape clause for emergencies, by allowing moral rules to be overridden by prudential considerations, obscures what is distinctive of the moral point of view'.[31] Laws forbidding torture cannot be set aside, 'because they express a moral rule' which cannot be 'altered or nullified by an act of will'[32] and, argues Nardin, public officials have no authority to waive them. For Nardin, the rule of law as a moral idea constrains the ability of public officials to justify extra-legal conduct taken for the public good since the justification for doing so is neither legal nor moral, but instrumental or prudential. But prudential reasons 'cannot "justify" illegal or immoral action if that word is to retain its core meaning as making an act just within a framework of legal or moral prescriptions'.[33] The argument here is a conceptual one, and Nardin insists that the idea of illegal action in an emergency cannot be reconciled *conceptually* with the rule of law.[34]

Along similar lines, Rueban Balasubramaniam,[35] using the experience of indefinite detention in Malaysia and Singapore by way of illustration and drawing on Lon Fuller's work, argues that liberal democracies, in attempting to reconcile indefinite detention with the rule of law, risk undermining the values of 'liberal political morality' to which they are otherwise committed.[36] Specifically, Balasubramaniam argues that an 'attempt to construct and maintain legal order as a stable framework for the

[28] *Ibid.*, p. 58.

[29] 'Emergency Logic: Prudence, Morality, and the Rule of Law' (Chapter 4), this volume, p. 103.

[30] *Ibid.*, p. 109. The act of founding a legal order, however, is 'necessarily extra-legal, a matter of expediency for the sake of a substantive end (in this case, establishing the rule of law itself), not a matter of legality (governing within the rules of an established legal order)' (at 105).

[31] *Ibid.*, p. 109. [32] *Ibid.*, p. 110. [33] *Ibid.*, p. 111. [34] *Ibid.*

[35] 'Indefinite Detention: Rule by Law or Rule of Law?' (Chapter 5), this volume.

[36] *Ibid.*, p. 119.

guidance of conduct involves a moral dimension that constrains the law-giver's capacity to use law for authoritarian purposes, because legal order is a reciprocal enterprise requiring cooperation between lawgiver and legal subject'.[37] Once a government commits to operating 'on the rule-of-law continuum, it cannot assert rule *by* law without contradicting its commitment to legality'.[38]

Nardin and Balasubramaniam share with Dyzenhaus a common goal, to draw out the implications for emergency governance of a state's commitment to govern through law. They also share Fuller's belief that a commitment to legality includes, but goes beyond, a commitment to clear, stable, accessible, prospective, consistent rules that are capable of being obeyed and faithfully enforced.[39] And their conception of legality also involves – whether conceptually, as Nardin explicitly argues, or normatively, as Balasubramaniam implies – a model of the rule of law that includes a substantive commitment to respect the rights of legal subjects, even in times of emergency. Normative theories would tend to regard law as providing a comprehensive and autonomous response to emergency powers, but they need not collapse in the face of a 'legal black hole'.[40] Rather, confronted with this reality, says Dyzenhaus, judges should strive to resist any attempt by the executive to govern beyond the reaches of the law.[41] Law is not necessarily comprehensive in its scope, but aspires to be so; it aspires to be autonomous, at least in the sense that it is independent from other considerations, including political ones.[42]

This picture of legality might be challenged in several ways, which variously question law's claim to comprehensive and autonomous control of the state in an emergency. For example, it might be challenged on the ground that black holes do not violate every aspect of the rule of law since the perimeters of the black hole and the conduct that places one into it might be clearly defined in advance. In this case, argues A.P. Simester, the requirement of prospectivity would be met, so those held

[37] *Ibid.*, p. 131. [38] *Ibid.*, p. 135 (emphasis added).

[39] L.L. Fuller, *The Morality of Law* (New Haven: Yale University Press, 1969).

[40] J. Steyn, 'Guantanamo Bay: The Legal Black Hole' (2004) 53 *International and Comparative Law Quarterly* 1.

[41] Dyzenhaus, Chapter 2, p. 55.

[42] This aspirational quality may well be a positive feature of the rule of law, as Johan Geertsema observes in 'Exceptions, bare life and colonialism' (Chapter 14), this volume: 'Like democracy, the rule of law is a project that can in principle never arrive, for the political process of actively interrogating, negotiating, and reflecting that is constitutive of democracy if it were, or were thought, to have arrived' (p. 358).

within the legal black hole would 'not be able to complain about lack of notice when they deliberately jump'.[43] This argument suggests that the reach of the law can be less than comprehensive and yet it might still conform to at least some of the requirements of legality. Alternatively, a normative model of legality might be challenged on the ground that the law's apparent inability to constrain the state in practice means that democratic, rather than legal, constraints are necessary. Specifically, Gross challenges Dyzenhaus's characterisation of the extra-legal measures model as a 'lawless void'[44] – a legal black hole in which the state acts unconstrained by law. The model, he insists, does not create a black hole; rather, it 'seeks to preserve the long-term relevance of, and obedience to, legal principles, rules, and norms' by showing how 'going outside the law in appropriate cases may preserve, rather than undermine, the rule of law in ways that constantly bending the law to accommodate emergencies and crises will not'.[45] It permits a 'little wrong' (going outside the legal order) to attain a 'great right, namely the preservation not only of the constitutional order, but also of its most fundamental principles and tenets'.[46] To substantiate his claim that actions taken by public officials under the extra-legal measures model do not take place in a legal void, Gross returns to the process of ratification, arguing that the law remains intact, as one benchmark against which to judge the conduct in question; yet the legal, social and political response might be different in times of crisis.[47] Drawing on an ethic of political responsibility on the part of public officials, he insists that those who engage in official disobedience remain answerable to the public for their actions, and that the uncertain prospect of ratification remains a formidable deterrent for public officials, in the grip of an emergency, who are considering resorting to extra-legal measures.

B. Political and sociological theories

Gross shares with normative theorists an aspiration to legality, but finds in law's inability to constrain the state a practical need for a non-legal

[43] 'Necessity, Torture and the Rule of Law' (Chapter 12), this volume, p. 311. 'One should certainly object to black holes', Simester argues, but the 'core of the objection needs no rule-of-law label. . . . If it is wrong to torture people, it is wrong [for the state] to empower people to torture' (p. 312).

[44] D. Dyzenhaus, *The Constitution of Law*, p. 1.

[45] O. Gross, 'Extra-Legality and the Ethic of Political Responsibility' (Chapter 3), this volume, p. 62.

[46] *Ibid.* [47] *Ibid.*, p. 64.

check on power. Others, however, articulate a more thorough-going scepticism concerning law's ability to constrain state power in an emergency and, more generally, the autonomy of law. Mark Tushnet,[48] for instance, argues that both Dyzenhaus *and* Gross rely too heavily on law to regulate emergency powers. Even in his so-called extra-legal measure model, Gross 'is committed to the proposition that law occupies the entire institutional space of normative evaluation of emergency powers'.[49] In contrast, Tushnet argues that the possibility of a 'moralized politics' in which political leaders within the institutions of government and in civil society 'appeal for support on the basis of moral claims in addition to appeal for support from constituents non-moral preferences'[50] can fill rule-of-law gaps or black holes and constrain the exercise of emergency powers. By way of illustration, Tushnet argues that the emergence of 'rule of law' procedural fairness requirements with the system of combatant status review tribunals in the United States can best be explained not by the slim prospect that the courts would evaluate these tribunals, but rather by reference to bureaucratic and professional interests, including codes of military honour and military lawyers' discomfort with procedural informality.[51] These are, of course, contingent factors, but, for Tushnet, the poor record of the courts suggests that sociological and political constraints may well have a significant role to play in constraining emergency powers.

Nomi Lazar,[52] for her part, highlights the importance of agency and discretion as well as informal constraints on power in response to emergencies. In stark contrast with Nardin's non-instrumental conception of law, Lazar begins with the proposition that the rule of law and the structure of institutions are instrumental to the attainment of other ends, including the prevention of tyranny. She argues not only that formal constraints are insufficient means for constraining power, but also that discretion and informal power well-used can further the aims of good government, even in times of emergency. Lazar is conscious that agency and discretion can be abused. But so too, she argues, can strict conformity to the rule of law, citing Indira Gandhi's invocation of emergency powers in 1975, which 'conformed exactly to [the] procedural requirements' but 'resulted in gross and arbitrary abuses of power'.[53] By the same token, 'the formal constraint of power can sometimes hamper the necessary and positive effects of power well-used'.[54] The problem with Dyzenhaus's argument,

[48] Chapter 6. [49] *Ibid.*, p. 146. [50] *Ibid.*, p. 151. [51] *Ibid.*, p. 155.
[52] 'A Topography of Emergency Power' (Chapter 7), this volume. [53] *Ibid.*, p. 166.
[54] *Ibid.*, p. 167.

says Lazar, is that it places too much faith in judges to preserve the rule-of-law project. But the effectiveness of judges itself depends on conditions of informal power; so 'it is not just the weakness of judges, but also the power of rhetoric and popular support [that determines] whether a matter will ever come before a judge'.[55] The problem common to Dyzenhaus's and Gross's theories is that both authors fail to acknowledge the central role that 'informal means of constraint and enablement' have in relation to emergency powers.[56]

According to Tushnet and Lazar, then, factors apart from the law, such as politics, informal power and discretion, operate to regulate and constrain state power in an emergency. There are stronger and weaker versions of this challenge to the scope and autonomy of law. Stronger versions would deny both that law is comprehensive (denying, perhaps, its reach in an emergency) and that it is autonomous (asserting, for instance, that law should not always trump other considerations). Schmitt's challenge to liberalism, which denies law's capacity to survive an emergency, is perhaps the strongest version of this claim. Weaker versions might deny the comprehensive coverage or the autonomy of law in emergency situations, viewing emergency measures, with Gross, as regulated not primarily by law but through informal constraints on power. Tushnet's account of the sociological and political constraints on the detention of 'enemy combatants' by the United States post-9/11 could also be interpreted as a claim of this sort.

On the other hand, Tushnet's more general claim that concepts such as the rule of law 'cannot succeed at all without sociology and politics at their back'[57] could be interpreted as consistent with normative theory, if what he is claiming is that legality requires a particular institutional and political culture to support it. Dyzenhaus seems to say as much when he accepts, as a precondition for judicial deference, the need for a 'culture of justification' – a legal culture which comes about 'when a political order accepts that all official acts, all exercises of state power, are legal only on condition that they are justified by law, where law is understood in an expansive sense, that is, as including fundamental commitments such as those entailed by the principle of legality and respect for human rights'.[58] It is also consistent with his argument in this volume that the 'liberal aspiration to have the rule of law rather than the rule of men requires

[55] *Ibid.*, p. 170. [56] *Ibid.* [57] Chapter 6, p. 155.

[58] See D. Dyzenhaus, 'Deference, Security and Human Rights' in B. Goold and L. Lazarus (eds.), *Security and Human Rights* (Hart Publishing: Oxford, 2007), p. 137 and n. 27, referring to the work of Etienne Mureinik.

not only a political struggle to subordinate politics to the rule of law, but also a political struggle within practice about how that is best done'.[59] Some versions of a sociological challenge to the autonomy of law might therefore be compatible with some normative theories of legality in times of emergency.

Sociological approaches need not, however, be sceptical of the role law plays in constraining power, as Colm Campbell's contribution shows. Along with Tushnet and Lazar, Campbell adopts an overtly sociological perspective on law, but not with a view to questioning law's ability to constrain the state; rather, he asks what signals the state sends dissident groups when it 'takes off the gloves'[60] – an inquiry into the impact of law on society from the perspective of social movement theory. Drawing on empirical data from Northern Ireland, Campbell shows how the indiscriminate use of emergency powers 'can have radicalizing effects by reinforcing a sense of membership of a victimized community, particularly in quasi-ethnic conflicts'.[61] Abuses of state powers that take place within a 'grey zone of conflict' in a rule-of-law state can lead to violent activism and, correspondingly, a visible commitment to legality on the part of the state can have an 'indirect damping effect' on the conflict.[62] According to Campbell, Dyzenhaus's rule-of-law approach demonstrates the relatively autonomous quality of law and shows how 'an ideological commitment to the rule of law can open some ground for legal challenge, even if it is likely to be weighted in favour of powerful social forces'.[63] Campbell expresses concern, however, about the messages that are sent when, as in Gross's model, the illegal conduct of a public official is publicly ratified. Such ratification is 'likely to enhance the salience and resonance within affected communities of the "injustice frames" and "rights-violation frames" articulated by violent challenger organisations, and therefore the viability of such groups' framing processes'.[64] The empirical data, Campbell argues, does not support the extra-legal measures model.

Most of the essays in this volume and indeed most accounts of the role of law in an emergency could, as a rough-and-ready classification, be plotted on a spectrum indicative of their respective degrees of confidence in the

[59] Chapter 2, p. 39. Similarly, William E. Scheuerman's account in this volume might be seen as an attempt to acknowledge sociological and institutional pressures on legality in an emergency, while maintaining that executive power can nonetheless be held in check through statutory and constitutional (although not primarily judicial) means: see 'Presidentialism and Emergency Government,' Chapter 11, this volume.

[60] 'Law, Terror, and Social Movements: The Repression–Mobilisation Nexus' (Chapter 8), this volume, p. 184.

[61] *Ibid.*, p. 186. [62] *Ibid.*, p. 188. [63] *Ibid.* [64] *Ibid.*, p. 190.

ability of law to constrain state power in an emergency. Some contributors do not see the law as able to constrain state power either for the political and sociological reasons just considered or, as we shall see, by reference to the complex geopolitical context in which law is invoked.[65] Most do think the law plays some role.[66] But even for those who hold some faith in law's ability to constrain the emergency state, an important cleavage separates those who see law as offering a suite of prospective constraints on emergency powers and those that view it as responding to the exercise of those powers after the fact.

III. Legal constraints on power: the temporal dimension

Even if law does or ought to play a central role in constraining state power in an emergency, it must yet be determined whether *ex ante* limits on state power, *ex post* checks, or some combination of the two is preferable. Specific, prior constraints on state power enhance certainty and predictably in times of heightened fear and emotion, and *ex ante* limitations are consistent with the demand of legality that any exercise of power – particularly coercive power – by the state be authorised by law. And yet, doubts persist. Although it might be true that our inability to anticipate the exigencies of any particular emergency is overstated by Schmitt and others,[67] there may yet be a need for flexibility to enable the state to respond and adapt quickly to the unique challenges of any particular emergency. *Ex post* checks on state power address this concern by allowing public officials to react, but then holding them accountable after the fact, legally or politically. This part of the chapter explores the parameters of these arguments in the context of the essays in this volume.

A. Prospective constraints on state power

Gross's extra-legal measures model is expressly based on *ex post* constraints on power.[68] And while Dyzenhaus, with Dicey, prefers *ex ante* constraints

[65] See K. Jayasuriya, 'Struggle over Legality in the Midnight Hour: Governing the International State of Emergency' (Chapter 15), and C.L. Lim, '*Inter Arma Silent Leges?* Black Hole Theories of the Laws of War' (Chapter 16), this volume.

[66] This includes not only the authors already mentioned, but also Johan Geertsema, Chapter 14.

[67] Scheuerman, 'Emergency Powers and the Rule of Law After 9/11'.

[68] Gross specifically addresses the temporal issue in Chapter 3, p. 64ff.

on power where governments have adequate time to craft them,[69] he acknowledges, again echoing Dicey, that in times of emergency, it may be necessary for the executive to act first, and seek legal permission retrospectively. They might, for example, 'justify themselves by a defence of necessity', in which case their actions had 'prior legal authorization in that they act on a correct appreciation of what the common law of necessity permits them to do'.[70] Alternatively, they might seek an Act of Indemnity, 'to bring them back within the law, to legalize their illegality, as long as what they did was both reasonable and not recklessly cruel'.[71] What distinguishes their responses to emergencies, then, is not primarily the temporal dimension of the constraints on power they advocate, but their adherence to the rule of law.

In his contribution, Tom Campbell states up front his wariness of the 'constant temptation in legal theory and in the practice of politics to expand the "rule of law" concept to contain norms such as substantive equality, material justice and various fundamental rights so that good form can be combined with good substance in a more pervasive constitutional bedrock'.[72] Rather, he explores the implications of his own positivist theory, *prescriptive legal positivism*, for emergency powers. According to prescriptive legal positivism, a government can best serve the common good and the 'interests of the vast majority of individuals when that government is conducted through law and that law is conceived in formal terms as authoritative rules that are expressed in general, clear, specific and prospective terms which can be understood and applied without drawing on controversial moral or speculative judgments'.[73] For Campbell, prescriptive legal positivism is consistent with a carefully crafted emergency powers regime which defines an emergency in precise, empirical terms, and specifies the powers that can be exercised when such an emergency arises.[74] Courts can usefully supervise the executive to ensure compliance with such formally good laws, but Campbell is sceptical of judicial review on the basis of fundamental constitutional rights, where 'out of

[69] See 'State of Emergency in Legal Theory' where he argues that 'governments that have the luxury of time to craft a response to emergency situations should do so in a way that complies with the rule of law' (at 83).

[70] Dyzenhaus, Chapter 2, p. 46. [71] *Ibid.*, p. 47.

[72] 'Emergency Strategies for Prescriptive Legal Positivists: Anti-Terrorist Law and Legal Theory' (Chapter 9), this volume, p. 205.

[73] *Ibid.*, p. 206.

[74] Compare K. Roach, 'Ordinary Laws for Emergencies and Democratic Derogations from Rights' (Chapter 10), this volume.

touch constitutional courts' may be 'insufficiently responsive to changed and catastrophic circumstances'.[75] So while Campbell is sympathetic to Dyzenhaus's attempt to subordinate emergencies to legality, he rejects the priority Dyzenhaus accords to judicial, rather than political, judgments. At the same time, he finds Gross's extra-legal measures model inadequate in as much as it permits public officials what Campbell regards as an 'unfettered power' which 'departs from key ingredients of the rule of positive law, particularly the prospectivity required of formally good law'.[76] To the extent, then, that law is able to do so, and Campbell is confident that it is, it should specify *ex ante* what the executive is empowered to do and prohibited from doing in an emergency.

Kent Roach is critical of much of the post-9/11 literature on emergency powers for neglecting non-violent emergencies.[77] But like Tom Campbell, he believes that emergency legislation can be drafted prospectively in anticipation of a broad range of emergencies. Roach provides a critical survey of what he refers to as the 'ordinary law of emergencies' in the United States (the National Emergency Act), the United Kingdom (the Civil Contingencies Act) and Canada (the Emergencies Act). He argues that the best practices exemplified in these statutes show how, through the use of *ex ante* restrictions and *ex post* checks involving all branches of government and (contrary to Tom Campbell[78]) the 'creative hybrids of different branches' suggested by Dyzenhaus,[79] the state can be effectively supervised and held accountable for its use of emergency powers. Where these ordinary laws are insufficient, however, Roach argues (again contrary to Campbell) that a temporary derogation from rights which is subject to *ex post* legislative and judicial review and is 'designed to maximize both political and legal deliberation about the justifications for derogation' is preferable to Gross's extra-legal measures model, which 'gives each member of the executive a discretion to decide when it is necessary to dispense with rights and laws in order to deal with an emergency'.[80]

Although his starting point differs from Tom Campbell's and Kent Roach's, William Scheuerman[81] reaches a similar conclusion concerning the need for constitutional or statutory pre-constraints on emergency powers. Scheuerman argues that both Gross and Dyzenhaus overlook the special challenges posed by presidentialism for liberal-democratic responses to emergencies. Presidentialism poses a special challenge because the 'incentives for declaring and perpetuating emergencies are particularly

[75] Chapter 9, p. 221. [76] *Ibid.*, p. 224. [77] Chapter 10. [78] Chapter 9, p. 220.
[79] Chapter 10, p. 256. [80] *Ibid.*, p. 257. [81] Chapter 11.

pronounced in the context of presidential regimes'.[82] By the same token, the ability of the President in times of crisis to define the terms of the political debate means that the prospect of a public debate over extra-legal measures taken by the executive will not have the deterrent effect Gross hopes it will. Dyzenhaus too, in relying on judicial checks on executive power, fails to appreciate the conservative tendencies of the common law tradition, which render the courts unable to provide an effective check on emergency power, particularly in Presidential systems:

> Congenital structural tendencies, which drive the president incessantly to expand emergency discretion means that the courts always lag behind, its review powers always outpaced in an institutional competition which the courts cannot possibly win: before our cautious common law judges have even begun to grapple with the ramifications of the last round of presidential emergency decrees, the executive has already undertaken new ones.[83]

It is better, Scheuerman argues, invoking Bruce Ackerman's recent proposal,[84] to introduce 'properly designed constitutional mechanisms... [that] establish useful prospective legal guidelines for emergency authority, help to create separation between ordinary and extraordinary law and provide standards by which we can delineate legal from illegal emergency government'.[85] Scheuerman's argument is not, he insists, that the 'institutional realities of presidential democracy preclude the achievement of the rule of law, but only that Dyzenhaus's overtly court-centred vision of the rule of law is likely to fail at effectively countering the pathologies of emergency government in the context of presidential democracy'.[86]

B. Judicial responses to official disobedience

There are, it seems, persuasive arguments in favour of *ex ante* constraints on state power: prospective constraints, if carefully crafted, promote liberty by making the exercise of state power more predictable and enable the state to respond to emergencies more effectively since the parameters of and limits on its powers are fixed in advance. Yet even outside the emergency context, modern administrative law reminds us of a corollary concern – the need for flexibility and discretion in the implementation of the law. All the more so, it would seem, in an emergency. Gross's appeal for flexibility[87] and

[82] *Ibid.*, p. 264. [83] *Ibid.*, p. 277.
[84] 'The Emergency Constitution' and *Before the Next Attack.*
[85] Chapter 11, p. 279. [86] *Ibid.*, p. 285.
[87] See Gross, 'Stability and Flexibility', and his arguments in this volume, Chapter 3.

Lazar's account of the need for discretion[88] are, in this respect, attractive. And if Gross is right that, in practice, official disobedience will inevitably take place, it is necessary to consider how to respond *ex post* to apparent excesses of state power in an emergency.

Notwithstanding the contested scope of legality, even the most parsimonious accounts of that concept hold that public officials are legally accountable for their misdeeds just as any other citizen.[89] A public official who disobeys the law in the name of national security (say, by torturing a terrorist suspect to prevent an apparently imminent threat) is subject to the ordinary law of the land, including the criminal law, as anyone else would be – unless, that is, she has a defence. But this approach to legality and official disobedience concerns Gross, who worries that legal recognition of such a defence is dangerous as it would normalise acts of official disobedience, including torture.[90] For Gross, the solution is an absolute prohibition on torture, coupled with his extra-legal measures model, which would leave open the possibility of public ratification of official disobedience in an extreme and tragic case. Dyzenhaus also insists on an absolute prohibition on torture, which he regards as 'unlegalizable,' but he makes this allowance: if 'officials consider that they have to torture to avoid a catastrophe – the ticking time bomb situation – such an act must happen extra-legally... All a court should say is that if officials are going to torture they should expect to be criminally charged and may try a defence of necessity'.[91]

Yet the availability of necessity in such cases is contentious, as Simester argues.[92] One view is that necessity could be invoked by public officials if the harm they were trying to avert (e.g., the detonation of a ticking time bomb) is greater than the harm they would inflict (e.g., torture). But this 'lesser evils' approach, as a 'fall-back, catch-all principle of ordinary law', poses serious rule-of-law difficulties – difficulties that Simester seeks to avoid.[93] So he argues for a conception of necessity as a rationale-based justification which focuses on the actor's reasons for acting. On this approach, Simester argues, most putative reasons for torture would be excluded. As for whether necessity or duress could be invoked as an excuse, Simester insists that, as a 'concession to human frailty',[94] it would

88 Chapter 7. 89 Dyzenhaus, *Law of the Constitution*, pp. 189–90.

90 O. Gross, 'Are Torture Warrants Warranted? Pragmatic Absolutism and Official Disobedience' (2004) 88 *Minn. L. Rev* 1481.

91 Dyzenhaus, 'The State of Emergency in Legal Theory', at 84. 92 Chapter 12.

93 *Ibid.*, p. 293. 94 *Ibid.*, p. 300, citing *Howe* [1987] 1 AC 417 at 432–5.

not be open to public officials – in their public capacity – to invoke it. Simester's analysis suggests that there is limited scope for a public official to act in a prima facie illegal way and claim a defence of necessity.

Simon Chesterman offers a different solution to the dilemmas faced by public officials in times of emergency.[95] He begins by challenging the practicality of Gross's extra-legal measures model, focusing on the covert nature of executive counter-terrorism measures. Specifically, he disputes Gross's claim that public officials have, on the extra-legal measures model, an incentive to come clean with their conduct in a way that facilitates public deliberation and accountability. Drawing on contemporary examples of counter-terrorism measures in the United States, including the use of aggressive interrogation methods bordering on torture, extraordinary rendition, secret detention centres and warrantless electronic surveillance, Chesterman argues that the possibility of *ex post* ratification is unlikely to be 'a practical constraint on otherwise unlawful behaviour that is normally intended to be shielded from public scrutiny'.[96] Instead, he proposes that official misconduct of the sort Gross describes is better handled through mitigation, whereby a formal legal sanction is imposed with a minimal penalty.[97] Unlike Gross, Chesterman does not believe that the prospect of ratification creates an incentive on the part of the executive to disclose 'alleged wrongs perpetrated in the name of national security'.[98] The advantage of a mitigation approach, claims Chesterman, is that by requiring a judicial process, it 'reduces the danger of an executive asserting for itself the right to approve conduct that is never scrutinized'.[99]

While Simester and Chesterman both address the legal principles by which the courts, viewing the conduct retrospectively, can respond to official disobedience, it is important to bear in mind that as between the two accounts, only mitigation is clearly an *ex post* response. For as Dyzenhaus observes, a defence of necessity, if accepted, represents a judicial affirmation of the 'prior legal authorization' of their conduct in the common law.[100] In contrast, for Chesterman, constraints operate *ex post* when the courts, moved perhaps by the plight of public officials confronted with tragic choices in an emergency, mitigate the penalties imposed. At least in this temporal respect, Chesterman's approach mirrors the extra-legal measures model; rather than specifying *ex ante* the circumstances in which

[95] 'Deny Everything: Intelligence Activities and the Rule of Law' (Chapter 13), this volume.
[96] *Ibid.*, p. 315. [97] *Ibid.*, pp. 327–32. [98] *Ibid.*, p. 332. [99] *Ibid.*
[100] See note 69.

public officials may depart from ordinary legal principles in time of crisis, the courts should respond *ex post*, crafting an appropriate response to specific instances of official disobedience while leaving the legal prohibition intact.

The tension between prospective statutory constraints or retrospective judicial checks on emergency powers should not be overstated, for as most accounts recognise, it is possible, even desirable, to have both. At the same time, though, neither form of constraint is immune from political manipulation. Prospective constraints can be interpreted narrowly when invoked in the heat of a crisis, as the Bush administration's interpretation of the post-9/11 Congressional Authorization for the Use of Military Force to detain terrorist suspects in Guantánamo Bay and subsequent litigation of these measures shows.[101] But if the politics of law tests our confidence in the capacity of law to constrain state power in the domestic sphere, it threatens to undermine our confidence altogether where neo-colonial agendas and *realpolitik* collide with aspirations of legality in the international sphere.

IV. Post-colonial and international perspectives

Our discussion of emergencies thus far has focused on domestic conceptions of legality, largely in a contemporary setting. But as chapters by Johan Geertsema, C.L. Lim and Kanishka Jayasuriya remind us, it is crucial to look beyond the domestic and contemporary sphere in considering the problem of legality. For one thing, the experience of colonialism – including the Jamaica affair,[102] to which many of the chapters refer – reminds us not just of the potential dangers of legality, but also of its capacity to serve as a safeguard against abuses of state power, a point stressed by Dyzenhaus and Geertsema. These chapters expose what we would today call the *global* dimensions of law that Jayasuriya explores in his chapter, and the complexities of international legality that Lim stresses.

Geertsema is critical of attempts to simplify the colonial legal experience by focusing too narrowly on the lawlessness and violence of the moment of conquest or regarding the colonies as zones of exception, arguing that such views overlook 'the complexities involved in the dialectic between the colonial and the indigenous that resulted in the emergence of the colonial

[101] The scope of the Authorization of the Use of Military Force was the subject of litigation in the United States Supreme Court's first significant post-9/11 case, *Hamdi* v. *Rumsfeld*.

[102] See R. Kostal, *A Jurisprudence of Power* (Oxford: Oxford University Press, 2005).

state' and neglect 'the role that law itself played in . . . colonial violence'.[103] At the same time, however, he recognises the dangers involved in reacting to the colonial experience by underestimating the role law can play in preventing the reduction of persons to 'bare life' – a term he borrows from Giorgio Agamben.[104] An examination of the experience of colonialism, Geertsema argues, 'encourages us to resist the temptation of limiting the reach of the rule of law' and 'alerts us to the tendency of the exception to produce bare life' which renders people expendable.[105]

While the colonial experience reminds us that legal discourse remains today, as it was before, transnational, contributions by Lim and Jayasuriya confront squarely the complex international and transnational dimensions of contemporary emergency powers. Jayasuriya explores the 'intriguing parallels with metropolitan responses to colonial emergencies within the liberal British empire'[106] and argues that the post-9/11 international state of emergency has resulted in a 'hybrid domain of emergency governance that cuts across and beyond the boundaries of liberal constitutionalism'.[107] By disrupting nationally-defined constitutional structures, the international state of emergency opens the door to a 'jurisdictional politics'[108] in which new, contested legal categories (such as 'enemy combatant') and spaces emerge which are distinct from ordinary law. Along similar lines, Lim criticises Gross's extra-legal measures model and Dyzenhaus's legality model for paying insufficient attention to the complexity of international legality. Specifically, he argues that both theories adopt what he called a 'flat' view of international legality which takes, for instance, the prohibition on torture as 'an absolute and unchanging international perception of acceptable conduct'.[109] Lim rejects this model as unrealistic and unreflective of the actual practice of international law. Through a close examination of the Bush administration's legal manoeuvres on the applicability of the Geneva Conventions to suspected terrorists and non-conventional combatants and in relation to the international prohibition on torture, Lim argues that a comprehensive theory of domestic legality in times of crisis must account for the 'textured' nature of international legality, which recognises its creative and doctrinally contested character. We need to pay much closer attention, then, to the interplay between

[103] Chapter 14, this volume, p. 355.
[104] D. Heller-Roazen (trans.), *Homo Sacer: Sovereign Power and Bare Life* (Stanford: Stanford University Press, 1998).
[105] Chapter 14, p. 356. [106] Chapter 15, this volume, p. 362. [107] *Ibid.*, p. 364.
[108] See L. Benton, *Law and Colonial Cultures* (New York: Cambridge University Press, 2002).
[109] Chapter 16, this volume, p. 399.

the 'jurisdictional politics' of international legal norms and practice, and domestic conceptions of legality in an emergency.

The importance of this international dimension of legality can be seen in the way that contemporary counter-terrorism efforts typically extend across national boundaries; and national counter-terrorism measures are increasingly subject to international scrutiny by human rights bodies, including the Counter-Terrorism Committee mentioned at the outset of this chapter, whose human rights mandate has also become much stronger. Equally, the importance of reflecting on the role of legality in colonial settings is evident given charges of neo-imperialism[110] in post-conflict reconstruction contexts, in which the rule-of-law rhetoric is particularly strong. These charges of neo-imperialism suggest the need to be alert to the dangers of hegemony and legal transplantation. Unless the lessons of colonial legality are properly understood, argues Geertsema, the 'imperial exception' threatens to 'locate authority outside legality' thereby undermining 'the very values that the (neo-)colonial empire was meant to export'.[111] Yet, if the rule of law can be theorised in a minimalist (though not necessarily formal) manner that is responsive to local needs and respectful of cultural sensitivities, it may yet make a positive difference where abuses of state power in the name of national security are prevalent.

V. The scope and limits of legality

The essays in this volume represent a collaborative attempt, through different disciplinary and methodological lenses, to explore the scope and limits of legality in times of emergency – to reflect on the promise of the law in constraining state power and on its conceptual and practical limits. This introductory chapter has identified three significant issues that arise from the problem of legality in times of emergency, relating to the scope and autonomy of the law in an emergency, the choice between *ex ante* and *ex post* mechanisms for controlling emergency powers and the neo-colonial and international dimensions of legality. The arrangement of the essays in this volume into parts reflects these themes. But there are, of course, other important themes and concerns that cut across the various chapters and parts. For instance, the tension between positivist

[110] J. Stromseth, D. Wippman and R. Brooks, 'Introduction: A New Imperialism?' (ch. 1) in *Can Might Make Rights? Building the Rule of Law after Military Interventions* (New York: Cambridge University Press, 2006), pp. 1–17.

[111] Chapter 14, p. 359.

and non-positivist theories of law surfaces in several chapters; we might, for instance, contrast Dyzenhaus's non-positivist approach with Tom Campbell's prescriptive legal positivism. The legal (or extra-legal) acceptability of torture in the most extreme cases (the so-called 'ticking time bomb' scenario) is another common concern, featured in chapters by Dyzenhaus, Gross, Simester, Chesterman and Lim. We might also, taking the lead from Tom Campbell and Kent Roach, hone in on the contentious notion of 'emergency', in its conceptual, normative and historical dimensions, to clarify its boundaries and coherence.[112] In this section, I consider the significance of methodological approaches to the way we understand legality in times of emergency before concluding with a brief caveat on the scope of this volume.

A. Methodological approaches and disciplinary perspectives

How might our methodological approaches and disciplinary perspectives shape our response to the limits of legality in times of emergency? There is, of course, a broad spectrum of approaches that might be employed in examining the scope and limits of legality – from a formal, legal, a priori approach to a contextual, political, empirical one. We have already observed the contrast between the normative approach to emergency powers employed by Dyzenhaus, Nardin and Balasubramaniam, on the one hand, and the sociological and institutional approaches adopted by Tushnet, Lazar, Colm Campbell and Scheuerman, on the other. The normative theories we have seen tend to adopt an internal legal perspective, asking questions about the normative implications of a commitment to legality in those systems. And while the conclusions reached might be stated in general terms, they are often premised expressly, though more often implicitly, on background assumptions about the kind of political system (a liberal-democratic one) and the particular kinds of institutions (independent courts, stable legal principles and practices) that are present. A sociological approach might regard law as one institution in a wider context, along with politics, religion, culture and other social phenomena; from this perspective, the critical issue is not simply whether formal legal institutions can control the exercise of emergency powers, but how their capacity to do so measures against the ability of other social institutions and informal mechanisms to do the same.

[112] I am grateful to Gregory Clancey and François Tanguay-Renaud for helpful exchanges on this point.

Does this mean that these two approaches will necessarily lead to inconsistent conclusions? Reflecting on the distinction between 'socio-legal' and 'philosophy of law' perspectives on emergencies, Colm Campbell argues that 'while there will be overlap in some areas, in others the perspectives are likely to be radically heterogeneous; different questions are asked, so it is unsurprising that answers may not be coterminous'.[113] And yet, one sub-discipline 'need not trump another, raising the possibility that the juxtaposition of a variety of sub-disciplinary perspectives may enhance understanding of the overall phenomenon'.[114] Dyzenhaus is less sanguine, however, in his critique of realism. Realism, he argues, 'denies the worth of legal theory altogether, seeing it as an attempt to hide the facts of power, in which legal considerations are but one of a number of, and far from the most important, considerations, when one is seeking to understand the constraints on the state'.[115] In doing so, however, it 'gives up on the aspiration of the rule of law to replace the arbitrary rule of men with something qualitatively better'.[116] In response, Dyzenhaus argues:

> This kind of theory of law goes much further than a claim that legal theory cannot be divorced from a political sociological understanding of the forces that shape the practice of law, a claim which I completely endorse. If, for example, the political and social forces in a presidential system of government incline the President to escape the limits of law, it is important for legal theorists to consider how such a system can nevertheless be subject to law. But this is a very different inquiry from the realist one, which seeks to move from contested facts about law's limits to the conclusion that legal theorists are both naïve about and blind to the reality of political power. Exactly that move is made, I contend, when it is alleged that in an emergency the executive is in fact unconstrained by law.[117]

At least for Dyzenhaus, then, methodology matters, and some methodological approaches cannot simply be reconciled with others. The disjunction between normative theory and realism leads Dyzenhaus to the conclusion we noted earlier, that the rule-of-law project invokes a 'regulative assumption [that] is made in order to bring a practice closer to its ideal realization; hence it both constitutes and guides that practice'.[118] Not surprisingly, Gross elsewhere criticises aspirational models, charging

[113] Chapter 8, p. 173. [114] *Ibid.* [115] Chapter 2, p. 38. [116] *Ibid.*
[117] *Ibid.*, pp. 37–8. [118] *Ibid.*, pp. 50–1.

them with 'naiveté and out-of-context idealism'[119] for their inability to constrain emergency powers when they are most needed.[120]

We might also consider who the intended primary audience is. Much of Dyzenhaus's work on the emergencies and legality is directed primarily at judges; his work is prescriptive and his implicit goal is to encourage judges to take seriously their role in constraining state power. In contrast, Gross's audience is distinctly *not* judges. Gross assumes that judges will, as a matter of empirical fact, tend to defer to the executive in times of crisis. In asking what we should do about this, his arguments appear to be directed, in part, at public officials in the executive branch of government. Faced with a tension of 'tragic dimensions',[121] these public officials should, conscious of whatever guidance the law can provide, take a considered and deliberate decision, mindful that the ultimate judgment on their conduct will rest in the hands of others.[122] Gross's arguments are therefore addressed, in part, to members of the executive confronted with the dilemmas of disobedience; they are also aimed at 'the people' who must later deliberate and stand in judgment of such conduct.

The lesson to be drawn, then, is that in seeking to make sense of the limits of legality in an emergency, we need not only to understand competing concepts and arguments, but to understand the methodological and disciplinary approaches employed. Some disciplinary approaches might complement one another, allowing us to see, as Colm Campbell reminds us, that an object described by different viewers as a circle and a triangle 'can only be a cone'.[123] But we should remain open to the possibility that some approaches are incompatible and irreconcilable.

B. The road ahead

Questions on the scope and limits of emergency powers are not new. Neither are theories of emergency powers. But in some important respects, times have changed. First, the international dimension of contemporary terrorism, facilitated by modern technology, means that non-state-based political violence (to use a less contentious term) is no longer limited primarily to domestic or geographically narrow regional disputes. This is not to suggest that political violence did not, in the past, have a global dimension, as anti-colonial political movements clearly did. But, as the 9/11 attacks demonstrate, political dissidents in seemingly far-away lands

[119] Gross, 'Chaos and Rules', at 1068. [120] *Ibid.*, at 1056–7.
[121] *Ibid.*, at 1027. [122] *Ibid.*, at 1123–4. [123] Chapter 8, p. 173.

can take their battle directly to the heart of the most powerful states. Second, the awesome political, economic and military clout of the United States has meant that few states could escape the legal and policy aftermath of the 9/11 attacks. Through its influence in the United Nations Security Council, the United States was able to persuade many states to adopt a broad counter-terrorism agenda under the supervision of the Counter-Terrorism Committee.[124] Third, this international dimension of contemporary political violence means that legal responses cannot be separated from geopolitical issues, including the alleged fault lines between East and West, North and South, and among 'civilisations' – or from the implications that geopolitics has on domestic politics, including multiculturalism, minority alienation and the politics of identity. Finally, the years immediately before 9/11 witnessed an expansion of the ideals of human rights, constitutionalism and legality in powerfully symbolic ways in South Africa and the United Kingdom, through the meteoric rise in the influence of the South African Constitutional Court's jurisprudence, and the adoption by the United Kingdom of the Human Rights Act 1998, together with constitutionally significant reforms in the structure of its judicial system. That the political and legislative responses to the attacks on the United States coincided with this rise in the legitimacy, practice and influence of constitutionalism means, at least in contemporary liberal democracies, that the legal framework for emergencies has to be reconciled with constitutionalism on a theoretical and practical level.

The essays in this volume might be seen as an attempt to examine critically the theoretical aspects of emergency powers against the backdrop of these recent developments. In so doing, they raise a range of important questions on emergency powers that invite further reflection and analysis. We should, however, be mindful of the inevitable limitations of a study of this nature. One limitation is the focus in many chapters on liberal-democratic states with a stable and developed legal-political infrastructure and an entrenched – though perhaps severely strained – culture of accountability. How much relevance does this discourse have for the developing world, where emergencies connote insurgency and prolonged armed conflict or military government? Or where a prolonged and complex process of post-conflict reconstruction involves, as it often does, the introduction of unfamiliar forms of wielding and constraining state power, the reduction or elimination of traditional forms of power and a

[124] Above, note 1.

direct challenge to the existing political elites? These questions are scarcely addressed in this volume, yet they are questions that must be confronted squarely. Alas, we must leave this task for another day. In the meantime, it is more than enough to grapple with the scope and limits of legality when established and otherwise stable legal systems are confronted with the challenge of an emergency.

PART ONE

Legality and extra-legality

2

The compulsion of legality

DAVID DYZENHAUS

I. Introduction

According to Carl Schmitt, the limits of law exposed by emergencies debunk not only legal theory, but also what we might think of as the political theory of liberal democracy, since Schmitt rightly took liberal democracy to be committed to the rule of law.[1] The considerable theoretical interest of Oren Gross's extra-legal measures model of how a liberal democratic state should respond to an emergency lies in how he might be said to turn Schmitt's claim that the 'exception proves everything' to liberalism's advantage.[2] Gross's argument is that one can and should accept Schmitt's claim that a state of emergency exposes the limits of law.[3] Nevertheless, the extra-legal measures model, in showing why it is appropriate for the executive to respond illegally in catastrophic situations, not only leaves liberal democracy and the rule of law intact, but even strengthened.

I will argue that unless we commit to governing through law in an emergency, we are forced into one of two unsatisfactory positions. The 'internal realist' position undermines law's claim to authority by creating a veneer of legality over what is really the exercise of power by the political elite, while the 'external realist' position suggests that the sovereign's power is not ultimately constrained by law. Gross's extra-legal measures model

I thank all the participants in the conference at which the papers in this volume were initially presented for a discussion which inspired me to rewrite entirely my own contribution. In particular, I thank Johan Geertsema and Victor V. Ramraj. Discussion with Johan has helped me to clarify some key ideas. Victor had the idea for and then organised the conference and his opening remarks at that event were crucial to the discussion that followed and thus to the reformulation of my own ideas.

1 C. Schmitt, *Political Theology: Four Chapters on the Theory of Sovereignty* (Cambridge, MA: MIT Press, 1988).

2 *Ibid.*, p. 15.

3 For his most recent statement of the model, see O. Gross and F. Ní Aoláin, *Law in Times of Crisis: Emergency Powers in Theory and Practice* (Cambridge: Cambridge University Press, 2006), pp. 110–72.

might seem to be a version of external realism but, as I will show, his position is subject to what I call the compulsion of legality: the compulsion to justify all acts of state as having a legal warrant, the authority of law. As a result of that subjection, Gross reproduces the normative instability in one of his chief sources of inspiration, John Locke's account of the prerogative, by vacillating between external realism and the robust account of legality offered by A.V. Dicey.[4] I will conclude that one should opt for Dicey's legalism, but I will also draw attention to some problems that such legalism faces. First, I wish to explore in some detail Schmitt's claim that the limits of law exposed by emergencies debunk legal theory.

II. The state of emergency in legal theory

States of emergency are said to show that that there are limits to law in the sense that in an emergency the sovereign has the authority to suspend or violate the law in order to deal with the emergency. If that is right, the state of emergency raises a fundamental question for legal theory, since legal theorists see the explanation of law's normative character – law's claim to authority – as part of their task of explaining what law is. To explain what law is one must also explain the claim made by those who wield legal power to have authority over those subject to that power because it is wielded through law. Both legal positivists and natural lawyers assume that this claim is an essential feature of law. They dispute only whether that authority is moral as well as legal.

According to many contemporary positivists, law's claim to authority is never in and of itself justified. It only becomes justified when law is also the instrument of morally correct judgments.[5] While natural law theory is often considered to contest legal positivism through an argument that law is necessarily the instrument of correct moral judgment, this is likely

[4] A.V. Dicey, *An Introduction to the Study of the Law of the Constitution*, 10th edn (London: MacMillan, 1959).

[5] This is the position developed under the influence of Joseph Raz's conception of authority. See Raz, 'Authority, Law and Morality' in Raz, *Ethics in the Public Domain: Essays in the Morality of Law and Politics* (Oxford: Clarendon Press, 1994), p. 194. It is of course the case for Raz's position that judgment as to justification is an all-things-considered one. The factors to be weighed by the conscientious citizen in considering whether to disobey a morally bad law could include the moral costs of disobedience, that there is widespread controversy within the society about this issue, that the law is the product of fair deliberative process within a democratic assembly, etc. But such factors simply complicate the process of individual moral reasoning. It remains the case that the law has authority only when it meets the requirement of what Raz calls the 'normal justification thesis'; see, *ibid.*, p. 198.

a mistaken view. Most, perhaps all, natural law theories place the burden of their claim about law's moral nature on an argument about legality – an argument that seeks to show that for law to be such it has to comply with criteria of legality that are also moral.[6] We might say that for natural law theory the moral nature of law is not based on the fact that it reflects correct moral judgment; rather, it is based on the fact that for X to be law, it must be legal. The intrinsic moral authority of judgments that are implemented through law comes not from their content, but from the fact that they are implemented through law.

Understood in this way, the natural law tradition supports the intuition that the rule of law is a moral good because it replaces the arbitrariness of the rule of men. One who governs through law will find that legality constrains political judgment so as to render it non-arbitrary. Legality or the rule of law provides a legal constitution which is the basis of the authority of those who have power to make law. If they should stray outside the limits of that authority, they lack not only legal authority, but also any authority at all. They act ultra vires, to use the technical term, so that their judgments have no legal force, whether or not their judgments are morally correct.

However, if the sovereign – the ultimate wielder of state authority – and the public officials who are his delegates have the authority to suspend or to violate the law in order to preserve the state in an emergency, this family of natural law ideas might be thought to be bankrupt. In that case, the state's authority comes ultimately not from a legal constitution, but from morality. It is this issue which, in my view, is raised for legal theory by the topic of emergencies and the limits of law.

It might seem that if there are legal limits to sovereign authority, legal positivism wins by default. As we have seen, for positivists since law is merely an instrument of judgment, its claim to be authoritative is justified if, and only if, it is the instrument of correct moral judgment. However, this position gives rise to an ambiguity between the claim that a morally

[6] See T. Nardin, 'Emergency Logic: Prudence, Morality and the Rule of Law' (Chapter 4), this volume, pp. 102–3. In my view, the best contemporary exponent of this tradition is L.L. Fuller, *The Morality of Law*, rev. edn (New Haven: Yale University Press, 1969). I do not consider Gustav Radbruch's position to be a natural law one. Rather, as I have argued elsewhere, it is positivism with a minus sign – law is positive law with the exception of extremely unjust laws that do not count as law because of their violation of criteria for injustice external to law. See D. Dyzenhaus, 'The Dilemma of Legality and the Moral Limits of Law', in A. Sarat, L. Douglas and M.M. Umphrey (eds.), *The Limits of Law* (Stanford: Stanford University Press, 2005), p. 109.

unjustified claim to authority has no authority of any sort and the claim that it might have legal authority but not moral authority. Put differently, the former claim is that X might be legally valid but lacking in authority because it is morally unjustified, while the latter is that if X is legally valid, it necessarily has legal authority, but will have moral authority only if it happens also to be morally justified.

This ambiguity recurs when it comes to the question whether states of emergency show that that there are limits to law, because the sovereign has the authority to suspend or violate the law in order to deal with the emergency. On the one hand, if morally unjustified law is not authoritative in any sense and the correct moral judgment in a state of emergency is that law should be suspended or even violated, not only is it the case that law's claim to authority resides in factors outside of the legal constitution, but also the sovereign's authority is prior to law. On the other hand, if legal authority and moral authority can conflict, one would conclude that the sovereign's moral but not his legal authority is prior to law. But in substance this is the same claim – the sovereign has moral authority prior to the law.

Given this, positivism, at least in its contemporary version, is just as threatened as natural law. The claim that law is merely an instrument of judgment can lead, as we have seen, to the conclusion that the state, represented by the sovereign, has the authority to act outside of the law. But positivists also share with natural lawyers the Identity Thesis, named by Hans Kelsen, that the state's authority is constituted by law.[7] For the state to act qua state, it must act within the limits of the law. All positivists deny is that the legal constitution is always a moral constitution. But since that denial explodes the Identity Thesis by discovering that the state's authority both precedes law and is not limited by law, the state of emergency's exposure of the limits of law also undermines legal positivism.[8]

One might conclude so much the worse for legal theory and the pretence of jurists to suppose that to understand law one must understand its normativity – its claim to (in some sense) justified authority. However, I will argue below that law's claim to authority in the face of the challenge

[7] See H. Kelsen, *Introduction to the Problems of Legal Theory*, S.L. Paulson and B. Litschewski-Paulson (trans.) (Oxford: Oxford University Press, 1992).

[8] This conclusion is of course somewhat puzzling, since positivism begins by denying a necessary connection between law and morality, thus suggesting that law's authority must be based on considerations that are not necessarily moral, and ends by denying that law has any authority whatsoever, if correct moral judgment requires the sovereign to act outside of the law.

posed by states of emergency can be salvaged by showing not only that the state's authority has to be exercised through law, but also that this requirement provides a moral basis for the state's claim to authority.

Before I begin to make that claim, I want first to explore a position that is quite happy with this conclusion. The realist position accepts that the state's authority is prior to law, but finds that the basis of that authority is not a moral but a political constitution – the informal or at least non-juridical factors that will determine whether the sovereign's judgments stick.

III. Realism and the political constitution

Realists are those who wish to understand law purely as a matter of political and social forces. For example, in a recent book of essays on democracy and the rule of law, the contributors argue that the normative conception of jurists, according to which government is always subject to the rule of law, is a 'figment of their imagination'. Law, they say, is not an autonomous constraint on actions but a constraint which those with political power will accept or not depending on their relative strength. If accepting the constraint is the only way elites can maintain their power they will, otherwise not. Not only is the choice to abide by the rule of law a matter of political incentives, the same is true of the choice to use rule by law to achieve one's ends. It follows that the weaker one's relative position, the closer one will find oneself to the normative rule-of-law end of the continuum that stretches between rule by law and rule of law. One who is in a very powerful position will submit to ruling at various points away from the rule-by-law end of that continuum only when it is expedient to do so.[9]

This kind of theory of law goes much further than a claim that legal theory cannot be divorced from a political-sociological understanding of the forces that shape the practice of law, a claim which I completely endorse.[10] If, for example, the political and social forces in a presidential system of government incline the President to escape the limits of law, it is important for legal theorists to consider how such a system can

[9] See J.M. Maravall and A. Przeworski (eds.), *Democracy and the Rule of Law* (Cambridge: Cambridge University Press, 2003), p. 1.

[10] For a fruitful example of how political sociology and legal theory can learn from each other, see C. Campbell, 'Law, Terror and Social Movements: The Repression–Mobilisation Nexus' (Chapter 8), this volume.

nevertheless be subject to law. But this is a very different inquiry from the realist one, which seeks to move from contested facts about law's limits to the conclusion that legal theorists are both naive about and blind to the reality of political power. Exactly that move is made, I contend, when it is alleged that in an emergency the executive is in fact unconstrained by law. Indeed, often it is thought that this alleged fact is most apparent in presidential systems.

In making these moves, realism denies the worth of legal theory altogether, seeing it as an attempt to hide the facts of power, in which legal considerations are but one of a number of, and far from the most important considerations, when one is seeking to understand the constraints on the state. However, in seeking to debunk legal theory and refocus our concerns on political and social forces, realism also gives up on the aspiration of the rule of law to replace the arbitrary rule of men with something qualitatively better. Realism is an account of the dynamics of power, not an account of authority. Moreover, it is an account of power which tries to cut the ground from under an account of authority. It does not simply mount an inquiry from a different theoretical perspective.[11]

Notice that realism is contestable on its own 'realistic' terms because it subscribes to what I call the myth of the given. From the fact that presidential systems have tended to put more strain on the rule of law than others, or that the executive generally tries to escape legal constraints in times of emergency, or that judges have a dismal record of deference to the executive in times of emergency, it concludes that things can be no different. It is a kind of historical inevitablism, with a rather partial view of the historical record, precisely because it excludes from its inquiry a normative account of law that raises questions about the givenness of its facts. If the reality of legal practice is that law's claim to authority shapes that practice, realism does not explain the real world of law.

Moreover, since within practice as in theory the basis of law's claim to authority is contested, realism neglects the potential for practice to change in response to normative argument made within practice about how to improve it. Such arguments involve a political contest about the most appropriate conception. The liberal aspiration to have the rule of

[11] I believe that this claim applies in different ways to N.C. Lazar, 'A Topography of Emergency Power' (Chapter 7), W.E. Scheuerman, 'Presidentialism and Emergency Government' (Chapter 11) and M. Tushnet, 'The Political Constitution of Emergency Powers' (Chapter 6) all in this volume. However, I accept that they have no desire to endorse Carl Schmitt's position, described below.

law rather than the rule of men requires not only a political struggle to subordinate politics to the rule of law, but also a political struggle within practice about how that is best done.[12] The individuals involved in that struggle are motivated by what they take to be the correct understanding of law's claim to authority. They participate in it because they fully appreciate that if the right sorts of institutions are put in place to realise that aspiration, legal practice will be different as institutions shape the individuals who participate in them by making available roles with different moral contours.

Finally, the most important problem with realism arises out of its determination to debunk normative conceptions of law. As I have already suggested, it is possible for legal theory and political sociology not only to coexist with but also to learn from each other. But realism wishes not merely to explain the political and social forces that shape law, but also to debunk law's claim to authority, and, in its hands, that turns out to be itself a normative claim.

Two dangers arise out of this feature of realism. Either it endorses a kind of internal normativity that legitimates anything the executive chooses to do in law's name. Or it requires a move to an external normativity, but one which is existential, which is to say unanchored in liberal democratic values.

In respect of internal normativity, the commitment to the normativity of law entails that jurists proceed as if law's claim to authority can be vindicated. Thus, for example, lawyers for the Bush administration and judges sympathetic to its policies, notably Justice Thomas of the USA Supreme Court, do not argue that the Bush administration has authority to act ultra vires – beyond the limits of the law – in its 'war on terror'. Rather, they claim that the administration has legal/constitutional authority to fight that war unlimited by legal restraints, except those to which it voluntarily submits. They thereby exhibit what I called the compulsion of legality – the compulsion to justify all acts of state as having a legal warrant, the authority of law.

Thus the functional equivalent of realism within juristic thought is a position which bestows the authority of law on the arbitrary rule of men. Law's claim to authority is preserved. But it is hollowed out of any substance, becoming truly a mask for the exercise of power by political elites. They are constrained only by their calculations of political prudence,

[12] See T. Campbell, 'Emergency Strategies for Prescriptive Legal Positivists: Anti-Terrorist Law and Legal Theory' (Chapter 9), this volume.

including calculations as to when it is prudent to submit themselves to or to pretend to submit themselves to legal constraints.

Elites who are willing to eschew the mask can simply say that their claim to authority is based not on law. Theirs is an external normativity, one which does not rely on law's authority, but on another source – their superior insight into how best to respond to what they perceive as an emergency. Their authority is not based on norms or principles; rather it is based on the ability effectively to decide and to enforce decisions. As Carl Schmitt put it, 'Sovereign is he who decides on the exception',[13] by which he meant that sovereign authority accrues to one who has the power to make an effective decision, both about whether there is an emergency and how best to respond to it.

So realism finds itself in an uncomfortable dilemma when it comes to the issue of the normativity of law. Either it turns out to be internal realism, a realism which endorses a counterintuitive and unattractive position on the rule of law, or it is external realism, which endorses a Schmittean claim that normativity accrues to the one who successfully exercises power.[14] Since the latter position is politically impossible in a liberal democracy, realism is more or less forced to adopt the former position, one which places a mask of liberal democratic legitimacy, derived from law, over the facts of sheer power.

IV. Extra-legal measures model

Gross contrasts his extra-legal measures model with two models which he takes to be its rivals: business-as-usual models, which deny that one need depart at all from the ordinary law because they deny that emergencies raise any special problem and models of accommodation that either seek to adapt the ordinary law, or which provide for its suspension under prescribed conditions.

Gross thinks that one should reject business-as-usual models because they are blind to the fact that true emergencies outstrip the resources of ordinary law. Further, one should reject models of accommodation

[13] Schmitt, *Political Theology*, p. 5.

[14] For a position which shuttles in between external and internal realism, see E.A. Posner and A. Vermeule, *Terror in the Balance: Security, Liberty and the Courts* (New York: Oxford University Press, 2007). In my view, the authors are really external realists – see their enigmatically qualified endorsement of Schmitt (pp. 38–9) – who occasionally have to make internal arguments in order to find a hook for the claim that the Bush administration is legally entitled to wage its 'war on terror' more or less as it pleases.

because attempts to make ordinary law flexible enough to respond to such emergencies lead to disrespect for the rule of law as its content gets diminished and create the danger of seepage of diminished rule of law into the rest of the legal order, as people become accustomed to its presence. So instead of trying to accommodate the rule of law to emergencies, liberal democratic societies should advise public officials to break the law, if need be, and then candidly confess to their illegality, thus throwing themselves on the mercy of 'the people'.

The people will then choose either to allow the officials to be punished with the full force of the law that prohibited their actions, or they will cause the penalty to be moderated, or they will find some way of exempting the officials from punishment, either through an Act of Indemnity, or through the prerogative of pardon, or through prosecutorial discretion. But since in all of these cases the ordinary law remains not only intact but also undiminished in its rule-of-law content, the rule of law is affirmed rather than undermined by the consequences of official illegality. Moreover, the risk of punishment should society not approve of the officials' illegal activity means that the officials will be slow to act illegally.

The case for the virtues of the model over its rivals is in part a consequentialist one. It depends on the extent to which officials will be slow to resort to illegal action, given that it is openly advocated to them and to the public as the appropriate way to respond to emergencies. It must be advocated in this way because for it to be a model, to be more than a description of the pattern of events that usually unfolds in the wake of official illegality, it must be openly prescriptive. In addition, the case for the model depends on the extent to which there will be genuine democratic deliberation about how to react to the action, given that the executive's ability to manipulate opinion in and outside the legislature is heightened during an alleged emergency. Finally, if the consequences are such that official resort to illegal action is usually excused rather than punished, one might worry that official illegality will become the norm – a kind of precedent – when officials deem there to be an emergency.

These considerations are of course very important. But my main focus in this chapter is theoretical. It is on the question states of emergency pose for legal theory – whether they expose the limits of law in such a way that law's claim to authority is debunked. Thus I wish to explore mainly the normative basis of the extra-legal measures model. As I will show, the extra-legal measures model is best understood as an unusual combination of normative legal theory with external realism. Law's claim to authority is preserved by preserving a business-as-usual model for ordinary times, while recognising that such a model is inadequate for emergencies. In emergencies, officials simply do what they think is appropriate – whatever it takes to bring the emergency to an end. In other words, external realism governs both the decision that there is an emergency and the decision about how best to respond to it. At the termination of the emergency, the officials are forced to account for their actions by the people, at which time the internal normativity of law enters the picture again.

V. Is the prerogative in or outside the constitution?

While Gross has acknowledged Schmitt – the external realist par excellence – as an intellectual forebear, he acknowledges him only for the insight that law runs out in an emergency. He prefers Locke's account of the prerogative in order to understand the constitutional stakes of an emergency, while, as we will see in the next section, he adopts Dicey's account of the after-the-fact response to official action to cure what he takes to be the main defect in Locke. As I will show in these two sections, Gross, despite his attempt to go further than Locke, in fact repeats the normative instability at the heart of Locke's theory of prerogative – a shuttle between external realism and legality. That same normative instability affects Gross's reliance on Dicey, with the result that Gross is not able fully to appreciate Dicey's claim that 'martial law is in England utterly unknown to the constitution'.[15]

Locke defined prerogative as 'nothing but the Power of doing publick good without a Rule', and elaborated that it is the 'power to act according to discretion for the publick good, without the prescription of the Law, and sometimes even against it'.[16] His position is that in ordinary times, government should take place within a framework of clear and determinate rules, established by the legislature. However, when situations arise which are both not covered by a rule and which are politically urgent in that they demand an instant response, the executive has the moral authority to respond as it sees fit, even though it lacks legal authority and even when it has to act illegally.

Locke's account of prerogative authority is highly ambiguous, the manifestation of a profound normative instability in his theory. The ambiguity comes about because Locke vacillates in his answer to the question whether the executive, personified in the figure of the prince, exercises the

15 Dicey, *Law of the Constitution*, p. 289.

16 J. Locke, *Two Treatises on Government*, P. Laslett (ed.) (Cambridge: Cambridge University Press, 1988), p. 375.

prerogative in his natural capacity or in his artificial role as the public official at the apex of the hierarchy of state.[17] If it is the former, then it seems that the authority comes not from his official position, but from whether he handles the emergency appropriately, an authority which depends on his moral character, and thus, ultimately on the political constitution. If it is the latter, then the authority is a constitutional authority, an authority bestowed on him by a legal albeit unwritten constitution. In sum, it is unclear whether Locke is an external or an internal realist on prerogative authority.

Locke does not seem perturbed by this issue. He assumes that in either case one can generally trust a prince to act, as he is required by his office, for the public good. If the prince does not, he is answerable to God. He is also ultimately answerable to his people if he acts in such an egregious fashion that he causes a revolt, though Locke does suppose that generally the people will acquiesce in what the prince does, whatever he does.

Gross prefers an external realist understanding, since he thinks it dangerous to claim that it is a necessary component of every legal constitution that it grants the executive a prerogative authority. To place an arbitrary power within the constitutional framework is to expand in potentially dangerous ways the government's powers under the constitution. Indeed, his main critique of Schmitt seems to be that Schmitt turns an external realist position, where the sovereign's constitutional authority stands 'outside, even above' the constitution and legal order into a kind of internal realism, where everything the sovereign does must be deemed legal – the sovereign cannot act illegally.[18] Gross argues that if one treats the Lockean prerogative as a 'pragmatically necessary, yet extra-constitutional, power', this allows for a 'government that is exercised by "established and promulgated laws" while giving government the flexibility that may be required in the face of crisis and exigency'.[19]

However, Gross also regards Locke's model as 'lacking a crucial accountability concept'. Locke's focus is on 'implicit, general, ex ante public acquiescence in the exercise of the prerogative power'. For him an 'appropriate exercise is legitimate per se and ex ante owing to the implicit acquiescence of the public to any such exercise, and does not require any further public involvement'. Locke thus conflates two issues: 'doing the pragmatic right

[17] Clement Fatovic suggests that this feature is not an ambivalence in Locke, but an advantage of his account; 'Constitutionalism and Contingency: Locke's Theory of the Prerogative' (2004) 25 *History of Political Thought* 276 at 288–90.

[18] Gross and Ní Aoláin, *Law in Times of Crisis*, p. 169.

[19] *Ibid.*, pp. 122–3.

thing' and 'deciding what is legally, politically and morally the right thing'. He thus fails to 'impose the ethic of responsibility that is central to the Extra-Legal Measures model'.[20]

The extra-legal model, in contrast to both Schmitt and Locke, opens the 'door for subsequent legal accountability'. Moreover, it is the people who have 'final authority' – 'they... decide on the exception through the process of ex post ratification or rejection'.[21] While the word 'final' might imply that the executive has some kind of provisional authority, it seems that Gross regards the authority that attends a use of the prerogative power as bestowed after the fact by the decision of the people. In sum, the sovereign has no constitutional authority, either within or without the legal constitution, to act illegally.

However, if the authority is located with the people, it is located ultimately in a decision, which supports Schmitt's claim that ultimate political authority rests not on norms or principles, but on decision. Indeed, there might be little difference between Gross's position and Schmitt's claim in his book on constitutional theory that the people's acquiescence does have a role in the constitution of sovereignty – they signal 'Yes' or 'No' to claims to sovereign authority by either acquiescing or not.[22] The difference perhaps between Schmitt and Locke, on the one hand, and Gross, on the other, is that Gross is not content with passive acquiescence. But he also offers no principled objection against such acquiescence, only a hope that there will be public deliberation followed by an explicit legal response to official illegality.

In my view, in focusing on legal responses, Gross reproduces the same ambiguity as one finds in Locke, although he locates it in a different place.[23] Whereas the ambivalence in Locke is between a personalised extra-constitutional authority of the prince qua natural person and a legal authority the prince wields as an artificial person, in Gross the ambivalence is between the people as a disparate group of natural individuals, who happen to make a decision, and the people in some artificial role, a role whose constraints require them to make a principled decision.

[20] *Ibid.*, p. 123. [21] *Ibid.*, p. 170.

[22] C. Schmitt, *Verfassungslehre* (Berlin: Duncker & Humblot, 1989), pp. 81–91.

[23] In an earlier essay, Gross seemed tempted to say that the authority is located in the legal constitution – see O. Gross, 'Stability and Flexibility: A Dicey Business' in V.V. Ramraj, M. Hor. and K. Roach (eds.), *Global Anti-Terrorism Law and Policy* (Cambridge: Cambridge University Press, 2005), pp. 90–106 at 97–8.

Gross has, of course, a clear preference for the latter. However, the measures to which he is drawn to have for the most part little to do with explicit public approval or disapproval. They are measures wielded by public officials such as judges or prosecutors or by executives, who usually wield the prerogative of pardon and who often will have control over the legislature if the reaction is a legislative one, as in an Act of Indemnity. Of course, public opinion will be a factor that politicians take into account, but Gross does not show how opinion in itself provides a basis for authority. Rather, when it comes to authority, he gravitates towards the legal constitution.

This normative ambivalence – the shuttle between a Schmittean personalised conception of natural authority and a legalistic conception is something Schmitt understood perhaps better than many liberal thinkers. His rather enigmatic claims that the exception both belongs to legal order and yet transcends it are not, in my view, intended to represent his position. Rather, he means them to describe the ambivalence liberals experience when they grant the existence of the exception or the state of emergency in Schmitt's sense, that is, as a state ungovernable by the rule of law and thus without law's limits. That grant necessitates recognition of a political, extra-legal authority. Since this recognition is anathema to liberals, they attempt to tame the exception through law.[24]

Put differently, only Schmitt is able consistently to make the following three claims. First, the fact of the matter is that the sovereign is he who decides, unconstrained by law, when there is an emergency and how to respond to it; second, no liberal sovereign can admit to that fact given that liberals must adopt the view, exemplified in Kant and Kelsen, that a condition of the authority of a political decision is that it is authorised by law; third, the initial fact of the matter hollows out legality, with the result that the fact prevails under the guise of legality. External realism seems in

[24] See Schmitt, *Political Theology*, ch. 1. In my view, one finds that ambivalence not only in Locke and Gross, but also in recent attempts to design Neo-Roman models of constitutional dictatorship, notably in Bruce Ackerman's work: *Before the Next Attack: Preserving Civil Liberties in an Age of Terrorism* (New Haven: Yale University Press, 2006). Ackerman reacts to the history of judicial failure to uphold the rule of law during emergencies in the face of executive assertions of necessity to operate outside of law's rule by constructing what he calls a political economy to constrain emergency powers. But that political economy still has to be located in law in order to be enforceable, which means that Ackerman cannot help but rely on judges. But why should we accept his claim that we can rely on judges when the executive asserts the necessity of suspending the constitution, when one of his premises is that we cannot so rely?

liberal hands to turn into internal realism.[25] However, as I will now argue, we need not accept this counsel of despair.

VI. Dicey's legality model

In Gross's more recent elaborations of the proper legal response to emergencies, he relies heavily on Dicey for support of the extra-legal measures model.[26] However, on Dicey's account, the state qua state may not act outside of the limits of the law. When it comes to emergencies, Dicey clearly prefers that the legislature enact a statute that gives officials the authority they need to act in a 'spirit of legality'.[27] Should there not be time to enact such a statute, officials must do what they think necessary to respond, in which case there are two options.

First, the officials will act in a way that does not take them outside the law, because they will be able to justify themselves by a defence of necessity, that is, they will be able to prove to a judge that what they did was strictly necessary to deal with an emergency. In this case, what they do has a prior legal authorisation in that they act on a correct appreciation of what the common law of necessity permits them to do. That their appreciation is correct will not be known until a court has certified that they were indeed justified in acting as they did, but that certification is no more retrospective than a court's certification that an official's act was intra vires, within the limits of his statutorily bestowed authority.[28] In the second case, the officials do act outside of the law. But they should be able

[25] Fatovic tries to distinguish Locke's conception of prerogative from Schmitt's: 'Constitutionalism and Contingency: Locke's Theory of the Prerogative', 296. I do not think a sharp distinction can be drawn. Fatovic is correct that Schmitt did not regard Locke as an intellectual predecessor, as he aligned Locke too quickly with Kant. See Schmitt, *Political Theology*, pp. 13–14. However, Schmitt was right to make this alignment, because, as he put it, the exception is 'incommensurable to John Locke's understanding of the constitutional state'; *ibid.*, p. 13.

[26] Gross and Ní Aoláin, *Law in Times of Crisis*, pp. 130–42.

[27] See Dicey, *Law of the Constitution*, pp. 224–33 and 280–90.

[28] Of course, one could retort that the certification is no less retrospective, if one takes the view that all judicial decisions on questions of law are discretionary in the sense of not legally determined. I do not want to enter into this debate with legal positivists in this chapter, except to note that the positivist idea of judicial discretion can be seen as presenting a mini emergency for a legal theory which sees legal order as consisting primarily in rules. Indeed, Schmitt's whole account of states of emergency has its roots in his first academic work, in which he tackled the problem of judicial interpretation of the law in precisely these terms: see C. Schmitt, *Gesetz und Urteil: Eine Unterzuchung zum Problem der Rechtspraxis* (Munich: C.H. Beck, 1969).

to count on an Act of Indemnity to bring them back within the law, to legalise their illegality, as long as what they did was both reasonable and not recklessly cruel, again factors that a judge will be entitled to review.

It is important to realise that Dicey, in setting out his views on Acts of Indemnity, seems to want to generalise from what we can think of as an emergency situation to how to respond to a state of emergency. An emergency situation is one where I reasonably suppose that I should act illegally in order to deal with some imminent threat. If such threats are widespread, the emergency situations might together amount to a state of emergency, so that not only is it the case that multiple illegal reactions are required, but it is better that the actions be undertaken by public officials in a deliberate and planned fashion. When the emergency is over, the state should respond to the widespread illegality by indemnifying officials who acted appropriately, as we would say today, in a proportionate fashion.

But it seems clear that Dicey has in mind that an Act of Indemnity is a statute that indemnifies action that could and should have been authorised in advance, had there been time. His discussion of *Habeas Corpus* Suspension Acts makes this point, with the only qualification that, in a time of emergency, officials should also be given some margin for error. Their evaluation of what has to be done, with or without advance legal authorisation, need not be correct – it need only be reasonable. However, it remains the case that advance authorisation, if there is time for it, should be procured. An Act of Indemnity, subject to the qualification just mentioned, thus brings officials within the law retrospectively who did what they should have been authorised in advance to do, had there been time so to authorise them.

Dicey, I should note, far from having a sophisticated understanding of the relationship between the judiciary and the administrative state, was in fact opposed to the very existence of such a state. His thoughts about the desirability of prior legislative authorisation are thus in tension with other parts of his position. But once that tension is resolved, it is possible that even the qualification is not required. If judges should in general defer to reasonable executive interpretations of particular legislative mandates, official action in terms of a prior authorising statute would be valid as long as it is based on a reasonable interpretation of the mandate of that statute.

However, the main point is that if there is no prior authorising statute, an Act of Indemnity should not purport to provide a blanket indemnity for all illegal activity, nor should it provide expressly that it covers bad faith acts or acts of reckless cruelty. The Act is meant to secure the rule of law, not to undermine it. While the rule of law includes a principle of non-retrospectivity, that principle can be outweighed by other principles of the rule of law, in this situation, the need to preserve legal order. But service to that need requires accountability to the rule of law in general, which requires observance of other rule-of-law principles, in this context the principles of proportionality which would govern official action, had there been a prior authorising statute. In a democracy, the rule of law should only be sacrificed for the sake of the rule of law and that condition imposes its own constraints on the sacrifice.

'Should' does not mean 'will', as Dicey well knew. His references to the 'Jamaica affair' in his discussion of martial law show that he was writing in keen awareness of the fact that his claim that the English constitution does not know martial law was a contested claim. In the same way, when he argued that an Act of Indemnity serves the rule of law only when it covers reasonable acts which are not recklessly cruel, he was aware of examples of such statutes, passed with the deliberate intention of covering literally everything that had in fact been done.

The Jamaica affair[29] arose because Eyre, the colonial governor, and his officials, had put down a local rebellion with means that were both unreasonable and recklessly cruel. They made no secret of what they had done, convinced that in the precarious situation of white colonial rule over a large population of black impoverished inhabitants, it was not only constitutionally appropriate but also politically necessary that the governor had a prerogative authority, located in the unwritten constitution, to declare martial law and do whatever it takes to put down unrest. Moreover, in Jamaica, that constitutional authority seemed to be explicitly confirmed by local statute and, Eyre, once he was sure the unrest had settled, ensured that an Act of Indemnity was passed which generously covered all that he and his officials had done.

However in England, the Jamaica Committee, which included John Stuart Mill, was formed in order to bring Eyre to account before the law, which of course required them to show that his understanding of his constitutional legal authority was wrong. The Committee must be said to have failed in one sense: the attempted prosecutions of Eyre and some of his officials failed in the face of the determination of magistrates and juries who were determined not to let the imperial side down. But the Committee succeeded in showing that if the officials who governed at home or abroad were committed to governing through law, they had

[29] See R. Kostal, *The Jurisprudence of Power: Victorian Empire and the Rule of Law* (Oxford: Oxford University Press, 2005).

to be aware that that commitment is to more than formal assertions of authority. The commitment also has to be to the rule of law, and thus to a set of constitutional principles to which they were as public officials accountable.

I want to highlight three features of the affair. First, it is striking that Eyre scrupulously took legal advice from his chief law officer before he declared martial law. However, once martial law was declared he saw no need for further advice given his belief, shared by his supporters in England and advocated by his lawyers as the controversy unfolded, that he could do as he pleased once he had the initial legal warrant. This feature tells us that for all the participants in the Jamaica affair, the compulsion of legality was a given. Politics, however brutal, were in Kostal's words, 'understood and transacted largely in terms of law and legality'.[30]

Second, the Jamaica Committee was not primarily motivated by concerns about black Jamaicans. It was concerned that if Eyre's position were right the government could rely on it against political opposition at home. It was no coincidence that its principal members were deeply involved in the political struggle to bring full suffrage to England's adult male population. As Rande Kostal remarks, 'at bottom, reform of the franchise and the Jamaica affair raised the same question: what was the nature of legal accountability in a constitutional state?'[31] This feature tells us that the members of the Committee would have rejected an argument that one should be wary of seeking to subordinate politics to the rule of law, because the constraints of the rule of law will constrain politics, permitting elites to hijack the democratic, political project. They saw what we might think of as the democratic political project and the rule-of-law project as intimately related.

The rule of law, in other words, is a necessary, though not sufficient condition for democracy. It is a necessary condition because it presupposes one kind of political accountability, the requirement that all acts of public power count as such only if they can trace their authority to a legal warrant. It is not sufficient because democracy requires other forms of political accountability in addition, mainly the accountability of the rulers to the people through elections. But because the rule of law is a necessary condition of democracy, it is a condition of an assertion of democratic authority that it can show a warrant in both politics and law. The idea that there is an extra-legal basis for authority is thus incompatible not only

[30] *Ibid.*, p. 18. [31] *Ibid.*, p. 133.

with law's claim to authority, but with a commitment to democracy and it is this incompatibility that results in the operation of the compulsion of legality in a democracy. The compulsion thus arises out of the normative commitments of democracy. But its own normative grammar, so to speak, is not reducible to democratic political commitments, since that grammar is based on the principles of legality, not on the principles of representative government, and so on.

Third, as Kostal is anxious to stress, the conclusion of the affair was indeterminate. The failure of the prosecutions of Eyre and others, together with the continued support at the highest levels of government for a constitutionally based prerogative of the executive to act as it pleased in a state of emergency, meant that the reassessment by the elites of the 'jurisprudence of power' was 'ultimately indecisive'.[32] This third feature serves to emphasise the politics of the rule of law. There is no Whiggish progression towards its realisation and, as I have suggested, there is also the issue of the political contest over what it is we are struggling to realise. A.W.B. Simpson in his 'General Editor's Preface' to Kostal's monograph, remarks that the 'issues which so excited the Victorian intelligentsia – the role of respect for legality in countering feared challenges to government under law – have a timeless quality, as is particularly obvious as I write this'.[33] That is, as governments react to 9/11, we are confronted by the same issues as were the Victorians. Thus Dicey, in his remarks about martial law and the English Constitution, was assuming a victory that had not yet been secured.

Dicey was prevented from his commitment to the claim that he was engaged in a project of descriptive legal science from seeing that this assumption is regulative.[34] A regulative assumption is made in order to

[32] *Ibid.*, p. 21.

[33] *Ibid.*, p. vii. See further the illuminating review essay by J.F. Witt, 'Anglo-American Empire and the Crisis of the Legal Frame (Will the Real British Empire Please Stand Up?)' (2007) 120 *Harvard Law Review* 754. For further discussion of Kostal in this volume, see J. Geertsema, 'Exceptions, Bare Life and Colonialism' (Chapter 14) and K. Jayasuriya, 'Struggle over Legality in the Midnight Hour' (Chapter 15). In my view, Jayasuriya's concerns about the imperialism of natural law are legitimate but pertain only to versions of natural law which say, somewhat like legal positivism, that law is the instrument of correct moral judgment. The concerns do not, that is, pertain to a natural law theory which is about the moral significance of the exercise of power through legality.

[34] A.W.B Simpson says that Dicey's claim about martial law is 'grossly and perversely misleading': Simpson, *Human Rights and the End of Empire: Britain and the Genesis of the European Convention* (Oxford: Oxford University Press, 2001), p. 60. While I agree with Simpson that the claim is misleading, my argument is that it misleads only in that it pretends to be a scientific description rather the product of a normative position.

bring a practice closer to its ideal realisation; hence it both constitutes and guides that practice. On this assumption, judges are entitled to do more than attribute an intention to the legislature and the executive always to comply with the rule of law. They may also expect that when they find that the legislature or the executive is failing so to comply that both institutions will find ways of responding positively to that finding. If the legislature makes plain its intention to override the rule of law, the judges may not have available to them the remedy of invalidation. But they can still signal to the public that the government of the day is determined to govern extra-legally, an informal equivalent of the remedy judges have under the United Kingdom's Human Rights Act (1998) of declaring incompatible with the jurisdiction's commitment to human rights a statute which is incapable of being interpreted as complying with that commitment. In doing that, they adopt the role I have described as the judge as weatherman, the judge who regards it as his duty to alert the public to the storm clouds on the horizon.[35] But whether the judge has the remedy of invalidation or only the formal or informal remedy of a declaration of incompatibility, she is not doing the equivalent of Gross's moral hero who decides to disobey the law in order to save the state. Rather, the judge is simply doing her duty to maintain the claim to authority that the state must make in order to continue governing as a state.

Gross's reliance on Dicey does not then help to flesh out the accountability component of the extra-legal measures model. Rather, that reliance demonstrates the compulsion of legality that operates in any authentic democratic account of the appropriate response to states of emergency. In fact, the extra-legal measures model has little to do with emergencies and the constitutional or legislative responses to them. Rather, it is concerned with the most extreme situations imaginable, exemplified in the so-called ticking bomb situation where a public official resorts to torture in a bid to extract urgently required information.[36]

[35] D. Dyzenhaus, *The Constitution of Law: Legality in a Time of Emergency* (Cambridge: Cambridge University Press, 2006), pp. 11–12. I accept fully Kent Roach's clarification of my position, 'Ordinary Laws for Emergencies and Democratic Derogation from Rights' (Chapter 10), this volume, p. 255, that I am committed to the proposition that the judges should fight the storm to the extent possible before taking this role.

[36] Note that in his response to my earlier critique of his work, Gross emphasised that he had said in his first statement of his model that it does not seek to do away with the traditional discourse over emergency powers, nor to exclude constitutional models of emergency powers; rather, it is for 'truly extraordinary occasions': O. Gross, 'Chaos and Rules: Should Responses to Violent Crises Always be Constitutional?' (2003) 112 *Yale Law Journal* 1011 at 1134. For the critique, see D. Dyzenhaus, 'The State of Emergency in Legal Theory' in

However, if this is what the extra-legal measures model amounts to, it is not a model of emergency powers, nor even it is a model for dealing with situations which are utterly unforeseen by the law, in the sense that there are in fact no legal resources to deal with them. Rather, it describes a category of emergency situations for which no advance legal provision should be made and where the illegal actions to which officials resort is not only illegal but unlegalisable, as I will now show.

VII. The unlegalisable

If an official decides to resort to action that is not only illegal but unlegalisable, he will by definition have to act in extra-legal space. The official is choosing to deal with an emergency situation by resorting to an extreme kind of illegality. But one cannot build a model from such examples. They remain emergency situations, to be dealt with on a highly individual basis. They never amount to a state of emergency.

While debate about what falls into the category of the unlegalisable happens to some extent outside of the law, in the realm of the moral rather than the legal, it is important not to exaggerate this distinction. For example, the debate about whether torture is morally permissible, and, if it is, whether it should also be legally authorised, is a debate that happened simultaneously in the legal and the moral realms. It is perhaps when international law hardened to the point where one could say that it was illegal to deport someone to a country where he might face torture that one could say with confidence that there was a moral consensus that torture is absolutely prohibited. Recent US official practices, Canada's Supreme Court's pronouncement that in exceptional circumstances national security grounds could justify a decision to deport to torture,[37] the United Kingdom Court of Appeal's dictum that under certain circumstances evidence obtained by torture might be admissible,[38] are all instances of attempts to reopen that debate by chipping away at the consensus.

Nevertheless, there do seem to be at least somewhat distinct categories of unlegalisable acts of which one is so because it includes acts such as torture which are unlegalisable primarily because they are in themselves morally wrong. Even if so-called torture warrants could be issued in accordance

Ramraj, Hor and Roach (eds.), *Global Anti-Terrorism Law and Policy*, p. 66; for Gross's response, see 'Stability and Flexibility: A Dicey Business', in the same volume, p. 90.

[37] *Suresh* v. *Canada (Minister of Citizenship and Immigration)* [2002] 1 SCR 3.

[38] *A.* v. *Secretary of State for the Home Department (No. 2)* (2005) 1 WLR 414.

with rule-of-law requirements, this would not render torture legalisable. Other acts, for example, lengthy or indefinite security detention might be unlegalisable, not so much because they are in themselves morally wrong, but because it is impossible, given concerns about confidentiality of information and so on, to police them in accordance with the rule of law.[39]

In regard to this second category, much more depends than in the first on legal practice. We might find out whether indefinite detention is unlegalisable only once the United Kingdom has fully developed its system of special advocates to test claims about the necessity to control suspected security risks, the Canadian Supreme Court has fully tested the constitutionality of Canada's system of security certificate detentions,[40] and once in the USA, Congress, the President and the Supreme Court have finished reacting to each other's moves in the legal situation arising out of the detention and trial of 'enemy combatants'.[41]

But whatever is properly within the categories of the unlegalisable, a rule-of-law model for dealing with emergencies cannot be built on the back of examples from these categories. A rule-of-law model seeks to show how to go about legalising prospectively those government acts that are normatively appropriate responses to an emergency. How the law should react when there is no time to engage in this process is an interesting question, but it is mostly interesting because of the light it sheds on how to craft legal responses when there is time. Thus when an act is unlegalisable it is, as it were, both legally and morally doomed to take place in extra-legal space. But precisely that fact is what makes examples from that space inapt for model building.

That the extra-legal measures model is built on the back of inapt examples explains what I perceive to be a deep tension in Gross's position. On the one hand, he argues against both the business-as-usual and accommodation models. On the other hand, he argues for the extra-legal measures

[39] For a similar point, see D. Cole, 'The Priority of Morality: The Emergency Constitution's Blind Spot' (2004) 113 *Yale Law Journal* 1753 at 1794–5.

[40] *Charkaoui* v. *Canada (Citizenship and Immigration)* [2007] SCC 9 has held the present system unconstitutional on the basis that people are detained in way that does not meet constitutional guarantees of 'fundamental justice'. But, for reasons I cannot go into here, it is not yet clear whether this decision is productive for the rule of law. I explore its flaws (including the fact that it did not address *Suresh*), in 'Cycles of Legality in Emergency Times' (2007) 18 *Public Law Review* 165.

[41] For a powerful statement of the claim that indefinite detention is unlegalisable, see R.R. Balasubramaniam, 'Indefinite Detention: Rule by Law or Rule of Law?' (Chapter 5), this volume.

model and at the same time claims that it does not seek to do away with the traditional discourse over emergency powers, nor exclude constitutional models of emergency powers. But it is the business-as-usual model which provides the strongest basis for asserting something like the extra-legal measures model, since the stance of business-as-usual leads to an all-or-nothing approach. Either officials must act within the law, which means the ordinary rule of law, or they must act illegally. There is no middle ground for discussing adaptations of the rule of law to respond prospectively to emergencies. Precisely that middle ground, the middle ground of legality, is, as I suggested above, provided by Dicey.

Gross might respond that the very recognition of the category of the unlegalisable commits me to accepting a version of the extra-legal measures model, but he would be wrong. Following Dicey, I accept that as a matter of fact when individuals are faced with what they perceive to be necessitous circumstances, they will act as they see fit, which might result in illegality.[42] But also with Dicey, I think there is no distinction here between public official and private individuals and that those who so act should be subject afterwards to the tribunal of law and, if they are found not to have met the requirements of the defence of necessity, to the tribunal of politics. Indeed, I myself doubt that anyone who resorts to torture should ever be allowed to plead necessity in his defence.[43]

A successful defence does not legalise a past illegality but finds it not to be illegal. If it is right that torture is morally impermissible, it cannot be allowed entry into the legal order, whether through prior carefully regulated authorisations or through the defence of necessity. At most, and I do not mean to concede that the following comment applies to torture, there can be a brute act of politics that uses law to legalise past illegality because it is considered that, in this exceptional situation, there was reason for society to immunise the individual from legal sanctions. But the point of the exercise is to preclude the idea that from the fact that

[42] Here I rely on Dicey, *Law of the Constitution*, pp. 284–94 and on the vocabulary in the wonderful passage at pp. 412–3: There are times of tumult or invasion when for the sake of legality itself the rules of law must be broken.... The Ministry must break the law and trust for protection to an Act of Indemnity. A statute of this kind is... the last and supreme exercise of Parliamentary sovereignty. It legalises illegality.... [It]... combine[s] the maintenance of law and the authority of the Houses of Parliament with the free exercise of that kind of discretionary power or prerogative which, under some shape or other, must at critical junctures be wielded by the executive government of every civilized country.

[43] See A.P. Simester, 'Necessity, Torture and the Rule of Law' (Chapter 12), this volume, for relevant discussion. I am grateful to Andrew for an extended discussion of these issues.

this individual was immunised in this situation, one can build a principled model.

In sum, given that Gross does not adopt the combination of the business-as-usual model and external realism that makes best sense of most of his claims, he offers us no model at all. Rather, he offers the correct observation that, while there are certain acts that a society which respects legality should never attempt to legalise, it might be the case that in some circumstances a society must consider whether it is fair to punish the person who did one of those acts. Moreover, that observation does not show, as Schmitt (and perhaps Gross) seem to think, that emergencies expose the fact that the political sovereign has an authority prior to law. Rather, it shows that it is morally permissible for the political sovereign on occasion to choose not to punish private individuals who have broken the law, and, I would add, a legality model must prefer that such choices are themselves law-governed.

But while I reject the extra-legal measures model, I accept that Gross's critiques of the other models are most valuable. In particular, he has powerfully argued against what he calls the assumption of separation between the ordinary and the exceptional and identified perspicuously the problem of seepage of the exceptional into the ordinary which affects all attempts to adapt the rule of law. Indeed, I believe his insights about the assumption of separation and the problem of seepage to be deeply connected, though not in a way he envisages.

Consider the claim that the Bush administration has since 9/11 accelerated a process in which the executive has been arrogating ever more power. That claim points out that even in ordinary times, the executive is prone to try to carve out exceptions for itself, so that it can act largely unconstrained by the rule of law. In other words, when one is confronting the problem of seepage, one should be aware that it is not a problem which follows legal responses to a state of emergency: the barbarian is already within the gates. However, one should at the same time recall that legislatures, judges and the executive itself have often been keenly aware of the need to subject executive discretion to rule-of-law controls and have found imaginative and productive ways of doing so. The myth that the regulatory state is unlegalisable and therefore immoral has long been shattered, so that those who are opposed to that state have to argue against it on the terrain of the politics of redistribution and not on the terrain of legality.

There is surely every reason to consider the feasibility of the rule-of-law controls developed for the regulatory state for executive responses to emergencies. In addition, the acceleration of executive arrogation of power in a time of emergency or alleged emergency might serve to draw our attention to more than the dangers during that time. It might, that is, draw our attention also to the arrogations that happened during ordinary times, so that the awareness of the need for rule-of-law reform extends beyond the emergency.

There are risks inherent in such rule-of-law projects, not least the pathology that ensues when the rule of law is reduced to a 'thin veneer of legality' such that it serves to cloak what is in substance arbitrary executive power. This phrase was recently used by an English judge[44] to describe the rule-of-law controls put in place on the control order regime presently in use in the UK for individuals who are alleged to be security risks. Indeed, one has to be aware that then the compulsion of legality might well turn out counter-productive, as it can set in motion two very different cycles of legality.

In one cycle, the institutions of legal order cooperate in devising controls on public actors which ensure that their decisions comply with the principle of legality, understood as a substantive conception of the rule of law. In the other cycle, the content of legality is understood in an ever more formal or empty manner. In this case, the compulsion of legality may result in the subversion of constitutionalism – the project of achieving government in accordance with the rule of law. The political constitution asserts itself under the guise of the legal constitution. Indeed, as I have indicated, the very requirement that all acts of public power have a legal authorisation might become counter-productive when the kind of power sought is of a kind that either cannot be legally controlled once authorised or is too morally repugnant to be considered for authorisation.

VIII. Conclusion

Recall the realist assertion that states of emergency expose the limits of law, thus undermining the central assumption of legal theory – that the state to act with authority must act within the limits of the law. This claim is as damaging to legal positivism as it is to natural law theories, because legal positivism, no less than natural law theories, claims that the state acts

[44] *MB* v. *Secretary of State for the Home Department* [2006] EWHC 1000 (Admin) at para. 103. Sullivan J. found that aspects of the control order regime imposed by Parliament (Prevention of Terrorism Act 2005) are incompatible with the Article 6.1 guarantee of a right to 'a fair and public hearing within a reasonable time by an independent tribunal established by law'.

authoritatively only when it acts through law. We have encountered this idea in Hans Kelsen's Identity Thesis. Its equivalent in the English tradition of legal positivism is H.L.A. Hart's rule of recognition,[45] which consists of the criteria in the legal practice of officials who have the authority to certify whether a law is in fact a valid member of their legal system.

Hart saw himself as curing a deficiency in the theory of his positivist predecessors, Jeremy Bentham and John Austin, whom he took to claim that the sovereign is legally unlimited. But it is doubtful that Bentham and Austin meant by this claim more than the sovereign is free to change the law through using recognised legal procedures, which means that he is also free to change the legal procedures, as long as he does so in accordance with the existing procedures. They did of course also argue that the authority of the sovereign is not limited by natural law, in the sense of moral limits inherent in legal order. But Hart, with some ambiguities, makes exactly the same argument.

Curiously it is Hobbes, often considered the most authoritarian thinker within the positivist tradition, who argued both that any legal order necessarily subscribes to the principles of natural law as a kind of unwritten constitution of law and that the sovereign, qua sovereign, is always subject to these principles, as much as the meanest of his subjects.[46] In Hobbes's view, the sovereign's authority to change the law does not thus extend to the laws of nature. It is precisely this thought that Dicey resurrected some centuries later, though, unlike Hobbes, he located the principles in the common law.

Both Hobbes and Dicey fall within the natural law tradition, on my conception of that tradition, since for them while particular laws are an instrument of sovereign judgment, what gives the laws their legal quality is their compliance with principles of legality. Moreover, such compliance does not overall seek to ensure (though it does in part) that the content of each particular law is determinate. It mainly seeks to ensure that the legal order as a whole, and thus each and every particular law, lives up to the moral point of law – service to the interests of those subject to its force.

Where positivism, on any version, differs from this conception of natural law is that the quality of legality is reduced to criteria or principles that seek to ensure that particular laws are as determinate as possible. It is

[45] H.L.A. Hart, *The Concept of Law* (Oxford: Clarendon Press, 1961), ch. 5.

[46] T. Hobbes, *Leviathan*, R. Tuck (ed.) (Cambridge: Cambridge University Press, 1997), p. 237. See further: D. Dyzenhaus, 'Hobbes' Constitutional Theory', in I. Shapiro (ed.), *Leviathan* (New Haven: Yale University Press, forthcoming).

this difference that makes positivism into an instrumental theory of law, not that natural law fails to see the importance of law as an instrument for conveying judgment. And it is the utter instrumentality of positivism that leads to the incoherence I have identified: that positivism both subscribes to the Identity Thesis and finds itself forced to conclude that the authority of the state is prior to the law. That incoherence, I have argued, makes positivism most vulnerable to the challenge to legal theory posed by states of emergency.

My conception of natural law is vulnerable to the challenge, but in a different way. Positivism is conceptually vulnerable, while natural law is not because for it the legal limits of law are also moral and thus the state has no authority at all prior to law. The state is, to repeat, completely constituted by law. Thus the vulnerability of a non-instrumental, natural conception of law is practical – whether legality can in fact control all exercises of public power in accordance with its principles; whether, to use the terms of the last section, the compulsion of legality must result in a cycle of legality subversive of the content of the rule of law.

However, this vulnerability should not be misconstrued. The test for the natural law conception is not whether power can override the principles of legality. If that were the test, then Dicey could not have coherently maintained both that in his legal order parliament was supreme and that the unwritten constitution of that legal order precluded the French idea of a state of siege, the idea of a state of emergency as space in which the military has an unfettered power to act. A supreme parliament can, that is, make it completely explicit that it does not wish the public officials to whom it is delegating power to abide by legality.

But while this situation raises important and complex questions about the appropriate institutional remedies for overrides of legality, it does not challenge the natural law conception of the limits of law. That conception does not claim that legality can withstand determined attempts by those who wield political power to override it. All it claims is that it is possible to exercise power through law in a way that sustains the aspirations of legality. This is important because, as we have seen, in the hands of both internal and external realists the challenge of states of emergency proceeds by, first, denying that possibility and, second, affirming the normative desirability of the idea that the authority of the state is prior to law. In other words, the challenge does not assume a political elite unwilling to attempt to govern under the constraints of the rule of law; rather, it argues that in a state of emergency such governance is impossible and draws normative conclusions from that alleged fact.

My argument depends on considerations which, as I have tried to indicate, require framing the questions in terms of the debates between the classics of legal and philosophy. Thus with Tom Campbell,[47] I believe that the challenge raised by states of emergency to legal theory might bring about a welcome return to these classics, because they saw the task of understanding the law as part of political philosophy. And again with Campbell, I believe that this normative political inquiry cannot be confined to some normative plane. It must also be consequentialist, at least in the sense that the test of good theory is ultimately its effects on practice. Where Campbell and I differ is in regard to our sense of which legal theory is superior, given this political, normative contest. I would venture that in the face of the challenge posed by states of emergency, positivism must lose. As Campbell's chapter shows, positivists (at least of his sort) will want to advocate a conception of the rule of law that is substantially richer or thicker than that endorsed by internal realism, yet are unwilling to grant judges the guardianship role that such a conception seems to require. That is, legal positivism will have to put forward a non-instrumental account of legality, which might require giving up most of what makes positivism distinctive.

There is a flip-side to this point. Internal realists cannot help but take a position in legal theory, as their realism is based on a conception of the rule of law that is utterly formal or thin, the position that is often associated with legal positivism.[48] External realism is excused this necessity, but only at the cost of allying itself with Schmitt and his claim that the sovereign is a pre-legal political entity, who has authority to do whatever he likes, constrained only by whatever social and political forces he deems prudent to take into account.[49] But whatever one's position in these debates, it is, or so I have argued, important to understand more precisely the depth and kind of challenge states of emergency pose for legal theory.

[47] 'Emergency Strategies for Prescriptive Legal Positivists: Anti-Terrorist Law and Legal Theory' (Chapter 9), this volume, p. 201.

[48] See Scheuerman, Chapter 11.

[49] Tushnet (Chapter 6) and Lazar (Chapter 7) seem to me to verge on accepting this position.

3

Extra-legality and the ethic of political responsibility

OREN GROSS

> Whoever wants to engage in politics at all, and especially in politics as a vocation . . . lets himself in for the diabolic forces lurking in all violence.[1]
>
> Would not the burden on the official be so great that it would require circumstances of a perfectly extraordinary character to induce the individual to take the risk of acting? The answer is of course yes, that's the point.[2]

I. Introduction

Public officials, like everybody else, ought to obey the law, even when they disagree with specific legal commands. However, there may be extreme exigencies when officials may regard strict obedience to legal authority as irrational or immoral. Public officials who believe that the law is so fundamentally unjust as to be devoid of both legitimacy and legality may exercise their discretion and refuse to apply, or seek actively to undermine, such law. The extra-legal measures model of emergency powers (ELM) invokes the possibility that public officials having to deal with extreme cases may consider acting outside the legal order while acknowledging openly their actions and the extra-legal nature of such actions and accepting the possible consequences.[3] ELM has been challenged as embracing brazen lawlessness by placing public officials in a 'legal black hole . . . a

[1] M. Weber, 'Politics as a Vocation' in H.H. Gerth and C.W. Mills (eds. and trans.), *From Max Weber: Essays in Sociology* (New York: Oxford University Press, 1946), p. 77 at 125.

[2] S.H. Kadish, 'Torture, the State and the Individual' (1989) 23 *Israel Law Review* 345 at 355.

[3] On the model see O. Gross, 'Chaos and Rules: Should Responses to Violent Crises Always Be Constitutional?' (2003) *Yale L.J.* 1011 at 1096–133; O. Gross and F. Ní Aoláin, *Law in Times of Crisis: Emergency Powers in Theory and Practice* (Cambridge: Cambridge University Press, 2006), pp. 110–70.

zone uncontrolled by law'.[4] This chapter begins to address some of those criticisms.[5]

II. Legal black holes: beyond the legal frontier?

David Dyzenhaus has been a thoughtful critic of ELM. In his excellent contribution to this volume he argues that ELM undermines, and is incompatible with, law's claim to authority, legal theory's central assumption that the state can only act with authority when it acts within the limits of the law, and the commitment to democracy.[6] If we accept, as he perceives ELM to do, that the sovereign has the authority to suspend or to violate the law in order to preserve the state in an emergency, then we accept that the state's authority derives, at the end of the day, not from a legal constitution but from a political constitution. The sovereign's authority is antecedent to law. As he notes elsewhere: 'It might seem . . . that the only conclusion to be drawn by someone committed to a substantive conception of the rule of law is [Carl] Schmitt's. One should concede that, in the state of exception or emergency, *law recedes leaving the state to act unconstrained by law*. Just this conclusion is reached . . . by Oren Gross'.[7]

Dyzenhaus describes ELM as a legal black hole constituting a 'lawless void'.[8] The concept of legal black holes was famously conjured up by Lord Steyn to describe and condemn the situation of detainees held by the

[4] D. Dyzenhaus, 'The State of Emergency in Legal Theory' in V.V. Ramraj, M. Hor and K. Roach (eds.), *Global Anti-Terrorism Law and Policy* (Cambridge: Cambridge University Press, 2005), p. 65.

[5] There are those who consider the model to be too wrapped-up in legalistic tradition and as paying too little attention to the political. See, for example, the contributions of M. Tushnet, 'The Political Constitution of Emergency Powers' (Chapter 6), N.C. Lazar, 'A Topography of Emergency Power' (Chapter 7) and to some extent W.B. Scheuerman, 'Presidentialism and Emergency Government' (Chapter 11) in this volume. Thus, for example, Mark Tushnet identifies the main drawback of ELM in that it operates within a 'conceptual framework in which only law has value that is simultaneously normative and institutional' (p. 145). According to Tushnet, ELM is committed to the proposition that 'law occupies the entire institutional space of normative evaluation of emergency powers' (p. 146): ELM sets forth legal criteria for identifying when public officials invoke ELM appropriately and the *ex post* ratification process is controlled and regulated comprehensively by and through law. In this paper I will mostly focus on the 'legal black hole' arguments against ELM and leave the discussion of the challenges from the political for another day.

[6] D. Dyzenhaus, 'The Compulsion of Legality' (Chapter 2), this volume.

[7] D. Dyzenhaus, *The Constitution of Law: Legality in a Time of Emergency* (Cambridge: Cambridge University Press, 2006), p. 50 (emphasis added).

[8] *Ibid.*, p. 1.

United States in the American naval base at Guantánamo Bay, Cuba.[9] Lord Steyn's powerful narrative invokes the image of detainees locked in a space that is both 'utterly lawless'[10] and allows no escape. This understanding of legal black holes is reminiscent of Giorgio Agamben's treatment of the state of exception. Equating it with the Roman *iustitium* – the general suspension of public business in times of emergency – Agamben argues that the state of exception 'is not defined as a fullness of powers, a pleromatic state of law . . . but as a kenomatic state, an *emptiness* and standstill of the law'.[11] It is 'a zone of anomie in which all *legal* determinations . . . are deactivated'.[12] Emergency powers exercised, and measures taken, in that space of juridical vacuum are therefore 'radically removed from any juridical determination . . . *and the definition of their nature . . . will lie beyond the sphere of law*'.[13] For Agamben, the state of exception constitutes an anomie that results from the suspension of law. It is not originary of law nor does it reflect a reversion to a state of nature:[14] 'The state of exception is not a special kind of law . . . rather, insofar as it is a suspension of the juridical order itself, it defines law's threshold or limit concept'.[15] Its definition is a negative one, that is, the state of exception is a state of not-law. But then Agamben has to acknowledge (as he does) the difficulty or, indeed, the impossibility, 'of thinking an essential problem: that of the nature of acts committed during the *iustitium*. What is a human praxis that is wholly delivered over to a juridical void?'[16] Those acts ostensibly undertaken in order to save the republic are 'produced in a juridical void' and as such are 'radically removed from any juridical determination'.[17] Nor can the legal status of such acts be pre-determined and prescribed *ex ante* (e.g., in the constitution or a statute). I will come back to this question below.

ELM neither describes nor establishes a legal black hole. On the contrary, it seeks to preserve the long-term relevance of and obedience to legal principles, rules and norms. It suggests that going outside the law in appropriate cases may preserve, rather than undermine, the rule of law in ways that constantly bending the law to accommodate emergencies and crises will not. While going outside the legal order may be a little wrong,

[9] J. Steyn, 'Guantánamo Bay: The Legal Black Hole' (2004) 53 *International and Comparative Law Quarterly* 1.

[10] *Ibid.*, at 15.

[11] G. Agamben, *State of Exception* (Chicago: University of Chicago Press, 2005), p. 48 (emphasis added).

[12] *Ibid.*, p. 50 (emphasis added). [13] *Ibid.* (emphasis added). [14] *Ibid.*, pp. 50–1.

[15] *Ibid.*, p. 4. [16] *Ibid.*, p. 49. [17] *Ibid.*, p. 50.

it facilitates the attainment of a great right, namely the preservation not only of the constitutional order, but also of its most fundamental principles and tenets. ELM seeks to promote, and is promoted by, ethical concepts of political and popular responsibility, political morality and candour. Indeed, ELM offers the possibility that public officials having to deal with extreme cases may consider acting outside the legal order. However, the model rejects the possibility of *ex ante* lawful override of concrete legal rules and principles or of the rule of obedience (to law) itself.[18] Under extreme circumstances public officials may regard strict obedience to legal authority as irrational or immoral because of a contextual rebalancing of values which takes place at a level that is antecedent to the relevant legal rule itself, that is, the level of the rule's underlying reasons or similar first-order content-dependent reasons that relate to obedience to the rule.[19] According to ELM, if an official determines that a particular case necessitates her deviation from the rule, she may choose to depart from that rule. But, and this is critical, when she acts her actions are extra-legal and she does not know what the personal consequences of violating the relevant rules are going to be. Not only does the basic rule continue to apply to other situations (that is, it is not cancelled or terminated), it is not even overridden in the concrete case at hand.[20] Rule departures constitute, under all circumstances and all conditions, violations of the relevant legal rule. Yet, whether the actor would be punished for her violation remains a separate question.

Under ELM, law does not recede and does not leave the state or its public officials to act unconstrained by law. The extreme case is not a space of juridical vacuum. Legal principles, rules and norms continue to be applicable throughout the exception and can serve as appropriate benchmarks by which to assess both the legality of, and the appropriate response to, actions taken by public officials in times of emergency. Such actions cannot, in and of themselves, change and modify the legal

[18] In contrast to the views expressed, for example, by T. Campbell, 'Emergency Strategies for Prescriptive Legal Positivists: Anti-Terrorist Law and Legal Theory' (Chapter 9), K. Roach, 'Ordinary Laws for Emergencies and Democratic Derogation from Rights' (Chapter 10) and Scheuerman, Chapter 11, in this volume.

[19] F. Schauer, *Playing by the Rules: A Philosophical Examination of Rule-Based Decision-Making in Law and in Life* (New York: Oxford University Press, 1991), p. 128; H.M. Hurd, 'Challenging Authority' (1991) 100 *Yale Law Journal* 1611 at 1625–8; F. Schauer, 'The Questions of Authority' (1992) 81 *Georgetown Law Journal* 95 at 110–15.

[20] Schauer, 'The Questions of Authority', 103 (suggesting 'the idea of overridable obligations that survive the override despite being overridden in a particular case').

terrain. They remain extra-legal. It is against the background of such legal benchmarks that we may continue to talk of 'extra-legal' measures. ELM suggests, therefore, that the appropriate response to Agamben's quandary regarding the nature of acts committed during *iustitium* is to be found in the legal sphere, for such actions, contrary to his claim, are not performed in a juridical void. However, the fact that the relevant acts have not been performed in a juridical void does not necessarily entail that the legal, political and social responses to those actions be the same as those that would have been given in times of peace and tranquility. It is precisely because the actions taken are extra-legal, and not made legal merely due to the decision of the acting official, that the question of implications for the actor is still relevant.

III. *Ex post* ratification

According to ELM, society retains the role of making the final determination whether the public official who acted extra-legally ought to be punished and rebuked or rewarded and commended for her actions. As Frederick Schauer notes, in the context of the United States: '[S]ociety presently strikes this balance pursuant to a procedure under which ex post justified acts of disobedience to the law on the part of officials are punished quite mildly, if at all, while ex post unjustified acts of disobedience to the law are punished somewhat more heavily than those same acts would have been punished merely for being bad policy'.[21] It is up to society as a whole, 'the people,' to decide how to respond *ex post* to extra-legal actions taken by government officials in response to extreme exigencies.

The people – acting either directly or indirectly, for example, through their elected representatives in the legislature – may decide to hold the actor accountable for the wrongfulness of her actions or may approve them. Even when acting to advance the public good under circumstances of great necessity, officials remain answerable to the public for their extra-legal actions. Society may determine that certain extra-legal actions, even when couched in terms of preventing future catastrophes, are abhorrent, unjustified and inexcusable. In such a case, the acting official may be called to answer for her actions and make legal and political amends. Alternatively, the people may approve the actions and ratify them.

[21] *Ibid.* at 114.

A. Modes of ratification

According to ELM, *ex post* ratification may be formal or informal, legal as well as social or political. Legal modes of ratification include, for example, the exercise of prosecutorial discretion not to bring criminal charges against officials accused of violating the law, jury nullification where criminal charges are brought, mitigation of penalties and sanctions that are imposed on the official when she is found liable (in criminal or civil proceedings) for violation of the law[22] and executive pardoning or clemency where criminal proceedings result in conviction.[23] Governmental indemnification of state agents who are found liable for damages in civil proceedings may also operate as *ex post* ratification of the extra-legal actions of those agents. In the United States, for example, constitutional violations might be remedied by way of money damages recovered in suits brought against government officials in their individual capacities. Individual responsibility of government officials serves as a mechanism to enforce constitutional rights.[24] A public official who acts extra-legally may be exposed to having a claim brought against her and to being found liable for damages to persons whose constitutional rights were violated by

[22] For discussion of mitigation in similar contexts see, for example, M. Byers, 'Preemptive Self-defense: Hegemony, Equality and Strategies of Legal Change' (2003) 11 *Journal of Political Philosophy* 171 at 185–8; T.M. Franck, *Recourse to Force: State Action Against Threats and Armed Attacks* (Cambridge: Cambridge University Press, 2004), pp. 174–91. See also S. Chesterman, 'Deny Everything: Intelligence Activities and the Rule of Law in' (Chapter 13), this volume, part III.

[23] On at least one occasion, presidential clemency was granted to eleven agents of the Israeli General Security Service, including the Head of the Service, *prior* to trial, blocking any future possibility of criminal proceedings being brought against them. H.C. 428/86, *Barzilai* v. *Gov't of Israel*, 40(3) (1986) P.D. 505. See also M. Kremnitzer, 'The Case of the Security Services Pardon' (1987) 12 *Iyunei Mishpat* 595; P. Lahav, 'A Barrel Without Hoops: The Impact of Counterterrorism on Israel's Legal Culture' (1988) 10 *Cardozo Law Review* 529 at 547–56; Y. Gutman, *Taltelah ba-Shabak: ha-yoets ha-mishpati neged ha-memshalah mi-parashat Tovyanski ad parashat Kav 300* (*A Storm in the G.S.S.*) (Tel Aviv: Yediot Aharonot, 1995), pp. 15–133; O. Gross, 'Are Torture Warrants Warranted? Pragmatic Absolutism and Official Disobedience' (2004) 88 *Minnesota Law Review* 1481 at 1523–4.

[24] *Bivens* v. *Six Unknown Named Agents of Federal Bureau of Narcotics*, 403 U.S. 388 (1971). See also 42 U.S.C. para. 1983 (1994) (permitting actions against state officials for violation of the Constitution and federal statutes, but providing no similar legislative mechanism against federal officials); A.R. Amar, *The Constitution and Criminal Procedure: First Principles* (New Haven: Yale University Press, 1997), p. 40; R.H. Fallon, Jr. and D.J. Meltzer, 'New Law, Non-Retroactivity and Constitutional Remedies' (1991) 104 *Harvard Law Review* 1733 at 1822.

her actions. Such threats, even if practically remote, play a role in providing added deterrence against acting extra-legally.[25]

Acts of Indemnity offer another route to *ex post* ratification. A.V. Dicey suggests that, 'There are times of tumult or invasion when for the sake of legality itself the rules of law must be broken. The course which the government must then take is clear. The Ministry must break the law and trust for protection to an Act of Indemnity'.[26] By enacting such Acts of Indemnity Parliament 'legalises illegality' and 'free[s] persons who have broken the law from responsibility for its breach, and thus make lawful acts which when they were committed were unlawful'.[27]

Political and social ratification is also possible. Charles Black suggested in a different, yet related, context, that once a public official violates the law, 'he should at once resign to await trial, pardon, and/or a decoration, as the case might be'.[28] Honorific awards can establish *ex post* ratification in appropriate circumstances. Withholding a decoration may also send a strong message of rejection and condemnation and serve as informal sanction that society may apply against officials for acting in violation of a recognised rule.[29] Indeed, such measures as impeachment combine political and legal modes of *ex post* ratification. In that respect, Mark Tushnet's assertion that that *ex post* ratification under ELM is limited to the realm of the legal as it is carried out 'by means of subsequent punishment or ratification, or restitutionary payments to victims . . . and the like'[30] ignores the significant role that other, non-legal, forms of ratification (or rejection) may occupy as part of the model.

By requiring a process of *ex post* ratification (or rejection), ELM emphasises an ethic of responsibility not only on the part of officials, but also of the general public. Thomas Jefferson analogised extra-legal actions

[25] C.T.L. Pillard, 'Taking Fiction Seriously: The Strange Results of Public Officials' Individual Liability Under Bivens' (1999) 88 *Georgetown Law Journal* 65 at 66 and 76–7; *Carlson* v. *Green*, 446 U.S. 14, 21 (1980); J.M. Byrd, 'Rejecting Absolute Immunity for Federal Officials' (1983) 71 *California Law Review* 1707 at 1718–21; J.C. Jeffries, Jr, 'In Praise of the Eleventh Amendment and Section 1983' (1998) 84 *Virginia Law Review* 47 at 51.

[26] A.V. Dicey, *Introduction to the Study of the Law of the Constitution*, 8th edn (Indianapolis: Liberty Classics, 1982), p. 272.

[27] *Ibid.*, pp. 10–11 and 142. For a fuller discussion of Dicey in this context see O. Gross, 'Stability and Flexibility: A Dicey Business', in Ramraj, Hor and Roach (eds.), *Global Anti-Terrorism Law and Policy*, p. 90.

[28] A.M. Froomkin, 'The Metaphor Is the Key: Cryptography, the Clipper Chip and the Constitution' (1995) 143 *University of Pennsylvania Law Review* 709 at 746 n. 153; R.A. Posner, *Catastrophe: Risk and Response* (New York: Oxford University Press, 2004), p. 241.

[29] Gross and Ní Aoláin, *Law in Times of Crisis*, p. 139.

[30] Tushnet, Chapter 6, p. 146.

taken by public officials on great occasions to acts of a guardian who is making an advantageous, albeit unauthorised, transaction on behalf of her minor ward. When the minor comes of age, the guardian must explain her actions thus: 'I did this for your good; I pretend to no right to bind you: you may disavow me, and I must get out of the scrape as I can: I thought it my duty to risk myself for you'.[31] During the process of ratification, members of the public become morally and politically responsible for the decision. '[D]ecent men and women, hard-pressed in war, must sometimes do terrible things', writes Walzer, 'and then they *themselves* have to look for some way to reaffirm the values they have overthrown'.[32] Yet, according to ELM, it is not only the actors who must attempt to find a way to reaffirm fundamental values they have violated in times of great exigency. Society too must undertake a project of reaffirmation. Members of society, in whose name 'terrible things' have been done, become morally responsible through the process of ratification or rejection.[33] It may well be easier today than in the past to access this process, e.g. through the now pervasive information technology. To be sure, each member of the general public will have different opportunities and venues through which to participate: some (including public intellectuals and scholars) would have greater ability to influence public opinion or be in a better position to take action (legal, political or otherwise), while others may have their opportunity to participate through the ballot box.

After the 2004 presidential elections in the United States, John Yoo, of the torture memos infamy, expressed the opinion that the debate on torture was over because the American public had its referendum on the matter in the elections.[34] This position has been strongly criticised. A *New York Times*'s editorial of 19 February 2005, called it the most bizarre claim of an electoral mandate.[35] Yoo's point was that the re-election of President

[31] Letter from Thomas Jefferson to John C. Breckinridge (12 August 1803) in Ford, *Thomas Jefferson*, pp. 1136 and 1138–39.

[32] M. Walzer, *Just and Unjust Wars: A Moral Argument with Historical Illustrations*, 3rd edn (New York: Basic Books, 2000), p. 325 (emphasis added).

[33] E.V. Rostow, 'The Japanese American Cases – a Disaster' (1945) 54 *Yale Law Journal* 489 at 533.

[34] J. Mayer, 'Outsourcing Torture' *The New Yorker* (14 February 2005). ('If the President were to abuse his powers as Commander-in-Chief, Yoo said, the constitutional remedy was impeachment. He went on to suggest that President Bush's victory in the 2004 election, along with the relatively mild challenge to Gonzales mounted by the Democrats in Congress, was "proof that the debate is over." He said, "The issue is dying out. The public has had its referendum."').

[35] Editorial, 'Time for an Accounting' *New York Times* (19 February 2005), p. A14.

Bush, despite the revelations of the abuses in Abu Ghraib, could be viewed as amounting to social and political ratification. I believe that he got it wrong (and not for the first time) on the merits. It is sufficient to point out that the Abu Ghraib abuses and the more general question of the use of torture in interrogations, had not been on the agenda during the presidential campaign.[36] When the question is not put squarely before it, it is hard to claim that the public has had its referendum on it. However, the fact that almost all of the main characters in the torture memos' saga have since been promoted – including to the bench and to the position of Attorney General – does work, to a certain degree, as an after the fact confirmation – most troubling to be sure – that what those individuals did was not so terrible. In fact, in Professor Black's terms, they received their decorations. That such a social and political affirmation need not have thick legal significance does not mean that it is devoid of any significance. Indeed, despite the fact that the American public has been aware of the abuses in Abu Ghraib, Guantánamo and other places, and the role that its government and its lawyers have played in those abuses and violations, it is very hard to point to any real, continuous, popular outcry. Even if many are disturbed by the direction the United States has been taking, most do not seem to care that much, or at least not care enough to actually do something about it. Inaction is not cost-free. It is imbued with moral and political significance. That is true for the public at large and true for its representatives who confirmed the nomination of Alberto Gonzales as Attorney General.

While this example is disheartening, it also holds a promise. Society can ratify and approve acts of torture, but it can also reject them and take actions against the perpetrators. The vigorous (and painful) public debate in Israel on those questions, since the establishment in 1987 of the Landau Commission is an example – albeit imperfect – of the process in action.

Government agents must decide whether or not to act extra-legally in times of crisis. They must face that question as moral agents. But their grappling with the question should then be followed by an assessment of that same question by an informed public. In this instance, however,

[36] In subsequent interviews, Yoo continued to make the referendum claim, but directed it at the President's general policies regarding the war on terror rather than the issue of use of torture in interrogation of suspected terrorists. See, for example, online: www.cbc.ca/fifth/badapples/interviews_yoo.html.

the answer carries not only moral significance, but also the potential for very real and tangible legal effects in the form of sanctions that would be imposed on the actor when the public rejects her illegal actions.

B. The effects of ex post *ratification*

What if the public does ratify *ex post* the extra-legal actions taken by public officials in times of emergency? How are we to understand the legal status of those actions once ratified? We already noted Agamben's acknowledgement of the impossible task inherent in the need to determine the nature of acts committed during *iustitium*: 'What is a human praxis that is wholly delivered over to a juridical void?'[37] Of course, for Agamben, this impossibility results from his conceptualisation of the exception as a juridical void and the corollary conclusion that such human praxis is 'radically removed from any juridical determination'.[38] It should by now be clear that determining the nature of extra-legal actions by public officials according to ELM, while possibly a difficult decision to be made in any particular case, is not impossible. In fact, there are legal benchmarks against which assessment of the act can be made.

The conspiracy of L. Sergius Catilina to take over the control of Rome by invading it with an army from Etruria was one of Marcus Tullius Cicero's greatest moments.[39] Acting as consul, Cicero foiled the conspiracy by mobilising troops to defend the city and capturing Catilina's accomplices. On 5 December, 63 BCE, Cicero assembled the Roman Senate in order to obtain its consent for the summary execution of five of those accomplices. Cicero believed that such action was necessary in order to safeguard the Republic. In his fourth Catilinarian Oration before the Senate, he conveyed the following description of what would have befallen Rome had the conspirators been successful: 'I imagine this city, the light of the world and the citadel of every nation, suddenly being burnt to the ground. I see in my mind's eye pitiful heaps of citizens unburied, in a country that has itself been buried . . . I cannot help but shudder at the thought of mothers

[37] Agamben, *State of Exception*, p. 49. [38] *Ibid.*, p. 50.

[39] E.G. Hardy, *The Catilinarian Conspiracy in Its Context: A Re-study of the Evidence* (Oxford: Basil Blackwell, 1924); Sallust, *The Jugurthine War and the Conspiracy of Catiline*, S.A. Handford (trans.) (Baltimore: Penguin, 1963), pp. 175–233; M. Cary and H.H. Scullard, *A History of Rome Down to the Reign of Constantine*, 3rd edn (New York: St. Martin's Press, 1975), pp. 246–7.

weeping, girls and boys running for their lives, and Vestal virgins being raped'.[40]

In light of this existential threat and because 'this prospect seems to me so dreadfully pitiful and pitiable', Cicero decided to take 'a firm and resolute stance against those who would perpetrate the atrocities'.[41] Yet, the execution without a proper trial of Roman citizens who were not previously declared 'public enemy' and who, at the relevant time, did not present an immediate threat to Rome, was outside the legal authority of the consul or, for that matter, of the Senate.[42] Although the Senate had previously declared a state of emergency (*tumultus*) and passed a resolution of last resort (*senatus consultum ultimum*), such proclamation could not legally confer new powers on the consul, notwithstanding Cicero's claims that it bestowed on him dictatorial powers including the right to order the summary execution of a Roman citizen.[43] Nevertheless, Cicero did go ahead and ordered the execution of the conspirators without trial.

Although Cicero was generally hailed as having saved the republic, the risk to himself of acting as he did was significant. Not long after the conspiracy was crushed, an attempt was made by new tribunes, led by one of Cicero's bitterest enemies, Publius Clodius, to impeach Cicero for the unlawful executions by passing a bill that any citizen guilty of putting another to death without trial would be sent into exile. With the political odds stacked high against him Cicero had to escape from Rome. Condemned by yet another bill as a criminal for his violation of the law, Cicero's house was demolished and his property confiscated.[44] A year later, when Clodius's term as tribune ended and new forces, backed by Pompey, assumed power in Rome, Cicero was recalled back after a vote of 416 to 1 in the Senate and a subsequent positive public vote.[45]

How are we to understand the nature of the actions by the liberator of Rome who is also a lawbreaker? ELM suggests that the answer depends on the nature of the eventual ratification. In Cicero's case, that ratification did not serve to legalise, *ex post*, the possibility of executing Roman citizens without proper trial nor did it don a cloak of legality over Cicero's actions

[40] M.T. Cicero, 'In Catilinam IV' in *Cicero: Political Speeches*, D.H. Berry (trans.) (Oxford University Press, 2006), § 11–12, p. 193 at 197–8.

[41] *Ibid.*; Hardy, *The Catilinarian Conspiracy*, p. 85.

[42] Cary and Scullard, *History of Rome*, p. 247; Hardy, *The Catilinarian Conspiracy*, pp. 86–7.

[43] Hardy, *The Catilinarian Conspiracy*, pp. 55–7 and 98–9.

[44] T. Holland, *Rubicon: The Triumph and Tragedy of the Roman Republic* (London: Abacus, 2003), pp. 238–40.

[45] *Ibid.*, pp. 253–4.

in the particular context of Catilina's conspiracy. Those remained unlawful and, once the political regime changed, Cicero was punished for them. The fact that, after much intervening political and legal uncertainty, Cicero was allowed to return to Rome did not expunge that earlier experience nor did it act to legalise his earlier actions. On the other hand, we have already seen Dicey's claim that an Act of Indemnity 'legalises illegality'.[46] Acts of Indemnity, according to Dicey, exculpate the actor from any legal responsibility for her actions by making such actions – which when taken were unlawful – lawful retrospectively. However, even where the illegal actions performed by public officials are taken to preserve and protect the nation, that alone does not, in and of itself, make those actions legal. Necessity does not make legal that which otherwise would have been illegal.[47] It may exempt the actor from subsequent legal liability, but only subsequent ratification *may* (but does not have to) transform the extra-legal nature of the relevant act into legality.[48] Extra-legal actions and constitutionally permissible acts are not equal in obligation and force under the constitutional scheme.[49] The former are not made legal or constitutional as a result of the necessity of the situation. The very fact that an action is branded 'extra-legal' raises the costs of undertaking it.

C. Ex post *ratification and legal black holes*

If *ex post* ratification also allows for the possibility of such ratification legalising that which otherwise would have been deemed unlawful then ELM becomes subject to the critique that it does not offer any meaningful method to maintain constitutional and legal constraints over public officials. Indeed, if a state of emergency permits stepping outside the legal system, no limits – certainly no legal limits – can be set on how far such deviations would go and how wide in scope they would be. Even if such limitations are conceivable, the scenario in which the unlawful becomes lawful *ex post* undermines ELM's claim that it upholds the rule of law. Even some who expressed sympathy with the possibility of exercising powers

[46] Dicey, *Law of the Constitution*, pp. 10–11 and 142.

[47] Compare A. Simester's contribution: 'Necessity, Torture and the Rule of Law' (Chapter 12), this volume, pp. 293–4.

[48] J. Lobel, 'Emergency Power and the Decline of Liberalism' (1989) 98 *Yale Law Journal* 1385 at 1390–97.

[49] *Marbury* v. *Madison*, 5 U.S. (1 Cranch) 137, 176–77 (1803); Schauer, 'The Questions of Authority', 102–3.

extra-legally have conceded these points.[50] Yet to acknowledge the possibility of extra-legal action is categorically different from accepting the spectre of limitless powers and authority in the hands of state agents.

According to ELM, when a public official acts outside the legal order in the face of exigency her actions are extra-legal. The urgency and necessity of the situation cannot legalise that which otherwise would have been illegal. However, when we turn our attention to the issue of *ex post* ratification of those actions, we realise that the actor may pay a significant price for her actions or may be praised and receive substantial benefits for undertaking them. Her actions may remain unlawful or they may be transformed and become lawful *ex post*. But even if the actions remain unlawful it may well be that the actor would not be subject to any sanctions related to these acts. The real state of affairs – with respect to the consequences for the acting official – remains unknown until the process of *ex post* ratification is concluded. Until then, uncertainty reigns.

Dicey clearly recognises the significant constructive value of this uncertainty when he suggests that 'there are one or two considerations which limit the practical importance that can fairly be given to an expected Act of Indemnity. The relief to be obtained from it is *prospective and uncertain*'.[51] Uncertainty and the prospective nature of the required *ex post* ratification may not only slow down the rush to act extra-legally in the first place. They may also facilitate meaningful limitations (legal and otherwise) on such actions once they are taken. By separating the extra-legal actions of public officials in extreme cases and subsequent public ratification, and by ordering them so that ratification follows, rather than precedes, action, ELM seeks to add uncertainty to the decision-making calculus of state agents which, in turn, raises both the individual and national costs of pursuing an extra-legal course of action and, at the same time, reinforces the rule of obedience.

With the need to obtain *ex post* ratification from the public, officials who decide to act extra-legally undertake a significant risk because of the uncertain prospects for subsequent ratification. The public may, for example, disagree after the fact with the acting officials' assessment of the situation and the need to act extra-legally. Ratification would be sought *ex post*, when calm and rationality, rather than heightened emotions, might govern public discourse and when more information about the

[50] See, for example, M. Tushnet, 'Defending *Korematsu*?: Reflections on Civil Liberties in Wartime' (2003) *Wisconsin Law Review* 273 at 306, n. 122.

[51] Dicey, *Law of the Constitution*, pp. 144–5 (emphasis added).

particular case at hand may be available to the public and possibly after the particular danger has been eliminated or averted.[52] Indeed, if the officials are successful and the harm to the nation is averted, the assessment of the legitimacy of acting extra-legally is likely to be more heavily weighted against them since no harm would be 'available' to the public to justify or excuse violations of the law.[53] Success of extra-legal actions may actually strengthen the case against the granting of *ex post* ratification to the acting officials, deterring them further from acting extra-legally.

Uncertainty is also important because it reduces the potential risk of under-deterrence that is involved in the possibility of *ex post* ratification. Under-deterrence may be a significant concern if public officials have good reasons to believe that ratification will be forthcoming in future cases when they act extra-legally.[54] Dicey openly acknowledges that the expectation of the executive that Parliament will pass Acts of Indemnity 'has not been disappointed' as a matter of history and experience.[55] Acts of Indemnity have, in fact, been 'passed by all governments when the occasion requires it'.[56] This would seem to eliminate, or at least significantly minimise, any uncertainty on the part of public officials about the prospects of *ex post* ratification. David Dyzenhaus argues:

> If the Extra-Legal Measures model were public, as it must be if it is to promote deliberation, the expectation would be generated of after-the-fact validation of illegal official acts. In an atmosphere of fear that expectation would likely be met rather easily, especially when the threat is, or is claimed to be, a constant one and the government successfully manipulates public opinion.[57]

Uncertainty results from acoustic separation between rules that guide public officials' conduct and those rules that govern the determination whether those who act extra-legally can be held responsible for their

[52] *Ibid.*, p. 145.

[53] See Gross, 'Chaos and Rules', in *Global Anti-Terrorism Law and Policy*, pp. 1039–40 (on the availability heuristic in the context of terrorist attacks).

[54] J.T. Parry and W.S. White, 'Interrogating Suspected Terrorists: Should Torture Be an Option?' (2002) 63 *University of Pittsburgh Law Review* 743 at 764–5; S. Levinson, '"Pre-commitment" and "Postcommitment": The Ban on Torture in the Wake of September 11' (2003) 81 *Texas Law Review* 2013 at 2045–8.

[55] Dicey, *Law of the Constitution*, p. 144.

[56] *Mitchell* v. *Clark*, 110 U.S. 633 at 640 (1884).

[57] D. Dyzenhaus, 'The State of Emergency in Legal Theory' in Ramraj, Hor and Roach (eds.), *Global Anti-Terrorism Law and Policy*, p. 65 at 72–3. See also H.P. Monaghan, 'The Protective Power of the Presidency' (1993) 93 *Columbia Law Review* 1 at 26.

behaviour.[58] Under-deterrence may result from conditions of low acoustic separation between such conduct and decision rules. Low acoustic separation increases the likelihood that officials will be familiar with both sets of normative messages and will be able to act strategically. This creates substantial risks of undesirable behavioural side effects on the part of officials, for example, by allowing decision rules – which recognise the possibility that agents who resort to extra-legal actions in extreme cases may be let off the hook – to affect the conduct of the officials in specific cases (i.e., state agents resorting to such extra-legal actions knowing, or at least having good reason to believe, that they will enjoy immunity against criminal charges and civil claims).[59] However, uncertainty acts to minimise the risks of behavioural side effects in the context of ELM. The more uncertain are the substance and the operation of the decision rules – which are, in the context of the model, directed at the general public as the *ex post* decision-maker – and the greater is the personal risk involved in wrongly interpreting either of those, the greater the incentive for individual actors to conform their action to the conduct rules – primarily the rule of obedience – and eschew the urge to act extra-legally.

Indeed, several critics have suggested that, if anything, ELM would result in over- rather than under-deterrence of public officials. Thus, for example, Jack Goldsmith notes that Alberto Gonzales and David Addington 'and their respective clients' (i.e. President Bush and Vice President Cheney) 'were not remotely interested in [ELM]'. He suggests that 'The post-Watergate hyper-legalisation of warfare, and the attendant proliferation of criminal investigators, had become so ingrained and threatening that the very idea of acting extralegally was simply off the table, even in times of crisis. The President had to do what he had to do to protect the country. And the lawyers had to find some way to make what he did legal'.[60] The problem, according to Goldsmith, is not that ELM's effect on public officials would be that of under-deterrence, but rather that it would act to over-deter them; instead of causing more official action than is optimal, ELM would lead to suboptimal action on the part of officials and may contribute to rigidity and paralysis where flexibility and action are called for.[61] Critics who make this charge against ELM often argue that the 'hyper-legalisation of warfare' was a major cause for the culture of

[58] M. Dan-Cohen, 'Decision Rules and Conduct Rules: On Acoustic Separation in Criminal Law' (1984) 97 *Harvard Law Review* 625 at 636–41.

[59] *Ibid.*, pp. 631–2. [60] Goldsmith, *The Terror Presidency*, p. 81.

[61] See also Posner and Vermeule, *Terror in the Balance*, pp. 172–3.

risk aversion and excessive caution that seized the intelligence community in the United States prior 9/11 and which prevented it from foiling the attacks.

Even if one accepts that there exists a good chance that *ex post* ratification will be forthcoming, there are still significant costs to acting extra-legally. For starters, there remains a degree of anxiety that ratification will not, in fact, follow. Likelihood and even high probability do not equate with certainty. More significantly, ratification may not be comprehensive or fully corrective. Again, Dicey notes: 'As regards . . . the protection to be derived from the Act [of Indemnity] by men who have been guilty of irregular, illegal, oppressive, or cruel conduct, *everything depends on the terms of the Act of Indemnity*'.[62] Subsequent ratification may, for example, shield the actor against criminal charges, but not bar the possibility of civil proceedings. It may also not shield the actor from liability for all of her actions. Similarly, when ratification assumes the guise of an executive pardon or clemency, it eliminates the criminal penalty that was imposed on the individual actor, but it neither removes the ordeal of criminal prosecution nor the condemnation associated with criminal conviction.[63] If we wish to increase the costs of extra-legal actions even further we can introduce a duty of compensation and reparations – which can be imposed on the individual public officials or on the state – to those who were the victims of such actions, whether or not the actions have enjoyed *ex post* ratification.[64]

When we consider international legal rules and norms, the costs and uncertainties that are involved in acting extra-legally increase further. Even if a particular extra-legal act is domestically ratified it may be subject to a different judgment on the international level. This may have significant consequences both for the individual public official and her government. Acting officials may still be subject to criminal and civil proceedings in jurisdictions other than their own, and may also be subject to international criminal prosecution. Thus, for example, Jack Goldsmith, while decrying the effects of the 'judicialization of warfare' on the ability of the United States to engage in forceful counter-terrorism measures, claims

[62] Dicey, *Law of the Constitution*, p. 145 (emphasis added).

[63] L. Sheleff, 'On Criminal Homicide and Legal Self Defense' (1997) 6 *Plilim* 89 at 111–12; Y. Kamisar, 'Physician Assisted Suicide: The Problems Presented by the Compelling, Heartwrenching Case' (1998) 88 *Journal of Criminal Law & Criminology* 1121 at 1143–4.

[64] See, e.g., Levinson, 'Precommitment', 2049–50; Tushnet, 'Defending Korematsu?', 307; Civil Liberties Act of 1988, Pub. L. No. 100–383, 102 Stat. 903 (Congressional formal apology and restitution to victims of the Japanese internment of World War II).

that Donald Rumsfeld 'worried more than ever' about that phenomenon and it 'wasn't only foreign courts that Rumsfeld worried about – it was international courts too'.[65]

As part of the compromise allowing free elections to be held in Chile, a general amnesty was issued in 1978, granting immunity from criminal proceedings for offences committed between 1973 and 1978. In addition, Augusto Pinochet, the former Chilean dictator, was given the title of senator-for-life, granting him immunity from prosecution under the Constitution. However, in October 1998, while visiting the United Kingdom for medical treatment, Pinochet was arrested on an arrest warrant – issued by a Spanish judge – for the murder in Chile of Spanish citizens while he was President. A further arrest warrant was issued soon thereafter, charging Pinochet with systematic torture, murder, illegal detention and forced disappearances during his rule in Chile. After a long legal battle Pinochet was released in March 2000 on medical grounds without facing trial in the United Kingdom. However, his arrest in the United Kingdom drew not only international attention to Pinochet's crimes but also changed Chile's own willingness to come to (new) terms with its past. After returning to Chile Pinochet was stripped of his immunity and was subsequently indicted with such crimes as kidnappings, torture, murder and tax evasion.[66] It is also noteworthy that in January 2005, the Chilean Army accepted institutional responsibility for past human rights abuses during the rule of the military junta.[67] The renewed public focus on the junta regime also led to new revelations about the CIA's involvement in assisting Pinochet and the junta in overthrowing the democratically elected Allende government.[68]

The emergence of political and legal willingness to prosecute former state leaders and other high-ranking state officials for human rights abuses that they had perpetrated, orchestrated, ordered or have otherwise been

[65] J. Goldsmith, *The Terror Presidency: Law and Judgment Inside the Bush administration* (New York: W.W. Norton & Co., 2007), p. 61.

[66] It should be noted that at the time of his death in December 2006, Pinochet had not been convicted of any crimes committed during his dictatorship. However, as this chapter went to print, a Chilean judge ordered the arrests of the widow and five of Pinochet's children as well as of 17 of his closest military and civilian collaborators on charges of misappropriating more than $20 million public funds. See P. Bonnefoy and A. Barrionuevo, 'Chilean Court Orders Arrests of Pinochet's Kin and Close Allies' *New York Times* (5 October 2007), p. A5.

[67] P. Kornbluh, 'Letter from Chile' *The Nation* (13 January 2005) available online at www.thenation.com/doc/20050131/kornbluh.

[68] P. Kornbluh, 'Chile and the United State: Declassified Documents Related to the Military Coup of September 11, 1973' (Nat'l Sec. Archive Briefing Book No. 8), available online at www.gwu.edu/~nsarchiv/NSAEBB/NSAEBB8/nsaebb8i.htm.

involved in, has had great effect on the conduct of such officials.[69] In recent years, a new international regulatory model emerged concerning violations of core human rights and war crimes – centred around individual legal criminal accountability.[70] A world in which domestic courts show willingness to exercise universal jurisdiction and in which international tribunals such as the International Criminal Court become active, exacerbates the uncertainty faced by public officials under ELM.[71]

Furthermore, to the extent that the relevant actions violate the nation's international legal obligations, especially its obligations and undertakings under the major international human rights conventions and are not covered by an appropriate derogation (or are in violation of non-derogable rights), state agents who engage in such acts expose their government to a range of possible remedies under the relevant international legal instruments and possibly in foreign jurisdictions as well.[72] Indeed by recognising what has occurred, a domestic *ex post* ratification may facilitate international remedies.

Thus, ELM imposes significant burdens on public officials. They must act in the face of great uncertainty. If they believe that the stakes are high enough to merit an extra-legal action, they may still decide to act extra-legally 'for the public good' and expect to be protected subsequently by some form of *ex post* ratification. At the same time, the model makes it extremely costly to resort to such drastic measures, limiting their use to exceptional exigencies. Thus Cicero:

> [I]f the immortal gods intend this to be the outcome of my consulship, that I should rescue you and the Roman people from a pitiless massacre,

[69] See S. Romero, 'Living in Exile Isn't What it Used to be' *New York Times* (7 Oct. 2007), p. 416.

[70] See K. Sikkink, 'From State Responsibility to Individual Criminal Accountability: A New Regulatory Model for Core Human Rights Violations' (July 2007) (on file with the author); S. Ratner and J. Abrams, *Accountability for Human Rights Atrocities in International Law: Beyond the Nuremberg Legacy*, 2nd edn (Oxford: Oxford University Press, 2001); A. Cassese, *International Criminal Law* (Oxford: Oxford University Press, 2003).

[71] See, for example, Guatemala Genocide Case, Judgment No. STC 237/2005 (Spanish Constitutional Tribunal, 26 September 2005), available online at www.tribunalconstitucional.es/jurisprudencia/Stc2005/STC2005-237.html (broad application of universal jurisdiction by the Spanish Constitutional Court); UN Security Council Resolution 1593, UN SCOR, 5158th mtg., UN Doc. S/RES/1593 (31 March 2005) (referring the situation in Darfur to the ICC Prosecutor). In April 2007, judges at the ICC issued arrest warrants for Ahmad Harun – a former Sudanese Minister of State for the Interior – and Janjaweed leader Ali Kushayb, for 51 counts of crimes against humanity and war crimes.

[72] But see *Jones* v. *Saudi Arabia* [2007] 1 All E.R. 113.

> your wives and children and the Vestal virgins from brutal rape, the temples and shrines and this beautiful homeland of each one of us from the most loathsome fire, and the whole of Italy from war and devastation, then I am willing to submit, alone, to whatever fortune may have in store for me.[73]

As Sanford Kadish notes, 'Would not the burden on the official be so great that it would require circumstances of a perfectly extraordinary character to induce the individual to take the risk of acting? The answer is of course yes, that's the point'.[74]

Even if we accept, *arguendo*, Dyzenhaus's assertion that under ELM taking illegal actions may be 'openly advocated to' public officials, that in and of itself, does not lower the risks that those officials face in so acting for there is nothing given to them by way of *ex ante* assurances. Jack Goldsmith, who notes the toll that over-legalisation took on the Bush administration's ability to fight successfully and forcefully the war on terror, describes what he perceives to be the plight of public officials in these words:

> In my two years in government, I witnessed top officials and bureaucrats in the White House and throughout the administration openly worrying that investigators acting with the benefit of hindsight in a different political environment would impose criminal penalties on heat-of-battle judgment calls. [They worried] because they would be judged in an atmosphere different from when they acted, because the criminal investigative process is mysterious and scary, because lawyers' fees can cause devastating financial losses, and because an investigation can produce reputation-ruining dishonor and possibly end one's career, even if you emerge 'innocent'.[75]

The more uncertain it is that ratification will be forthcoming, the more uncertain its potential scope and the greater the personal risk involved in wrongly interpreting either of those is, the greater the incentive for individual actors to conform their action to the existing legal rules and norms and not risk acting outside them. The burden lies squarely on the shoulders of the public officials who must act, sometimes extra-legally, without the benefit of legal pre-approval of their actions by the courts or the legislature. Public officials have no one to hide behind. They must put themselves on the front line and act at their own peril. Thomas Jefferson observed:

73 Cicero, 'In Catilinam IV', in *Cicero: Political Speeches*, p. 193.

74 S.H. Kadish, 'Torture, the State and the Individual' (1989) 23 *Israel Law Review* 345 at 355.

75 J. Goldsmith, *The Terror Presidency*, p. 69.

> The officer who is called to act on this superior ground, does indeed risk himself on the justice of the controlling powers of the constitution, and his station makes it his duty to incur that risk... The line of discrimination between cases [where such action is necessary and where it is not] may be difficult; but the good officer is bound to draw it at his own peril, and throw himself on the justice of his country and the rectitude of his motives.[76]

The argument that ELM puts public officials in a 'zone uncontrolled by law'[77] underestimates the significance of such disincentives to step outside the legal framework and of the possibilities for external supervision, both by the public and by other branches of government.

Indeed, Dyzenhaus himself seems to recognise these disincentives. He suggests that for Dicey 'an Act of Indemnity should not purport to provide a blanket indemnity for all illegal activity, nor should it provide expressly that it covers bad faith acts or acts of reckless cruelty. The Act is meant to secure the rule of law, not to undermine it... In a democracy, the rule of law should only be sacrificed for the sake of the rule of law and *that condition imposes its own constraints on the sacrifice*'.[78] Once again, even according to Dyzenhaus's reading of Dicey that an Act of Indemnity could only indemnify an action that could and should have been authorised in advance had there been sufficient time,[79] there exists a marked difference between an *ex ante* authorisation for such an action and a possible, yet uncertain, *ex post* ratification of it. Dyzenhaus finds that Governor Eyre's actions in Jamaica in 1865 exhibited what he terms 'the compulsion of legality'. Politics was 'understood and transacted largely in terms of law and legality'.[80] Dyzenhaus notes, for example, that Eyre was scrupulous in taking legal advice from his chief law officer before he declared martial law. In light of this scrupulousness is it not possible to assume that the

[76] Letter from Thomas Jefferson to John B. Colvin (20 September 1810), in Ford, *Thomas Jefferson* (New York: G.P. Putnam's Sons, 1986), p. 1231 at 1233. See also A. Reichman, '"When We Sit to Judge We Are Being Judged": The Israeli GSS Case, Ex Parte Pinochet and Domestic/Global Deliberation' (2001) 9 *Cardozo Journal of International & Comparative Law* 41 at 67–8.

[77] D. Dyzenhaus, 'The State of Emergency in Legal Theory' in Ramraj, Hor and Roach (eds.), *Global Anti-Terrorism Law and Policy*, p. 65.

[78] Dyzenhaus, Chapter 2, pp. 47–8. (emphasis added).

[79] This is by no means as clear as Dyzenhaus tries to make it. Note again in this context, Dicey's own words: 'As regards... the protection to be derived from the Act [of Indemnity] by men who have been guilty of irregular, illegal, *oppressive, or cruel conduct*, everything depends on the terms of the Act of Indemnity' (above, note 62). Hence, according to Dicey, an Act of Indemnity could, in fact, cover within its ambit acts that are 'oppressive or cruel'.

[80] Dyzenhaus, Chapter 2, p. 49.

Governor would have been a bit more circumspect and his actions a bit more cautious and less flagrant had the compulsion of legality not been satisfied *ex ante*, i.e. where he was not armed with a legal opinion clearing the road, *ex ante*, for the imposition of martial law and the measures that followed? We can expect that an official who takes action without having the benefit of an authoritative legal opinion that states the legality of her action and 'immunizes' the official against future claims and charges to be more hesitant and cautious before acting as compared with an official who acts with the certainty and security offered by such an opinion.

The threshold of illegality provides an intrinsic limit against a rush to employ unnecessary measures. We can and should expect public officials to feel quite uneasy about possible resort to extra-legal measures, even when such actions are deemed to be for the public's benefit.[81] Jack Goldsmith writes: 'It may be hard to believe that executive branch officials, many of whom risk their lives to protect the nation, really care much about criminal law, investigation, and possibly, jail. But they do care – a lot'.[82] This feeling of uneasiness would be even more pronounced in nations where the 'constitution is old, observed for a long time, known, respected, and cherished'.[83] The knowledge that acting in a certain way means acting unlawfully is, in and of itself, going to have a restraining effect on government agents, even while the threat of catastrophe persists. Officials, as individuals, are not immune to self-regulation that results, among other things, from their internalisation of socially accepted moral and legal norms and that pushes them to value observing those norms and be weary of norm-violating conduct. When we add the spectre of having to give reasons to the public for one's illegal actions after the crisis is over, it seems likely that the mere need to cross the threshold of illegality would serve as a further limiting factor against a governmental

[81] Weber, 'Politics as Vocation', in Gerth and Mills, *From Max Weber: Essays in Sociology*, p. 121.

[82] Goldsmith, *The Terror Presidency*, p. 69.

[83] G.H. Dodge, *Benjamin Constant's Philosophy of Liberalism: A Study in Politics and Religion* 101 (Chapel Hill: University of North Carolina Press, 1980) (quoting Benjamin Constant). Constant recognised that in nations where the constitutional experience is as described in the quoted excerpt, the constitution 'can be suspended for an instant, if a great emergency requires it.' He distinguishes this case from the following: '[I]f a constitution is new and not in practice nor identified with the habit of a people, then every suspension, either partial or temporary, is the end of that constitution'. See also G.L. Negretto and J.A.A. Rivera, 'Liberalism and Emergency Powers in Latin America: Reflections on Carl Schmitt and the Theory of Constitutional Dictatorship' (2000) 21 *Cardozo L. Rev.* 1797 at 1800–03.

rush to assume unnecessary powers.[84] Furthermore, in a democratic society, where values such as constitutionalism, accountability and individual rights are firmly entrenched and traditionally respected, we can expect that the public would be circumspect about governmental attempts to justify or excuse illegal actions. That being the case, 'Any suspicion on the part of the public, that officials had grossly abused their powers, might make it difficult to obtain a Parliamentary indemnity for things done'.[85] The public may also determine that the extra-legal actions violated values and principles that are too important to be encroached upon, as a matter of principle or in the circumstances of the particular case. The greater the moral and legal interests and values infringed upon, the less certain the actor can be of securing ratification. For ELM, Dyzenhaus's strong words in 'a democracy, the rule of law should only be sacrificed for the sake of the rule of law and that condition imposes its own constraints on the sacrifice' certainly ring true.[86]

IV. Candour

I argued earlier that the more uncertain it is that ratification will be forthcoming, the more uncertain its potential scope and the greater the personal risk involved in wrongly interpreting either of those is, the greater the incentive for individual actors to conform their action to the existing legal rules and norms and not risk acting outside them. But rather than incentivise rule-obedience on the part of public officials, could not such grave uncertainty lead officials to disguise their actions and coat them with secrecy rather than seek to conform their actions to the law?[87] After all, if the public does not learn of the extra-legal action to start with there would be no opportunity for passing judgment *ex post* over such actions. In other words, public officials may neither be likely to disclose their actions nor admit that such actions, even if made public, had been extra-legal. Instead, they may opt for secrecy or for arguments utilising open-ended constitutional language to claim that their actions have, in fact, been legal. Yet, according to ELM, public officials who act extra-legally in extreme cases need to acknowledge openly the nature of their actions and attempt to justify both their actions and their undertaking of those

[84] Gross and Ní Aoláin, *Law in Times of Crisis*, pp. 155–6.
[85] Dicey, *Law of the Constitution*, p. 145. [86] Dyzenhaus, Chapter 2, p. 48.
[87] See, for example, S. Chesterman, Chapter 13.

actions.[88] The open acknowledgement and engagement in public justificatory exercise are critical components in the moral and legal choices made by the officials.

In his contribution to this volume, Simon Chesterman notes that in the context of the current war on terror, 'Much, in the end, was debated publicly though this tended to be the result of investigative journalism or disclosures in legal action on behalf of affected individuals. There was little evidence of a willingness on the part of the executive to have arguments over legality "openly, candidly, and fully disclosed." On the contrary, questionable conduct was asserted – at times improbably – to fall within the law. The most troubling conduct was simply denied.'[89] Thus, after reviewing issues concerning torture, extrajudicial detention and warrant-less surveillance, he concludes that 'public deliberation on the legality of the practice clearly was never intended by the relevant officials'.[90] Of course, if this is the case (and I believe it is) then we must conclude that in none of these examples did the officials live up to the requirements of ELM. But we cannot content ourselves in making this argument for in turn it opens the ELM to the further challenge of being utopian and not useful in real life. As Chesterman suggests 'It appears unrealistic, therefore, to put much hope in the prospect that such decisions will ever be made either openly or candidly.'[91]

Such critique seems to rely heavily on a sense of separation between 'investigative journalism' and the willingness of public officials to be open and candid about their actions. However, such separation is, in and of itself, unrealistic and misses the interplay between the two in nations that enjoy a robust and engaged civil society. Modern reality indicates that the ability of public officials to keep their actions secret and hidden from public view is significantly limited. Investigative journalism, both by traditional media and such developing tools as web-based blogs, all but ensures that, in due course, much, if not everything, is going to be exposed. A threat may, indeed, be stronger than its ultimate execution and thus it may well be that the very real threat of subsequent publicity, no matter how hard officials try to hide their actions, would have a significant braking power on the road to illegality no matter how noble the call for action may be.

This is especially true when we consider matters from a broader, long-term, historical perspective. High-ranking officials may care deeply about

[88] M.R. Kadish and S.H. Kadish, *Discretion To Disobey: A Study of Lawful Departures from Legal Rules* (Stanford: Stanford University Press, 1973), pp. 5–12.

[89] Chesterman, Chapter 13, p. 320. [90] *Ibid.*, p. 326. [91] *Ibid.*, p. 327.

their place in history and how they are perceived. They would be aware that skeletons in their proverbial closets may adversely affect history's judgment of their actions. As Justice Jackson noted: 'The chief restraint upon those who command the physical forces of the country . . . must be their responsibility to the political judgments of their contemporaries and to the moral judgments of history'.[92] Furthermore, if the truth about the extra-legal actions comes about not through open and candid (and one may add, timely) disclosure by the relevant officials but rather through 'investigative journalism' it may well affect the public perception of those actions and the public's willingness to accord them its *ex post* ratification. In this respect it may be said that open, candid and timely disclosure by the acting public official works as a powerful de facto condition for the official's ability to escape sanctions and perhaps be heralded for her heroic efforts on behalf of the nation.

There may be additional strong (and potentially more troubling) incentives for acting officials to disclose their actions openly and in a timely manner. The closer in time is the disclosure to the actual emergency the more likely it is that the public, still under the strong impression of the crisis, will ratify the measures. Moreover, the executive is often the first to act in the face of emergency and its actions are most visible. 'In drama, magnitude and finality his decisions so far overshadow any others that almost alone he fills the public eye and ear'.[93] When added to the consensus-generating quality of emergencies[94] that means that the other branches of government will have to catch up with the executive (should they at all wish to) and react to its actions. The agenda, including the legislative agenda, will be dictated and dominated by the executive.[95] Such domination is facilitated further by the realities of party politics. In parliamentary systems the government is supported by a majority in parliament. In fact, times of acute crises may also lead the opposition to mute its criticisms of the government or even join the government itself as part of a coalition of national unity. While in presidential systems such control of the legislature is not guaranteed, in countries such as the United States the realities

92 *Korematsu* v. *United States*, 323 U.S. 214, 248 (1944) (Jackson J. dissenting).

93 Youngstown, 343 US 579 at 653 (1952) (Jackson J. concurring).

94 Gross, 'Chaos and Rules', 1035–6.

95 C.L. Rossiter, *Constitutional Dictatorship: Crisis Government in Modern Democracies* (Princeton: Princeton University Press, 1948), pp. 240–55; H.H. Koh, *The National Security Constitution: Sharing Power after the Iran-Contra Affair* (New Haven: Yale University Press, 1990), pp. 117–23; M. Tushnet, 'Controlling Executive Power in the War on Terrorism' (2005) 118 *Harvard Law Review* 2673 at 2677.

of the modern political party system have benefited the executive. Once again, it was Justice Jackson who noted perceptively that, 'Party loyalties and interests, sometimes more binding than law, extend [the President's] effective control into branches of government other than his own and he often may win, as a political leader, what he cannot command under the Constitution'.[96] In addition, the fact that in periods of emergency, conflicts that seem to be mere partisan politics are set aside ensure that 'When government is unified, in the sense that the President and Congress are in the hands of the same party, and that party is itself more unified than ever, Congress will probably authorize anything for which the President asks. When government is divided, with at least one house of Congress not controlled by the President's party, the story is more complicated, but broad authorizations still seem likely'.[97] The executive's 'first mover' advantage in this area pertains not merely to the other branches of government but also to the general public. Executive branch officials may well prefer to disclose their actions early and gain control, at least initially, over the way in which such actions are presented and discussed in public rather than risk that the public deliberation would be initiated by external disclosures and revelations that may also undermine their ability to manipulate the story and give it the desired spin.

This potential for manipulation exacerbates another risk of ELM. Taken to its logical extreme, the model does not seem to incorporate substantive limitations on the range of possible extra-legal actions taken in the face of emergency that may later be ratified. There is nothing to prevent such ratification from being given to egregious actions. One way around this challenge is to incorporate into the model substantive elements, such as Bruce Ackerman's entrenchment of fundamental rights against constitutional revision and amendment or John Hart Ely's protection of certain minority groups.[98] Yet, if we accept the possibility, in extreme cases, of governmental actions that are extra-legal so long as they are taken to advance the public good, there can be no constitutional or legal limitations on such governmental exercise of power. If we accept that the executive may act outside the law in order to avert or overcome catastrophes, there is nothing to prevent the wielder of such awesome powers from exercising

[96] *Youngstown*, 343 US 579 at 654 (1952) (Jackson J. concurring); Tushnet, 'Controlling Executive Power', 2678–9.

[97] *Ibid.*, at 2679.

[98] B. Ackerman, *We the People: Foundations* (Cambridge: Belknap Press, 1991), pp. 320–1; J.H. Ely, *Democracy and Distrust: A Theory of Judicial Review* (Cambridge: Harvard University Press, 1980), pp. 135–79.

them in violation of any constitutional and legal limitations on the use of such powers.

In 1944, Judge Learned Hand, speaking in Central Park at a swearing-in ceremony of naturalised citizens told his audience:

> I often wonder whether we do not rest our hopes too much upon constitutions, upon laws and upon courts. These are false hopes... Liberty lies in the hearts of men and women; when it dies there, no constitution, no law, no court can save it; no constitution, no law, no court can even do much to help it. While it lies there it needs no constitution, no law, no court to save it.[99]

At the end of the day, ideas such as liberty, freedom, democracy and rule of law must exist in the hearts of the people if they are to survive the whirlwind of crisis and emergency. If they are not there to begin with, no model of emergency powers is likely to help much. As Carl Friedrich notes: 'there are no ultimate institutional safeguards available for insuring that emergency powers be used for the purpose of preserving the Constitution. Only the people's own determination to see them so used can make sure of that.'[100] Whether that determination exists will be reflected, among other things, in the process of *ex post* ratification (or rejection) of extra-legal measures taken by public officials. The ethics of popular responsibility that is advocated by ELM seeks to avoid that which Justice Brandeis identified as the greatest menace to freedom – an inert public: 'Those who won our independence believed... that the greatest menace to freedom is an inert people; that public discussion is a political duty; and that this should be a fundamental principle of the American government'.[101]

V. Institutional arrangements

Many of the critics of ELM put their faith in *ex ante* procedural and institutional arrangements. Thus, for example, William Scheuerman, another

[99] L. Hand, *The Spirit of Liberty: Papers and Addresses of Learned Hand*, I. Dillard (ed.) (New York: Legal Classics Library, 1989), pp. 189–90. See also G. Gunther, *Learned Hand: The Man and the Judge* (New York: Knopf, 1994), pp.547–52 and 639–43.

[100] C.J. Friedrich, *Constitutional Government and Democracy: Theory and Practice in Europe and America*, 4th edn (Waltham: Blaisdell Publishing Co., 1968), p. 570.

[101] *Whitney* v. *California*, 274 U.S. 357 at 375 (1927) (Brandeis J. concurring).

thoughtful student of emergency regimes and a self-proclaimed legal formalist,[102] supports suggestions such as Bruce Ackerman's 'escalating cascade of supermajorities' (ECS) as possible constitutional mechanisms to curb the rush to use – and abuse – emergency powers:[103] Based on the constitutional framework that is introduced in Article 37 of the Constitution of South Africa, Ackerman's proposal of ECS seeks to reduce the possibility of emergency powers becoming entrenched and 'normalised' by insisting on the temporary nature of such measures and making extensions thereof increasingly harder. Scheuerman argues that only such legal formalist suggestions pay sufficient attention to the 'institutional dynamics' of the 'modern executive.'[104] According to Scheuerman, the current jurisprudential debate about emergency powers suffers from insufficient consideration to the 'broader social and political context in which competing conceptions of emergency government operate.'[105] Specifically, in the American context, that debate fails to account for the changing nature of the executive branch.[106]

However, legal formalism does not fare well under Scheuerman's own yardstick for evaluating the different positions in the debate. In the first place, many of the particular proposals put forward by legal formalists in the context of emergency powers already exist in several constitutional regimes around the world and experience shows that they have not done well in practice.[107] While in many cases such failures may reflect issues of constitutional and political cultures, they also result from the problematic nature of attempts to provide *ex ante* for what is, in essence, unforeseen events. That difficulty was captured cogently by Alexander Hamilton when he wrote that, 'it is impossible to foresee or to define the extent and variety of national exigencies, and the correspondent extent and variety of the means which may be necessary to satisfy them. The circumstances that endanger the safety of nations are infinite'. It was for this reason, he argued, that 'no constitutional shackles can wisely be imposed on the

[102] W.E. Scheuerman, 'Emergency Powers' (2006) 2 *Annual Review of Law and Social Science* 257.

[103] B. Ackerman, 'The Emergency Constitution' (2004) 113 *Yale Law Journal* 1029 at 1047–49.

[104] Scheuerman, 'Emergency Powers' at 258. [105] *Ibid.*

[106] *Ibid.* See also, W.E. Scheuerman, 'Rethinking Crisis Government' in D. Sherman and T. Nardin (eds.), *Terror, Culture, Politics: Rethinking 9/11* (Bloomington: Indiana University Press, 2006), p. 214; W.E. Scheuerman, 'Emergency Powers and the Rule of Law After 9/11' (2006) 14 *Journal of Political Philosophy* 61.

[107] See generally Gross and Ní Aoláin, *Law in Times of Crisis*, pp. 35–66.

power to which the care of it is committed'.[108] Second, Scheuerman himself acknowledges that, 'In the face of institutional deadlock, and stymied by a hostile legislature or courts, presidents may opt to operate outside the boundaries of legal normalcy, enlivened to violate the regular operations of the rule of law'. That this is the case is explained by structural institutional dynamics including the tendency for presidents 'to see themselves as the most immediate embodiments of a unitary popular will, standing above normal politics and in possession of super-mundane talents and a special aura.'[109] But if Scheuerman is correct in this assessment then surely proposals that are designed to make extension of executive emergency powers more cumbersome are likely, if anything, to exacerbate the potential for presidential opting to operate outside the boundaries of legal normalcy in the face of 'institutional deadlock' when the stakes are high enough. As Scheuerman readily acknowledges: 'In practical terms this means that the executive is likely to latch onto more-or-less serious challenges to the political community and refashion them into life-or-death threats, or if the crisis at hand is indeed a dire one, milk it for everything it is worth politically even at the cost of undermining the rule of law'.[110] Under such circumstances, and in light of the plethora of institutional dynamics that Scheuerman identifies, ECS may well result in executive claims that Congress (or Parliament) is hampering the war effort and stifles the executive's ability to fight terrorism successfully and therefore Congress and the particular procedures that allow it to act in such manner must be by-passed for the greater good of the nation.

Third, different institutional dynamics also suggest that the potential effectiveness of ECS would further undermine it. Governments enjoy significant support, at least in the initial stages of emergency periods. James Madison noted that constitutions originated in the midst of great danger that led, among other things, to 'an enthusiastic confidence of the people in their patriotic leaders, which stifled the ordinary diversity of opinions on great national questions'.[111] Conflict is deemed dysfunctional for the

[108] C. Rossiter (ed.), *The Federalist Papers*, No. 23 (New York: New American Library, 1961), p. 153 (Alexander Hamilton). See also J. Hatchard, *Individual Freedoms and State Security in the African Context: The Case of Zimbabwe* (Harare: Baobab Books, 1993), p. 2; H.P. Lee, *Emergency Powers* (Sydney: Law Book Co., 1984), p. 5.

[109] Scheuerman, Chapter 11, p. 266. [110] *Ibid.*

[111] C. Rossiter (ed.), *The Federalist Papers*, No. 49 (New York: New American Library, 1961), p. 315 (James Madison). See also K.R. Popper, *The Open Society and Its Enemies*, 5th edn (Princeton: Princeton University Press, 1971), vol. I, pp. 43 and 198; E.L. Quarantelli

maintenance or survival of the relevant social system and the public as well as the courts and the legislature, tend to 'rally round the flag'.[112] Furthermore, crises present the executive with the advantage of the 'first-mover'. The combination of these phenomena and the potential success of proposals such as Ackerman's in curbing and restraining the executive responses to terrorism and external threats, may push presidents to capitalise on the early broad support that they are likely to receive and to aggregate as many broad powers as possible at that point for fear that such powers and measures will no longer be available to them at a later point in time in light of the need to ensure increasing legislative supermajorities.[113] Kent Roach observes that violent emergencies tend to bring about a rush to legislate. The prevailing belief may be that if new offences are added to the criminal code and the scope of existing offences broadened and if the arsenal of law enforcement agencies is enhanced by putting at their disposal more sweeping powers to search and seize, to eavesdrop, to interrogate, to detain without trial and to deport, the country will be more secure and better able to face the emergency.[114] It is often easier to pass new legislation than to examine why it is that the existing legislation and the powers granted under it to government and its agencies was not sufficient. This allows government to demonstrate that it is doing something against the dangers facing the nation rather than sitting idly. The need to respond quickly to future threats – as much as to assure the public that its government is acting with a vengeance against past and future terrorists – frequently results in rushed legislation, often without much debate and at times foregoing normal legislative procedures. Proposals such as ECS may, in fact, exacerbate such race against the clock problems. At the same time, the requirement of ECS combined with the above-noted phenomenon of early rally around the flag, may encourage individual legislators to not oppose initial executive measures based on the assumption that such measures are going to be temporary and expire shortly (if only due to

and R.R. Dynes, 'Community Conflict: Its Absence and Its Presence in Natural Disasters' (1976) 1 *Mass Emergencies* 139 at 140 and 145.

112 B. Russett, *Controlling the Sword: The Democratic Governance of National Security* (Cambridge: Harvard University Press, 1990), p. 34; G. Barzilai, *A Democracy in Wartime: Conflict and Consensus in Israel* (Tel Aviv: Sifriyat Poalim, 1992), pp. 248–60.

113 E.A. Posner and A. Vermeule, *Terror in the Balance: Security, Liberty and the Courts* (New York: Oxford University Press, 2007), p. 168.

114 K. Roach, 'The Dangers of a Charter-Proof and Crime-Based Response to Terrorism', in R.J. Daniels, P. Macklem and K. Roach (eds.), *The Security of Freedom: Essays on Canada's Antiterrorism Bill* (Toronto: University of Toronto Press, 2001), pp. 131 and 138–42; Gross, 'Chaos and Rules', 1031–4.

the executive's inability to garner the requisite supermajority).[115] This, in turn, may give further incentive to the executive to push for (overly) broad emergency powers and authorisation of sweeping initial measures which may not only be unnecessary, but once granted and accepted may become entrenched.

In addition, the perception that a robust ECS may hamper the executive's ability to fight successfully future crises – including such crises that may be unforeseen at present – may well encourage the legislature to accept the need for exceptions to be carved out to the 'normal' procedural requirements of the 'escalating cascade of supermajorities'. This is a recognised feature of many constitutional arrangements around the world: for example, a constitution may mandate that a 'normal' declaration of emergency be made by parliament while recognising special circumstances when the authority to so declare is vested in the President.[116]

Fourth, institutional proposals such as ECS come with a clear vision of emergency regulation that may not prove realistic. As noted above, ECS seeks to reduce the possibility of emergency powers becoming entrenched and 'normalised' by insisting on the temporary nature of such measures and making extensions thereof increasingly harder. But how, then, would ECS achieve that goal if one considers such possibilities as legislative accommodation through the modification of ordinary laws or the various forms of interpretive accommodation, i.e. forms of accommodating for emergency powers without, necessarily, invoking the need for an 'official' proclamation of emergency or for special emergency legislation? The former suggests that 'Legislative provisions that are born out of the need to respond to an emergency situation find their way into ordinary legislation and become part and parcel of the ordinary legal system . . . the legal framework used for applying emergency measures is the ordinary one as so modified'.[117] The latter means that 'Existing constitutional provisions, as well as laws and regulations, are given new understanding and clothing by way of context-based [judicial] interpretation without any explicit modification or replacement'.[118] These forms of 'dispersed emergency regulation'[119] are not easily, if at all, amenable to mechanisms such as ECS.

[115] Posner and Vermeule, *Terror in the Balance*, p. 168.
[116] Gross and Ní Aoláin, *Law in Times of Crisis*, pp. 54–8.
[117] *Ibid.*, p. 67. [118] *Ibid.*, p. 72.
[119] N. Hussain, 'Beyond Norm and Exception: Guantánamo' (2007) 33 *Critical Inquiry* 734 at 751.

Finally, Scheuerman and others have suggested that, faced with 'an executive outfitted with awesome symbolic authority and capable of propagating effective daily reminders of the immediate dangers at hand amid an atmosphere of ubiquitous fear, even the most courageous citizens may opt to shut their mouths. Contra Gross, the extra-legal model by no means seems destined to enliven public deliberation'.[120] Yet Scheuerman also argues, in support of Ackerman's ECS proposal, that 'as the initial emergency passes and the general climate of fear subsides, opposition legislators will discover their own political reasons for questioning controversial, repressive emergency measures'.[121] Rallying around the flag may be a relatively short-lived phenomenon in the context of controversial counter-terrorism measures and as the initial trauma wears off Congress's (and others') ability to stand up to the President may improve. If this is correct then surely it applies with at least as much force to ELM.[122] In fact, ELM seeks to foster robust public deliberation as part of its ethic of accountability and (public) responsibility. Because the use of extra-legal measures by public officials during an emergency involves significant risks to the actors, it is likely that upon the termination of the crisis the legislature will be called upon to review and ratify governmental actions by, for example, passing Acts of Indemnity. This process presents the legislative branch of government with an opportunity to review the actions of the executive and assess them *ex post*, relieved from the pressures of the crisis, before deciding whether to ratify them. The appeal to the legislature to ratify the actions of the government may, for its part, further invoke public deliberation and force the legislature to take an affirmative stand on issues connected with the emergency. This is of special significance in light of the general reluctance of legislatures to assume responsibility in times of emergency, satisfying themselves with acquiescence in actions taken by the executive.[123] Moreover, open acknowledgement of extra-legal measures taken by government agents will contribute to reasoned discourse and dialogue not only between the government and its domestic constituency, but also between the government and other governments, and between the government and non-governmental or international organisations. The benefits of the *ex post* justificatory exercise are not confined to the domestic sphere. Such exercise has international implications, both

[120] Scheuerman, Chapter 11, pp. 271–2. [121] Scheuerman, 'Emergency Powers' at 273.
[122] In fact, this may apply with greater force to ELM due to the extra-legal nature of the initial actions undertaken by public officials.
[123] Koh, *The National Security Constitution*, pp. 117–33.

political and legal. The reasons put forward by a state to justify its actions may be subject to scrutiny by other governments and non-governmental organisations as well as by international and regional judicial and quasi-judicial bodies.[124] The need to give reasons *ex post*, that is, the need to publicly justify or excuse (not merely explain) one's actions after the fact, emphasises accountability of government agents. The fact that specific emergency powers used by the government are extra-legal preserves the need not only to give reasons for such actions, but also to give reasons that go beyond pure pragmatic excuses or justifications for the specific conduct in question.[125] Faced with the need to give reasons for her actions, a public official may well decline to engage in extra-legal measures and actions unless she is confident that the people and their representatives will come to see things her way and regard her action as necessary and legitimate. Even then she may still hesitate to act unless she is confident that she will not suffer personally for taking such actions.[126]

VI. Final remarks

Rather than placing state agents in a zone uncontrolled by law, ELM subjects them to an extremely heavy – perhaps even unfair – burden. The notion that a valiant public official out to save the nation may be forced to employ illegal means and 'throw himself on the justice of his country'[127] is difficult to accept. Frederick Pollock, commenting on the view that the necessity that leads to the use of martial law may not make, of its own accord, measures taken to protect the nation legal if otherwise such measures would have been illegal, suggested that such a theory,

[124] For the idea of two-level games in international relations, see R.D. Putnam, 'Diplomacy and Domestic Politics: The Logic of Two-Level Games' (1988) 42 *International Organizations* 427.

[125] Kadish and Kadish, *Discretion To Disobey*, pp. 5–12. But see C.L. Eisgruber, 'The Most Competent Branches: A Response to Professor Paulsen' (1994) 83 *Georgetown Law Journal* 347 at 360 (arguing that Justice Jackson's dissent in *Korematsu* suggests that the executive branch does not have to offer reasons beyond the pragmatic).

[126] F. Schauer, 'Giving Reasons' (1995) 47 *Stanford Law Review* 633 at 656–7; Bessette and Tulis, 'Constitution, Politics and Presidency', 10; Finn, *Constitutions in Crisis*, pp. 30–36; D.L. Shapiro, 'In Defense of Judicial Candor' (1987) 100 *Harvard Law Review* 731 at 737; D.G. Adler, 'The Steel Seizure Case and Inherent Presidential Power' (2002) 19 *Constitutional Commentary* 155 at 174–5.

[127] Letter from Thomas Jefferson to John B. Colvin (20 September 1810), in P.L. Ford (ed.), *The Writings of Thomas Jefferson* (New York: G.P. Putnam's Sons, 1986) p. 1231 at 1233.

> imputes gratuitous folly to the common law, which cannot be so perverse as to require a man in an office of trust to choose between breaking the law and being an incompetent officer and a bad citizen . . . It seems, therefore, that the acts which every courageous and prudent magistrate would certainly do in the circumstances supposed are not a kind of splendid offence, but are . . . 'justifiable and lawful for the maintenance of the Commonwealth'.[128]

I readily admit that such 'gratuitous folly' is what ELM, in fact, prescribes. As Sanford Kadish suggests, the basic idea is to impose such a heavy burden on officials that it would require circumstances of a perfectly extraordinary character to induce the individual to take the risk of acting.[129] Consider Jean-Jacques Rousseau's analysis of Cicero's fortunes and misfortunes in the context of the Catilinarian conspiracy: '[I]f, in the first transports of joy, [Cicero's] conduct was approved, he was justly called, later on, to account for the blood of citizens spilt in violation of the laws . . . He was therefore justly honoured as the liberator of Rome, and also justly punished as a law-breaker. However brilliant his recall may have been, it was undoubtedly an act of pardon'.[130] By separating the issues of action and ratification or rejection (with the possibility of sanctions), conceptually as well as chronologically – with action subject to *ex post* ratification or rejection – we add an element of uncertainty to the decision-making calculus of public officials. That uncertainty raises the costs of pursuing an extra-legal course of action. For all the impositions on officials such as Cicero, the alternatives – amounting, in effect, to amending the law so as to permit the execution without a proper trial of Roman citizens – impose a higher social cost. Hard cases make bad laws. Emergencies make some of the hardest of cases. ELM attempts to keep the ordinary legal system distinct from the dirty and messy reality of emergency so as to prevent the perversion of that system in order to give answers to the hard exceptional cases. According to the model, ordinary rules need not necessarily be modified or adapted so as to facilitate governmental crisis measures. Insofar as exceptional measures are required to deal with the

[128] F. Pollock, 'What is Martial Law?' (1902) 70 *Law Quarterly Review* 152 at 156.

[129] Kadish, 'Torture', 355.

[130] J. Rousseau, *The Social Contract and Discourses*, G.D.H. Cole (trans.) (New York: Everyman Library, 1993), pp. 295–6. See also M. Walzer, 'Political Action: The Problem of Dirty Hands' in M. Cohen, T. Nagel and T. Scanlon (eds.), *War and Moral Responsibility* (Princeton: Princeton University Press, 1974), p. 62 at 81.

crisis, these measures are viewed precisely as such, 'exceptional'. One of the main goals of terrorism is to push the state to adapt itself to meet the terrorist threat on its own turf. Under ELM, while government and its agents sink lower in their fight against terrorism, the legal system remains afloat above the muddy water's surface.

PART TWO

Conceptual and normative theories

4

Emergency logic: prudence, morality and the rule of law

TERRY NARDIN

Whether executive action contrary to law in an emergency can be justified depends not only on contingent circumstances – the credibility of an alleged danger, its gravity, its imminence – but on our understanding of law. It matters whether we understand law in prudential terms as instrumental to achieving desired goals or morally as prescribing goal-independent limits on the pursuit of goals. The word 'moral' in this context signals a non-instrumental relationship in which human beings treat one another not as obstacles to be overcome or resources to be used, but as persons whose autonomy should be respected. If law is instrumental, it can serve to oppress and exploit. Only if we think of law as ultimately moral in the sense defined do we approach a concept of legality that is distinct from arbitrary rule.

The premise of this chapter is that the prudential and the moral are distinct kinds of relationship, and that the arguments defining each belong to different universes of discourse. Emergency arguments work differently in each realm. Where law is understood in prudential terms as an instrument of policy, defending extra-legal acts does not change the kind of argument that is being made – we remain within the realm of prudential reasoning. To reason prudentially is to consider alternative outcomes and to weigh benefits and costs. Prudential reasoning is not necessarily self-interested because one can act prudently for others as well as for oneself. But if law is understood in moral terms, extra-legal action cannot be justified. If a legal order is understood morally, rationalising extra-legal action involves a modal shift from the non-instrumental to the instrumental. One of the fears about emergency departures from the rule of law is that they will normalise extra-legal government, creating within the state an extra-moral world in which human beings are related to *one another* in the same way they are related to non-human *things.*

My claim is that the expression 'rule of law' is properly used to distinguish a legal order in which law meets criteria that presuppose a non-instrumental, and in that sense moral, understanding of law from one in which law is understood instrumentally. But the expression is also used in other ways, so I begin by defending my claim that the rule of law entails a moral understanding of law (Part I). This is a purely theoretical proposition, neither prescriptive nor descriptive. Its purpose is to define, distinguish and explain, not to prescribe conduct or to describe the contingent features of any particular legal order. The prudential and the moral are abstract types of human relationship, not actual normative orders. Any particular legal order – the American legal system, for example – is an ambiguous mixture of instrumental and non-instrumental rules.

I then argue (Part II) that the rule of law bars emergency exceptions to laws with substantive moral content or to procedurally fundamental rule-of-law principles, such as those that forbid enacting secret or retroactive laws or imposing extra-legal punishment. If by the rule of law we mean a mode of association among persons who are entitled to respect – a moral mode of association – exceptions to at least some laws cannot be accommodated within the rule of law because it does not fall within the proper authority of governments to transgress moral limits. In an emergency, public officials can make a prudential case for violating merely instrumental laws. But they cannot justify violating laws that protect moral rights or, more generally, evading rule-of-law principles. Officials often do act immorally. But they cannot logically offer *moral* reasons for violating a *moral* rule: to do that would be self-contradictory. They can plead that the end justifies the means, but that is a prudential argument, not a moral one.

In my view, the distinctive contribution of legal *theory* to the post-9/11 debate on emergency powers is not to solve a practical problem but to identify the presuppositions and assess the coherence of alternative understandings of extra-legal executive action. I therefore conclude (Part III) by discussing what it means to justify executive action contrary to law, using Oren Gross's argument as an example of how the issue of justification is obscured if one fails to distinguish considerations of right from those of desirability. I suggest that illegal acts cannot be *justified* – that is, made just within the moral universe of the rule of law. They can only be *rationalised* in prudential terms as consequentially desirable or else *excused* as admittedly wrongful but nevertheless non-culpable responses to necessity.

I. The idea of the rule of law

The 'rule of law' is one of those terms, like 'democracy' or 'human rights', that has become obscure from overuse. So those who want to use the expression must first say what they mean by it. Perhaps all they mean is that people should obey the law. But this is clearly an inadequate definition of the rule of law because it leaves open the meaning of the word 'law'. The commands of an autocrat may be called law but a state ruled by such commands is ill-described as a rule-of-law state. The rule of law implies a constitution – written or unwritten – specifying procedures for enacting, interpreting and enforcing law. Why speak of the rule of law if one is indifferent to the distinction between arbitrary and limited rule? The idea that a rule-of-law state is one in which government itself is constrained by law is more promising, but it still leaves the main question unanswered: What do we mean by 'law'? What is the character of this law that public officials as well as citizens must respect?

Two ideas about 'law' need to be distinguished if we are to make sense of the phrase 'rule of law'. The first is that law can be an instrument for achieving particular substantive ends: safe streets, economic growth, secure borders and the like. Such laws can be seen as instrumental to the outcomes they are designed to produce. Their rationale is that they effectively produce those outcomes. If not, they may be replaced by more effective laws. Instrumental laws reflect the imperatives of social policy, not the internal demands of legality as an aspect of civil life in which individuals look to law rather than force to redress wrongs. For this reason, it is a mistake to see all law in instrumental terms. When that happens, legality itself becomes subordinated to utility, as in economic theories of law, which are concerned with how legal rules can be made to serve the demands of policy, not with the idea of legality as a kind of relationship that is distinct from an essentially economic one.[1] An instrumentalist conception of law erodes the distinction between legality and utility, between law and policy and ultimately between law and force.

The second idea about law, then, is that it can be a purpose-independent constraint on the pursuit of purposes. The rationale of at least some laws is not that they advance or retard particular ends but that they protect the right of persons to pursue ends of their own. Such laws are non-instrumental because they concern the manner of the pursuit, not the

[1] E.J. Weinrib, *The Idea of Private Law* (Cambridge: Harvard University Press, 1995), pp. 46–8.

substance of the end pursued. By determining the conditions under which people pursue their ends, they draw a line between proper and improper means. Non-instrumental laws must be respected, no matter what one's ends, because they ensure procedural fairness and protect basic rights. In this respect they are like rules of a game. In applying them, judges are umpires adjudicating conflicting claims under the law, not policy makers seeking the best outcomes for society. Non-instrumental laws imply an idea of the state as an association whose members are equally free to pursue their own self-chosen ends, provided they respect one another's freedom to do the same. That proviso requires that each person know what the rules are and refrain from improper interference.

The idea of non-instrumental law can be extended from the conduct of private persons to that of public officials. Government is not only the source of law but is itself constrained by law. Respect for law can be demanded not only in transactions among private persons but also in the conduct of official business. The expression 'rule of law' is often used to pick out this aspect of legality: that public officials as well as private persons are constrained by law. But that formula takes no account of the distinction between instrumental and non-instrumental law. A government that enacts laws that strip citizens of their moral rights and faithfully adheres to those laws cannot be said to exemplify the rule of law because that expression properly designates a legal system that enables the coexistence of autonomous persons by providing a framework of non-instrumental constraints. The problem for the legal theorist is to understand the relationship between instrumental and non-instrumental law.[2]

Instrumental laws are consistent with the idea of the rule of law, provided those laws and the policies they enable are constrained by non-instrumental laws, for it is the latter that constitute a state whose citizens are moral equals. The rule of law does not exclude the administrative and judicial actions needed to make law work in the contingent circumstances of an actual state. To regulate the affairs of a state, officials must issue administrative rules, render judgments, impose penalties, collect taxes and so forth. Courts must apply general rules to particular cases. A legal

[2] The place of non-instrumental principles – moral principles inherent in law itself – in private law is emphasised by Weinrib, *Idea of Private Law*, pp. 48–50. Their importance in public law is implicit in T.R.S. Allan, *Constitutional Justice: A Liberal Theory of the Rule of Law* (Oxford: Oxford University Press, 2001) and D. Dyzenhaus, *The Constitution of Law: Legality in a Time of Emergency* (Cambridge: Cambridge University Press, 2006).

system must provide for redress when people are convicted of failure to observe their legal obligations. Officials must be able to compel the performance of actions ordered by a court. What distinguishes such instrumental rules and orders from general laws is that they concern particular actions, persons or events. They are devices that link general rules to particular situations. Their effectiveness is a contingent condition for realising the rule of law in an actual state.

The rule of law exists only where law both limits official discretion and respects the personality, dignity, freedom or moral rights of legal subjects. Both requirements must be met. It is not enough to say that the rule of law exists when public officials and private persons obey the law because that assertion ignores the character of the laws that are obeyed. So-called 'thin' or 'inclusive' definitions of the rule of law, by stripping it of any moral element, permit the theorist to bring a wide range of systems under the rule-of-law umbrella. But such definitions fail to distinguish the rule of law from mere law.[3] My claim is stronger: that such definitions not only fail to distinguish the rule *of* law from rule *by* law, but that rule by anything properly called 'law' presupposes the rule of law. To assert that legal order can exist without the rule of law is to erase the distinction between legally constrained and unconstrained power. The rule of law is realised in a state to the degree that its subjects are related on the basis of non-instrumental law, not on the basis of relative power. No state fully embodies the rule of law, which is an abstract type of association rather than a description of any actual legal system. Thin and thick conceptions of the rule of law can coexist within a given legal system.[4] But one must not confuse a *concept* with the contingent and always conceptually ambiguous *features* of an actual historic state.

The rule of law, as a type of association, defines the proper end of government, which is to govern in a way that respects the equal freedom of those who fall within its jurisdiction. The distinction between instrumental and non-instrumental rules expresses a distinction between what is desirable, given certain goals, and what is morally required, given a certain view of what it means to be a human being. Consequentialist legal

[3] Minimalist definitions of the rule of law are favoured by theorists whose understanding of law is positivist and utilitarian, like T. Campbell, 'Emergency strategies for prescriptive legal positivists: anti-terrorist law and legal theory' (Chapter 9), this volume, and by scholars of comparative law wishing to avoid the charge of Euro-centrism, like some of the contributors to R. Peerenboom (ed.), *Asian Discourses of Rule of Law* (London: Routledge, 2004).

[4] P. Craig, 'Formal and Substantive Conceptions of the Rule of Law: An Analytical Framework' (1997) *Public Law* 467–87.

theories, realist or utilitarian, give insufficient attention to distinguishing the desirable from the obligatory. The consequentialist rationale for a rule is that it produces a beneficial outcome, not that the conduct it prescribes is right for reasons that are independent of that outcome. If law is to be connected with its moral presuppositions as a distinct kind of human association and not merely with policy, if it is to be about what is right or just and not merely about what is desirable or expedient, it must be understood as at least in part an order of non-instrumental rules determined by moral and not only by utilitarian considerations. The idea of the rule of law captures the essential connection between legality and morality. Let me further explicate this connection.

The familiar rule-of-law principles are non-instrumental principles. They presuppose the idea of law as a framework within which free persons are related on the basis of common rules and they implement that presupposition by forbidding arbitrary, retroactive, or secret laws, arbitrary exemption from legal duties, punishing or detaining the innocent, arbitrary services or punishments, legal remedies that are disproportionate to the harm done and the like. Such principles serve among other things to protect citizens from tyrannical government because they focus on the potential misconduct of officials. But they also reinforce the idea that in a rule-of-law state citizens are joined as moral equals within an order of non-instrumental rules. This does not mean that every rule enacted within a legal order is a non-instrumental rule. It does mean that enacted instrumental rules do not offend the idea of legality expressed in rule-of-law principles. Practically speaking, rule-of-law principles constrain legal enactment; theoretically speaking, they determine what is properly called law. Those principles are *moral* principles in at least three ways.

First, they do more than simply forbid arbitrary power, for the arbitrary conduct of public officials that they forbid is arbitrary in a fundamental way. It is arbitrary with respect to basic moral rights, above all the right to be free in the sense of setting goals for oneself and pursuing them while respecting the equal freedom of others to pursue their own goals. Rule-of-law principles display the fundamental quality of a moral principle, which is to presuppose the autonomy of every human being and therefore of the subjects of a legal order.

Second, rule-of-law principles, like other moral principles, rest on reason, not legislation. They are inherent in the idea of enacted law, in so far as it respects the autonomy of legal subjects, but they are not themselves enacted law. Their authority is constitutional, not statutory. They are criteria of legality presupposed by enacted law, the premise, not the product, of legislative enactment.[5] Because rule-of-law principles are not enacted, they cannot be repealed or annulled. No decision can alter them.

Third, like other moral principles, rule-of-law principles provide a standard by which to judge enacted law. But they are not 'natural law' understood as rules distinct from enacted law. Nor are they 'higher law' – that is, principles that are above enacted law.[6] They are what might be called 'immanent law' – moral principles inherent in the idea of laws as rules regulating the transactions of free and equal persons. These principles are inherent in law itself, understood as the ground of association among autonomous persons and therefore as presupposing both agency (the capacity to make decisions) and individuality (the wish to make one's own decisions instead of having decisions made for one by others). They forbid a government to impose substantive ends that would interfere with the freedom to choose one's own ends and that are therefore not properly enforced by law. For this reason, rule-of-law principles are uniquely appropriate for judging the propriety – the justice or rightness – of enacted laws. In a rule-of-law state, those principles have legal force and legal consequences. They are not only moral principles; they are also *law* because they limit the enactment and administration of law. Enacted law that violates rule-of-law principles has not been properly enacted and is, for that reason, not properly law.

The rule of law implies a moral standard, one derived not from an arbitrary notion of the good but from the idea of human beings as autonomous persons who articulate their own conceptions of the good. To those who are sceptical of morality, defining the rule of law in moral terms may seem an invitation to anarchy. Enacted law is definite and clear, they think, and morality contested and amorphous. But the reverse view is equally plausible: that legal rules, being products of decision and therefore of power, stand in need of the correction that only a moral perspective can provide. If by morality we mean a set of considerations arising from the idea of human personality and the respect for persons it properly demands, it is easy to grasp the impermissibility of force and fraud, of slavery and cruelty

[5] This point is made by Michael Oakeshott in an essay seldom cited by legal theorists, 'The Rule of Law', in *On History and Other Essays* (Oxford: Basil Blackwell, 1983), pp. 140–1 and examined by R. Friedman, 'Michael Oakeshott and the Elusive Identity of the Rule of Law' in C. Abel and T. Fuller (eds.), *The Intellectual Legacy of Michael Oakeshott* (Exeter: Imprint Academic, 2005), p. 173.

[6] A point emphasised by L.L. Fuller, *The Morality of Law* (New Haven: Yale University Press, 1964), p. 96. Fuller's 'inner morality of law' (pp. 42–3) equivocates, however, between an aspiration to have 'good laws' and the duty to subscribe to such laws.

and the permissibility of using force to defend the innocent from violence. The basis of law, from this perspective, is the idea that human beings – creatures with the capacity to think and choose – should not interfere with one another's freedom to exercise that capacity except to thwart impermissible interference. And given that capacity, it seems evident to modern defenders of human rights, as it did to ancient defenders of natural law, that human beings are included within the realm of law by nature, not by convention – that is, as being human, not as beneficiaries of a sovereign decision. If such inclusion were determined by convention ('decision'), some human beings would have access to the legal relationship and others would be excluded from it.[7] If law represents a distinct kind of relationship between human beings, no government can claim the authority to decide who is and is not human. There is no juridically empty space of the sort imagined by Carl Schmitt and Giorgio Agamben – a space inhabited by human beings placed outside the realm of law by being deprived of legal personality and civil rights.[8] Under the rule of law, no government can deprive a human being of moral personality or moral rights, which means that human beings in all circumstances retain legal as well as moral personality and civil as well as human rights. Rule-of-law principles are inherent in the idea of law itself in so far as we understand law to be, as Michael Oakeshott puts it, a mode of association among human beings on the basis of common rules, not association on the basis of some putative good and rules instrumental to achieving that good.[9]

The idea of the rule of law serves no useful purpose if any system of enacted rules can qualify as law. Only a non-instrumental conception of law can distinguish a rule-of-law state from a state that compels legal subjects to support religious, economic or other ends that are not their

[7] R.B. Friedman, 'Some Thoughts on Natural Law and International Order' in D.R. Mapel and T. Nardin (eds.), *International Society: Diverse Ethical Perspectives* (Princeton: Princeton University Press, 1998), p. 78. Johan Geertsma explores the boundary between natural and juridical life in his contribution to this volume: 'Exceptions, Bare Life and Colonialism' (Chapter 14).

[8] C. Schmitt, *Political Theology: Four Chapters on the Concept of Sovereignty* (Chicago: University of Chicago Press, 2005); G. Agamben, *Homo Sacer: Sovereign Power and Bare Life* (Stanford: Stanford University Press, 1998) and *State of Exception* (Chicago: University of Chicago Press, 2005).

[9] Oakeshott's version of this understanding is developed most fully in his essay 'On the Civil Condition' in M. Oakeshott, *On Human Conduct* (Oxford: Clarendon Press, 1975). For my reading of Oakeshott's theory of civil association, which is also a theory of the rule of law, see T. Nardin, *The Philosophy of Michael Oakeshott* (University Park: Penn State Press, 2001), ch. 5.

own. If we define the rule of law simply as government according to law, we cannot distinguish between a morally licit state and one that permits some to use others as resources for achieving their ends. Nor can we distinguish between a state governed by the rule of law and one in which the rule of law is struggling to find a foothold. In a state like Iraq or Timor Leste, the challenge is to establish conditions under which the rule of law can emerge. That project is an instrumental one, for creating the conditions for a legal order should not be confused with governing within the constraints of such an order. The act of founding a legal order is necessarily extra-legal, a matter of expediency for the sake of a substantive end (in this case, establishing the rule of law itself), not a matter of legality (governing within the rules of an established legal order). To the objection that a non-instrumental understanding of the rule of law ignores the extent to which government in a modern state is a substantive enterprise, the answer is obvious: the more a state acquires a substantive character by organising its citizens to pursue an overarching purpose to which their own ends must give way, the less it is a rule-of-law state. The rule of law lies not in policy but in subordinating policy to non-instrumental legality.

II. The logic of exception in the rule of law

The context of the current debate on executive action contrary to law is 'the war on terrorism'. Let's take the war metaphor literally for a moment and consider the case for violating the laws of war in an emergency.

War is not the opposite of law but a condition regulated by law. The laws of war give expression to the rule of law by limiting the use of force by states. International law regulates war by specifying the conditions under which a state may resort to force and by prescribing limits on the conduct of military operations. These conditions and limits effectively constrain, if not the actions of states, at least the arguments they can mount to defend their actions. The Bush administration, for example, has offered several political justifications for invading Iraq, including self-defence, preventive war and humanitarian intervention, but lacking Security Council authorisation, its strictly legal case eschewed all of these in favour of the narrow claim that the invasion was merely a continuation of the first Gulf War, which the Security Council had endorsed.[10]

[10] S. Toope, 'Human Rights and the Use of Force after September 11th, 2001', in D.J. Sherman and T. Nardin (eds.), *Terror, Culture, Politics: Rethinking 9/11* (Bloomington: Indiana University Press, 2006), p. 252.

The laws of war make room for the idea of military necessity, which permits directly harming enemy combatants and indirectly harming non-combatants if harming them cannot be avoided. Military necessity therefore reflects instrumental considerations. But it operates as an argument within the law to limit permissible violence, forbidding destruction that does not advance the pursuit of legitimate military ends, is disproportionate to these ends or is aimed at non-combatants either as an end in itself or as a means to an end. It is not an overriding permission that legalises otherwise illegal acts, such as killing prisoners of war to ensure the success of an operation or bombing cities to hasten an enemy's defeat by demoralising its population. Military necessity can justify inflicting harm only where the laws of war permit it. Those laws already incorporate considerations of military necessity, so a plea of necessity cannot be invoked to justify exceptions to them. Many 'necessary' (expedient) acts are categorically forbidden, such as feigning truces or surrenders, denying enemy soldiers the right to surrender, torturing or humiliating prisoners of war, taking hostages and imposing collective penalties. The Geneva Conventions and related treaties – which with respect to these prohibitions codify customary international law, apply in civil as well as international wars and are incorporated in national military codes – do not permit such acts on grounds of military necessity.[11] In short, military necessity is a recognised plea *within* the laws of war; it is not a recognised plea for *violating* the laws of war.

If follows that when necessity is invoked to defend violating the laws of war, it cannot be military necessity as defined by the laws of war. It must be a higher necessity that alters the ordinary laws. The plea must be that an exceptional situation warrants violating the rules that normally apply. The uneasiness of those who make this plea is evident in the words they choose: the normal rules are 'overridden', 'suspended' or 'set aside' – not 'violated'. And the situation that triggers the violation is said to be one of '*extreme* necessity'[12] or '*supreme* emergency'.[13] The intensifying adjectives imply that the state whose officials violate the law faces no

[11] This standard understanding of the limits of military necessity in justifying illegal action is accepted by O. Gross and F. Ní Aoláin, *Law in Times of Crisis: Emergency Powers in Theory and Practice* (Cambridge: Cambridge University Press, 2006), p. 334.

[12] T. Franck, 'Interpretation and Change in the Law of Humanitarian Intervention' in J.L. Holzgrefe and R.O. Keohane (eds.), *Humanitarian Intervention: Ethical, Legal and Political Dilemmas* (Cambridge: Cambridge University Press, 2003), p. 216.

[13] M. Walzer, *Just and Unjust Wars: A Moral Argument with Historical Illustrations*, 4th edn (New York: Basic Books, 2006), pp. 251–68.

ordinary emergency, like an earthquake or civil disturbance, but a situation of imminent and general catastrophe.[14] Two kinds of catastrophe are usually invoked. The first is a conquest that would extinguish a state, that is, terminate its independence. It is not the death of citizens that distinguishes a supreme emergency but the death of the state. The second is conquest by an adversary posing a threat to civilization itself. Military defeat cannot justify gross violations of the laws of war, according to this argument, unless one of these conditions is met. Michael Walzer defends Britain's deliberate destruction of German cities beginning in 1940 on the grounds that Britain was fighting to survive and to defeat an enemy of civilization, for Nazism was 'evil objectified in the world'.[15] Similar arguments are invoked in the war against terrorism. The question is: may a state violate the laws of war on such grounds?

A moralist who thinks that a people is defined by its moral beliefs would reject this argument from extremity. A community is constituted by its morality, so when its leaders choose to act immorally on its behalf they destroy it as a community. And a community that supports such leaders (by an act of *ex post facto* ratification, for example) loses its integrity and its moral rationale.[16] To defend the violation of moral constraints on a plea of necessity is to argue that a community can survive by expedients its constitutive morality condemns as immoral. In using those expedients, the community seeks to protect itself while denying the principles that make it the community it is. The problem does not arise for political realism, which treats both morality and law as conventional and instrumental and therefore assumes that a community can transgress its principles without destroying its integrity. The realist thinks that one can do evil and remain unchanged. But, the moralist might reply, war destroys character as well as lives and goods. The Britain that emerged from the Second World War, having indiscriminately bombed German cities, was not the Britain that went to war with just cause in 1939. The same holds for the United States, whose incendiary and atomic attacks on Japan were a barbaric response to Japanese barbarism. One does not defend civilisation by means like

[14] *Ibid.*, p. 251. As Walzer observes, 'everyone's troubles make a crisis. "Emergency" and "crisis" are cant words, used to prepare our minds for acts of brutality'. Hence the need for criteria (like seriousness and imminence) to distinguish authentic emergencies.

[15] *Ibid.*, p. 253. 'Evil' is arguably another cant word used to prepare our minds for brutality.

[16] A. Donagan, *The Theory of Morality* (Chicago: University of Chicago Press, 1977), pp. 180–3; J.B. White, *When Words Lose Their Meaning: Constitutions and Reconstitutions of Language, Character and Community* (Chicago: University of Chicago Press, 1984), pp. 59–92.

these. New versions of the constitutive argument have emerged post-9/11 in the assertion that the terrorists win if we fight them by adopting their methods.

The argument is rhetorically powerful but it is compromised by ambiguities in its reliance on the idea of communal integrity: it is not clear, for example, whether the claim that acting immorally destroys the integrity of the agent is conceptual or contingent. If the claim is a contingent one, it might be false. A community that acts barbarically might strengthen its moral integrity as a result of that experience: post-war Germany is an example. If the claim is conceptual, the argument is that the crime stains the character of a person or a community and must be redressed. The suggestion that officials who do wrong must present themselves for judgment addresses this issue, as does the call for collective reparations to expiate collective guilt.

If moral wrongs must be acknowledged and moral principles vindicated, one is conceptually barred from offering moral reasons for violating a moral rule. To do so would be self-contradictory. The only way to avoid paradox is to distinguish different meanings of morality. Morality is often confused with prudence and where that is the case we can avoid the paradox by making the distinction clear. We can say without self-contradiction that there are prudential reasons for acting immorally or moral reasons for acting imprudently. But we cannot offer moral reasons for violating a moral rule. So even if an immoral policy like area bombing can be shown to have saved a community, the principle that justifies it cannot be a moral one. Officials acting in an emergency might on prudential grounds rationalise violating a prescription of the laws of war, such as the rule forbidding one to directly attack non-combatants as an end in itself or as a means to an end. But because that prescription expresses the moral principle that it is wrong deliberately to harm the innocent, those officials could not logically offer a *moral* justification for the forbidden act. Morality cannot permit the violation of its own categorical precepts, such as the precept that forbids deliberately killing innocents. How can it be 'just' (and therefore 'justified') to deliberately kill the innocent? Acts that do that, like judicial murder or destroying cities, are paradigm cases of injustice and only a debased moral vocabulary that erases the distinction between justice and expediency can make the argument plausible. A self-consistent moralist *must* hold that to pursue a good end by morally forbidden means is to violate the fundamental moral principle that evil may not be done for the sake of good. Most legal systems permit officials to suspend instrumental laws in situations of emergency and the practice of using emergency powers to deal with threats to public order or national security is as old as the state. But the emergency argument does not work when it is used to justify violating moral rules. We cannot defend acts that do that without bringing morality itself into question.

In morality, as I understand it, the rightness of an act is determined by internal considerations. Reasoning morally means looking inside and back to interpret principles, not outside and ahead to calculate results. Principles may imply policies, as in the case of beneficence, which requires us to adopt a policy of helping others so far as we reasonably can. But the *calculations* we make in acting on the principle of beneficence are not moral. They are prudential calculations needed to carry out the policy and acting on those calculations is constrained by moral considerations: we are to pursue beneficent ends only by morally permissible means. Moral reasoning is hermeneutic, not computational. Its criteria of rightness are non-instrumental principles that are binding regardless of one's aims. One is obligated to observe them not because doing so will produce good results but because their authority is presupposed.

This priority of principles over outcomes distinguishes the understanding of morality advanced here from theories like political realism or utilitarianism, which understand rules in instrumental terms as expedients for bringing about desired states of affairs. Such outcome-oriented or consequentialist theories postulate ends that determine the rightness or wrongness of acts or policies. A non-consequentialist theory of morality does not postulate such ends: ends are chosen by individuals, not prescribed by morality, though morality does constrain their choices. Morality rests on the presupposition that people pursue different ends and prescribes that they respect one another's autonomy in doing so. What makes an act right, on this view, is not that it is directed to a good end but that it does not violate limits grounded on the idea of mutual respect. An act cannot be right if it violates these limits, even if its consequences are good. Only if it respects these limits can it be said to be morally right. The argument that moral constraints may be violated in an emergency reverses this relationship between moral and prudential considerations. An escape clause for emergencies, by allowing moral rules to be overridden by prudential considerations, obscures what is distinctive of the moral point of view.

Now if the rule of law has moral significance, as I argued in the preceding section it does, this understanding of morality has implications for the argument that public officials in a rule-of-law state may violate the law in an emergency. On this understanding, the law may *not* be violated because rule-of-law principles are moral principles. In violating enacted law, officials also violate the principles of legality that underlie that law. This can happen in two ways. First, officials may violate a non-instrumental law that has intrinsic moral importance, such as a law forbidding murder. Second, officials may violate an instrumental law that lacks intrinsic moral importance, but whose violation nonetheless breaches the procedural requirement that officials respect enacted laws. That requirement is part of the rule of law. Rule-of-law principles constrain administering as well as enacting law, and although these principles may leave room for legislation to alter the laws by defining states of emergency, they do not permit administrators to violate laws in an emergency. To hold otherwise is to reject the logic of legal order and to subordinate law to policy, decision and discretion, which is the antithesis of the rule of law.

In a rule-of-law state, I have argued, law has two aspects, one genetic and the other conceptual. First, it is enacted by authority. Second, it satisfies criteria of legality that are not themselves enacted. Such criteria are non-instrumental and therefore moral. It is the second aspect, not the first, that bars public officials in a rule-of-law state from violating the law. From the standpoint of prudence, there can be no principled objection to officials acting contrary to human laws – laws enacted for human convenience – if that convenience is better served by violating those laws than by observing them. Enacted law can be amended within certain limits for the common good, and in an emergency in which a civil order is threatened a case might be made for violating at least some enacted laws to protect that order. But some laws, like those forbidding torture, cannot be set aside because they express a moral rule. They are in the jargon of the law 'non-derogable'.[17] A moral rule is not an enactment that can be altered or nullified by an act of will. Only that which has been made by authority can be unmade by authority. Public officials can have no authority to waive the moral law. They might be given authority to suspend some enacted laws but morally speaking they cannot have authority to suspend enacted laws that protect basic moral rights. Nor can they suspend the un-enacted principles of legality that distinguish the rule of law from law as a mere instrument of power.

[17] So, for example, the International Covenant on Civil and Political Rights categorically forbids, inter alia, the arbitrary deprivation of life (Article 6); torture, cruel and unusual punishment or coerced participation in medical or scientific experiments (Article 7); slavery (Article 8); punishment for acts not criminal at the time performed (Article 15) and coerced religious belief (Article 18).

III. What does it mean to 'justify' action contrary to law?

I have argued, so far, that the rule of law implies a dual concept of law as comprising rules authoritatively enacted according to moral principles (expressed in non-instrumental rule-of-law criteria) that are not themselves enacted, and therefore that although public officials might be *morally* justified in violating *enacted* law they cannot logically offer a *moral* justification for violating *moral* principles. So to the extent that the rule of law is a moral idea, it constrains the ability of officials to justify illegal actions taken for the public good. In a rule-of-law state, the justification for *violating* law – that is, for suspending a law without proper authority – cannot be either legal or moral, for even if the violated rules are merely instrumental, they have been made according to procedures that have a moral basis in the idea of the state as an association of persons related to one another on the basis of law. Public officials may choose to violate the law for prudential reasons, but those reasons cannot make the violation just. They might be reasons why considerations of justice must give way to prudential considerations: reasons that invoke the goal of public order, national survival, the defence of civilisation or some other overriding good. But prudential reasons cannot 'justify' illegal or immoral action if that word is to retain its core meaning as making an act just within a framework of legal or moral prescriptions. All that such reasons can do is rationalise illicit acts in terms of the desirability of the consequences they are supposed to produce. Prudential arguments are consequentialist. And because the consequences that public officials most often presume to matter are those affecting the security of a state, such arguments are recognisably a version of the realist doctrine of reason of state, if we take that expression to identify the view that law and even morality must give way to prudence when a state's vital interests are threatened.

The debate on emergency powers might be said to proceed on two levels. The first is the level of practice: whether public officials *should* act illegally if illegal action is needed to deal with an emergency or instead find ways of responding that are consistent with the rule of law. The second level is that of theory: whether the *idea* of illegal action in emergencies can be reconciled *conceptually* with the idea of the rule of law or is, on the contrary, incompatible with it. These levels represent not a distinction between prudence and morality, both of which are within the realm of practice, but between the practical and the theoretical.

Issues of practice and legal theory are mixed together in this debate and need to be distinguished. Arguments about policy – arguments that are practical because they yield a prescription for action – turn on factual contingencies. Assessing contingencies is a part of prudential reasoning, for whether a policy is prudent depends on how its benefits and costs are identified and measured. But assessing contingencies is irrelevant in a theoretical inquiry, which abstracts from contingencies to uncover presuppositions. The tension between practice and theory persists even when practical concerns are generalised. The practical question of how officials should respond in an emergency should not be confused with the theoretical question of whether emergency powers are compatible with the rule of law. That question turns not on contingencies but on the concept of the rule of law. It depends on logic, not on events. Consistency in theory is a matter of conceptual coherence, not contingent probability. The question is not whether illegal action is likely *in fact* to erode the rule of law but whether the idea of illegal action is compatible with the *idea* of the rule of law.

To grasp the significance of the debate over emergency powers for legal theory, then, we need to separate the conceptual questions it raises from contingencies of fact and policy. The theoretical issue is not, as Oren Gross argues, whether public officials may justifiably violate the law in an emergency or whether such violation is likely to 'preserve the long-term relevance of and obedience to legal principles' and therefore to 'preserve, rather than undermine, the rule of law'.[18] It is what these practical claims imply about the relationship between the ideas of emergency and law – in particular, whether the proposition that officials may act illegally in an emergency can be reconciled conceptually with the idea of the rule of law.

Gross's argument is practical, not theoretical. His central claim is that '*public officials* . . . *may* act extra-legally when they believe that such action is *necessary* for protecting the nation and the public in the face of *calamity*, provided that they openly and publicly acknowledge the nature of their actions', at which point it is 'up to *the people* to decide . . . how to respond'.[19] Some of his critics engage this argument at the level of practice, arguing that the proposal is an undesirable solution to the problem of how governments should deal with emergencies. Rather than join that debate, I want to examine Gross's argument at the level of theory, focusing on some of the

[18] O. Gross, 'Extra-Legality and the Ethic of Political Responsibility' (Chapter 3), this volume, p. 62.

[19] O. Gross, 'Chaos and Rules: Should Responses to Violent Crises Always be Constitutional?' (2003) 112 *Yale Law Journal* 1023 and Gross, Chapter 3, p. 64. See also O. Gross and F. Ní Aoláin, *Law in Times of Crisis: Emergency Powers in Theory and Practice* (Cambridge: Cambridge University Press, 2006), p. 11.

key terms he uses in stating it (which I have italicised). 'Illegal' would be a better word than 'extra-legal' for the kind of action Gross proposes. 'Extra-legal' means not regulated by law and is misleadingly applied to violations of law, which is what Gross really means here.[20] Both the argument itself and the vocabulary used to state it are familiar from Roman law and rhetoric and have been part of European political debate since the Middle Ages: *salus populi suprema lex.* I can do no more than offer a few passing comments in relation to this larger context.

Public officials. Thomas Jefferson, in a passage that Gross quotes to support his version of reason of state, speaks of *citizens* rather than of *public officials*: 'A strict observance of the written laws is doubtless *one* of the high duties of a good citizen, but it is not the *highest.* The laws of necessity, of self-preservation, of saving our country when in danger, are of a higher obligation'.[21] Perhaps this is not surprising for a statesman who was also a revolutionary – for it was the *citizens* of British America who saved their country by resisting the written laws that ruled them. Gross might argue that only public officials are authorised to act on behalf of the community and he would have a point. But public officials are authorised to act for the common good only within the law. They cannot be *authorised* to act ultra vires beyond their legal authority. Arguably, their responsibility to respect the law is more serious than that of the ordinary citizen.

Comparing the duties of officials and citizens raises the question of the connection between illegal action by officials and civil disobedience by citizens. The chief justification of civil disobedience is to dramatise the injustice of a law, but this justification is not part of the idea of reason of state. Gross's defence of official disobedience in an emergency is like the defence of civil disobedience in requiring those who break the law for the public good to acknowledge the illegality of their action and submit to judgment. The difference is that if civilly disobedient citizens must submit to *legal* judgment, Gross's disobedient officials stand to have their illegalities ratified not in a court of law but politically. If we choose the logic of emergency over the logic of law, in acting illegally officials succeed in putting themselves beyond the reach of law.

May. Gross's central claim is that public officials *may* act illegally when they believe such action is necessary to protect their nation from calamity.

[20] As Gross now clarifies: 'Rule departures constitute, under all circumstances and all conditions, violations of the relevant legal rule'. Gross, Chapter 3, p. 63.

[21] Gross, 'Chaos and Rules', 1106; Gross and Ní Aoláin, *Law in Times of Crisis*, p. 124.

Leaving aside the subjective element in the phrase 'they believe' and the ambiguities of the word 'necessary', we can ask what might be meant by the word 'may'. What kind of permission does this claim assert? It would seem not to be a legal permission, for the law cannot logically permit law to be violated. If the law authorises official discretion in emergencies and provides a procedure for deciding when a state of emergency exists, actions taken under that authority and according to that procedure are not illegal – the authority legalises the action. Elsewhere Gross switches from 'may' to words like 'should' and 'ought' that imply obligation rather than permission. He seems to have in mind an 'ought' that is either moral or prudential, but it is not clear which, for he seems at times to equate morality and prudence. He suggests in some places that extra-legal action is desirable, in others that it is appropriate. But desirability and propriety are not synonyms. Propriety implies a standard of right and wrong that is missing in the broader notion of desirability. An action is *desirable* if performing it will have good consequences. It is *proper* only if it is consistent with antecedently authoritative rules of conduct.

Necessary. The word 'necessary' is a key term in the lexicon of political realism. Its ambiguities are many and they have often been discussed. One must, for example, distinguish the claim that something is beyond the realm of human choice from the claim that it is an indispensable means for executing human choices. If the latter, one must distinguish the truly necessary from the merely expedient and what is believed to be necessary from what is actually necessary. And, as I suggested in discussing the idea of military necessity, one must distinguish necessity as a recognised defence within the law from necessity as an exceptional ground for violating the law.[22] It is the latter that defines the doctrine of reason of state. Law must give way to prudence when a state's vital interests are threatened.

Gross denies that his argument is realist. He distinguishes his position from political realism on the grounds that the realist is indifferent to law, whereas his own concern is to preserve the law.[23] But he reads realism uncharitably, targeting a rather feeble version of it: that realists are not concerned with preserving legal order and that they regard it to be without value. But the core of political realism is not a mere dismissal of law. It

[22] 'The defence, if properly understood and applied, is no malleable tool with which to negotiate the rule of law'. On the contrary, 'it offers a mechanism by which the conduct of officials falls to be normatively regulated, by the courts, *within* the legal system'. A.P. Simester, 'Necessity, Torture and the Rule of Law' (Chapter 12), this volume, p. 299.

[23] Gross, 'Chaos and Rules', 1024. See also Gross and Ní Aoláin, *Law in Times of Crisis*, pp. 3, 11 and 112.

is the claim that recognises the authority and binding force of law, yet argues that law may be violated for the sake of law itself. This is the idea of reason of state. The state is a legal order and to preserve that legal order those charged with its preservation may find it expedient to perform illegal acts. Just as the act of founding a legal order is extra-legal – the founding act cannot be one that is retrospectively authorised by the legal order it establishes, and must be illegal in the legal order it overturns – so maintaining a legal order can require extra-legal actions. There is a distinction, emphasised by Machiavelli in the *Discourses*, between *ruling* within an order of law and *maintaining* that order. The first involves interpreting and applying general laws in particular situations, which is essentially a judicial function. The second is concerned with securing the conditions for law's effectiveness and is essentially a matter of prudence and policy, exercised normally within the law but exceptionally outside it. Realists can be read as debating the boundary between law and policy, between ruling within the law and acting to maintain a legal order in the face of various threats. What Gross calls political realism is a version of the tradition that in treating legal considerations as mere niceties dismisses law as unimportant. But if law is unimportant, it can be ignored not only in emergencies but also in non-emergency situations. Because he identifies political realism with legal scepticism, he fails to see that his own argument is a form of political realism. What Gross calls political realism is one point on a continuum of realist arguments. As a political doctrine, reason of state is precisely the Weberian 'ethic of responsibility' that he invokes.

Calamity. The word 'emergency' has been tarnished by being invoked to justify acts that have less to do with preserving a community than with increasing the power of officials to pursue other ends. I have already mentioned that defenders of lawbreaking in emergencies imagine they have strengthened their argument by adding intensifying adjectives to produce expressions like extreme or supreme emergency. Gross's references to 'acute violent crisis', 'great calamity', 'extremely grave national dangers' and the like provide further examples. The adjectives signal that the word invoked is imprecise and cannot be relied upon, but the expression produced by adding an adjective is no more precise or reliable. Often, instead of the response being tailored to the calamity, the calamity is tailored to the response, as when leaders exaggerate the stakes in a war to which they have foolishly committed.

The people. The illegal action must be approved *ex post facto* by 'the people' who may express their approval through prosecutorial discretion, jury nullification or executive pardon; awarding honours; indemnifying those wronged or indemnifying those doing the wrong.[24] The last is illustrated by Dicey's proposal that ministers who act illegally 'in times of tumult or invasion' for the sake of legality itself should be cleared by an act of indemnity designed to 'free persons who have broken the law from responsibility for its breach, and thus make lawful acts which when they were committed were unlawful'.[25] But this formula obscures the distinction between excusing an act and justifying it. To excuse an offence is to defeat a charge of culpability on the grounds that an offender, though acting wrongly, is not responsible for the act because it was done in ignorance, under duress, as a result of mental impairment or under some other excusing condition. An excuse may lessen responsibility and therefore blame but it cannot justify the wrong – that is, make it just or lawful – though it may mitigate the penalty.[26] You cannot legalise an illegal act by excusing those who commit it from responsibility for violating the law. Much depends on who (the electorate, courts, parliament) does what (legalises, excuses, mitigates) in respect of the illegality.

Like many who defend discretionary executive action in emergencies, Gross quotes Jefferson's assertion that to lose one's country by a scrupulous adherence to written law would be to lose the law itself, thereby sacrificing the end to the means.[27] But the law that Jefferson says may be set aside in emergencies is *enacted* ('written') law. He does not urge violation of the unwritten *moral* law, of what in those days lawyers called 'the law of nature and of nations'. When officials violate the rule of law, their offence is moral and not merely political. They should be judged and held accountable. But if their plea is not to be judged in a court of law, it should be judged in the court of 'mankind' rather than that of 'the people'. We may ask why Gross imagines that the people who are to judge an illegal act are the citizens of

[24] See Gross, Chapter 3, p. 65, for discussion of these and other forms of *ex post facto* ratification.

[25] A.V. Dicey, *Introduction to the Study of the Law of the Constitution*, 8th edn (London: Macmillan, 1915), p. 228.

[26] J.L. Austin, 'A Plea for Excuses' in his *Philosophical Papers*, 3rd edn (Oxford: Oxford University Press, 1979). Donagan distinguishes 'first-order' questions of permissibility from 'second-order' questions of the culpability. *Theory of Morality*, pp. 52–7. Dicey does clearly distinguish the two in discussing martial law: an act of indemnity, he writes, is a statute that aims (1) 'to make legal transactions which, when they took place, were illegal' *or* (2) 'to free individuals to whom the statute applies from liability for having broken the law'. Dicey, *Law of the Constitution*, p. 547; see also p. 47. For further discussion, see A.P. Simester, Chapter 12, and S. Chesterman, 'Deny Everything: Intelligence Activities and the Rule of Law' (Chapter 13), this volume.

[27] Gross, 'Chaos and Rules', 1106; Gross and Ní Aoláin, *Law in Times of Crisis*, p. 124.

a given state when the law that is violated may extend beyond that state because it is a part of *international law* or because it is a violation of *moral law* as embodied in a bill of rights, doctrine of due process or conception of the rule of law. To the degree that enacted and moral law are entwined, as I think they are in the idea of the rule of law, I do not see how popular approval can repair the wrong.

5

Indefinite detention: rule by law or rule of law?

R. RUEBAN BALASUBRAMANIAM

I. Introduction

Global terrorism is thought to herald a paradigm shift within constitutional liberal democracies where liberty must give way to security creating a new normality.[1] Such a situation differs from a classically conceived state of emergency because it does not precipitate a temporary suspension of the rule of law. In response, post-9/11, constitutional liberal democracies, like the United States, the United Kingdom and Canada, therefore, contemplate the use of indefinite detention without trial (indefinite detention) as a counter-terrorism measure that should possess rule-of-law legitimacy.[2]

Indefinite detention raises problems for morality and the rule of law. It is morally troubling though it is far from clear that indefinite detention is inherently immoral and intolerable. From the perspective of the rule of law or legality, a question arises whether law can meaningfully regulate indefinite detention. If such control is impossible, then constitutional liberal democracies run the risk of creating rule by law not the rule of law. The rule of law contrasts with arbitrary power while, rule by law,

I thank all the participants in the symposium at which the papers in this volume were presented for discussion on an earlier version, especially Victor V. Ramraj for his editorial suggestions. I would also like to thank my colleagues at the Centre for Ethics for feedback on an even earlier draft. And, finally, I am especially grateful to David Dyzenhaus, Michael Hor, Rinku Lamba, Lindy Ledohowski, Mathias Thaler, Rayner Thwaites and Lars Vinx for helpful comments.

1 See Lawyers Committee for Human Rights (now known as Human Rights First), *Assessing the New Normal: Liberty and Security for The Post September 11 United States* (United States of America: Lawyers Committed for Human Rights, 2003), available at www.humanrightsfirst.org/us_law/loss/assessing/assessingnewnormal.htm.

2 The legislation need not explicitly create indefinite detention, but its practical use against suspected terrorists gives rise to indefinite detention. In the Canadian context, for example, immigration laws are used to deport suspected terrorists but indefinite detention arises when individuals cannot be deported to torture. See H. Stewart, 'Is Indefinite Detention of Terrorist Suspects Really Constitutional' (2005) 54 *University of New Brunswick Law Journal* 235.

on the other hand, involves the use of the legal form to cloak arbitrary power.[3]

In this chapter, I explore the lessons that constitutional liberal democracies can learn from Malaysia and Singapore where indefinite detention has been a long-standing feature of the legal landscape under internal security legislation. This power has been used as a tool of abuse and is now justified in the name of counter-terrorism. I shall begin by describing how the use of indefinite detention in both countries has led to rule by law, with the result that rule by law undermines the rule of law. Then I utilise the lessons of the study to show how rule by law is dependent upon the rule of law. Central to this argument is Lon Fuller's claim that state power filter through principles of legality requiring that laws are public, intelligible, non-contradictory, stable over time, generally prospective, and, importantly, that official action match declared rule, amount to an 'internal morality' of law that work in favour of the moral interests of legal subjects, including liberty.[4] I conclude by arguing that constitutional liberal democracies seeking rule-of-law legitimacy for indefinite detention risk weakening their culture of legal argument, ultimately jeopardising important values of liberal political morality, such as liberty and equality affirmed by their laws.

II. Indefinite detention in Malaysia and Singapore

Upon gaining independence from the British, Malaysia and Singapore both inherited a Westminster system of government where appointments to the office of Prime Minister and Cabinet derive from the majority party in Parliament. A constitutional monarch, a King known as the Yang Di-Pertuan Agong, is head of state in Malaysia while an elected president is the official head of state in Singapore.[5] The idea that political stability and the common good should override individual rights is a defining feature of politics in both countries. In Malaysia, the difficulties of managing ethnic interests that are not easily subject to compromise underlie the emphasis on political stability over rights.[6] And as Malaysia has developed

[3] For a discussion of the distinction, see B.Z. Tamanaha, *On the Rule of Law: History, Politics, Theory* (Cambridge: Cambridge University Press, 2004), pp. 92–3.

[4] L.L. Fuller, *The Morality of Law*, 2nd edn (New Haven: Yale University Press, 1969), ch. 2.

[5] See K.Y.L. Tan and P.E. Lam (eds.), *Managing Political Change in Singapore: The Elected Presidency* (London and New York: Routledge, 1997).

[6] See A. Lijphart, *Democracy in Plural Societies: A Comparative Exploration* (New Haven: Yale University Press, 1977).

economically, its government also argues that political stability and the subordination of individual rights is a precondition for economic progress. A similar argument holds sway in Singapore, reaching its height when former Prime Minister, Lee Kuan Yew, defended political rule that emphasises discipline and duty over individual rights in the name of 'Asian values'.[7] In both countries, the same ruling parties have successfully retained a supermajority in Parliament at every election. Political opposition is weak thus giving the ruling parties the power to institute rule by law. But since neither government is wholly unresponsive to the populace, political scientists describe them as 'semi-democratic'.[8]

With respect to legal order, Malaysia and Singapore share in a common law heritage that protects foundational moral interests of legal subjects that underpins a supreme written constitution containing a bill of rights that protects the right to life, liberty and due process, the principle of equality before law, and civil and political rights.[9] These features suggest a commitment to the rule of law. But given the capacity of both governments to institute rule by law, there have been constitutional amendments and legislation that allow for authoritarian control over such rights.

It is in this context that indefinite detention finds its basis in the legal order. Article 149 of both constitutions permits the enactment of 'special anti-subversion' legislation 'inconsistent' with the right to life, liberty and due process. Concerned about a communist insurgency that rocked Malaysia during the 1940s and 1950s, both legislatures enacted internal security legislation in 1960 to affirm earlier legislation introduced by the British allowing for indefinite detention.[10] The Malaysian legislation allows the Minister of Home Affairs to detain a person for up to two years 'if satisfied that he has acted or is about to act or is likely to act in any manner prejudicial to . . . security . . . or to the maintenance of

[7] See M. Jacobsen and O. Bruun (eds.), *Human Rights and Asian Values: Contesting National Identities and Cultural Representations in Asia* (Surrey: Curzon Press, 2000).

[8] See W. Case, *Politics in Southeast Asia: Democracy or Less* (London: Routledge Curzon, 2002).

[9] Article 5(1) of both constitutions protects the right to life, liberty and due process, stating 'No person's right to life or liberty shall be deprived save in accordance with law'. The rest of Article 5 protects the writ of habeas corpus, the right to be told of grounds of an arrest, the right to appear before a judge within 24 hours of arrest and the right to counsel.

[10] Indefinite detention pre-dates the internal security legislation. British colonial authorities introduced it in Malaya (as it was then known) in the 1940s to combat the communists. For an account of the insurgency and the British response, see T.N. Harper, *The End of Empire and the Making of Malaya* (Cambridge: Cambridge University Press, 1999), ch. 4.

essential services therein or the economic life thereof'.[11] The Singaporean provisions are identical except that the President must be satisfied that detention is necessary.[12] In both countries, detention orders are subject to unlimited renewals creating a system of indefinite detention.

The legislation contains procedural controls that try to discipline the detention power so that it is not wholly arbitrary, but these are ineffective. The controls suggest that the government bears a justificatory burden to show that its decision to detain is fair, impartial and reasonable. Article 151 of both constitutions stipulates that the government must specify the precise grounds of detention and supply sufficient facts to the detainee to challenge the decision to detain before a three-member Advisory Board. The Board may comprise an active or retired judge or someone qualified to be a judge and two civil servants, although in Singapore, it is not unusual that non-governmental people may be appointed. The Board can call witnesses, examine documents and hear arguments from the government and the detainee who may use legal counsel. On the other hand, a major weakness is that there is no formal mechanism for the detainee to make representations directly to the Minister or the President. And the effectiveness of the Board is ultimately undermined by the fact that the government can withhold sensitive information on 'national interest' grounds from the Board and the detainee. Finally, the Board's decision is merely advisory although its decision potentially has more purchase in Singapore if the President concurs with the Board's decision that the detention is unjustified; such concurrence leads to the automatic invalidation of a detention order.[13] In general, however, the Board appears to be nothing more than a mere fig leaf for the rule of law that does little to protect against arbitrary power.[14]

Nevertheless, one might argue that procedural controls evidence a legislative intention to protect the detainee and is a foothold for judges to adopt a more charitable interpretation of the statute that would give greater effect to legality. They might insist on a high degree of procedural rectitude and invalidate a detention order for the slightest procedural failure. The basis for such an argument is the idea that procedural failures are substantive rule-of-law failures. As Trevor Allan argues, procedures lay

[11] Internal Security Act 1960 (Act 82, Laws of Malaysia), s.8(1); Internal Security Act (Cap. 143, 1985 Rev. Ed. Sing.), s.8(1). The legislation also grants a detention power to the police but my focus is on the Ministerial power of detention.

[12] Internal Security Act, s.8(1). [13] Internal Security Act, s.13A.

[14] For critical analysis of the effectiveness of the Advisory Board, see M. Hor, 'Terrorism and the Criminal Law: Singapore's Solution' (2002) *Singapore Journal of Legal Studies* 30.

down a framework that allows an affected party to enter into dialogue with the decision-maker.[15] Dialogue facilitates more accurate decision-making because the decision-maker gains more information. But procedures also speak to the legitimacy of the decision since by requiring the decision-maker to explain and justify the decision to the affected party, the former recognises the inherent rationality and dignity of the latter thereby giving the decision rule-of-law legitimacy. By implication, to use Allan's words, 'infringements of procedural legality will tend to undermine . . . confidence in, and respect for, law'.[16] In this regard, the internal security legislation in both countries permits judicial review for procedural irregularities, but the problem is that a finding of such irregularity will not stop the Minister of Home Affairs from issuing a further detention order.

When the communist threat remained a real concern to national security, Malaysian and Singaporean judges resisted a strict approach to procedural defects. In the 1969 decision of *Karam Singh* v. *Menteri Hal Ehwal Dalam Negeri (Minister for Home Affairs)*, Malaysia's highest court, the Federal Court, held that procedural defects are mere defects of form.[17] Judges asserted that Parliament could control the executive under the Westminster system and showed unwillingness to second-guess government decisions on national security. They upheld the 'subjective satisfaction' of the Minister that detention is necessary and ultimately felt that indefinite detention is a necessary and justified qualification to the rule of law in light of the threat of subversion.[18] In taking this highly deferential stance in favour of the government, the judges stripped any rule-of-law significance from procedural controls in the legislation. In the 1971 decision of *Lee Mau Seng* v. *Minister for Home Affairs*, the head of Singapore's highest court, the Court of Appeal, Wee Chong Jin C.J., echoed this view and declared that indefinite detention under the security legislation is 'purely executive'.[19] The court affirmed the so-called 'subjective test' for judicial review and overlooked the rule-of-law significance of procedural irregularities despite the absence of any formal legal barrier to reviewing

[15] T.R.S. Allan, 'Procedural Fairness and the Duty of Respect' (1998) *Oxford Journal of Legal Studies* 497.

[16] *Ibid.*, at 505. [17] [1969] 2 MLJ 129.

[18] For a detailed analysis of the case, see R.R. Balasubramaniam, 'The Karam Singh Case' in A.J. Harding and H.P. Lee (eds.), *Constitutional Landmarks in Malaysian Law: 50 Years of the Malaysian Constitution* (Kuala Lumpur: Malaysian Law Journal, 2007).

[19] [1971] 2 MLJ 137 at 140–2.

decisions expressing such irregularities, thus practically giving the government a legally uncontrolled power.[20]

By the 1970s and 1980s, however, the communist insurgency was no longer a realistic threat to political stability, which made it difficult to see why governments should possess the power of indefinite detention.[21] Nevertheless, governments in both countries continued to assert the primacy of stability and the interests of the collective over individual rights, using that assertion to justify using indefinite detention to squash dissent of governmental policy and practice. Indefinite detention had become a useful authoritarian tool.

This problem was rife under the rule of Dr Mahathir Mohammad, who was Prime Minister of Malaysia from 1981 until 2003. As a populist, he was resistant to concepts such as the separation of powers and judicial review.[22] Although he professed a commitment to the rule of law, Dr Mahathir felt that the law should not obstruct official judgments about how best to exercise state power serving the common good, especially in the national security context. The Prime Minister was therefore critical of judicial review, describing it as 'undemocratic'. In the mid-1980s, judges tried to affirm the importance of constitutional values through judicial review of legislative and administrative action, but Dr Mahathir publicly argued that judges were undermining the government's specific intent in creating a law. Judges tried to explain, from the bench, that this objection misunderstood their role under the rule of law.[23] But the Prime Minister expressed the desire to find ways of stopping judges from doing so.[24]

In fact, Dr Mahathir overtly resorted to rule by law along with political moves designed to weaken judicial review. In 1987, in the midst of an

[20] A detainee could still challenge the validity of a detention order on grounds of bad faith, but this argument was notoriously difficult to prove. See the dictum of Abdoolcader J. in *Yeap Hock Seng* v. *Minister for Home Affairs Malaysia and Others* [1975] 2 MLJ 279.

[21] Thus, it is argued that the security legislation has now lapsed and is no longer constitutionally valid but no Malaysian or Singaporean court has accepted this argument. See N. Fritz and M. Flaherty, *Unjust Order: Malaysia's Internal Security Act* (New York: Joseph R. Crowley Program in International Human Rights, Fordham Law School, 2003), pp. 40–1.

[22] For analysis of Dr Mahathir's rule, see R.S. Milne and D.K. Mauzy, *Malaysian Politics under Mahathir* (London: Routledge, 1999).

[23] For analysis of Dr Mahathir's attack on the rule of law, see H.P. Lee, *Constitutional Conflicts in Contemporary Malaysia* (Kuala Lumpur and New York: Oxford University Press, 1995), especially Chapter 3.

[24] See his comments in an interview aptly entitled, 'I Know How the People Feel' *Time Magazine* (24 November 1986).

economic recession, his government was the subject of several political and financial scandals and faced harsh criticism from the political opposition, the press, civil society and the public. In addition, members of his own ruling party doubted his leadership and the party divided over whether to endorse him as their leader. This posed a very serious political threat to his status as Prime Minister since, by convention, the leader of the ruling party is Prime Minister. Dr Mahathir reacted by detaining over one hundred people, including opposition leaders and some of his own party members, portraying the detainees as security threats because their criticism of government threatened to destabilise racial harmony.[25]

Much to his chagrin, the courts departed from their posture of strict deference to the government and released several opposition figures on procedural grounds.[26] Although judges never expressly challenged the basis behind these decisions to detain, they argued that the subjective test was unsatisfactory and led to unfairness to detainees. The problem with the subjective test was that it allowed the government to claim rule-of-law legitimacy for its actions despite the fact that under that test, governments could effectively exercise a wholly arbitrary power. Courts argued that the test should go and that a proper interpretation of the internal security legislation would require that the government meet an 'objective test', where the government would have to adduce evidence to substantiate the claim that detainees posed a threat to national security that judges could assess for reasonableness.[27]

One should note, however, that no court ever went so far as to apply the objective test, as judges would advert to it merely by way of *obiter dicta*. And where they had seemed to apply it, judges acted as if the law had not departed from the subjective approach.[28] Practically, however, a barrier to the application of the objective test is that the government's ability to retain sensitive information limited the test to obvious cases of unreasonableness, such as mistaken identity or outright fabrication. Instead, the test seemed

[25] For a detailed account of what happened, see R. Yatim, *Freedom Under Executive Power in Malaysia: A Study of Executive Supremacy* (Kuala Lumpur: Endowment Publications, 1995).

[26] See *Karpal Singh* v. *Menteri Hal Ehwal Dalam Negeri* (High Court), [1988] 2 MLJ 468; *Lim Kit Siang and Others* v. *Menteri Hal Ehwal Dalam Negeri* (High Court), [1988] 2 MLJ 95.

[27] See the *dictum* of Edgar Joseph, Jr, S.C.J. in *Yit Hon Kit* v. *Minister for Home Affairs; Malaysia and Another* (Supreme Court), [1988] 2 MLJ 638.

[28] In one case, the court described as far-fetched the detention of a bank official suspected of defrauding a bank on the basis that clients who comprised members of the armed forces may violently revolt. See *Tan Sri Raja Khalid bin Raja Harun* (High Court), [1988] 1 MLJ 182.

to play a rhetorical role in expressing judicial rule-of-law concerns. In my view, judges were trying to protect detainees without expressly declaring that the government was abusing power, a declaration that would be hard to avoid if courts had tried to apply the objective test.

Despite its rhetorical role, the judiciary's stance in favour of the objective test was significant because it forced the government to do more than assert rule-of-law legitimacy for its use of indefinite detention. Now it had to defend its preference for the subjective test on the terrain of legal argument. In addition, judicial emphasis on procedure in evaluating the legitimacy of decisions to detain also conveyed that unless the government does take its procedural obligations seriously, it could not claim rule-of-law legitimacy for its actions. In the words of the then head of the judiciary, Tun Salleh Abas L.P., '[in] a democratic society in which the government is not absolute but a limited one, there is a duty on the part of the executive to act with fairness and follow fair procedures'.[29] The idea here is that the government was failing in its duty to uphold the rule of law and could not assert rule-of-law legitimacy without taking seriously the legal subject's right to impartial exercises of power cognisant of their interests in the protection of liberty.

Implicit in this argument against the government is the idea that the rule of law depends on governmental willingness to self-correct and to perfect its duties towards legality if legal subjects challenge a government's claim to rule-of-law legitimacy. But the Malaysian government answered in an authoritarian manner. As part of an overall attempt to weaken the judiciary's power of judicial review, which included the government's desire to insulate itself from an accounting in court for its use of detention without trial, Dr Mahathir made good on his expressed desire to find a way to control the courts. He successfully secured the dismissal of Salleh Abas L.P. and two other judges of the highest court on grounds of 'misconduct'. Under Malaysian law, the dismissal of judges depends on a decision of a tribunal appointed by Parliament, comprising active and retired judicial officers from Malaysia and elsewhere in the Commonwealth.[30] The tribunal must determine whether there are grounds for misconduct and report this conclusion to the Prime Minister who then advises the Yang di-Pertuan Agong who makes the decision to suspend or dismiss the judge. There were several serious problems with the legality of the tribunal's

[29] *Theresa Lim Chin Chin and Others* v. *Inspector General of Police* (Supreme Court), [1988] 1 MLJ 293 at 297.

[30] Art.125(3).

proceedings, not the least of which was a problem with its impartiality. One of its members stood to replace Salleh Abas L.P. as the head of the judiciary should the tribunal decide that there were grounds for misconduct.[31]

In addition to dismissing judges, the government passed a constitutional amendment to make judicial review more difficult. The government amended constitutional provisions providing for the judicial power of the courts, that is, the power of the courts to adjudicate disputes between legal subjects and between subjects and the state. Article 121 had stated that 'the judicial power of the Federation shall be vested in two High Courts . . . and in such inferior courts as may be provided by federal law'. But the amendment, Article 121A, deletes the term 'judicial power' and declares that the jurisdiction of the courts shall be subject to 'federal law'. The idea behind the amendment is to facilitate the legislative use of privative clauses limiting or banning judicial review.[32] The government weakened constitutional provisions recognising the importance of judicial independence and the separation of powers as institutional features necessary for the protection of the rule of law.

In Singapore, the government also made questionable use of indefinite detention, again, facilitated by the fact that it could rely on the subjective test to avoid accounting meaningfully for its use in court. And like Dr Mahathir in Malaysia who challenged the importance of judicial review, the Singaporean Prime Minister, Lee Kuan Yew, had openly declared unwillingness to have to justify fully decisions to detain in court especially when it came to dealing with 'subversives'.[33] Such an attitude generated the danger that the government was willing to use indefinite detention without justifying itself, with the risk that it could use the power as an authoritarian tool.

This danger materialised in *Chng Suan Tze* v. *Minister for Home Affairs*.[34] The case involved five appellants whom the government had detained as 'Marxist conspirators' threatening to overthrow the government. It was not clear what evidence the government had to this effect, since the detainees merely appeared to be Christian activists seeking to spread awareness

[31] Lee, *Constitutional Conflicts in Contemporary Malaysia*, ch. 3, p. 65.

[32] See A.J. Harding, *Law, Government and the Constitution in Malaysia* (Kuala Lumpur: Malayan Law Journal, 1996), pp. 133–6.

[33] See B. Frank *et al.*, *The Decline in the Rule of Law in Singapore and Malaysia: A Report of the International Committee on Human Rights of the Association of the Bar of the City of New York* (New York: Association of the Bar of the City of New York, 1990), p. 55.

[34] [1989] 1 MLJ 69.

on pressing political issues through a variety of media including drama groups and clubs. The government worried that their activities could ultimately lead to violence but it did not disclose any evidence to support this concern. As Michael Hor points out, it was unclear that the activities of the appellants posed any imminent threat to national security.[35] The government's decision seemed too speculative. Perhaps in the face of such doubts, the government televised the detainee's confessions to a Marxist conspiracy. But when the Home Minister issued alternative orders releasing the detainees, they retracted their confessions, claiming that these were coerced. The Singaporean government quickly re-detained the appellants who were then unsuccessful in seeking habeas corpus in the lower courts.

There were serious doubts about the legitimacy of the government's decision that would linger without a full disclosure of the basis of that decision. But the Singaporean court was likely aware that a full frontal attack against the government's decision that openly suggested it was abusing powers might lead to a government backlash that could seriously damage the rule of law although they could not allow the government to act arbitrarily in this case and sought to send a clear message to the government that the courts would not condone an abuse of power. This meant, as Hor puts it, the courts needed to find a 'face-saving' solution.[36]

To protect the appellants and secure their release, the Court of Appeal invalidated the detention order. Wee Chong Jin C.J. delivered the court's judgment, arguing that the government had not proven presidential satisfaction that the detainees were a security threat. On this technical point of procedure, the court ordered the release of the detainees.[37] But to highlight doubts about the legitimacy of the government's actions, Chong Jin C.J. engaged in a lengthy *obiter dictum*, attacking the subjective test and backtracking from his earlier position in *Lee Mau Seng* in support of that test where he had declared that indefinite detention under the internal security legislation is 'purely executive'.

The judge made several points, observing that other countries in the Commonwealth had already departed from that test in favour of the objective test and that Malaysian judges had criticised the subjective test. He

[35] M. Hor, 'Law and terror: Singapore Stories and Malaysian Dilemmas' in V.V. Ramraj, M. Hor and K. Roach (eds.), *Global Anti-Terrorism Law and Policy* (Cambridge: Cambridge University Press, 2005), pp. 281–2. I largely follow Hor in my analysis of *Chng Suan Tze*.

[36] *Ibid.*, p. 284.

[37] The point is technical since the government could have easily cured the defect and proven Presidential satisfaction by issuing an affidavit signed by the President himself. On the facts, however, the government issued an affidavit signed by the Permanent Secretary.

also argued that the internal security legislation does not envisage a legally untrammelled power in light of its procedural controls, such that the government only possessed a limited detention power. But his primary argument was that the subjective test was unconstitutional under Singaporean law. Starting with the principle that the security legislation operates under the Article 149 derogation power, Chong Jin C.J., correctly argued that the derogation should receive a narrow reading that should not impinge upon other constitutional values untouched by the derogation, such as 'equality before law', 'fairness', 'natural justice' and the concept of 'judicial power'.[38] On this view, the subjective test was an incorrect reading of the internal security legislation because it was in tension with these constitutional values.

But instead of self-correcting and responding in a way that fulfils a commitment to legality, the Singaporean government answered the decision by invoking rule by law. The government amended the Constitution to extend the scope of the derogation clause to cover provisions previously untouched by it. In addition, the government enacted a privative clause banning judicial review of the President's decision except on 'procedural matters'.[39] Although the clause seems to leave space for procedural challenges, it is reasonable to infer that the government did not anticipate such challenges to be serious obstacles to their use of indefinite detention. This is evidenced by a further amendment stating that the law of judicial review under the security legislation would be as decided on 13 July 1971, the date *Lee Mau Seng* was decided.[40] These amendments try to eviscerate sources of legal arguments available to legal subjects that push the government meaningfully to account for its actions under the rule of law.

Since *Chng Suan Tze*, the Singaporean judiciary has affirmed the subjective test.[41] And post-9/11, the Singaporean government has invoked the threat of global terrorism as a justification to retain indefinite detention, using the power against individuals suspected of terrorist links or activities.[42] Malaysia, too, has used indefinite detention with respect to suspected terrorists.[43] Like its Singaporean counterpart, the Malaysian legislature introduced a new section 8B to the internal security legislation

[38] *Chng Suan Tze* at 81–2. [39] S. 8B(2). [40] S. 8B(1).

[41] See *Teoh So Lung* v. *Minister for Home Affairs*, [1989] 1 SLR 499.

[42] See Hor, 'Terrorism and the Criminal Law'. See also the Singapore government's account of these arrests in its White Paper entitled *The Jemaah Islamiyah Arrests and the Threat of Terrorism*, Cmd. 2 of 2003 (Singapore, 7 January 2003).

[43] See T. Lee, 'Malaysia and the Internal Security Act: The Insecurity of Human Rights after September 11' (2002) *Singapore Journal of Legal Studies* 56.

containing a privative clause banning judicial review of Ministerial decisions to detain save on 'procedural grounds'. However, recent cases suggest that Malaysian judges are unwilling to be entirely passive in the face of the government's use of indefinite detention, at least in the context of police powers under the internal security legislation.[44] But judges have not challenged the constitutional validity of the privative clause so the subjective test continues to apply to Ministerial detention orders.[45]

Despite the threat of global terrorism, there remains heavy criticism of indefinite detention in both countries. The worry is that the incidence of rule by law undermines the overall legitimacy of the legal order. The case study shows that where governments act out of an authoritarian impulse and impose rule by law, they do so at the cost of institutional features of the legal order designed to protect the basic rights of legal subjects. The whittling away of such features arises out of an official unwillingness to engage legal challenges that spotlight the significance of such rights. By enacting changes in the legislation to insulate against judicial review, effectively, putting in place rule by law, the Malaysian and Singaporean governments' implicit claims to rule-of-law legitimacy for their use of indefinite detention are in tension with the damage done to the rule of law. I shall now use legal theory to sharpen this difficulty before arguing that it raises particular problems for constitutional liberal democracies.

III. Rule by law and rule of law

Although there is agreement that the principles of legality, among them that laws are general, public, clear, coherent and consistently enforced, are core features of the rule of law, legal theorists debate about whether the rule of law is a morally substantive idea at all.[46] At first glance, the principles of legality appear to be merely procedural rather than substantive moral constraints on state power. This view is prevalent amongst legal positivists who subscribe to the Separation Thesis – the thesis that there is no necessary connection between law and morality. Positivists argue that

[44] See *Abdul Ghani Haroon* v. *Ketua Polis Negara and Another Application* (High Court), [2001] 2 MLJ 689; *Mohamad Ezam bin Mohd Noor* v. *Ketua Polis Negara and Other Appeals* (Federal Court), [2002] 4 MLJ 449.

[45] See J.D. Ciorciari, 'A Half-Way Challenge to Malaysia's Internal Security Act (*Mohamad Ezam bin Mohd Noor* v. *Ketua Polis Negara*)' (2004) 3 *Oxford University Commonwealth Law Journal* 237.

[46] See P. Craig, 'Formal and Substantive Conceptions of the Rule of Law: An Analytical Framework' (1997) *Public Law* 467.

law is a social creation such that the moral goodness of the law or a legal order is contingent upon the moral character of its lawmaking officials and/or the community. On that view, law can be pressed in the service of morality in as much as it can be made to serve immorality.

In articulating his version of legal positivism, H.L.A. Hart argues that the validity of legal norms within any given legal order depends on criteria set out in the legal system's master rule of recognition.[47] The rule of recognition delivers certainty in the identification of law so that law can effectively guide conduct.[48] Law's capacity to guide conduct breaks down if there are doubts about what is to count as an authoritative rule of conduct.[49] And it is a master rule because its existence does not depend on the existence of any prior rule. Hart explains that the rule of recognition manifests in the practice of legal officials whose task is to identify what counts as valid law. But consistent with the Separation Thesis, he tells us that official practice need not guarantee the moral goodness of laws. In fact, Hart warns that officials may join forces and use law as a tool for abusing legal subjects.[50] If this is right, then the principles of legality are not only consistent with tyrannical rule, they may be a useful tool of tyranny.[51]

I think there is a crucial difference between tyrannical rule and rule by law. But for the moment, I want to consider the plausibility of Hart's claim that the rule of law is compatible with tyrannical rule. Presumably, in Hart's view, the rule of recognition would stipulate that the law is whatever the tyrant decides is law. But if the rule of recognition is meant to deliver certainty in the law that speaks to law's capacity to guide conduct, the suggestion is that legal decision-making about questions of legal validity is somehow disciplined such that legal officials cannot make decisions merely by reference to their subjective preferences. One might say that such decision-making must express a commitment to a degree of impartiality. But a moment's reflection would suggest that no tyrant would wish to bind himself to a duty of impartial rule making it difficult to see how Hart's rule of recognition could find a foothold within a tyranny.[52]

[47] H.L.A. Hart, *The Concept of Law*, 2nd ed. (Oxford: Oxford University Press, 1994), ch. 6.

[48] *Ibid.*, pp. 94–5. [49] *Ibid.*, p. 93.

[50] See L. Green, 'The Concept of Law Revisited' (1996) *Michigan Law Review* 1687; J. Waldron, 'All We Like Sheep' (1999) *Canadian Journal of Law and Jurisprudence* 169.

[51] For another influential articulation of this view, see J. Raz, 'The Rule of Law and its Virtue' in J. Raz, *The Authority of Law: Essays on Law and Morality* (Oxford: Oxford University Press, 1979).

[52] See J. Finnis, *Natural Law and Natural Rights* (Oxford: Clarendon Press, 1980), p. 273.

The more general point is that legal order, as a system of rule-governed behaviour cannot emerge if those who wield political power are indifferent to the legal subject as a rational self-directing agent bearing moral interests. For legal rules to be capable of guiding conduct, it is necessary to comply with the principles of legality. But once one accepts this general point, and then one also has to acknowledge that attention to the moral interests of the legal subject is material to law's claim to respect and the successful creation of legal order. Thus, whatever the conception of political rule in play, the moral interests of legal subjects are germane if such rule depends upon the allegiance of legal subjects. Even Hart acknowledges this point in saying that every legal order must reflect some 'minimal moral content' in recognising basic moral interests such as the protection of life and property.[53]

The idea that legal subjects are rational self-directing agents with moral interests lies at the core of Lon Fuller's claim that the principles of legality amount to an 'inner' or 'internal' morality of law that are incompatible with the use of law for injustice. For Fuller, any attempt to construct and maintain legal order as a stable framework for the guidance of conduct involves a moral dimension that constrains the lawgiver's capacity to use law for authoritarian purposes, because legal order is a reciprocal enterprise requiring cooperation between the lawgiver and legal subject. Unless the former takes seriously the legal subject's concern for impartial rule and a concern to protect basic moral interests such as the legal subject's interests in liberty, the latter will not develop a sense of respect for legality. And without that sense of respect, legal order is doomed to fail.

The key point in Fuller's analysis is that the appropriate lens through which to analyse the idea of legal authority is the perspective of the legal subject.[54] Once we take that perspective seriously, we can see that law's commitment to impartial rule derives from the legal subject's concern that important moral interests receive legal protection. The fact that Hart acknowledges such protections as the minimal moral content towards which every legal order must aspire, vindicates the idea that no legal order can get off the ground unless such interests are adequately protected. Of course, Hart does not go so far as to say that the existence of such content makes legality a moral idea. In his view, the principles of legality are merely procedural and not substantive moral principles that underlie legal order.

[53] Hart, *The Concept of Law*, pp. 193–200.

[54] See K. Winston (ed.), *The Principles of Social Order: Selected Essays on Lon L. Fuller* (Oxford: Hart Publishing, 2001), pp. 36–7.

However, if the perspective of the legal subject is the primary lens through which to analyse legal authority, then the procedural-substantive distinction is mistaken. The problem with positivism is that it analyses legal authority from an erroneous 'top-down' view of law as a 'one-way projection of authority' from ruler to the ruled.[55] On this top-down view, law is a tool for transmitting preordained content, content decided by the lawmaker. This explains why positivists argue that the moral goodness of law depends on the moral character of whoever holds lawmaking power and why they see the principles of legality as nothing more than procedural preconditions for law to effectively transmit such content. The problem with the top-down view of law is that the perspective of the legal subject drops out of the analysis of legal authority so that the subject's moral interests and corresponding interest in impartial rule do not appear to be essential factors for legitimate legal authority.

Positivists fail to see that constructing and maintaining legal order is a dynamic enterprise in the sense that the lawgiver must be constantly mindful of whether his actions promote the legal subject's concern for impartial and moral rule. So every exercise of political power claimed under the rule of law involves a choice by the lawgiver that may enhance or reduce the legal subject's respect for law. In Fuller's words, a commitment to the rule of law is one that needs to be constantly 'renewed'.[56] Where exercises of power diverge from the duty of impartial rule and the moral interests of legal subjects, the latter's sense of respect for legal order weakens. And where such divergence is persistent and endemic, this undermines the claim that one is in fact ruling in accordance with legality.

Fuller's view is appealing because it also allows one to think of the rule of law as operating on a continuum, which more clearly highlights why the principles of legality ultimately operate as a moral constraint on political rule.[57] At one end, one might posit a legal order that securely protects the moral interests of legal subjects, perhaps in the form of a robust constitutional liberal democracy, and at the other end, is rule by law. The rule of law is compatible with a variety of different political philosophies, all of which can claim to fall on the rule-of-law continuum so long as they reflect a commitment to impartial rule and recognise the

[55] Fuller, *The Morality of Law*, pp. 200–23.

[56] L.L. Fuller, 'American Legal Philosophy at Mid-Century' (1954) 6 *Journal of Legal Education* 467.

[57] See D. Dyzenhaus, *The Constitution of Law: Legality in a Time of Emergency* (Cambridge: Cambridge University Press, 2006), p. 231.

basic moral interests of the legal subject as constitutive elements necessary for successful legal order.[58]

This brings me to the distinction between rule by law and tyranny. The latter has no place on the rule-of-law continuum because nothing mediates the tyrant's exercise of power in the service of his own interests. The perspective of the legal subject is not intrinsically relevant to the tyrant such that there is no plausible basis to think that law does mediate an exercise of power. Talk of rule by law crucially depends on there being some basis for claiming a position on the continuum of legality since rule by law captures the idea that an exercise of political power is at odds with an underlying commitment to legality. Rule by law is out of place within a tyranny where the claim that law rules is doubtful.

It is important to note that rule by law is an unavoidable feature of legal order because the law may sometimes fail to facilitate and control an exercise of political power in a manner that remains faithful to the interests of legal subjects. This explains why legal reform is part of any attempt to maintain legal order. To use language from the case study, rule by law in this event is a reason for a legal order to self-correct and perfect a commitment to legality. However, as the Malaysian and Singaporean case studies show, rule by law can arise out of an authoritarian impulse to exercise arbitrary power hidden beneath a false claim to rule-of-law legitimacy. This is a danger that faces any legal order. As Fuller puts it, 'the lawgiver or law-enforcer is subject to a constant temptation to cheat on the system, and to exercise a ruleless power under the guise of upholding a system of rules'.[59] Such a claim to legitimacy is fake and cannot escape being in opposition to an underlying commitment to legality.

The case study illustrates this point. Governments in Malaysia and Singapore can make a plausible claim to respect legality because they are not outright tyrannies. Rather they are 'semi-democratic' regimes where governments are still responsive to popular will even if there is limited space for the exercise of individual rights. Importantly, both political cultures recognise the role law plays in mediating judgments about the legitimate exercise of state power. Together, these factors have enabled the maintenance of a workable legal order, placing them on the rule-of-law

[58] In this regard, consider Robert Alexy's point that the 'claim to correctness' is a conceptual prerequisite for the rule of law. See R. Alexy, *The Argument for Injustice: A Reply to Legal Positivism*, B.L. Paulson and S.L. Paulson (trans.) (Oxford: Clarendon Press, 2002), pp. 31–5.

[59] See L.L. Fuller, 'A Reply to Professors Cohen and Dworkin' (1965) 10 *Villanova Law Review* 655 at 657.

continuum.[60] But when both governments change the law to give formal validity to arbitrary exercises of power that unreasonably disrupt the moral interests of legal subjects in the protection of their liberty and other rights, they are cheating on the system. They are seeking to capitalise on the legal subject's sense of deference to law in an attempt to project rule-of-law legitimacy for arbitrary power.

In this regard, it is no defence for these governments to assert, as they sometimes do, that the importance of political stability requires that one accept a narrow formalistic view of legality where there is rule of law as long as official action coincides with formally valid law.[61] On this view, the distinction between rule of law and rule by law supposedly collapses, so that rule by law should receive real rule-of-law legitimacy.

But this argument is unconvincing. The case study reveals that an assertion of formal legality through rule by law ignores the legal subject's concern for impartial and moral rule and rides roughshod over features of the legal order that give effect to that concern. One of the lessons of the case study is that governments are likely to resort to a combination of authoritarianism (as occurred in the Malaysian case with the removal

[60] Some participants at the symposium suggested that Singapore, in particular, is a counter-example to Fuller's claim that a commitment to the rule of law generates moral constraints on state power. Singapore is highly regarded for efficient and transparent governance, while holding a poor human rights record. Thus, it is argued that adherence to principles of legality may generate efficient and transparent governance, making legality a moral idea, but Fuller is wrong to think that a commitment to the principles of legality can generate more robust moral constraints on state power.

I find this objection problematic for several reasons. First, it suggests that one could establish a rule-of-law abiding society without respecting foundational moral interests of legal subjects. As I argue in the text, no legal order can get off the ground without such respect. Second, using efficiency and transparency as primary markers for identifying the rule of law misses the point that these are rule-of-law virtues because they derive from the interests of legal subjects in impartial and moral governance. Third, I suspect that those who pose this objection would point to the dismal record of judicial review in Singapore to vindicate their claim. This record of failure is cause for serious concern but, again, we can use the language of rule by law to say that such a record is at odds with Singapore's commitment to the rule of law. I do not think that one can point to such a record as sufficient evidence to substantiate the claim that the Singaporean government is indifferent to human rights. One has to study political behaviour in that country to see if government policies are indifferent to foundational moral interests of legal subjects, the substance of such rights. In this regard, political science does not yield such a conclusion.

[61] For an argument exploring the plausibility of the narrow conception of legality in the Singaporean context, see V.V. Ramraj, 'Four Models of Due Process' (2004) 2 *International Journal of Constitutional Law* 492; K. Jayasuriya, 'The Exception Becomes the Norm: Law and Regimes of Exception in East Asia' (2001) 2 *Asian Pacific Law and Policy Journal* 108 at 114–17.

of judges and detention of critics) with attempts to affect an ideological shift among legal subjects aimed at convincing them that they should not assert the importance of individual rights. One might treat the Singaporean government's attempt to emphasise 'Asian values', for example, as an attempt to convince legal subjects that collective interests and a sense of duty over individual rights. But that argument has since waned as governments now emphasise the threat of global terrorism to make a similar claim against the expression of individual rights. The narrow conception of legality does not deliver any genuine rule-of-law legitimacy, which is why governments must resort to such strategies. As Victor V. Ramraj observes in the Singaporean context, attempts to rely on a formal conception of legality (the equivalent of rule by law) fly in the face of constitutional furniture that protects the foundational moral interests of legal subjects and sets out a framework for impartial rule.[62] This tension vindicates Fuller's point that authoritarian rule and rule by law strain the principles of legality; the tension strains the internal morality of law.

In sum, once a government makes a plausible claim to operate on the rule-of-law continuum, it cannot assert rule by law without contradicting its commitment to legality. Whatever the political motivations of a government in choosing to exercise political power, it must address the legal subject's concern for impartial and moral rule. In this regard, the rule of law becomes a litmus test of legitimacy that allows legal subjects to evaluate and challenge political arguments posed by governments when justifying state power claimed in the name of the common good. With this idea in mind, let me turn to explicating why constitutional liberal democracies need to be wary of the risk that unresponsiveness to such interests when engaging indefinite detention may lead to a backslide on the rule-of-law continuum.

IV. Indefinite detention and legal archetypes

I began by noting that the moral status of indefinite detention is murky since it is unclear whether indefinite detention is inherently immoral and unclear whether indefinite detention can be effectively controlled by law in a manner that assures adequate respect for legality. As David Dyzenhaus observes in this volume, such difficulties contribute to uncertainty over whether indefinite detention is 'unlegalisable' and doomed to take place

[62] Ramraj, 'Four Models of Due Process', 523.

in an extra-legal space.[63] In the face of such uncertainty, he argues that constitutional liberal democracies should engage in imaginative experiments of institutional design to try to keep indefinite detention within the rule of law, rather than choosing to depart from legality. But there is a risk attendant to such attempts, because such experiments may only yield rule by law thus allowing governments to enjoy false rule-of-law legitimacy for exercising essentially arbitrary power. To check this danger, Dyzenhaus argues that such experiments must pass constitutional muster, whether that constitutional test is embodied in a written constitution that enshrines fundamental liberties or whether that test is to be found in an unwritten common law constitution reflecting values affirming liberty.

In this regard, recent judicial pronouncements from the highest courts in the United Kingdom, the United States and Canada suggest that achieving constitutional consistency is difficult.[64] Indefinite detention puts pressure on constitutional values such as the right to liberty, procedural due process and the principle of equal protection under law, moral interests crucial to legal subjects that are foundational to liberal political morality. Courts have so far declared that regimes of indefinite detention fall short of such values though no court has declared that indefinite detention is unlegalisable. In reaction to these decisions, no government has chosen fully to derogate from its commitments to the rule of law, perhaps because it now seems politically unthinkable to do so, especially if the threat of global terrorism is indefinite and does not precipitate a state of emergency. To use a more contemporary term, no government wants to declare that it wishes to exercise power by creating a 'legal black hole', a lawless zone.[65]

However, in choosing to stick with the rule of law, constitutional liberal democracies will face two related challenges. First, as already noted, they will have to find a way to come up with some alternative arrangement that is sufficiently respectful of liberal political morality embedded in their law. This can be especially difficult when governments persist in relying on secret information, which makes it difficult for any adequate testing of whether there is a defensible basis for the detention of individuals in

[63] D. Dyzenhaus, 'The Compulsion of Legality' (Chapter 2), this volume, p. 53.

[64] See *A* v. *Secretary of State for the Home Department* (House of Lords) [2005] 2 WLR 87; *Hamdi* v. *Rumsfeld* 124. S. Cr. 2633 (2004); *Charkaoui* v. *Canada (Citizenship and Immigration)* (2007) SCC 9.

[65] J. Steyn, 'Guantanamo Bay: The Legal Black Hole' (2004) 53 *International Comparative Law Quarterly* 1.

given cases.[66] The failure to address this problem also calls into question the efficacy of indefinite detention laws as attempts to guard against global terrorism. We cannot know if indefinite detention is effective unless we can ascertain that detainees are in fact terrorists.[67] Second, if a concern to respect liberal political morality remains on the table, constitutional liberal democracies will have to answer the further question of why those suspected of terrorist acts should not be prosecuted under the regular criminal law and given full access to constitutional rights. If the rule of law in such countries embodies a respect for moral principles, principles that equally underlie the idea of human rights, it is unclear why a government is entitled to withhold recognition of such principles even to non-citizens.[68]

My point is that constitutional liberal democracies must give a convincing reply to both questions, without which they can expect legal subjects to continue to mount challenges of constitutionality. In this regard, the case study suggests that the absence of a convincing answer to these questions triggers challenges by legal subjects even within semi-democratic regimes.

In the context of a constitutional liberal democracy, it is reasonable to suppose that legal subjects within such societies are likely to make such challenges through a view of law as aspiring towards what Ronald Dworkin describes as 'integrity' of moral principle.[69] Legal subjects will tend to see legitimate legal authority as aspiring towards a coherent commitment towards liberal moral values like justice, equality, liberty and fair process. They are likely to challenge the legal legitimacy of indefinite detention from that perspective, thus informing their legal arguments. For Dworkin, a culture of legal argument founded on integrity, ties closely to a society's claim to be a constitutional liberal democracy. In his view, law fuses personal moral convictions and public legal argument giving the society a vehicle for articulating its moral commitments.[70] A commitment to law as integrity makes the community a 'fraternal' community, where law is a tool for affirming a commitment to treating its members as moral equals.[71]

[66] See S. Chesterman, 'Deny Everything: Intelligence Activities and the Rule of Law' (Chapter 13), this volume.

[67] D. Cole, 'The Priority of Morality: The Emergency Constitution's Blind Spot' (2004) 113 *Yale Law Journal* 1753.

[68] See O. Fiss, 'The War Against Terrorism and the Rule of Law' (2006) 26 *Oxford Journal of Legal Studies* 235.

[69] See R. Dworkin, *Law's Empire* (Harvard: Harvard University Press, 1986).

[70] *Ibid.*, pp. 188 and 213. [71] *Ibid.*, pp. 195–202.

This account of legal argument gives expression to the Fullerian view that the attempt to maintain legal order must track the moral interests of legal subjects. And as I argued in the previous section, the rule of law becomes a litmus test for conceptions of political rule that claim concern for the common good. Dworkin's claim about the close connection between coherence of moral principle and liberal democratic identity explains why constitutional liberal democracies sit closer to the upper end of the rule-of-law continuum; foundational moral interests are crucial to their culture of legal argument and play a pervasive role in judgments on legitimate legal and political authority.[72]

Building from this picture of legal argument within constitutional liberal democracies, I worry that rule by law in the context of indefinite detention risks damaging core legal principles protecting liberal values of political morality. Such principles are 'legal archetypes', a legal standard that has 'significance beyond its immediate normative content, a significance stemming from the fact that it sums up or makes vivid to us a point, purpose, principle, or policy of a whole area of law'.[73] An example of a legal archetype is the principle against torture; it exemplifies the law's commitment to non-brutality. Another archetype is the writ of habeas corpus which exemplifies the law's commitment to the protection of liberty. Legal archetypes operate to fortify arguments about the morality and legality of issues that legal subjects are less confident to assert. Thus, the prohibition against torture might help to fortify an argument objecting to the constitutionality of 'coerced confessions' by highlighting how the law commits to the idea of non-brutality. Legal archetypes enable legal subjects to work out what a commitment to a liberal political morality demands in less clear cases and contribute to law's function as a 'matrix' for thinking through moral issues especially in a liberal democratic setting.

Once we notice the prevalence of legal archetypes in legal argument within constitutional liberal democracies, we can see that the imposition of rule by law in the context of indefinite detention might put pressure on legal archetypes and undermine the power of legal argument as a site for legal subjects to articulate their moral interests. If constitutional liberal

[72] For a developed version of Dworkin's idea, see R.R. Balasubramaniam, 'Our Law: An Argument for Jurisprudence from the Inside-Out', MPhil Dissertation, Australian National University (2001).

[73] J. Waldron, 'Torture and Positive Law: Jurisprudence for the White House' [2005] 105 *Columbia Law Review* 1681 at 1723.

governments cannot supply convincing arguments in reply to the two challenges posed earlier they must brace for legal challenges that invoke legal archetypes. Thus, indefinite detention strains a number of legal archetypes including habeas corpus and the principle of equal protection under law. As the case study reveals, a government that is prone to authoritarianism may elect to deprive legal subjects of sources in the law that include such archetypes thus calling into question the legitimacy of the entire legal order.

In raising this danger, I am not suggesting that governments in constitutional liberal democracies are likely to respond by eviscerating legal archetypes as sources of legal argument. But the murky moral status of indefinite detention and consistent doubts that it can be made subject to legal control is likely to contribute to pressure on governments to meet challenges of constitutionality at the level of principle, a challenge expressed through the idea of law as integrity. And when forced to defend indefinite detention on the terrain of legal argument, my concern is that the absence of a convincing reply to the two challenges noted above may push governments to institute rule by law and suppress the availability of legal archetypes so that they can try to claim rule-of-law legitimacy for indefinite detention. Given the intimate connection between a culture of legal argument expressing a commitment to integrity of principle and the liberal democratic identity, there is a real danger that such a move will lead to regress along the rule-of-law continuum.

Given this danger, Dyzenhaus is right in thinking that experiments of institutional design taking place in constitutional liberal democracies that try to serve the rule of law are risky, especially if they may threaten legal archetypes. And he is right to argue that they should pass constitutional muster. But the risk to legal archetypes also suggests that constitutional liberal democracies need consistently to address the question: is it worth engaging such experiments at all given the difficulties posed by indefinite detention for the rule of law? In asking this question, I am not arguing against institutional experimentation sympathetic to the rule of law in the face of the terrorist threat. It is not my view that one should allow governments to exercise power extra-legally circumscribed primarily by political checks because I think the option to act extra-legally opens the door to a moral corruption of the legal order.[74]

[74] See O. Gross and F. Ní Aoláin, *Law in Times of Crisis: Emergency Powers in Theory and Practice* (Cambridge: Cambridge University Press, 2006).

The option to act extra-legally relies on the presupposition that we can construct a sharp boundary between politics and legality but as my overall argument suggests, this idea is dangerous and itself the product of faulty thinking about the relationship between law and political morality. Moreover, the idea that governments should be allowed to act extra-legally requires what I see as misguided trust in governments not to abuse powers.[75] In this regard, it is instructive to notice that constitutional liberal governments post-9/11 have done little to safeguard important values of liberal political morality, while courts in such societies have been more successful in asserting the importance of the rule of law. This does not necessarily mean that courts are therefore better suited to protect legality. Rather, the significance of court decisions that affirm the rule of law should remind us that a culture of legal argument committed to moral values like liberty and equality must infuse political discourse. A firm commitment to responding to threats to national security from within the rule of law is paramount in upholding the identity of the legal order as a constitutional liberal democracy premised upon the rule of law. In the post-9/11 context, this may require experiments in institutional design undertaken with the openness to learning that such experiments may reveal certain actions to be unlegalisable and therefore intolerable.

To conclude, the possible strain on legal archetypes suggests that it may be necessary to reconsider the claim that we now live in a new normality that should justify extending rule-of-law legitimacy to measures that strain the importance of core values like liberty. The risk to legal archetypes I have highlighted links to a more general argument made in this chapter, the argument that legality is a litmus test for claims of political legitimacy. The continuing relevance of the rule of law to the legitimacy of state power post-9/11, even in the new normality, cuts both ways. While governments may desire the extension of rule-of-law legitimacy to counter-terrorism

[75] Oren Gross's arguments for the view that officials should be able to act extra-legally to avert catastrophe are, I think, motivated by the desire to avoid *ruat caelum* absolutism. The risk of catastrophic moral horror forces constitutional liberal democracies to make difficult choices and these may include the choice to permit extra-legal powers. I agree that the prospect of catastrophe forces hard choices but I fear that Gross overlooks a different and more fundamental choice that such democracies can make out of concern to preserve the integrity of the rule of law. Citizens could choose to live more courageously in the face of such a risk rather than countenance departures from legality. Nothing about the fear of catastrophe necessitates loosening a commitment to the rule of law. See J. Waldron, 'Security and Liberty: The Image of Balance' (2003) 102 *The Journal of Political Philosophy* 191.

measures like indefinite detention, they should not lose sight of their duty to self-correct in order to perfect a commitment to the rule of law. The operation of the rule of law as a litmus test on conceptions of political rule extends to the duty to question whether the new normality is an idea that leads to fuzzy thinking about the rule of law that gets in the way of a conscientious commitment to legality.

PART THREE

Political and sociological theories

6

The political constitution of emergency powers: some conceptual issues

MARK TUSHNET

How are norms regulating the organised exercise of public coercion – that is, state power – embedded in institutions? Legal scholars tend to assume that law provides the only institutional form for the normative regulation of state power. Starting from the competing positions of Professors Dyzenhaus and Gross, I argue here that we can regulate state power through a normatively infused politics. My argument is largely conceptual – that is, aimed at establishing the possibility of such a politics. I leave to another day the identification of the empirical circumstances under which such a politics can arise and offer a realistic alternative to legal regulation of state power.[1]

Professors Dyzenhaus and Gross disagree over *how* law should regulate the exercise of emergency powers, but, I will argue, both start from a conceptual framework in which only law has value that is simultaneously normative and institutional.[2] Strikingly, Professor Dyzenhaus, who seems more deeply committed to the exclusivity of law as a system of normative regulation of state power, actually leaves more space for a normatively infused politics than does Professor Gross. I will argue as well that we ought to acknowledge the possibility, and the fact (on occasion), that the institutions of ordinary politics can be the vehicle for normative

[1] As all participants in the discussion of the legal control of emergency powers agree, courts in general have not imposed strong constraints on the exercise of such powers. The standard metaphor is that courts are weak reeds that bend under pressure and upon which little weight should be put. The standard for a normatively infused politics as a realistic alternative to legal control, then, must be that such a politics is no weaker a reed than are the courts, not that it is a strong protection against abusive exercise of power.

[2] I do not contend, that is, that either author denies the possibility of normative evaluation of how emergency power is exercised, in the register of morality. I do argue, though, that they see law as the only institutional form that normative evaluation can take.

regulation of the exercise of emergency powers.[3] If I am correct, we should add a third model to those proposed by Professors Dyzenhaus and Gross, a model in which we would pay close attention to the ways in which politics, in its operation, can (sometimes) control the exercise of emergency powers.[4]

Even though Professor Gross attaches the label *extra-legal* to his model, he is committed to the proposition that law occupies the entire institutional space of normative evaluation of emergency powers. This comes out in several ways. First, Professor Gross insists that the boundaries of his model are themselves set by law.[5] Of course he does not contend that officials can *always* act outside the law and accept the possibility of subsequent legal evaluation of their actions. Rather, he offers criteria – legal criteria – for identifying when officials permissibly invoke the extra-legal measures model. Second, again obviously, the retrospective evaluation he commends is done through law, by means of subsequent punishment or ratification or restitutionary payments to victims of what come to be seen as improper exercises of emergency powers and the like.[6] Third, consider the possibility, which everyone who has addressed Professor Gross's model thinks is large,

[3] I note that one could challenge the opposition I draw by observing that the institutions of politics are themselves constituted by law and so that in the last instance law does indeed provide the only institutionalised means of normative evaluation. I am not sure that much turns on this point, but if it does I would defend my position with a version of the proposition, important in what follows, that the institutions of law are constituted (in the last instance) by social practices, which, if they are normatively freighted, are so antecedent to the law.

[4] Two additional preliminary notes: (1) This third model was, I now think, what I was grasping for when I came up with the term *extra-constitutional* to describe an alternative to Professor Gross's 'extra-legal measures' model. See M. Tushnet, 'Defending Korematsu?: Reflections on Civil Liberties in Wartime' (2003) *Wisconsin Law Review* 273. I no longer think that that term is useful. (2) I have begun to give some empirical flesh to the conceptual model in works in progress. See M. Tushnet, 'The Political Constitution of Emergency Powers: Some Lessons from Hamdan' (2007) 91 *Minnesota Law Review* 1451; M. Tushnet, 'The Political Constitution of Emergency Powers: Parliamentary and Separation-of-Powers Regulation' (2008) 3 *International Journal of Law in Context* 275.

[5] See L.M. Seidman, 'The Secret Life of the Political Question Doctrine' (2004) 37 *John Marshall Law Review* 441.

[6] Professor Gross suggests that this formulation overlooks the social and informal sanctions and approvals that might be applied retrospectively. I am not persuaded. His examples involve formal acts – awarding or withholding decorations and promotions – that occur within the legal system. Actions by civil society, such as invitations to conferences or awards from non-governmental organisations are so obviously subject to partisan manipulation that I doubt that they could ever satisfy the requirements of Professor Gross's model.

that those contemplating extra-legal action will come to expect *ex post* endorsement rather than *ex post* repudiation, at least within their lifetimes. From one common point of view, the practices in which such officials engage take on normative weight – that is, become law – as the actions accumulate. Practice becomes a non-judicial precedent in shaping the law. In these ways, the space is comprehensively occupied by law: ordinary law outside the boundaries of the extra-legal measures model and retrospective law within its boundaries.

Most of Professor Dyzenhaus's discussion is devoted to examining precisely how far we can get with the assumption that law can and should control the exercise of emergency powers.[7] He argues, for example, that courts should strive to interpret statutes authorising extraordinary measures to comply with basic rights, and that they should interpret narrowly statutes that purport to deprive courts of jurisdiction to evaluate exercises of emergency powers for consistency with the rule of law. Suppose, though, that a legislature adopts a privative clause whose terms are unequivocal. Doing so does not, according to Professor Dyzenhaus, relieve the legislature of the obligation to comply with the rule of law in its substantive enactments. Indeed, he argues, the privative clause may simply bring to the fore the legislature's ever-present obligation to comply with the rule of law. In this sense, Professor Dyzenhaus is committed to the proposition that politics is normatively infused.

Politics is the obvious alternative to law as a means of regulating the exercise of emergency powers – not politics as mere preference or the exercise of power for its own sake, but a principled or moralised politics. The combination of law, including requirements for clear statements of the sort Professor Dyzenhaus thinks desirable and a moralised politics might do quite well – that is, might satisfy any reasonable requirements we might think a decent rule-of-law system must satisfy.

Oddly, I think the best way to make credible the component involving a moralised politics is via Carl Schmitt.[8] To start, we can consider the implications of the proposition that the sovereign is the person – or, importantly, institution – that has the power to determine 'the exception',

7 For a more extended development of the argument in this paragraph, see M. Tushnet, 'Book Review' [2007] *Public Law* 604, reviewing Dyzenhaus, *The Constitution of Law: Legality in a Time of Emergency* (Cambridge: Cambridge University Press, 2006).

8 I do not pretend to be a scholar of Schmitt's thought and so use his work (to the extent I understand it) as the vehicle for laying out my views.

that is, to determine when the regime of ordinary law is to be displaced by something else.[9] How does this play out in a reasonably well-functioning democracy confronted with a situation that some significant political actors contend presents an emergency that requires the displacement of ordinary law?[10]

Suppose, then, that the nation's constitution purports to limit the circumstances under which the regime of exception can displace ordinary law.[11] The US Constitution, for example, allows Congress to suspend the privilege of the writ of habeas corpus only 'when in Cases of Rebellion or Invasion the public Safety may require it'.[12] Suppose that the President decides on his own to suspend the writ and that someone challenges the action in court. Nothing rules out, conceptually, the possibility that the courts will declare the President's actions unconstitutional either because the President may not suspend the writ without congressional approval (perhaps retrospective, perhaps not) or because the circumstances did not present a 'rebellion' or 'invasion'.[13] And – the crucial point here – nothing

[9] I have sometimes puzzled over the distinction between ordinary law and the exception within a legal realist universe: As I understand it, the regime of the exception is one in which the decision-maker exercises discretion uncontrolled by law. But, to a legal realist, decision-making pursuant to ordinary law is fully discretionary and uncontrolled by law, though subject to other constraints. I take up aspects of this perspective later. My puzzlement about the distinction is deepened when I consider that Schmitt's 'decisionism' seems to me quite similar to, if not the same as, American legal realism's view of legal decision-making; if that is correct, or even close to correct, the distinction between ordinary law and the regime of exception seems to me exceedingly difficult to sustain.

[10] I put the question in this way to emphasise that 'emergencies' do not present themselves as forces of nature independent of whatever people do. The claim that a nation faces an emergency is just that, a claim inserted into the regular operation of political life and – therefore – subject to contestation by other significant political actors, if they choose to do so. For an argument that US Supreme Court Justice Oliver Wendell Holmes, Jr, believed, to the contrary, that the existence of an emergency was a matter of ordinary fact, see A. Vermeule, 'Holmes on Emergencies' (forthcoming).

[11] I draw here on my discussion in M. Tushnet, 'Comment: Meditations on Carl Schmitt' (2006) 40 *Georgia Law Review* 877.

[12] U.S. Const. Art I, s.9, cl.2.

[13] I emphasise that my concern here is with conceptual possibilities, not empirical ones, and am not contending that as a matter of present-day US constitutional law the courts would in fact find the President's actions unconstitutional. The proposition that suspension of the writ requires congressional approval seems nearly universally accepted by constitutional scholars, and has not been rejected even in the aggressive litigating positions taken by the Bush administration. Justice Antonin Scalia asserted, without supporting argument, that Suspension Clause claims are non-justiciable. *Hamdi* v. *Rumsfeld* 542 US 507 (2004).

I am sceptical about that assertion, at least with respect to the question of whether the condition of 'invasion' or 'rebellion' exists. For a broad argument that Suspension Clause rules out, conceptually, the possibility that the President will accede to the courts' determination.[14] In such circumstances, on Schmitt's account the courts are sovereign, but so what? My point here is simply H.L.A. Hart's – that a legal system's rule of recognition is determined by habits of acquiescence on the part of officials, which habits are routinely although not always followed.[15]

My point here is quite general. As Tom Campbell, and Eric Posner and Adrian Vermeule, in their own ways, argue, we can readily construct systems regulating emergencies that have two components.[16] In one, there are rule-like conditions under which emergencies can be declared and an enumeration of the special powers government actors have and the rights that may (and cannot) be altered during the emergency. As Campbell emphasises, there is no conceptual reason why we could not have one set of rules for one type of emergency, another set for another – as we have different rules applicable to zoning in urban and rural areas.[17]

Schmitt argued and most commentators, including Campbell, and Posner and Vermeule, seem to agree, this component is always going to be incomplete. Circumstances will present themselves in which important legal actors contend, and with some reason, that the situation they face

claims are justiciable, see A.L. Tyler, 'Is Suspension a Political Question?' (2006) 59 *Stanford Law Review* 333.

[14] Much of the literature I have read on the relevance of Schmitt to contemporary law assumes, perhaps accurately, that executives will rarely, or perhaps never, accede to such judicial rulings. My point here is a conceptual one, but it may be worth noting the remarkable events described in G. Williams, 'The Case That Stopped a Coup? The Rule of Law and Constitutionalism in Fiji' (2002) 1 *Oxford University Commonwealth Law Journal* 73 (describing a judicial decision holding a military coup unlawful, to which the military rulers acceded). Canada's Emergencies Act 1985, c.22, s.62(2) requires that exercises of power during emergencies be reviewed by a parliamentary committee that includes at least one member from each party that has a membership of twelve or more in the House of Commons, and one member from each party in the (appointed) Senate. The provision has not been implemented since enactment, but its clear intention is to ensure that the executive government submit its actions to review by members of parties that might not share the executive's view of the emergency's nature.

[15] See Dyzenhaus, *The Constitution of Law*, p. 38.

[16] T. Campbell, 'Emergency Strategies for Prescriptive Legal Positivists: Anti-Terrorist Law and Legal Theory' (Chapter 9), this volume; E.A. Posner and A. Vermeule, *Terror in the Balance: Security, Liberty and the Courts* (New York: Oxford University Press, 2007), pp. 38–9.

[17] Canada's Emergency Act distinguishes among public welfare emergencies (arising from natural disasters or epidemics), public order emergencies (mostly, domestic disorders), international emergencies (essentially, international disputes short of war) and war emergencies. Each type of emergency has different procedural and substantive effects.

falls outside the rule-based component, either because the events do not neatly fit the triggering conditions or because the situation demands more power or greater restrictions on rights than are authorised by the applicable rule. Then the second component of the system could come into play. Here the law states a general standard.[18] Government actors do what they think the law authorises and their actions are assessed (later) by the courts. Conceptually, nothing prevents the courts from determining that what the actors did failed to satisfy the requirements of the legal *standard*.[19]

From a legal realist perspective, one might say that the courts qua sovereign are not constrained by law and so they are simply exercising *their* power under the guise of law.[20] But even the most hard-line legal realists contend only that courts are not constrained *by law*, not that courts are unconstrained. For realists, constraints on the exercise of legal power result from sociology and politics. Judges, for example, may feel themselves bound to act in one rather than another way because of the norms of their profession, including a norm that a judge must understand his or her decisions to follow from law rather than mere power. They might be selected through political processes that significantly limit the range of preferences judges have, so that when they simply exercise their sheer power they do so for relatively conventional ends.

18 The Spanish term 'extraordinary and urgent necessity' seems a good example. Constitution of Spain 1978, Art. 86.

19 Again, two points. (1) The only difference between the retrospective evaluation of compliance with a standard and Gross's extra-legal measures model, it seems to me, is that under the latter, actors acknowledge at the time of action that their decisions are illegal while under the former they contend that their actions are lawful. In both, though, there is a retrospective evaluation of the actors' decisions. (And, frankly, it seems to me unrealistic to think that, given the openness of any set of legal provisions under even a moderate legal realist view, any legal actor would ever find it necessary to acknowledge illegality rather than assert legality.) (2) Even under the first rule-based component of the system I am describing, evaluation is inevitably retrospective because there is always a temporal lag between action and evaluation, except to the extent that officials might be more reluctant or slower to 'breach' a clear rule – and move into the standard-based component if there is one. Here my sense is that discussion has been distorted by a continental sense that legal actors always comply with clear rules and do not, for example, seek to exploit their ambiguities.

20 I do not want to make anything of the fact that in the scenario I have described, the courts intervene to stop the executive's exercise of emergency powers, because I believe that nothing conceptually rules out the possibility that the courts themselves could declare that an emergency exists, driving home the point that in systems where significant political actors regularly accede to judicial decisions, the courts are the sovereign in Schmitt's sense.

Although for expository purposes I have developed the argument with reference to courts, the basic point is quite general: sovereignty in Schmitt's sense – the power to determine when the regime of exception comes into play – is lodged *institutionally*[21] and the institution in which it is lodged is not necessarily the highest official in the executive branch. That leaves room for politics to constrain the exercise of emergency powers.[22]

Suppose we agree with Dyzenhaus that courts quite frequently flag in their defence of the rule of law. On the view sketched here, that is not a counsel of despair or only a goad for urging the courts to do better. We can consider the possibility that politics conducted in parliaments, separation-of-powers legislatures, bureaucracies and civil society will fill in the 'rule-of-law' gaps – not black holes – that the courts put up with or create. The kind of politics I have in mind is a (partly) moralised politics, in which political leaders appeal for support on the basis of moral claims in addition to appealing for support on the basis of constituents' non-moral preferences.[23] So, for example, leaders might contend, as they have, that engaging in torture is simply not what we as Americans *do*.[24] Once again, there is nothing in the concept of politics that excludes the possibility that these appeals will succeed.[25] The institutional location of sovereignty in a system characterised by a partially moralised politics opens up the possibility of real-world limits on the exercise of emergency powers.

To this point, I have argued (a) that nothing conceptually interesting follows from the proposition that sovereignty is lodged in the institution

[21] It has occurred to me that this point is obscured by the conventional English translation of Schmitt's famous opening sentence as 'Sovereign is *he* who decides on the exception' (emphasis added).

[22] Although I do not provide it here, a full account would examine the politics of – that is, within – executive bureaucracies, to undermine the proposition that a nation's president or prime minister can simply sit down and decide to declare a state of emergency all on his or her own.

[23] Tushnet, 'Some Lessons from Hamdan', argues that even a purely interest-based politics can produce restrictions on the exercise of power during emergencies.

[24] Obviously this is not an empirical claim by the leaders. Rather, it is a moral one: we ought not understand ourselves as Americans to be a people who treat torture as a permissible practice.

[25] I suspect that someone with a Schmittian view of politics as 'friend versus enemy' would contend that the very concept of politics excludes moralised appeals of this sort. For what it is worth, I note that I find Schmitt's notion of the exception more interesting than his 'friend–enemy' analysis of politics. Perhaps my reference to a moralised politics in which 'who we are as Americans' plays a role reflects an implicit commitment to the 'friend–enemy' conception, but I think not, or at least not in any interesting way: all that conception requires is *some* enemy and conceptually 'space aliens' would do, preserving liberalism's commitment to a universalism among 'persons'.

that determines when to create a state of exception and (b) that the interesting questions are how, when and whether sociological and political constraints operate in the institutional processes for determining to create a state of exception. These latter questions are of course empirical and not conceptual ones. The *whether* question is a particularly important one. Sociological and political constraints, being empirical, can fail to operate or be absent.[26] Many commentators worry that modern conditions make such failures more likely. The form of the usual argument is incomplete, in my view. Commentators observe that chief executives over the course of the past century have made increasingly strong *claims* about the necessity of accreting power to them and that sometimes power has actually so accreted. What is missing in the discussion, though, is an analysis of exactly why the political and sociological constraints on the success of such claims failed. Often the examples come from political systems that were not well-functioning democracies prior to the emergency's declaration or express worries about what either did turn out to be or in the case of the current situation in the United States, might turn out to be relatively short-term problems.[27]

I conclude with a brief discussion on how the perspective developed here might inform our understanding of what Professor Dyzenhaus and others call legal black holes.[28] These are areas (physical or legal) in which the courts play no role whatever in regulating the exercise of power. At least in US constitutional law, the proposition that there are legal black holes is actually uncontroversial. The so-called political questions doctrine identifies questions of constitutional law on which the courts simply will not rule.[29] No one worries much, except as a matter of abstract theory,

[26] I try to identify the circumstances in which political constraints (thought not necessarily sociological ones) might be prone to fail in a US-style separation of powers system in Tushnet, 'Some Lessons from Hamdan', and suggest that failure of political constraints is more likely, though not guaranteed, in systems of parliamentary supremacy in Tushnet, 'Parliamentary and Separation-of-Powers Regulation'.

[27] I am inclined to think that a formulation that is simultaneously more general and more precise would include well-functioning democracies and moderately authoritarian systems and would take the criterion to be whether the deviation from the system's normal – that is, non-emergency – functioning is large enough to make plausible the claim that a spiral into complete authoritarianism is quite likely.

[28] The 'black holes' metaphor blends two allusions. The first is to the Black Hole of Calcutta, a single cell in which nearly 150 soldiers were confined overnight and where many died. The second is to the black holes of astrophysics, concentrated dots of matter with such high masses that light cannot escape, and which suck all matter nearby into them.

[29] *Nixon* v. *United States* 506 US 224 (1993).

about the existence of black holes of this sort and for good reason: political questions can be identified in substantial part by considering whether the political constraints on decision-makers are at least as strong as those that would be applied were the courts to intervene.[30]

The Military Commissions Act of 2006 purports to deprive the federal courts of all jurisdiction over some claims by those held by the United States as unlawful combatants.[31] Assume that, as a matter of positive US law, this denial of judicial intervention is constitutional. The Military Commissions Act would thus create a legal black hole.[32] The concern with such black holes is that they may exist within an otherwise reasonably well-functioning democratic system.[33]

Yet, the perspective developed here requires that we look beyond the fact that courts will not intervene, to ask whether there are political constraints on the exercise of power over enemy combatants. Without contending that those now being detained have always been treated in a manner comporting with minimal human rights requirements,[34] I think there is reason to believe that there are such constraints now operating. Public revelations about executive officials' behaviour have generated legislative

[30] See M. Tushnet, 'Law and Prudence in the Law of Justiciability: The Transformation and Disappearance of the Political Question Doctrine' (2002) 80 *North Carolina Law Review* 1203.

[31] The Act authorises some degree of review of the determination of *whether* a person is properly held as an enemy combatant, but none, as far as appears, over claims that the conditions under which the person is held satisfy minimum constitutional requirements, including the requirement that persons held under the authority of the United States, and within its jurisdiction, not be subjected to cruel and unusual punishment. (The review of a person's designation as an enemy combatant may be so limited as to be one of Professor Dyzenhaus's 'weak reeds'.)

[32] It may be worth noting that, in the United States, for a long time prisons generally were such black holes. See *Ruffin* v. *Commonwealth*, 62 Va. (21 Gratt.) 790, 796(1871) (describing prisoners as 'slaves of the State').

[33] And thereby lack one of the characteristics of physical black holes, the power to suck into their domain everything in their neighbourhood. Sometimes one hears a concern expressed that recognising the existence of one legal black hole threatens liberty generally, because the principles used to justify the existence of one black hole are available to justify the existence of many more. Yet, we can see that legal black holes do not *inherently* suck everything into their domain by observing that US constitutional law goes along well enough to satisfy sensible requirements for a 'rule-of-law' system despite the existence of the political question doctrine.

[34] I note that examples of gross human rights violations have not yet been legally validated in the United States; that is, we do not yet know whether such violations did in fact fall into a legal black (or grey) hole. Again I emphasise that we cannot show that there are legal black holes by identifying *claims* made by executive officials (or non-policy making commentators or advocates) that their actions are in fact not subject to judicial evaluation.

pressure on those officials and one way to avoid new regulations is to show, credibly, that minimum requirements of decency are being met. More important, in my view, are internal bureaucratic constraints. The best example comes from the procedures used to determine who is an enemy combatant, through 'combatant status review tribunals' (CSRTs). The CSRTs already used, and even more so those to be used in the future if proposed modifications go into effect, satisfy 'rule-of-law' requirements of procedural fairness.[35] To take one example: these tribunals will consider hearsay evidence, giving it the weight it rationally has. This is different from the rule applied in criminal trials in the United States, but legal systems around the world admit hearsay evidence routinely. The fact that it is admitted in the CSRTs does not show that the tribunals fail to satisfy 'rule-of-law' requirements.

Why did the United States develop CSRTs that satisfy 'rule-of-law' requirements when these tribunals were not subject to judicial evaluation for fairness?[36] At the first level, the reasons, I believe, combine bureaucratic and professional interests.[37] The CSRTs are at the end of a funnel with a fairly broad mouth. Those fighting US armed forces in the field were first given a rough-and-ready field assessment by field officers themselves, as minor participants or as serious threats. That assessment was then reviewed, again within the zone of active combat, by a group of officers. Some were found not worth holding, and others were transferred to prisons, and eventually to Guantánamo Bay, where a yet more formal evaluation process occurred. The CSRTs are the culmination of these processes. Here I think we are observing a bureaucratic impulse to increase formality at successive stages of review.[38]

[35] This is not to say that the CSRTs always reached the right result, or did so quickly enough. No procedural system is 100 per cent accurate, and many of the delays were occasioned by ordinary bureaucratic slowness and logistical difficulties, which do not, in my view, come close to creating a violation of the rule of law. Some, though, were attributable to apparent violations of human rights by agents of the Central Intelligence Agency, who were not covered by applicable US law (and who appear to have received exemptions from prosecution for war crimes in the Military Commissions Act). The military officials who initially detained enemy combatants in the field, and who hold them in custody at Guantánamo Bay, are and always have been restricted in what they could lawfully do by US law.

[36] One possibility, which (based on my reading of the publicly available information) does not seem to me to have played a large role, is that the CSRTs' creators thought that there was some possibility, albeit a small one, that the courts would in fact evaluate the CSRTs.

[37] I do not know the full details of how the CSRTs were developed; I have drawn on public accounts and made some inferences that I believe those accounts support.

[38] It is clear from press accounts that not every person held at Guantánamo Bay was *correctly* designated an enemy combatant, nor was every person put through every stage of the review

In addition, there are the professional interests of lawyers and military officers. Press accounts make it clear that military officials and lawyers within the military were rather strong voices favouring CSRTs (and trial-forms for those charged with offences) that satisfied 'rule-of-law' requirements. The reasons are professional: military officials have a sense of military honour and a concern for reciprocity, deeply imbued in their training, that push in the 'rule-of-law' direction. Lawyers, of course, are increasingly comfortable as procedural formality increases, at least up to the 'rule-of-law' threshold.[39]

These bureaucratic and professional interests are the proximate reason for the adoption of procedures generally consistent with rule-of-law requirements for the CSRTs. Behind them, though, lies what I have called a moralised politics. Bureaucrats and, even more, professionals, define their roles with reference to norms they have internalised. And, empirically, among those norms for the relevant bureaucrats and professionals is some degree of commitment to the rule of law. The legal black holes may be law-free zones, but they are not rule-of-law-free zones, because they are created and sustained in part by a moralised politics.

It would be foolish to contend, and I do not, that the sociological and political constraints I have sketched always have or always will keep the exercise of emergency powers within 'rule-of-law' bounds. Sociology and politics cannot prevent real black holes from coming into being. But, I would stress, neither can the *concept* of the rule of law.[40] True, concepts cannot fail in the way that politics can. They cannot succeed at all, though, without sociology and politics at their back.

process before reaching the CSRT. But – it should go without saying – having a procedurally fair system, one that satisfies 'rule-of-law' requirements, does not guarantee correct results in every case. I do not think we have enough information available to conclude that the CSRT process makes so many errors that it fails 'rule-of-law' requirements.

39 The analysis of the possibility of torture, inhuman or degrading treatment at Guantánamo Bay is more complex and less comforting to the position I sketch here. I would note, though, that reciprocity considerations do seem to have played some role in the equilibrium apparently reached at Guantánamo Bay and that conditions there are not dramatically different from those in high-security prisons within the United States, which are subject to judicial supervision for compliance with constitutional norms.

40 Parallel to my point that occasional failures in particular cases does not undermine the claim that, in general, politics and sociology can produce a system that operates within 'rule-of-law' bounds is the proposition that even the most vigorous defenders of the rule of law do not contend that occasional *violations* of the rule of law undermine the claim that a system in general satisfies all the 'rule-of-law' requirements we could reasonably impose.

7

A topography of emergency power

NOMI CLAIRE LAZAR

I. Introduction

People are ends in themselves, and states and institutions are means to their well-being. This essay argues that making emergency powers more conducive to that end requires a shift in focus. We have tended to think of emergency institutions in terms of legal norms and exceptions. But safe emergency powers depend primarily on whether public officials behave themselves, and this, in turn, depends on the landscape of formal and informal power and constraint which officials inhabit. Hence, if the well-being of people is our central concern even in times of crisis, we must move beyond a perspective which emphasises boundaries of law to concentrate on this broader terrain. For, bounded and formally delineated law never rules on its own. Law and other institutions are shot through with individual agency not just in times of crisis but every day, and this agency and informal power is a central, not peripheral element of rule.

Agency, the central element of informal power, has traditionally been associated with arbitrariness and opposed to the rule of law. Correlatively, agency is associated with a prudential mode of politics while the rule of law is associated with a principled mode. But agency is a necessary part of all institutions, both logically and normatively. Because circumstances are always variable and people unpredictable, without the benefit of flexibility which agency provides, institutions and laws could not do the moral work we set for them. The dangers of centralising individual agency and informal power mean we must be conscious not only of enabling flexibility but of constraining it also, which in turn will also require attentiveness to the informal aspects of power if such constraint is to be effective. If

My thanks are due to the participants in the symposium on law in a time of crisis at the National University of Singapore, in particular Victor V. Ramraj and Rueban Balasubramaniam for their editorial suggestions and William E. Scheuerman for his trenchant and helpful criticism. Thanks are also due to Avrim Lazar and Valerie Clements for their admirable patience.

agency and institutions are bound together as tightly as I mean to suggest, then informal power and its informal constraint suggest a different kind of geography: not a map of the boundaries and transgressions of emergency powers, but a topography of emergency power, with the normative imperative that emergency institutions, like all institutions, take each as an end and never as a means only.

To establish that flexible institutions are not only consistent with, but are also required by political ethics I argue in Part II that institutions are means to normative ends. If this is so, then we are obliged to employ the most moral means to reach these ends, and I show, in Part III that means and ends, principles and consequences, are related in complex and often contradictory ways. One part of the moral character of means, I argue, is their effectiveness at achieving moral ends, if we take those ends seriously. Hence, understanding institutions as means need not commit us to a strict consequentialist ethics with all the potential horror that could entail in cases of emergency, nor is it a Machiavellian claim in the simplistic sense of ends justifying means.[1]

If institutions are means to moral ends, then, as I argue in Part IV, if political circumstances are changeable things, it follows that institutions must be flexible in order to conform to circumstances. But because flexibility is also dangerous, enabling and constraining this informal power requires an institutional structure for crises and also for normal times that attends to the whole topography of formal and informal power and constraint. So, in Part V, I conclude that to make emergency powers safer and more conducive to meeting the ends of political life – a good life for people, who are ends in themselves – requires a topography of emergency power with an eye to flexibility and to helping us effectively orchestrate informal constraints.

II. Institutions as means to moral ends

Normative questions in matters of politics concern ends, things of intrinsic value such as a condition of respecting inherent human dignity, or liberty, equality and justice somehow understood. Our most fundamental political contestations concern which of these ends are central. Thus, we deliberate over the content of our ethical-political ends, but when we

[1] I have argued elsewhere, however, that Machiavelli's claim is in fact more nuanced, particularly in the emergency context. See N.C. Lazar, 'Must Exceptionalism Prove the Rule?' (2006) 34 *Politics and Society* 245.

deliberate over possible institutional structures, we are concerned primarily with questions of fact: how best to achieve these ends where 'best' takes account of the secondary impact of our institutions on other values we have established as ends and of the practical likelihood of success. A state, on this view, and the institutions through which it takes on agency, is inherently instrumental. When constitution framers contemplate institutions, tradition and experience – which lend a sense of intrinsic value – play some role, but the needs and ends of a specific nation form the primary grounds. Over time institutions may come to have a value of their own through the fondness that comes of long use, custom, etc., but our primary sense of their worth comes from the reflected glory of values they are intended to further.

This perspective stands in contrast to one in which the institutions of a state are conceptualised as manifestations of particular values. On this view, the institutions of a state are fixed because they are deduced from first principles. The normative values of a state are embodied in its institutions and the presence of the institutions themselves constitutes fulfilment of the state's basic normative aspirations: a just state is one with institutions derived from an abstract conception of justice. Here, for example, the separation of powers as a feature of constitutions is cast as intrinsically necessary for justice.[2]

There are several reasons to prefer the first approach. Critically, when institutions are primarily designed in this way – that is, with an eye to the well-being of people and the stability of the state, given local conditions, it suggests the central importance of people as the ultimate end and aim. It emphasises that the state exists not for its own sake, but as Aristotle tells us, for the sake of a good life. Were a set of radically different institutions to emerge that had been long tested under similar conditions elsewhere, which resulted in a more peaceful, more just and fair and more contented mode of life for the inhabitants of the state, it would be reasonable and normatively desirable to try them. This is true even if their form differed radically from those we now consider just. If this seems intuitive, then so must the idea that institutions are means.

Each of these alternative modes of understanding liberal institutions – the view that institutions are means to serve principled ends and the view

[2] See, for instance, I. Kant, *The Metaphysics of Morals*, M. Gregor (trans.) (Cambridge: Cambridge University Press, 1991). In section 45 in 'Public Right', Kant argues that a constitution with three separate powers (Kant uses the word *Gewalten*), as derived from the Principle of Right, counts as normative.

that institutions are embodiments of first principles – has long roots in the history of political thought which reflect the history of our confusion on the subject of emergencies.[3] The view that institutions are means to principled ends can be found, for instance, in the work of John Locke and that of Thomas Jefferson.[4] Locke's empiricism and correlative pragmatism yield an instrumental understanding of institutions and offices. Take, for example, his account of why powers ought to be separated: empirically, kings have a poor track record of keeping their hands to themselves and judging justly.[5] Because of this fact about the world and in order to reach the principled end of *salus populi*, there must be checks and balances, some right of appeal, to keep kings trustworthy. The separation of powers is prudent as much as it is rational. Institutions are instrumental. Hence, it makes sense to take account of situations where those institutions might not meet their ends, as Locke does in his account of the prerogative power. Officers must have flexibility and judgment plays a significant role in Locke's account. Indeed, an officer's human-ness, his capacity for judgment is an intrinsic part of the office itself. There is a recognition of the messiness of human affairs and of the multiplicity of often conflicting principles which governs them. To the extent that there are cases where institutions work against their own principled purpose, Locke's liberalism provides means of overriding them for the sake of this same purpose.

By contrast, what serve as means for Locke are instantiations of ends in the political philosophy of Kant and in some contemporary neo-Kantian strands of liberal and libertarian theorising, particularly in the work of theorists like Robert Nozick. Here, emergency has posed a paralysing or at least paradox-generating problem. Institutions, on this view are themselves intrinsically normative. If, as for Kant, the content of right is the sort of thing we can deduce a priori, we must advocate those institutions that embody and reflect the Principle of Right. Institutions would then necessarily be inflexible, since it is this very inflexibility which provides the impetus for the conception of right in the first place. As Kant makes

[3] This argument is developed at length in N.C. Lazar, *States of Emergency in Liberal Democracies* (Cambridge: Cambridge University Press, forthcoming 2009).

[4] See C. Fatovic, 'Constitutionalism and Presidential Prerogative: Jeffersonian and Hamiltonian Perspectives' (2004) 48 *American Journal of Political Science* 429–44 at 434. See also Letter from Jefferson to Claiborne (3 February 1807) quoted in M. Dennison, 'Martial Law: The Development of a Theory of Emergency Powers, 1776–1861' (1974) 18 *The American Journal of Legal History* 52–79 at 58.

[5] J. Locke, *Two Treatises of Government*, P. Laslett (ed.) (Cambridge: Cambridge University Press, 1988), § 91.

clear in the *Metaphysics of Morals*, moral laws 'hold as laws only insofar as they can be seen to have an *a priori* basis and to be necessary' and one who hoped to come to knowledge of the moral law or the principles of right in some other fashion 'would run the risk of the grossest and most pernicious errors'.[6] Empirical knowledge, because uncertain and incomplete, can never yield knowledge of what is right and what is just. 'Like the wooden head in Phaedrus' fable, a merely empirical doctrine of right is a head that may be beautiful, but unfortunately it has no brain'.[7] Kant goes on to deduce which institutions are in accordance with these a priori principles and such institutions necessarily take on a rigidity that would seem to preclude emergency powers. Kant's own engagement is therefore tense and inconsistent. It would be natural to assume that Kant would reject the possibility of emergency powers outright as a fine example of the clouding of the moral law by a moral judgment subject to inclination and nationalist sentimentality. Emergencies seem to require institutional, and hence moral flexibility. But emergencies are somehow different and Kant is, surprisingly, an avid advocate of unbridled executive power in such cases. For example, an executive may 'impose an enforced loan . . . by the right of majesty', despite Kant's insistence elsewhere that taxes must be consented to and soldiers seem suddenly to serve as means only.[8] Robert Nozick fares little better: his only comments on matters relating to necessity or emergency come in the form of dismissive footnotes. For example, with respect to rights, Nozick has this to say: 'The question of whether these side constraints are absolute, or whether they may be violated in order to avoid catastrophic moral horror, and if the latter, what the resulting structure might look like, is one I hope largely to avoid'.[9]

Hence, critics of liberalism who look to the epistemological heirs of Kant, and liberals who tacitly employ related methodologies, are bound to serve up confirmation for Carl Schmitt's charge that liberalism cannot confront emergencies without collapsing. Institutions which are rigid, which are embodiments of first principles rather than means to serve such principles, would seem to preclude flexibility and a central role for agency in government. This means that when such thinkers really confront

[6] Kant, *The Metaphysics of Morals*, p. 43. [7] *Ibid.*, p. 55 and also p. 123.

[8] *Ibid.*, p. 135. Against this right there is no appeal or counter-right of rebellion, even in the case of tyrannical misuse of this power, as we read in I. Kant, 'Perpetual Peace' in H. Reiss (ed.), *Kant's Political Writings* (Cambridge: Cambridge University Press, 1970), pp. 126–7.

[9] R. Nozick, *Anarchy, State and Utopia* (New York: Basic Books, 1974), p. 30.

emergencies, it is either with an air of paralysis or else truly as an 'exception' outside the government of norms.

Hence, in addition to the intrinsic normative and logical reasons to prefer the instrumental understanding of institutions, set out at the start of this section, there are moral-prudential considerations also. This shows a direction for answering Schmitt's challenge without removing emergency powers from the sphere of liberal moral norms.

III. Multiple moral ends and the most moral means

Now, the most apparent objection to this mode of understanding institutions is this: allowing instrumental or prudential considerations to enter into moral matters is wrong. Even if human well-being is the ultimate end, that does not mean it can justify 'the means'. Hence, we must simply confront and accept that the flexibility required by emergency powers is unjust. Sophisticated relatives of this position are espoused in the arguments of Terry Nardin (Chapter 4) and Rueban Balasubramaniam (Chapter 5), in this volume. Nardin argues that the prudential and the moral are strictly separate realms. He offers a choice of understanding law 'in prudential terms as instrumental to achieving desired goals, or morally as prescribing goal-independent limits on the pursuit of goals'.[10] Balasubramaniam, following Lon Fuller, suggests that a legal order must also be a moral order because 'legal order, as a system of rule-governed behaviour cannot emerge if those who wield political power are indifferent to the legal subject as a rational self-directing agent'.[11] But these critiques of 'institutions as means' rest on a misconception about the relation of means and ends in political life. Hence, in the interests of establishing the normative credentials of an institutions-as-means position we now turn to considering what this relation might be. I will argue that treating a person as an end in herself is not incompatible, indeed might necessitate, using the most moral means to meet that normative end. If this is so, then, *if* flexibility in institutional structures is necessary to meet the moral ends of institutions, it might be morally required. Whenever a duty has serious moral weight, so by extension does the most moral means of meeting it. In this way, so far from being anathema, the prudential must be *central* to the moral if

[10] T. Nardin, 'Emergency Logic: Prudence, Morality and the Rule of Law' (Chapter 4), this volume, p. 97.

[11] R.R. Balasubramaniam, 'Indefinite Detention: Rule by Law or Rule of Law?' (Chapter 5), this volume, p. 131.

we take our ends seriously. When this seems to entail moral conflict we should remember that strict moral consistency often comes at the expense of accuracy in normative matters, and it is largely because of the existence of real moral conflict that agency and judgment are important parts of political institutions.

Those who worry that prudential considerations would infect the realm of ethics worry that we might treat others as means, not as ends in themselves. But how does one treat a person as an end in herself, a rational self-directing agent? At the most basic, one acknowledges that one is interacting with a being with dignity. One confronts the rights and interests of each individual with due seriousness. To treat someone as an end in himself and never as a means only, means acting with due consideration for him: everyone matters, *everyone* counts for one and no one counts for more than one. But because valid interests conflict, because, indeed, rights conflict, to say that everyone matters, that everyone must be treated as an end and never only as a means cannot mean that no one's rights may ever be derogated, nor that the interests of some may never win out over the interests of others. Treating people as ends in themselves requires that everyone be taken into account, but it guarantees no particular outcome. In justice systems where a person who is demonstrably dangerous can be held on remand awaiting trial, for example, treating this person with respect, as an end in herself, means providing her with access to counsel and a chance to speak. But we need not let her go free to await trial, even though, arguably, this form of constraint on someone who has as yet been found guilty of nothing is a violation of her rights. Indeed, some might argue that any form of detention, even after conviction, constitutes a rights derogation, even if we feel it is 'justified'. This is so unless we consider rights to be defeasible in the first place, contingent on good law-abiding behaviour.

Because treating each with dignity is not equivalent to having for each her optimal outcome, institutions like criminal justice systems can be both prudential and moral: moral to the extent that they take citizens as ends in themselves but prudential to the extent that it matters morally whether such institutions work. Even in times of normalcy, citizens' rights are often derogated and this is always wrong. Recognising that this is the case means never taking such derogation lightly, or as is all too common, entirely ceasing to see them as derogations. Prudential concerns should never come into play without at the same time treating each as an end in herself, and never without recognising such sacrifices with due concern, regret or even shame. But such recognition in no way precludes prudential considerations.

Hence separating out prudential and moral concerns is not as clear-cut as the traditional debate between the consequentialists and the deontologists suggests. To say that everyone matters is to say that how our actions affect others matters: the consequences of our actions matter. What we will to be a universal law is grounded on the consequences of so willing. While Kant held these consequences to be logical, the problem of contradiction in the kingdom of ends is famously only really apparent in Kant's single case of truth telling. Dishonesty does not make sense without the assumption of honesty. But the reason we do not will adultery to be a universal law is not that this would be logically contradictory, but that it would cause unhappiness and social dysfunction. Ethics is about how our actions affect people. But the reason why it matters to us how our actions affect people is not itself consequentialist. The value we place on human dignity and human well-being, on humans as ends in themselves, cannot be derived from purely consequentialist arguments. It is foundational. Hence, it is difficult to imagine a purely deontological or purely consequentialist approach to ethics which is actually functional. Consequences matter, but which consequences matter depends on foundational moral commitments. So, even the classic Benthamite formulation, that 'everyone counts for one and no one counts for more than one' constitutes, itself, a deontological principle, even if it is operationalised in terms of consequences.

This comes out even in Balasubramaniam's own argument when he asserts implicitly and sometimes explicitly the reasons a legal system must treat people as ends in themselves. Roughly, if subjects or citizens do not feel that they are respected, if the legal system which mediates their affairs is not universal, prospective, etc., they will lose respect for the law, and this will make it difficult to govern them.[12]

This blurring of principles and consequences is reflected in the complexity of means and ends relationships in general. Just as it is fallacious to claim that prudential and moral considerations can be kept separate, it is fallacious to claim that there can be a strict separation between the moral character of means and that of ends. No moral aim, indeed no aim of any kind, can be met without means. Hence, if fulfilling some duty is an utmost moral imperative, then, by necessary implication, we are obligated

[12] Balasubramaniam, Chapter 5, p. 131.

to employ means to that end. That is to say, we are obligated to try to 'bring it about'. Who wills the ends wills the most moral means. For example, to feed one's children – a moral duty – one could grow a garden, get a job or rob a bank. The most moral means will take into account the likelihood that the garden will produce enough with enough consistency to fill the children's bellies, as well as the fact that robbing a bank is illegal, causes fear, might provoke violence and fails to respect property rights. One is obligated to find some means to feed one's children and the means one ought to use are those which are themselves 'most moral'. But it would be difficult to discern how the duty to feed one's children was somehow separate from the duty to find a means of doing so.

Hence, whatever the ends of political life might be – and we can here leave this matter open – if they are of sufficient value, if they are worth enough to us, we are obliged to construct *effective*, ethical institutions to meet them. If flexibility really is necessary for institutions to be effective, as I intend to show below, then flexibility within limits might be a moral imperative too.

The important difference between this claim and a simple claim that the end justifies the means, or simplistic consequentialist claim that the 'right' thing to do is what brings about the greatest good for the greatest number, is that it allows that we can acknowledge moral complexity. An action can be morally obligatory and at the same time have externalities that are profoundly even prohibitively morally regrettable. There are some means which no end, no matter how morally obligatory, could make us will. Strict consequentialism does not allow the commission of a morally necessary act to be, at the same time, regrettable, and strict Kantian style deontology does not allow that the omission of a morally necessary act on the grounds that it requires a morally prohibited means can be equally regrettable. Judgment, agency, is what navigates these tangles.

Nardin might object that to say that a morally offensive act is at the same time morally justifiable is contradictory.[13] But why should we expect abstract 'consistency' from moral principles? While ethics itself is timeless, the concepts, idea and principles we use to *talk about ethics*, ideas like rights, have grown out of particular times and circumstances, in response to particular social and political circumstances. To the extent that new problems, or new manifestations of old problems arise, our mode of understanding how best to apply highly abstract principles and values will

[13] Nardin, Chapter 4, p. 97.

surely shift. I am not suggesting that ethics are simply contextual, but rather that our ways of talking about ethics are contextual, and hence, potentially prone to contradiction. Hence this is not relativism but a descriptive kind of pluralism.

We should not expect our language-bound ethical principles to exhibit pure logical consistency, and an action can, at the same time, be right and regrettable. Even in those cases where, for example, lying might seem justifiable, we do not need to say that it was, strictly speaking, a good and moral thing to do. It is because of the indignity of being lied to (and the indignity of being a liar) that lying is always wrong. The man who lies to save a life has treated the person to whom he lied with disrespect, has dehumanised him, but it was right that he save the life, which required that he lie. Conversely, had he not lied, he would have treated the person whose life was lost as worthless, or at least, of very little worth. It would be right to tell the truth, but it would be quite wrong to allow someone to die. An action can be both morally wrong and morally obligatory. To insist on abstract consistency must stem from a misguided desire for the imposition of order or simplicity on complexity. Conceptual clarity may come at the expense of moral clarity.

The rightness and wrongness of lying and saving lives stem from the intrinsic value and dignity of humanity. This is deontological. But to the extent that we must deliberate on how our actions affect human dignity, we are concerned with our actions' consequences. This brings us back to the question of crisis government because states of emergency constitute a dilemma from precisely this perspective. They raise a complex mixture of conflicting ends which seem to require radically opposed means and these means all too often should give us serious pause. The ends relate to the fourfold sense of safety implicated in emergency powers' exercise. Safe emergency powers must be able to (1) secure the state (as itself a means to the promotion and protection of moral ends) and (2) its individual citizens, without (3) itself causing excessive harm to citizens,[14] and without (4) causing excessive damage to other values which define the ends of the state. It is because these claims for safety pull in different directions that emergency powers are precarious. They seem to require individual rule in place of rule by law, prompting a push-pull between the question of

[14] I say 'excessive harm' because all states necessarily harm their citizens somewhat, unless we define harm as damage which is 'unjustifiable' such that any damage which can be justified would not count as 'harm'. But that would be a very dangerous and somewhat sophistic move.

providing latitude or *Spielraum* to statesmen and administrators, necessary for (1) and (2) and the question of bounding that space for the sake of (3) and (4). Hence, it is common to oppose the rule of law and individual rule in the study of emergency powers because individual rule seems prominently in line with the first dyad and the rule of law with the second. The first means enables, the second constrains. On this view, it is the rule of law which constrains arbitrary power and arbitrary power is sometimes defined as power unconstrained by law. The next two sections show that this is not quite so.

Until now I have argued that institutions are means to principled ends, and that who wills the end wills the most moral means. I have suggested the conflicts that arise from such an approach are an inevitable, if regrettable part of all moral and political life if we avoid imposing a false order on a natural disorder. The nature of the conflicting ends involved in crisis government suggest the need for flexible institutions and I now turn to showing how this flexibility is not necessarily as terrible as we have often assumed nor is the need for it confined to crises.

IV. Flexibility and agency in political institutions

If we embrace agency, how do we restrict excess? There are good historical reasons to question whether formal constraints, such as laws and formal institutions, are enough on their own to constrain power ill-used. Substantial informal power in the form of personal authority can enable a political actor to behave tyrannically, but technically in accordance with the law and the constitution. Indira Gandhi's 'declaration' of a state of emergency in June of 1975 serves as a good example. While, at the time, opinion was divided regarding the justification of the emergency, hindsight leaves the case fairly clear that the move was dubious and self-serving. Technically, the President had to declare the state of emergency and this declaration had to be ratified by the Cabinet. Mrs Gandhi conformed exactly to these procedural requirements. But her personal power was such that no one was likely to oppose her. The emergency resulted in gross and arbitrary abuses of power, but this was made possible by strict conformity to the rule of law. The rule of law was subverted through informal mechanisms of power. The President signed the document put in front of him; Cabinet fell into line.[15] Hence, law might not go far enough, might

[15] See P.N. Dhar, *Indira Gandhi, the 'Emergency' and Indian Democracy* (New York: Oxford University Press, 2000); P. Gupte, *Mother India: A Political Biography of Indira Gandhi*

be insufficient as a means of constraining bad behaviour in emergency circumstances.

Conversely, the formal constraint of power can sometimes hamper the necessary and positive effects of informal power well-used. The rule of law was, as I have suggested, intended originally to constrain individual rule, to set limits on individual agency. And indeed, unconstrained agency is demonstrably disastrously dangerous. But the positive worth of individual agency to good government, given the proper incentives and disincentives, is often under-emphasised due to our habit of opposing the rule of law and individual rule. If we take seriously the idea that institutions are means to moral ends and we concede that some form of flexibility is then necessary, it makes sense to consider this landscape of formal and informal power together, what I am calling a topography of emergency power. We now turn to this task.

V. Formal and informal power and constraint

Action of any sort requires power and public officials employ two forms – forms which, while they may shift their 'market share', are consistent between times of normalcy and times of crisis. The first is the formal power which an office bestows on its holder to enable her to fulfil the tasks and duties associated with it. This is similar to the form of power that the Romans called '*potestas*', the capacities that make up an office. In addition to this formal *potestas*, informal power is necessary for achieving the aims associated with an office. This other form of power embraces, for example, both influence and authority. A formal capacity is pragmatically insufficient because orders can always be refused and rule entirely through violent coercion is morally illegitimate (as an assault on human dignity), prohibitively expensive and entirely precarious.[16]

Because attaining an office requires informal power and because the status of an office sometimes bestows it, *potestas* rarely exhausts a public official's power. This means not only that such an official is more likely to have the capacity to effectively meet the aims which have been set for

(New York: Scribner's, 1992); V. Iyer, *States of Emergency: The Indian Experience* (New Delhi: Butterworths, 2000); R.L. Park, 'Political Crisis in India' (1975) 15 *Asian Survey* 996–1013.

[16] The fact that we always govern in part through violent coercion is noteworthy. The law does not just appeal to our reason, it threatens penalties and these penalties are enforced. This suggests the extent to which a state cannot govern while treating everyone purely as rational beings, as ends in themselves.

her and which her status as an office holder makes morally obligatory, it also means that she has the capacity to act beyond those aims unless she meets with effective constraint. This has both benefits and drawbacks. It can provide the means for truly heroic action and it can provide the means for terrible abuse of power. Hence, all good sets of institutions have, as one aim, the constraint of informal power. Formal constraint of informal power is law. But constraints on political behaviour have informal aspects also. These include social mores and moral norms, the informal power of others and structures of incentives, political, monetary or otherwise.

Since enablement and constraint go well beyond law, while attention to law as a boundary or conduit is necessary, it is far from sufficient to addressing the emergency powers problem with its fourfold ends and seemingly opposed means. We should not conceptualise the emergencies problem as one of a choice between arbitrariness and responsible government, where arbitrariness is associated with individual rule and responsible government with the rule of law. If institutions are means to moral ends, we must make this more complex landscape of enablement and constraint our focus and not a peripheral concern. While it is the very essence of informality that emergencies can never be made safe, without a detailed and accurate understanding of the informalities of emergency, no set of formal powers can have much hope of bounding crisis or bounding crisis action.

The debate over extra-legal measures, were it to focus on boundaries and where with respect to them political actors are standing, would thus raise serious tensions. We can think of a rule-of-law focused approach to the question of emergency and extra-legal measures as analogous to a political map: one which focuses on jurisdiction, on borders and boundaries, on inclusions and exclusions. Just as boundaries between jurisdictions are symbolic of political membership, so legal boundaries relate to certain rights and entitlements. In breaking the law, in acting outside of it, one forfeits aspects of the right to liberty and property, for example.[17] In both cases, 'inside' means 'in good stead'.

But borders are porous: in the same way that they can mislead us with respect to who actually dwells in a state, to rely primarily on an 'inside/outside' conception of emergency powers is apt to misconstrue the complexities of the landscape. Emergency powers are just one, formal

[17] This is so even if such forfeiture is done in accordance with due process of law, unless we are willing to think of rights as contingent in the first place.

aspect of emergency power which embraces not only the formal constraints and enablements of law, but political power in general. One way to conceptualise this difference is to consider how it resembles a topographic, rather than a political, map, one which shows the physical features of a landscape: its pathways and physical barriers. These physical features can be understood to affect each other. Mountains channel the flow of rivers (as, with respect to politics, the new institutionalists demonstrate), but rivers erode their banks. Political agency structures and consistently remolds institutions. The fluid aspects of power shape the formal aspects over time and sometimes find their way over or around the barriers which formal power erects. Since institutions are means, and effective means require flexibility, this 'topographic' approach suggests the ways that law and human agency are always intertwined.

It is for this reason that we cannot simply take the approach of David Dyzenhaus. He has argued that, to exclude the Schmittian shadow of exceptions we must accept Kelsen's view that there is only one legal order, regardless of whether the state is in crisis. If a state is ruled not only by law, but also under Dyzenhaus's robust conception of the rule of law, then even in those cases where exigency presses, we need not and cannot resort to extra-legal measures. Instead, we should follow Dicey, who demonstrates an approach which aims to envelope crisis action in what Dyzenhaus refers to as a spirit of legality.[18] All agents, political, administrative and judicial, on this account, are supposed to be participating in what Dyzenhaus has called the 'rule-of-law project'. Formal correctness is insufficient, as 'wicked regimes' demonstrate. If an executive is granted prerogative powers, which, while they are formally correct, lack legal authority on account of flouting the rule-of-law project, they ought to be rejected and judges should have the legal authority to do so.

Dyzenhaus's perspective underplays the empirically grounded claim which Epstein *et al.*, and others have made that in times of serious crisis, judges do not do much good.[19] While evidence from the European Court of Human Rights suggests that the threat of imminent review can have at least some sobering effect on state action,[20] no similar body, comparatively

[18] D. Dyzenhaus, *The Constitution of Law* (Cambridge: Cambridge University Press, 2006), p. 54.

[19] See, e.g., Lee Epstein *et al.*, 'The Supreme Court During Crisis: How War Affects Only Nonwar Cases' (2005) 80 *New York University Law Review* 1–116.

[20] C. Schreuer, 'Derogation of Human Rights in Situations of Public Emergency: The Experience of European Convention' (1982) 9 *Yale Journal of World Public Order* 113–32. While Gross and Fionnuala Ní Aoláin contest this, their claim is that, after the fact, the courts tend

isolated from political pressures, governs most states, and even this body has been more effective as a deterrent than as a means of response.[21] The reason that judges do not do much good is that, politically and morally, it is not always wise or sensible for them to do good, given the fourfold nature of 'safety' in emergencies. While the threat of review well after the fact could certainly have a sobering effect on administrative or executive action, this threat is intrinsically dependent on both the likelihood of getting caught and the political will to prosecute. Each of these, in turn, is reliant on conditions of informal power. Hence, it is not just the weakness of judges, but also the power of rhetoric and popular support in determining whether a matter will ever come before a judge. The rule of law here, invokes a spirit of good intentions. It may well be true that judges *ought* to do good. But as institutional means to good ends, we need more.

Neither Gross's nor Dynzenhaus's approach is safe on its own. Informal means of constraint and enablement do the central, not peripheral, work of safety. And it is this informal flow of power, encumbered but not obstructed by the law, which we must understand if we wish to get a firmer grasp on the emergencies problem.

The functions of government, its institutions, are shot through with agency at every level. Human agency makes the laws and consents to them. Human agency enforces, executes and sometimes adapts policies, and human agency enforces the law or not, according to discretion. Judges hear arguments aimed to sway their judgment because law is something uncertain and deliberation, as an activity makes sense only with respect to what is uncertain.[22] In this respect, agency and discretion are not opposed to law. They are necessarily constant companions both in times of normalcy and in times of crisis. The inside/outside conception of the behaviour of statesmen and officers is thus misleading, whether in a crisis or otherwise. Informal constraints and informal power through individual agency are both critical means and potentially the most moral means to just outcomes. To rely on some aspect of the geography of emergency power without attending to the landscape as a whole is dangerous for *people*, who are, after all, ends in themselves.

to be supportive of the executive in countries with normally democratic institutions. This is potentially consistent with Schreuer's claim that before the fact executives may somewhat temper their behaviour. Gross and Ní Aoláin, *Law in Times of Crisis*, ch. 5.

21 Of course, supranational courts are subject to plenty of political pressures, but the key to their effectiveness is that the pressures which may have led to emergency action in the first place will not be the same as those which affect the likelihood of review.

22 As we learn from Aristotle, *Nichomachean Ethics*, §1112b, and in many of his other texts.

VI. Conclusion

Since men always rule, even when law rules, whether they rule inside or outside of the law is secondary to the question of whether they rule well with respect to meeting the underlying normative requirements which the state should uphold and further. How well we are governed, whether in an emergency or not, depends on whether our leaders and administrators behave well. This is not a curable, or even necessarily a regrettable, condition. Rather it is both necessary, and to a great extent desirable, because agency, when properly channelled and constrained by law and importantly by informal incentives, is one instrument of good government.

Because so many elements intervene in human affairs – the vicissitudes of human error, the ultimate unpredictability of human agency, even the weather – judgment and agency are necessary elements of effective institutions. I have argued that because government, and particularly crisis government requires flexibility it requires that experience, prudence and agency enter into the design of institutions as well as the administration of law. Political action in the service of principled ends must take account of new circumstances, not just in a crisis, but always. This is why government can never be a machine that runs itself. In this respect, emergency powers are continuous with, not an exception to, the normal case: they are only one instance among many where law and agency are bound up.

Hence we should centralise agency in our study of emergency noting that, while it will always be dangerous and conceptually problematic in the context of government, it is also fundamental. The broader question of how to manage it (enabling it, as well as constraining it) effectively for ends must be at the core of our institutional inquiry, and indeed of a moral inquiry into crisis government if we take the role of institutions as means for normative ends seriously. Any such inquiry will require sophisticated attention to informal considerations, and might consider concepts of earned discretion, good procedures and informal encouragement toward transparency and accountability.

Moral life and political life are invariably messier than the consistency requirements of philosophical discourse like to allow. Hence, to attempt to secure human dignity and to further liberal democratic values under emergency conditions we must contend with the topography of risk and enablement, formal and informal power. Emergency powers can never be made safe, but this paper has gestured toward a potentially promising approach for the study of how to make them safer.

8

Law, terror and social movements: the repression–mobilisation nexus

COLM CAMPBELL

A striking feature of the legal literature on the 'war on terror' is the dearth of empirically based socio-legal input. For the most part, lawyers have engaged with the issue as a philosophy of law exchange on law's role (or Schmittian influenced non-role) in counter-terrorism, shading at the edges into a law-and-policy debate. This approach has obvious strengths – within the internal logic of its discourses the philosophical quandaries are real and the policy dilemmas pressing – but it has also certain weaknesses, not least in what is not said.

The socio-legal gap may be explained partly in terms of the difficulty of conducting original, particularly empirical, research in the area; partly in terms of timing and partly in terms of the novel challenge of theorising a situation in which the world's only remaining superpower apparently retreats from legality in the pursuit of hegemony. The sensitivity of the field means that the state may place formidable obstacles in the way of gathering empirical data on the internal dynamics of its 'counter-terrorist' legal armoury. Assembling original quantitative data (for instance on the operation of emergency courts and tribunals and on interrogation practices) is likely to require high levels of official clearance in a situation in which the state may have a vested interest in avoiding public examination of its record and where security concerns may be strongly articulated.

The view of law 'from below' – in part the perspective of the communities from which violent actors spring – is also likely to be difficult to research. This may be particularly the case where the perspective is that of the violent actors who are the stated targets of counter-terrorist measures. Quantitative methodologies become largely redundant when researching

I wish to thank the participants at the Singapore symposium for their helpful comments, particularly Victor V. Ramraj and David Dyzenhaus; thanks too for the excellent assistance provided by my Research Associate, Ita Connolly, Transitional Justice Institute, University of Ulster.

underground groups and attempts to employ qualitative methodologies must engage with a group's concern with security that is likely to be at least as strong as that of the state. Even where access from the state and/or its violent challengers is granted, the collection and analysis of empirical data are time-consuming, with the result that a long time lag is virtually inevitable. It is unsurprising, therefore, that little primary empirical socio-legal research on the 'war on terror' has yet been published. What is surprising is that socio-legal frameworks theorising the role of law in conflicted societies have rarely been drawn upon and that empirical data from socio-legal studies in such conflict sites as Northern Ireland, apartheid-era South Africa and Israel/Palestine have frequently been overlooked.

Employment of the term 'socio-legal' refers not simply to the sociology of law, but following William Twining, it also refers to the relationship between law and social theory and social history.[1] Doing so opens the field of inquiry to a cluster of fresh theoretical insights and points to the utility of a variety of quantitative and qualitative research methodologies. This is not to suggest an hermetic division between 'socio-legal' and 'philosophy of law' sub-disciplinary categories,[2] but while there will be overlap in some areas, in others the perspectives are likely to be radically heterogeneous; different questions are asked, so it is unsurprising that answers may not be coterminous. To employ a geometric metaphor, the same object may be described as a circle or as a triangle by different viewers, yet both apparently contradictory descriptions may be accurate. One sub-discipline need not trump another, raising the possibility that the juxtaposition of a variety of sub-disciplinary perspectives may enhance understanding of the overall phenomenon. To complete the geometric metaphor: if both descriptions are assumed to be correct, the object can only be a cone.

Juxtaposition of perspectives has the effect of forcing attention on divergent sub-disciplinary assumptions, structures of argumentation and methodologies. While a variety of socio-legal streams offer potentially valuable insights on the 'war on terror', this chapter focuses mainly on that

[1] W. Twining, 'Schauer on Hart' (2006) 119 *Harvard Law Review Forum* 127, n. 24 and W. Twining, 'Reviving General Jurisprudence' in M. Likosky (ed.), *Transnational Legal Processes* (Cambridge: Cambridge University Press, 2003), pp. 3, 17 and n. 58, reprinted in W. Twining, *The Great Juristic Bazaar: Jurists' Texts and Lawyers' Stories* (Aldershot: Ashgate, 2002) pp. 335, 356–7 and n. 58.

[2] See for example Tamanaha's engagement with H.L.A. Hart's work in B.Z. Tamanaha, *A General Jurisprudence of Law and Society* (Oxford: Oxford University Press, 2001). On Hart's resistance to an earlier approach by Twining along related lines see Twining, *Schauer on Hart*, p. 122, n. 3.

relating to law and social movement struggles. A contrast is offered with the dominant 'counter-terrorist' legal conversation through an exploration of three key themes: 'decentred' versus 'top-down' views of law; law-as-norm versus law-as-communication and methodological issues. Drawing on research published by the author and a collaborator, an alternative socio-legal model is sketched, suggesting a much more ambivalent picture of law's place in violent political conflict. This exploration is then drawn upon to critique elements of the Gross–Dyzenhaus debate. Finally, some conclusions are offered about legal research and the 'war on terror'.

I. Perspective matters: the need for self-consciousness

The dominant legal conversation either explicitly or implicitly employs a top-down view of law. This is most clearly the case with that stream of thought associated with, or reacting against, Carl Schmitt. Schmitt's perspective on law is that of the 'sovereign', indeed definitional of the sovereign is the choice to act outside law in the initiation and execution of the state of exception (the assertion that the 'sovereign is he who decides on the exception'[3] has taken on the aura of a tedious mantra in the current debate). The sovereign not only makes the law, it (the top) decides on the extent to which it is to be bound by it in its dealings with those below. Much of the voluminous discussion of legal 'black holes' in the 'war on terror' also incorporates an implicit top-down view of law.[4] If the sovereign has the capacity to exempt itself from law, a 'black hole' is created, however limited this may be in practice. One effect of this perspective is to diminish the importance of legal claims-making (successful or otherwise) on the part of those on whom the sovereign's actions impinge in the supposed 'black hole'.

Schmitt was famously dismissive of liberal conceptions of the 'rule of law', but another stream of 'top-down' thought in this area is careful to employ the language of the 'rule of law' and 'human rights' (even if the discourse becomes remarkably thin at this point). Dershowitz recommends entrusting the administration of a system of 'torture warrants' to the courts.[5] Law then becomes the vehicle for empowering the state to

[3] C. Schmitt, *Political Theology: Four Chapters on the Concept of Sovereignty*, G.D. Schwab (trans.) (Cambridge, Massachusetts and London: MIT Press, 1985), p. 5.

[4] J. Steyn, 'Guantánamo Bay: The Legal Black Hole' (2004) 53 *International and Comparative Law Quarterly* 1.

[5] A. Dershowitz, *Why Terrorism Works* (New Haven: Yale University Press, 2002).

impose a system of torture on those within its custody. Ignatieff's major contribution in the field[6] likewise appears to envisage the use of law in the creation of a system that would inflict on detainees something close to what international human rights law would consider 'inhuman and degrading treatment' (though his later contributions seem to mark a retreat from this position).[7]

The point here is not to suggest that 'top-down' views of law are necessarily invalid, rather that theirs is not the sole perspective. By contrast, 'decentred' or 'bottom-up' approaches emphasise the use made of law by social movements (a broad term encompassing movements for social change, outside political parties, with varying degrees of organisation).[8] As a distinct body of legal thought, the emergence of the study of law and social movements can be traced to the failure of Legal Formalism in the US to deliver on the promise expected by its liberal adherents, particularly the progressive promise of litigation strategies. Rejecting a liberal 'myth of rights'[9] that failed to take account of the hegemonic tendency of law to buttress the status quo, legal scholars drawing on emerging social movement theory tended to emphasise the instrumental use of legal claims-making, and of law in general, by campaigning organisations. This value arose not only from incorporation of legal claims-making in an overall campaigning strategy, but also from the capacity of legal claims-making to act as a catalyst for group mobilisation. Viewed in these terms, legal claims-making could contribute to advancing the mobilisation of the group, even, or sometimes especially, in the face of a court's hostility to a claim. While recognising law's hegemonic quality, this perspective accorded to law a 'relatively autonomous'[10] quality – with a tendency to buttress the status quo, while simultaneously presenting some meaningful possibility of legal challenge. From this perspective, what is important is not the top-down effect of court judgments, but rather the messages and 'signals' sent by the courts to a variety of social movement actors – agents rather than

[6] M. Ignatieff, *The Lesser Evil: Political Ethics In An Age of Terror* (Edinburgh: Edinburgh University Press, 2004).

[7] M. Ignatieff, 'If Torture Works' *Prospect Magazine* 121:34 (April 2006).

[8] See M.W. McCann (ed.), *Law and Social Movements* (Aldershot: Ashgate, 2006) and B. Rajagopal, *International Law from Below: Development, Social Movements and Third World Resistance* (Cambridge: Cambridge University Press, 2003).

[9] S. Scheingold, *The Politics of Rights: Lawyers, Public Policy and Political Change* (New Haven: Yale University Press, 1974), p. 6.

[10] For an exploration of the relative autonomy of law in Apartheid-era South Africa, see R. Abel, *Politics by Other Means: Law in the Struggle Against Apartheid, 1980–1994* (New York: Routledge, 1995).

reactors to judicial command. The importance of this messaging in tactical judgments by movement actors means that law can be understood in part as 'particular traditions of knowledge and communicative practice',[11] rather than simply a system of norms emanating from 'above'.

All inquiry involves a methodology of sorts, whether explicit (as with the quantitative and qualitative techniques mentioned above), or implicit (often the case in the philosophy of law). Within discrete fields of inquiry, these methodologies are likely to be intimately linked to sets of primary assumptions or hypotheses and to particular modes of argumentation. It is these (frequently unstated) assumptions and modes that make the chosen methodologies appropriate.

In the dominant 'counter-terrorist' legal conversation, the favoured methodological device is the hypothetical. This typically involves a captured terrorist who is known to have planted a bomb, which is shortly to explode, and the location of which only the terrorist knows[12] (the first 'Dirty Harry' film uses a similar device to evoke sympathy for Harry Callahan's ill-treatment of a particularly loathsome villain). If the prisoner is successfully tortured to reveal the location of the bomb, many lives will be saved; accordingly the law should either be amended to allow torture or a theory of extra-legality is required that might allow the torturer to escape punishment. Empirical data are rarely drawn upon, and where they are, they tend to be secondary or tertiary.[13]

Typically, this device is utilised as part of a strategy of argumentation that rests upon simple models and metaphors (contributing to hypotheses of sorts), and equally simple notions of 'effectiveness': terrorism represents a crisis to which the state must respond (the 'crisis-response' model). A revised or attenuated legal framework, loosening restrictions on security agencies, is required in this response. At this point a (linear) 'balance' metaphor is frequently drawn upon. At one end are the rights of 'terrorist suspects' and on the other are the rights of 'society'; predictably the former must be diminished, with the assumed result that the latter are enhanced. In the more thoughtful versions of this discourse it is accepted that the result of the balance struck must be shown to be effective. This partly provides the basis for the normative question as to what role (if

11 McCann, *Law and Social Movements*, p. xii.

12 See especially Dershowitz, *Why Terrorism Works*, pp. 142–63.

13 This is true of 'terrorism' studies in general. See D. Brannan, P. Esler and N. Strindberg, 'Talking to "Terrorists": Towards an Independent Analytical Framework for the Study of Violent Substate Activism' (2001) 24 *Studies in Conflict and Terrorism* 3 and M. Crenshaw, 'The Psychology of Terrorism: An Agenda for the 21st Century' (2000) 21 *Political Psychology* 405 and 410.

any) law *should* play? The 'ticking bomb' hypothetical is then employed to demonstrate the effectiveness of torture in the individual case, or coercive techniques are assumed, without the necessity for further proof, to produce positive results in individual interrogations. The arguments are then transposed from the individual case to dealing with terrorism in general. By this means, a narrow hypothetical is taken to prove a much broader and frequently ill-defined hypothesis, producing the familiar normative argument for a legal regime that either provides for torture or something close to inhuman treatment or an extra-legal one that may permit a torturer to escape punishment. Similar structures of argumentation are employed in relation to issues other than torture.

As with the issue above about 'top-down' approaches to law, my critique at this point is not that such hypotheses, methodologies and transpositions are necessarily invalid (they are discussed further below). It is rather that there is a need for self-consciousness in articulating them: the hypotheses (such as they are) are not given; the hypothetical is one methodological device among many and the transposition of notions of effectiveness from the individual case to the general may or may not be appropriate.

II. Law, repression and mobilisation

Viewing the relationship of law, terrorism and political violence in general from a decentred perspective produces a somewhat different result. Research published by Campbell and Connolly in 2006[14] attempted to explore such a picture, first by setting out a decentred theoretical framework of law's place in the interaction of the state and its violent challengers in a state with an ideological commitment to the 'rule of law' (however imperfect in practice), and second by applying and grounding this framework using fresh empirical data from interviews with those formerly engaged in violent challenge to the Northern Ireland state. Rather than pointlessly reproducing the text of the article here, what will be done is to set out the architecture (though not the detail) of the theoretical

[14] C. Campbell and I. Connolly, 'Making War on Terror? Global Lessons from Northern Ireland' (2006) 69 *Modern Law Review* 935. The arguments are further developed in C. Campbell and I. Connolly, 'A Deadly Complexity: Law, Social Movements and Political Violence' (2007) 16 *Minnesota Journal of International Law* 265. For analyses pointing to similar conclusions (though from a different theoretical base) see, V.V. Ramraj, 'Counter-Terrorism Policy and Minority Alienation: Some Lessons From Northern Ireland' (2006) *Singapore Journal of Legal Studies* 385 and M. O'Connor and C. Rumann, 'Into the Fire: How to Avoid Getting Burned by the Same Mistakes Made Fighting Terrorism in Northern Ireland' (2003) 24 *Cardozo L. Rev.* 1657.

frame and the main empirical findings in a way that contrasts with the dominant 'counter-terrorist' conversation, and to use the resulting insights to explore elements of the Gross–Dyzenhaus debate. Finally, the framework is used to identify elements of the new legal research agenda sketched in the conclusion.

Whereas the crisis-response model employed in much anti-terrorist discourse is uni-directional and uni-dimensional, the framework set out by Campbell and Connolly is interactive, drawing on social movement theory's exploration of a complex 'repression–mobilisation nexus'.[15] Empirical studies of the interaction of the state and its violent challengers result in strong confidence about one dynamic in the nexus: violent challenger mobilisation always induces some degree of state repression[16] (defined as 'obstacles by the state (or its agents) to individual and collective actions by challengers').[17] As regards the other dynamic (impact of repression on mobilisation), no one picture has emerged: repression is sometimes

[15] The literature is vast. Material drawn upon includes: C. Davenport and D.A. Armstrong II, 'Democracy and the Violation of Human Rights: A Statistical Analysis from 1976 to 1996' (2004) 48 *American Journal of Political Science* 538; R. Francisco, 'Why Are Collective Conflicts "Stable"?' in C. Davenport (ed.), *Paths to State Repression: Human Rights Violations and Contentious Politics* (Lanham: Rowman & Littlefield Publishers Inc, 2000); R. Francisco, 'The Relationship Between Coercion and Protest: An Empirical Evaluation in Three Coercive States' (1995) 39 *Journal of Conflict Resolution* 263; M.I. Lichbach, 'Protest: Random or Contagious? The Postwar United Kingdom' (1995) 11 *Armed Forces and Society* 581; D.T. Mason and D.A. Krane, 'The Political Economy of Death Squads: Towards a Theory of the Impact of State-Sanctioned Terror' (1989) 33 *International Studies Quarterly* 175; C. Lee, S. Maline and W.H. Moore, 'Coercion and Protest: An Empirical Test Revisited' in C. Davenport (ed.), *Paths to State Repression: Human Rights Violations and Contentious Politics* (Lanham: Rowman & Littlefield Publishers Inc, 2000); W.H. Moore and K. Jaggers, 'Deprivation, Mobilization and the State: A Synthetic Model of Rebellion' (1990) VI *Journal of Developing Societies* 17; M. Ellina and W.H. Moore, 'Discrimination and Political Violence: A Cross-National Study with Two Time Periods' (1990) 43 *The Western Political Quarterly* 267; K.D. Opp, 'Repression, Micromobilization and Political Protest' (1990) 62 *Social Forces* 521; K. Cavanaugh, 'Interpretations of Political Violence in Ethnically Divided Societies' (1997) 9 *Terrorism and Political Violence* 33; R. White, 'On Measuring Political Violence: Northern Ireland, 1969–1980' (1993) 58 *American Sociological Review* 575; R. White, 'Issues in the Study of Political Violence: Understanding the Motives of Participants in Small Group Political Violence' (2000) 12 *Terrorism and Political Violence* 95 and R. White and T.F. White, 'Repression and the Liberal State: The Case of Northern Ireland, 1969–1972' (1995) 39 *Journal of Conflict Resolution* 330.

[16] See C. Davenport, 'Repression and Mobilization: Insights from Political Science and Sociology' in C. Davenport, H. Johnston and C. Mueller (eds.), *Repression and Mobilization: Social Movements, Protest and Contention Vol. 21* (Minneapolis: University of Minnesota Press, 2005), p. xvi.

[17] C. McPhail and J.D. McCarthy, 'Protest Mobilization, Protest Repression and Their Interaction' in Davenport, *Paths to State Repression*, p. 3, drawing on C. Tilly, *Popular Contention in Great Britain, 1758–1834* (Cambridge: Harvard University Press, 1995), p. 136.

effective, sometimes counter-productive and sometimes makes little identifiable difference. The literature stresses two related elements in explaining why some social movement organisations (including violent groups) are resistant to, or can apparently thrive on, repression: a capacity for 'adaptation' by the organisation in the face of a variety of repressive state strategies and the role of movement 'entrepreneurs' (protester/rebel leaders) who are assumed to make choices and maximise the uptake of available resources according to a rational actor model.

Exploration of such phenomena as adaptation and entrepreneurship is located by reference to the three main analytical devices employed to explain the emergence and development of social movements (including such particular 'social movement organisations' as guerrilla or terrorist groups)[18]: 'political opportunities', 'mobilising structures' and 'framing processes'. 'Political opportunities' refers to the 'structure of political opportunities and constraints confronting the movement'[19] (including such factors as the nature of the state [democratic versus authoritarian], and of electoral arrangements). 'Mobilising structures' refers to 'collective vehicles, informal as well as formal, through which people mobilise and engage in collective action'.[20] Successful structures are taken to have developed in order to make efficient use of available resources. 'Framing processes' refers to the 'conscious strategic efforts by groups of people to fashion shared understandings of the world and of themselves that legitimate and motivate collective action'.[21] Under this banner comes a range of cultural and ideational elements, providing collective actors with a shared frame of reference. While many of these analytical devices can be applied both to authoritarian and democratic states, the literature also recognises that the dynamics of protest in democratic states have particular features, expressed most importantly in Tilly's assertion that the democratic state's mechanisms tend to 'dampen the processes that generate violent contestation'.[22]

[18] For a social movement theory exploration of German and Italian terrorist groups see, D.D. Porta, *Social Movements, Political Violence and the State: A Comparative Analysis of Italy and Germany* (Cambridge: Cambridge University Press, 1995). On social movement organisations, see D. McAdam, J.D. McCarthy and M.N. Zald, *Comparative Perspectives on Social Movements: Political Opportunities, Mobilizing Structures and Cultural Framings* (Cambridge: Cambridge University Press, 1996).

[19] McAdam, McCarthy and Zald, *Comparative Perspectives on Social Movements*, p. 2.

[20] *Ibid.*, p. 3. [21] *Ibid.*, p. 6.

[22] C. Tilly, *The Politics of Collective Violence* (Cambridge: Cambridge University Press, 2003), p. 44.

Campbell and Connolly's framework was constructed by taking these three analytical devices and locating law's place in them in a way that drew upon the 'legal mobilisation' literature (relating to largely peaceful groups) mentioned above, and some socio-legal literature on violently conflicted societies.[23] Within this framework, law in a state with an ideological commitment to the 'rule of law' was viewed as having a 'relative autonomy'. Whereas dominant 'counter-terrorist' discourse frequently employs a metaphor of the legal 'black hole' to express the normative problem of deliberate lawless state action, Campbell and Connolly's framework employs the concept of legal 'grey zones' to describe the actuality of violent political contestation. Such conflict tends to be characterised by ambiguity, opacity, lack of accountability and indeterminacy as regards the lawfulness of state action. This is particularly true of covert action by intelligence agencies whose behaviour may leave few traces which legal mechanisms are designed to track and where strategies of denial are likely to be routine.[24] Yet even in these legal grey zones, legal claims-making is almost certain to continue.

Within this overall framework, law has a Janus-like quality – it is both a tool of repression and a site of resistance. Counter-terrorist law has the potential to close political opportunity structures (for instance by banning organisations or by restricting media access), but it may also provide a vehicle for resisting closure though legal claims-making ('law as a shield') or for assisting opening ('law as a sword').

Anti-terrorist law typically incorporates measures designed to deny resources to terrorist groups (for instance by providing for the sequestration of suspect funds), but law may also provide a resource which disenfranchised groups may be able to employ to grow their mobilising structures. Legal claims-making (perhaps in launching a challenge to 'unjust' 'counter-terrorist' powers), can act as a catalyst for mobilisation, even, or sometimes especially, when legal challenge fails (if the challenge succeeds, the powers are 'proved' to be unjust; if the challenge fails, the 'system' is shown to be unjust). The capacity to harness such a resource successfully is likely to depend at least partly on the relative ability of challenger 'entrepreneurs'. Attempts by the state to close political opportunity structures by trying rebel leaders may likewise present a resource, when challengers can successfully present the proceedings as 'show trials' and therefore in a way that stimulates resistance.

23 R. Abel, *Politics by Other Means: Law in the Struggle Against Apartheid, 1980–1994* (New York: Routledge, 1995).

24 See S. Chesterman, 'Deny Everything: Intelligence Activities and the Rule of Law' (Chapter 13), this volume.

'Anti-terrorist' powers tend to be designed to be executive-orientated, 'catch-all' and 'judge-proof';[25] all of this contributes to the 'grey zone' effect whereby the legality in the claimed exercise of such powers can be difficult to determine. Such use may have a radicalising effect within affected communities and to that extent amount to a potential resource for challenger groups, either by providing recruits or by promoting toleration or support for their activities. In some instances, the state's use of such powers may be demonstrably outside the grey zone in the sphere of illegality; in such cases, law in the 'rule-of-law' state is implicated by a failure of reach – a failure to live up to a claimed ideological commitment to the rule of law.

In employing such powers, particularly when this is largely within minority communities, the state may engage in markedly negative messaging – an obvious example is the semi-random use of abrasive powers to stop, search and question. The messaging here is likely to be multi-layered and partly contradictory: within the visible state; between the visible and the covert state; between the state (visible or covert) and the state's challengers; between the state (visible or covert) and the societies from which challengers spring and between the societies in question and violent challengers. The literature identifies 'injustice frames' and 'rights frames' as enduring elements of social movement framing processes.[26] This points to potentially paradoxical views of law (often 'anti-terrorist' law) as a source of injustice and rights violation, but also potentially as contributing to defining movement goals, in that identifying an injustice or a violation as a *legal* failing may implicitly make the case for a *legal* 'fix'.

The hypothesis that emerges from this is that the dynamics of the operation of law in a violently conflicted 'rule-of-law' state are intimately linked to its operation in social conflict in general. 'Counter-terrorist' law and extra-legal 'counter-terrorist' initiatives may simultaneously repress and contribute to the mobilisation of the state's violent challengers. Some powers may have strong repressive value and contribute weakly to mobilisation; with others, the situation may be reversed. Strong mobilisation is likely to depend in part on the capacity of violent entrepreneurs to adapt and to maximise the uptake of available resources. Where harsh repression acts as a resource-provider which the entrepreneurs harness effectively in

[25] See D. Bonner, *Emergency Powers in Peacetime* (London: Sweet and Maxwell, 1985) and C. Campbell, *Emergency Law in Ireland, 1918–25* (Oxford: Oxford University Press, 1994).

[26] See R.D. Benford and D.A. Snow, 'Framing Processes and Social Movements: An Overview and Assessment' (2000) 26 *Annual Review of Sociology* 611–39 and 619.

building violent organisations, there could be said to be an element of reciprocity in the actions of the state and those of its violent challengers. Law is implicated in a complex process of messaging within state structures (visible and covert) and also involving challenger organisations and affected communities.

While the 'rule-of-law' state can never fully live up to its ideological commitments, law is likely to have a damping effect on conflict, both by restricting the degree to which the state can engage in harsh repression and also perhaps by restricting the actions of violent challengers. The latter effect may occur indirectly, where there is some degree of reciprocity between the actions of the state and its challengers, or more directly, where challenger organisations articulate some adherence to international humanitarian standards.

In the Campbell and Connolly research, this framework was applied and grounded using in-depth qualitative interviews with 16 former prisoners from Northern Ireland who were released early as part of the peace process. All had been imprisoned for offences linked to the main violent anti-state organisation in Northern Ireland, the Provisional Irish Republican Army (IRA). The study paid careful attention to methodology (within the limits inherent in any study of an underground organisation): the group (which incorporated a slice of IRA middle management [violent entrepreneurs]), included female and male respondents and individuals from urban and rural backgrounds. Interviews were transcribed and coded using the QSR NUD*ST qualitative data analysis package.

Analysis of the data focused on life patterns, particularly relating to involvement in political violence and on the impact of the state's 'counter-terrorist' strategies, many of which employed extensive emergency legislation. The findings germane to the present discussion can be grouped under three data headings: early experiences; patterns of mobilisation; and law, 'damping' and framing processes.

As regards early experiences, two patterns emerged: the first was a marked emphasis on the impact of British army mass house raids on their parents' homes, when the respondents were young children, particularly amongst urban respondents in the 1970s. The impact appears to have been compounded by subsequent mass use of indiscriminate stop and search powers.[27] The second pattern was that the incidence of forced

[27] For a study of perceptions of experience of such powers see R. McVeigh, '"*It's Part of Life Here...*": *The Security Forces and Harassment in Northern Ireland*' (Belfast: Committee on the Administration of Justice, 1994).

house movement as a result of the conflict, when respondents were at and around early teenage years, was much higher than could have been the case in the general population. In some cases, expulsion from the home was linked to collusion between elements in the security forces and rival quasi-ethnic factions. The accounts paint a picture of these early experiences not directly propelling the respondents into violent activism, but of having a radicalising effect – of cementing a sense of (quasi-ethnic) identity as a member of a victimised community and of contributing to a predisposition towards violent activism.

The second data heading covers patterns of mobilisation. Very clear lines emerged: most respondents had become involved in violence either in the early 1970s or the early to mid 1980s. This was true both of male and female respondents, casting doubt on simplistic gendered accounts of violent activism.[28] The early 1970s cluster corresponded with the introduction of internment without trial, the 'Bloody Sunday' killings by paratroopers, the effective end of the Northern Ireland Civil Rights Association (NICRA) and the peak of IRA violence. The 1980s cluster corresponded with the prison protests and fatal hunger strike by IRA prisoners and with a partial reverse in the decline of IRA violence. The qualitative data in this regard are easily 'triangulated' against quantitative data on levels of violence.

Accounts relating to the two big clusters of IRA recruitment had three elements in common, separating them from the cases of outliers: the first is that perceptions of egregious repression directed at a group with whom the respondents identified appeared to function as 'tipping factors'. Both clusters involved perceptions of prisoner ill-treatment and multiple deaths for which respondents blamed the state. The second is that, particularly in the case of the 1972–3 cluster, and to some extent in the 1981–3 group, the activities giving rise to these perceptions corresponded with the pattern of legal grey zones set out earlier: activities of doubtful or heavily contested compatibility with domestic and/or international law norms, where the reach of the law was limited.

The final data heading is 'law, damping and framing processes'. While Northern Ireland saw incidents of horrific violence, analysis of casualty figures nevertheless suggests greater discrimination in use of violence than

[28] For a critique of simplistic gendered accounts see, M. Alison, 'Women as Agents of Political Violence: Gendering Security' (2004) 35 *Security Dialogue* 447 and B.L. Nacos, 'The Portrayal of Female Terrorists in the Media: Similar Patterns in the News Coverage of Women in Politics and in Terrorism' (2005) 28 *Studies in Conflict and Terrorism* 435.

is the norm in many situations of insurgency.[29] There must therefore have been factors at work tending to limit both the use of violence by organisations such as the IRA and the use of force by the state. Respondent accounts paint a picture of communal support and/or toleration for IRA violence being at its greatest when state repression was at its highest, corresponding with a time when a commitment to legality on the part of the state was at its lowest. Support for the IRA is painted as declining both when repression decreased and when the IRA inflicted civilian casualties. The IRA appears to have been heavily reliant upon (and to that extent responsive to) a narrowish band of hardcore support that was unwilling to tolerate civilian casualties, particularly when repression wound down. Beyond this was a variable outer band within the broader Irish nationalist community that accorded varying degrees of toleration or neutrality. The picture that emerges is of a complex semaphore of triangular messaging around law, involving the state, violent challengers and affected communities. Severe repression and a retreat from legality appeared to send a message from the state to affected communities that the 'gloves are off', leading the communities in question to message support or toleration for anti-state violence. Security force behaviour meant that the IRA's employment of repression-based 'injustice' frames, appeared, in social movement terms, to have 'salience' and 'resonance' with the communities in question,[30] and therefore to become more effective.

When the state retreated from severe repression in the direction of legality and Weberian 'formal rationality', this seemed to send a message to affected communities that the 'gloves are on', prompting the communities to send a restraining message to the IRA. The dynamics portrayed are similar to those portrayed in security force discourse as 'the battle for hearts and minds'. Law therefore appeared to have an indirect damping effect on IRA violence, on the basis of an enforced reciprocity of sorts with the state. These limitations in any case resonated with the IRA's

[29] There is some disparity in statistics. The deaths of 911 security force members and 642 civilians are attributed to the IRA in D. McKittrick *et al.*, *Lost Lives: The Stories of the Men, Women and Children Who Died as a Result of the Northern Ireland Troubles* (Edinburgh and London: Mainstream Publishing, 2001), p. 1504. Malcolm Sutton's 'Index of Deaths' in relation to the conflict attributes 517 civilian and 1011 security force deaths to the IRA, online: Conflict and Politics in Northern Ireland at http://cain.ulst.ac.uk. McKittrick *et al.*, *Lost Lives*, pp. 1498–1500, list an overall total of 2051 civilian and 1012 security force deaths in the conflict.

[30] On the 'salience' and resonance of 'frames', see Benford and Snow, 'Framing Processes and Social Movements', 619.

portrayal of itself as fighting a 'war' (rather than a terrorist campaign) and the respondents' frequent invocation of the example of such national liberation movements as the ANC.

The second way in which law could be said to have a damping effect on IRA violence had to do with law's place in the process of conflict resolution. In their 'diagnostic framing' (identification of opponents' failings), respondents frequently cited the injustice of the old Northern Ireland state and the state's violent response to the law-based Civil Rights Movement. This focus on the nature of the problem as 'legal' appears to have expanded within the IRA and its political allies in Sinn Féin towards the end of the conflict, paving the way for an acceptance of law as a key part of a political solution, in a way that portrayed law as a vehicle for 'capturing' political gain. This shift was one factor in a process that eventually led the Northern Ireland peace process to an abandonment of violence.

The final point to emerge about respondent framing processes and law was their exclusionary dimension: while there was a heavy emphasis on the substance and the mobilising effects of state repression and legal failings on Irish nationalist communities, respondents' accounts of IRA failings tended to focus on 'mistakes' where civilians were killed or injured. But there were several areas of IRA activities that seemed to have entailed systematic violations of 'laws of war' standards. These included: the infliction of 'punishment' shootings and beatings on individuals accused of 'anti-social activities'; the use of bombs against commercial premises even if warnings were generally given; the targeting of civilian defence contractors and the ill-treatment of suspected informers. The rights violations that figured in respondent accounts were those that had instrumental value to the movement's political goals; others seemed generally invisible.

In the case of the state, there were pronounced temporal and institutional dimensions to the damping effect of law on its conflict-related behaviour. As regards the visible state, the picture was largely one of an increasing commitment to legality over time. For instance, abuse of prisoners was at its highest in the early 1970s and at its lowest (though still a problem) in the 1990s.[31] Likewise, emergency and anti-terrorist

[31] On the enduring problem in the 1990s see Report to the Government of the United Kingdom of the Visit to Northern Ireland Carried out by the European Committee for the Prevention of Torture and Inhuman or Degrading Treatment or Punishment (CPT), CPT/Inf (94) 17 [EN] and Report to the Government of the United Kingdom on the Visit to Northern Ireland Carried out by the European Committee for the Prevention of Torture and Inhuman or Degrading Treatment or Punishment (CPT), CPT/Inf (2001) 7. For earlier time periods see *Ireland* v. *UK* 25 Eur. Ct. H.R. (ser. A); Committee Against Torture, Consideration of

legislation became increasingly hedged with safeguards. As regards the covert state, the picture is more ambiguous. It is now clear that elements in the security force were engaged in collusion with loyalist paramilitary groups in assassinations throughout the conflict[32] and this collusion appears to have been largely unaffected by an increasing approximation of the visible state to formal rationality. On this analysis, law operates not as a guarantee of legality in a violently conflicted rule-of-law state; rather it operates to dampen the extent of illegality in which the state can be seen to engage.

The empirical data therefore tended to support the hypothesis set out above and to ground it in three respects. It suggests that indiscriminate mass use of relatively low-level powers such as those to stop and search and to search houses, can have radicalising effects by reinforcing a sense of membership of a victimised community, particularly in quasi-ethnic conflicts. This can help create a predisposition to violent activism. Second, it identifies 'tipping factors' to violent activism: (a) where there has been prior mass protest mobilisation, (b) organised at least in part around claims of prisoner ill-treatment, and (c) coinciding with multiple deaths for which the state is blamed. Typically, these occur in the legal grey zone of conflict in the 'rule-of-law' state. Third, it suggests that the damping effect of law on conflict can be explained at least partly by the need of violent challengers to heed their support base, imposing a system of reciprocity of sorts with the actions of the state.

Reports Submitted by State Parties under Article 19 of the Convention, Initial State Reports Due in 1990, Addendum United Kingdom, para. 67, UN Doc. CAT/C/9/Add.6; Committee Against Torture, Summary Record or 92nd Session, UN Doc. CAT/C/SR.92, para 61. See also other parts of the Summary Record at UN Doc. CAT/C/SR.91 and the UK's report at UN Doc. CAT/C/9/Add.6; UN Doc. CAT/C/XVI/CRP.1/Add.4; UN Docs. CAT/C/SR.354, 355 and 360 and CAT/C/44/Add.1.

[32] See Police Ombudsman for Northern Ireland, 'Statement by the Police Ombudsman for Northern Ireland on her Investigation into the Circumstances Surrounding the Death of Raymond McCord Junior and Related Matters', Statement under Section 62 of the Police (Northern Ireland) Act 1998, (22 January 2007), at www.policeombudsman.org//Publicationsuploads/BALLAST%20PUBLIC%20STATEMENT%2022–01-07%.20FINAL%20VERSION.pdf and Houses of the Oireachtas, Joint Committee on Justice, Equality, Defence and Women's Rights, 'Final Report on the Report of the Independent Commission of Inquiry into the Bombing of Kay's Tavern, Dundalk', November 2006 (Prn.A6/2026), at www.oireachtas.ie/documents/committees29thdail/committeereport2006/Kays_Tavern_Final_Rep.pdf. See also, *Finucane* v. *UK*, (2003) 37 EHRR 29 and *Shanaghan* v. *UK*, Appl. no. 37715/97.

III. Implications for Gross–Dyzenhaus

At first sight, the Gross–Dyzenhaus debate appears to map relatively neatly onto the contours of the dominant conversation described above (indeed it has been partly constitutive of it). Both contributors employ a top-down view of law; both call upon A.V. Dicey in support of their arguments (though the interpretation of each is somewhat different). While David Dyzenhaus is careful to assert that his concern is a normative one, neither writer aims to engage with the issue as an abstract theoretical puzzle: Oren Gross proposes an 'extra-legal' *model* which he clearly envisages as being applied in the real world, while Dyzenhaus insists on a consequentialist dimension to his arguments: 'the test of a good theory is ultimately its effects on practice'.[33] Each contributor also engages with the issue of 'messaging' around the law, suggesting that the debate may not be simply reducible to a philosophy of law exchange. This chapter aims not to enter into the exchange between Gross and Dyzenhaus per se; rather it proposes to assess the implications for each in turn of the socio-legal framework described above and thereby offer some pointers on the debate.

Dyzenhaus's core concern is to offer a substantive conception of the rule of law that can apply as a normative framework in states of emergency. Illegality in state action is seen as inconsistent with this conception; furthermore he explicitly points to the existence of legal 'grey holes' where procedural rights may be formally available to victims of governmental abuse, but which may be devoid of any substance. He also explicitly acknowledges the mutual benefits that can accrue from the juxtaposition of normative and socio-legal analyses such as that set out above[34] and his conception of 'grey holes' provides a normative account corresponding in part to the phenomenon described by Campbell and Connolly as 'legal grey zones'.

Both Dyzenhaus and Gross articulate a commitment to the maintenance of the rule of law. While Dyzenhaus sees illegality as inconsistent with the rule of law as normative framework, Gross suggests that extra-legal, counter-terrorist action by state operatives, may in certain circumstances, legitimately and formally go unpunished, and he sees this as paradoxically capable of contributing to the maintenance of the rule of law.

Dyzenhaus constructs his substantive conception of the rule of law partly by drawing on the jurisprudence of Commonwealth courts during

[33] D. Dyzenhaus, 'The Compulsion of Legality' (Chapter 2), this volume, p. 59.
[34] Dyzenhaus, Chapter 2, n. 10.

emergencies. He successfully demonstrates the courts' articulation of a concern with the rule of law that goes beyond mere procedural dimensions, although he does not demonstrate a complete doctrinal consistency in the courts' articulation, except at a very high level of abstraction. In terms of the socio-legal framework set out by Campbell and Connolly, what is important is that he demonstrates a sufficient degree of doctrinal basis for an *ideological* commitment to the rule of law by key elements of the state apparatus. This is consistent with law's having a relatively autonomous quality: an ideological commitment to the rule of law can open some ground for legal challenge, even if it is likely to be weighted in favour of powerful social forces. Dyzenhaus's focus on the courts as articulators of a substantive conception of the rule of law also explains his particular focus on messaging – mainly that between courts and the executive and parliament.[35]

Campbell and Connolly's framework, drawing on Tilly, suggested that law could have a damping effect on conflict because of the intimate link between the rule of law and liberal democracy. The implication of this analysis is that the thicker the conception of the rule of law, the greater the damping effect was likely to be. Dyzenhaus therefore could be said to provide a normative framework likely to enhance this damping.

The damping effect might manifest in the state's behaviour in such areas as limiting the arbitrariness of security force powers (for instance to stop and search); by ameliorating the interrogation regime; by reducing the use of lethal force and by a credible commitment to punish security force wrongdoers. In the case of the state's violent challengers, Dyzenhaus's formula might operate first, to keep political opportunity structures partly open and therefore to draw the challengers into a law-based discourse. Second, less use of indiscriminate abrasive powers, abusive interrogations and lethal force could lessen the process of radicalisation, and might therefore cut down on the recruits and communal toleration that provide a resource for challenger organisations. And third, a demonstrable commitment to the rule of law would seem likely to reduce the salience and resonance of 'injustice frames' and 'rights violation frames' canvassed by challenger organisations within communities affected by emergency conditions.

As regards Gross's contribution, the starting point is to locate the order of claim being made – normative framework, policy prescription,

[35] D. Dyzenhaus, *The Constitution of Law: Legality in a Time of Emergency* (Cambridge: Cambridge University Press, 2006), pp. 106 and 169.

socio-legal analysis or a combination of some or all?[36] Gross takes from Schmitt the idea that the emergency can never be entirely knowable, with the result that the law cannot provide for all circumstances in advance, creating a consequent need to act beyond the law, but he differs radically from Schmitt as regards the apparent normative disjunction involved (commitment to versus departure from rule of law). For Schmitt no problem exists, since liberal conceptions of the rule of law are untenable (indeed the exception proves the point). Gross however articulates a commitment to the rule of law, with the result that his analysis becomes in part an attempt to address this apparent disjunction by developing a normative account of extra-legality consistent with the rule of law in a democratic state. He then draws on Dicey in addressing this normative conundrum (discussed further below).

But Gross does not restrict himself to abstract theoretical inquiry: he is concerned to prove the necessity for taking extra-legal measures by invoking the 'ticking bomb' hypothetical.[37] He also pays considerably more attention to the question of messaging and law than does Dyzenhaus and he labels the outcome of his project as a 'model'.[38] Gross's analysis can therefore be considered as to have elements of normative inquiry, socio-legal analysis and policy recommendation.

Gross's discussion of messaging draws on Meir Dan-Cohen's work on the criminal justice system.[39] For Dan-Cohen, the system involves two separate sets of messages: one directed at the general public (conduct rules) and one directed at officials who make decisions with respect to actions taken by members of the public (decision rules). For instance, the prohibition on torture constitutes a conduct rule, while provisions governing the decision when prosecutions for torture are to be mounted constitute decision rules. Where a security operative can simultaneously access both sets of messages, conditions of 'low acoustic separation' are said

[36] See, O. Gross, 'Chaos and Rules: Should All Responses to Violent Crises Be Constitutional?' (2003) 112 *Yale Law Journal* 1011; O. Gross, 'Are Torture Warrants Warranted? Pragmatic Absolutism and Official Disobedience' (2004) 88 *Minnesota Law Review* 1481, O. Gross, 'Torture and the Ethics of Responsibility' (2007) 3 *Law, Culture and the Humanities* 35 and O. Gross and F. Ní Aoláin, *Law in Times of Crisis: Emergency Powers in Theory and Practice* (Cambridge: Cambridge University Press, 2006).

[37] See O. Gross, 'Chaos and Rules', 1097–8.

[38] O. Gross, 'Extra-Legality and the Ethic of Political Responsibility' (Chapter 3), this volume, pp. 66, 73–4.

[39] See Gross's discussion in 'Are Torture Warrants Warranted', 1531, n. 185, and Gross, Chapter 3, pp. 73–4, drawing on M. Dan-Cohen, 'Decision Rules and Conduct Rules: On Acoustic Separation in Criminal Law' (1984) 97 *Harvard Law Review* 625.

to obtain. This creates an environment in which the operative may decide to ignore a particular conduct rule on the basis of an accurate assessment that invocation of the decision rule will result in non-prosecution. Gross recognises a potential problem here, but feels that uncertainty of outcome as to the application of the decision rule will be sufficient deterrent to routine non-compliance with the conduct rule.

A broader concept of messaging would see that dissonance between the conduct rules (torture is prohibited) and the decision rules (there may be no sanction for infraction) itself sends a message which may be particularly significant in communities experiencing the brunt of the state's counter-terrorist actions. Where it was publicly acknowledged that a lawbreaker was not to be punished (as in Gross's model), this would seem likely to enhance the salience and resonance within affected communities of the 'injustice frames' and 'rights violation frames' articulated by violent challenger organisations and therefore the viability of such groups' framing processes.

Experience in Northern Ireland was that the longer the conflict persisted the greater the commitment of the visible state to legality in 'counter-terrorist' measures. As regards the invisible state, the picture was somewhat different in that, as noted above, elements in the security forces continued to collude in assassinations with pro-state paramilitary groups through the conflict. On Gross's account, therefore, the prime actions that would fall to be dealt with under his extra-legal model in the Northern Ireland example would be assassinations and inhuman treatment/torture of prisoners, supporting Dyzenhaus's contention that the sphere of extra-legality was that of the 'unlegalisable'.[40] But the empirical data in the Campbell and Connolly study suggested that perceptions of state involvement in prisoner abuse and multiple deaths were particularly implicated in violent mobilisation, acting as tipping factors for violent activists, and enhancing degrees of support or toleration for violent challengers within communities most affected by 'counter-terrorist' policies. Gross's formula therefore brings particular risks of contributing to radicalisation and ultimately to violent mobilisation by enhancing access to and uptake of these resources by violent entrepreneurs. Since Gross relies upon the 'ticking bomb' hypothetical rather than empirical data to support his argument, his model overlooks the real problem here. As regards 'damping' and the state's behaviour, the effect could also be expected to be reduced by a

[40] Dyzenhaus, Chapter 2, Part VII.

model that made prior provisions for extra-legality. Such damping might evaporate entirely where recourse to acknowledged extra-legal action became routine, though Gross's insistence on a formal commitment to the rule of law would seem likely to mean that some damping effect would remain.

This raises the question of how credible Gross's model is, not simply as normative framework but as a prescriptive (policy) device? There may be a temporal dimension here. Gross correctly identifies the dilemmas faced by a state when it is forced to confront a legacy of illegal action by its agents committed in the context of violent conflict, in a situation in which some ideological commitment to the rule of law must be articulated: to punish, to mitigate punishment, to pardon? But were the state to publicly employ the device *seriatim* during conflict, with consequent regular mitigation or pardoning (and presumably some punishment), the resulting messaging seems almost certain to have a cumulative effect producing a growing lack of adherence by state officials to legal standards and therefore undermining a claimed ideological commitment to the rule of law. If the law enforcement official who has acted illegally is assumed to be a rational actor (as the violent challenger is), why publicly admit the illegality and risk punishment? Surely a self-interested actor is more likely to rely upon a strategy of silence and obfuscation, on the basis that this is less likely to result in punishment and more likely to result in reward (such as promotion or an official award). Empirical support for the course of action recommended by Gross is thin on the ground: the general pattern is that illegal behaviour of the kind in question falls into legal grey zones of denial, obfuscation and cover-up. Post-conflict however, the situation is likely to be different: Gross's dilemmas are the classic quandaries of 'transitional justice', at which point Gross's analysis collapses into that discourse. The official lawbreaker may be incentivised to 'come clean' by the payoff of an amnesty delivered through some truth-recovery process. This aspect of Gross's argument may therefore work better retrospectively than as a prospective device.

To return to the question of the apparent normative disjunction with which Gross is faced and its possible implications for the question of violent mobilisation, Gross draws upon Dicey to demonstrate how a commitment to the rule of law can yet square with the condoning of illegal actions by state officials,[41] but this may risk distorting what Dicey is saying about action

[41] Gross, Chapter 3, pp. 71 and 79.

in situations of emergency beyond that mandated by statutory powers. The point can be illustrated by briefly locating Dicey's contribution in the context of developing common law doctrines of non-statutory powers to deal with violent social conflict.

In medieval times, the power to wage war within the kingdom (or to impose 'martial law') was a prerogative one, recognised by law, and expressed in the institution of the 'Court of the Constable and the Marshal'.[42] The power is sometimes referred to as a 'common law prerogative', but this title probably only serves to obscure the issue. By the end of the seventeenth century the royal prerogative to impose martial law within the kingdom was generally viewed as being defunct, primarily as a result of the Petition of Right 1628. This prerogative power therefore seemed unavailable to deal with the emergence of a round of class-based social conflict early in the nineteenth century associated with the beginnings of the industrial revolution (although it is arguable that some prerogative public order powers subsisted in England and that the existence of prerogative powers outside England remained unaffected). To fill the perceived gap, a separate stream of 'common law' non-statutory powers emerged with judicial support. This also had ancient roots (going back to the '*posse commitatus*'), and relied on notions of 'repelling force by force', a formulation that proved extremely malleable. This malleability was manifest when the doctrine was exported to the colonies in the nineteenth century as a 'martial law' variant, distinguishable from its prerogative rival and was again employed during the Boer War.[43] Martial law was then imported to what was viewed in British constitutional law as metropolitan UK to deal with insurrections in Ireland in 1916 and in 1920–1[44] (though earlier constitutional divergence in Ireland meant that some still supported the

[42] On the development of prerogative and common law theories of martial law see the symposium at 1902 LQR: W.S. Holdsworth, 'Martial Law Historically Considered' (1902) 18 *Law Quarterly Review* 117; H.E. Richards, 'Martial Law' (1902) 18 *Law Quarterly Review* 133; C. Dodd, 'Case of Marais' (1902) 18 *Law Quarterly Review* 143 and F. Pollock, 'What is Martial Law' (1902) 18 *Law Quarterly Review* 152. See also Campbell, *Emergency Law in Ireland, 1918–25*; S.G. Greer, 'Military Intervention in Civil Disturbances: The Legal Basis Reconsidered' (1983) *Public Law* 573 and J.V. Capua, 'The Early History of Martial Law in England From the Fourteenth Century to the Petition of Right' (1977) 36 *Cambridge Law Journal* 152–73.

[43] See *Ex parte Marais* [1902] AC 109, and *Tilonko* v. *Attorney General of Natal* [1907] AC 93.

[44] *R* v. *Allen* [1921] 2 IR 241, *R (Garde and Others)* v. *Strickland* [1921] 2 IR 317, *R (Ronayne and Mulcahy)* v. *Strickland* [1921] IR 333, *Higgins* v. *Willis* [1921] 2 IR 386, *Re Clifford and O'Sullivan* [1921] 2 AC 570.

alternative, older 'prerogative theory').[45] It ('common law' martial law) was also applied in India in 1919.

It was this common law stream of jurisprudence that Dicey was drawing upon in his claim that he was merely articulating the law as it then stood. This helps to explain his statement that 'martial law . . . is unknown to the law of England',[46] one that Simpson points out is quite misleading[47] (a point that Dyzenhaus also acknowledges).[48] While the older prerogative theory, which corresponded more closely with continental models of martial law, was now 'unknown', some of the same juridical effect could be achieved under the common law theory. The point of this brief historical excursion is to demonstrate that Dicey's central concern is not with a normative reconciliation of illegality (or extra-legality) in emergency conditions with the rule of law. Rather, his project is to render *legal* actions taken during insurrection without statutory mandate, that would otherwise be illegal, and this legality was effected by invoking such notions as the 'common law right of the Crown and its servants to repel force by [reasonable] force.'

While Dyzenhaus is largely celebratory of Dicey's concern with legality and while the latter writer's test of what might be permissible under 'common law' martial law is more demanding than that suggested by some of his contemporaries,[49] it could also be argued that what Dicey provides is a gloss of legality, devoid of substance, typical of what Dyzenhaus describes as legal 'grey holes'.[50] While Dicey cannot be blamed for subsequent purported reliance upon his theories, the historical record provides ample evidence of conflict-escalation correlating with deployment of variants of the common law theory: in Ireland in 1920–1 the executions and reprisals that characterised martial law can be correlated to a rise in insurgent effectiveness.[51] Martial law in India saw the Amritsar

[45] Cf. *Egan* v. *Macready* [1921] I IR 265 and *R (Childers)* v. *Adjutant-General of the Provisional Forces* [1923] I IR 5. See also, Campbell, *Emergency Law in Ireland, 1918–25*. The Petition of Right is thought not to have applied to Ireland.

[46] A.V. Dicey, *An Introduction to the Study of The Law of the Constitution* (London: Macmillan, 1885), p. 294.

[47] A.W.B. Simpson, *Human Rights at the End of Empire: Britain and the Genesis of the European Convention* (Oxford: Oxford University Press, 2001), p. 60.

[48] Chapter 2, p. 50.

[49] Contrast Dicey's view as set out in the *Law and the Constitution* with the more expansive views set out by Pollock, 'What is Martial Law' and Richards, 'Martial Law'.

[50] Dyzenhaus, *The Constitution of Law*, pp. 3 and 42.

[51] Campbell, *Emergency Law in Ireland, 1918–25*, Graph B, p. 26 and pp. 29–38.

massacre (1919).[52] When the troops were deployed in Northern Ireland in 1969, those providing legal advice to the Secretary of State for Defence again (confidentially) defined the army's non-statutory powers in largely Dicean terms.[53] Although there was no formal proclamation of martial law, the local GOC (General Officer Commanding) took it upon himself to impose a non-statutory curfew that resulted in a number of civilian deaths, in an episode that is generally considered to have been one of the key escalatory contributions to the initial phase of the conflict.[54] The salient point is that the destructiveness of these various episodes of military intervention is not a chance phenomenon, but is directly related to the radical open-endedness of the common law theory, an open-endedness flowing from a highly elastic notion of legality.

Two final points can be briefly made about the implications of this historical material for the Gross–Dyzenhaus debate. The first is that Dyzenhaus's survey of common law jurisprudence in relation to states of emergence might benefit from a greater attention to the case law from Ireland under British rule. The second is that while the political and the legal prerogative are clearly distinguishable, they are also linked. Both Gross and Dyzenhaus pay careful attention to the Lockean conception of the former, but ignore the latter. This may be an omission worth remedying, particularly in view of the apparent revival of prerogative powers in the public order sphere in the UK in the 1980s.[55]

IV. What's new? Elements of a legal research agenda on the 'war on terror'

It might be claimed that the 'war on terror' is a completely new phenomenon,[56] either because of the novelty of the terrorist threat or because

[52] For a discussion of the legal issues surrounding the Amritsar massacre, see Simpson, *Human Rights at the End of Empire*, pp. 64–6.

[53] MOD Signal Message Form, MOD (Army) [from CGS] to NORIRELAND [to GOC], 6 December 1968, DEFE 24/882 PRONI; Attorney-General to Secretary of State for Defence, 13 December 1968, DEFE 24/882, PRO Kew; 'Military Aid to the Civil Power in Northern Ireland', Chief of the Defence Staff to Secretary of State, 9 December 1968, DEFE 24/883 PRO Kew and 'Military Aid to the Civil Authority in Northern Ireland', Attorney-General to Secretary of State for Defence, 13 December 1968, DEFE 24/882 PRO Kew.

[54] C. Campbell and I. Connolly, 'A Model for the "War against Terrorism"?: Military Intervention and the 1970 Falls Curfew' (2003) 30 *Journal of Law and Society* 341.

[55] *Ex parte Northumbria Police Authority* [1989] 1 QB 26 (CA).

[56] See K. Jayasuriya, 'Struggle over Legality in the Midnight Hour' (Chapter 15), this volume, p. 361.

the extent of US global hegemony has produced a radical shift in legal norms. If so, much of the discussion of law's role in other conflict sites might be irrelevant.

This chapter argues that while the current 'war' has novel features, variants of the legal analytical toolkits developed in earlier conflicts involving 'rule-of-law' states can usefully be applied. To return briefly to the question of hegemony, I have argued elsewhere that the British experience in Northern Ireland provides some pointers on the tendency of international law to accommodate itself to the requirements of powerful states, particularly at the outbreak of insurgency.[57] That example also suggests that international law displays resilience: the longer a conflict persists the greater the extent to which norms are likely to 'bite' and the post-conflict environment creates a context in which retrospective judgment of the state's behaviour is likely to be considerably harsher than that evident while violence persisted. Britain's position as former global hegemon and colonial power, coupled with its assumption of the role of 'vicarious hegemon' in the current conflict, may offer particularly valuable pointers for assessment of the legal implications of the current role of the US.

If the world at the time of the Iraq invasion had a uni-polar appearance, captured in Hubert Vedrine's depiction of the US as an 'hyperpower',[58] the effects of the Iraq debacle and the general quagmire of the 'war on terror' have been to highlight the limits of effective US power: the world increasingly appears uni-multipolar. While the exercise of hegemony may lead to some degree of norm-shift, there are complex reasons why strong countervailing pressures towards norm-compliance are likely to manifest.[59] At the international law level, therefore, a continuing retreat from legality in the exercise of hegemony is unlikely to prove a viable option. The record of the legal systems of democratic states involved in the 'war

[57] See C. Campbell, '"Wars on Terror" and Vicarious Hegemons' (2005) 54 *International and Comparative Law Quarterly* 321.

[58] H. Védrine and D. Moisi, *France in an Age of Globalisation* (Washington DC: Brookings Institute, 2001).

[59] M. Byers and G. Nolte (eds.), *United States Hegemony and the Foundations of International Law* (Cambridge: Cambridge University Press, 2003); M. Byers, 'Preemptive Self-defence: Hegemony, Equality and Strategies of Legal Change' (2003) 11 *Journal of Political Philosophy* 171; N. Krisch, 'International Law in Times of Hegemony: Unequal Power and the Shaping of the International Legal Order' (2005) 11 *European Journal of International Law* 369; and C. Bell, C. Campbell and F. Ní Aoláin, 'The Battle for Transitional Justice: Hegemony, Iraq and International Law', in K. McEvoy, J. Morison and G. Anthony (eds.), *Judges, Transition and Human Rights Cultures: Essays in Honour of Stephen Livingstone* (Oxford: Oxford University Press, 2006).

on terror' suggests that parallel processes are identifiable in the domestic legal system: the 'shock' effect of the eruption of conflict may create an environment conducive to a governmental retreat from legality, but with the passage of time, the bite of the law increases. There are good reasons, therefore, for suggesting that the exercise of hegemonic power need not invalidate the applicability of analytical frameworks such as that set out above.

Rather than representing a completely new phenomenon, the global nature of the 'war' points to the viability of the transnational transposition of analyses of law's relative autonomy and of the importance of conflict-related legal claims-making in democratic states. This claims-making frequently originates in peace and human rights-oriented social movement organisations. For example, there is a clear pattern in both the US and the UK of increasing judicial activism in the face of governmental claims, putting limits on the extent to which the threat of terrorism can be invoked to trump due process and rights-based claims.[60] Transnational patterns are also emerging of the use of law as a shield in conflict-related criminal claims by peace activists or conscientious objectors in the UK,[61] the Republic of Ireland[62] and Germany.[63]

The use of 'extraordinary renditions' by the US, which appears to have involved use of the territory and/or airspace of several European states, has

[60] See: *Hamdi* v. *Rumsfeld*, 124 S.Ct. 2633 (2004); *Hamdi* v. *Rumsfeld* (03-6696) 542 U.S. 507 (2004), and *Hamdan* v. *Rumsfeld*, 548 U.S. (2006). Regarding the 29 June 2007 Supreme Court decision on writs of certiorari, online, see Supreme Court of United States www.supremecourtus.gov/orders/courtorders/062907pzor.pdf. In the UK, see: *A and Others* v. *Secretary of State for the Home Department; X and another* v. *Secretary of State for the Home Department* [2005] 3 All ER 169; *R (On the Application of Al-Skeini and others)* v. *Secretary of State for Defence*, House of Lords Opinions of the Lords of Appeal for Judgment in the Cause, [2007] UKHL 26, [2007] All ER (D) 106 (Jun), (Approved judgment), (13 June 2007); *Secretary of State for the Home Department (Appellant)* v. *JJ and others (FC) (Respondents)*, House of Lords Opinions of the Lords of Appeal for Judgment in the Cause [2007] UKHL 45 (31 October 2007).

[61] R. Norton-Taylor, 'Protesters at RAF Base Guilty of Damaging US Vehicles' *Guardian* (7 July 2007), online: www.guardian.co.uk/antiwar/story/0,,2120842,00.html and C. Dyer, 'Freed Activists Accused of US Bomb Carrier Damage Face Retrial' *Guardian* (16 September 2006), online: Guardian Unlimited www.guardian.co.uk/antiwar/story/0,,1873846,00.html.

[62] See 'Not Guilty Verdict in Third Trial of Anti-War Activists', *Irish Times*, (26 July 2006).

[63] See Ruling of the 2nd Wehrdienstsenat (Military Service Division) of the Bundesverwaltungsgerich – BverwG – German Federal Administrative Court (Supreme Court) of June 21, 2005 – BverwG 2 WD 12.04 (English translation, p. 5). The English translation can be found online: Lawyers' Committee on Nuclear Policy www.lcnp.org/global/Germanrefusercase.pdf.

contributed in particular to a novel geography of legal claims-making, with law being deployed as a sword to challenge irregular rendition in Italy[64] and Germany,[65] and with EU[66] and Council of Europe[67] mechanisms being employed to challenge apparent US practice. Even if a significant proportion of this claims-making ultimately fails, its overall effect is likely to be to dampen the behaviour of the US and the UK.

As regards terrorist and insurgent groups involved in the conflation of conflicts that is the 'war on terror', the employment of the analytical devices set out above may help to identify important differences between these various groups and differences between them and the violent groups that featured in earlier conflicts. For instance, the mobilising structures and framing processes of Jihadi groups appear much more diffuse than

[64] See D. Bhat and agencies, 'Italian Judge Orders First "Rendition" Trial of CIA Agents' *Times Online* (17 February 2007), online: Times Online www.timesonline.co.uk/tol/news/world/europe/article1395637.ece. The trial was subsequently stopped, on 18 June, pending a Constitutional Court ruling due in October 2007. See, M. Tran and agencies, 'Judge Freezes CIA Kidnap Trial', *Guardian* (18 June 2007), online: Guardian Unlimited www.guardian.co.uk/international/story/0,,2105801,00.html.

[65] The Complaint against Rumsfeld and others was lodged with the German Federal Prosecutor on 14 November 2006. For a translation of part of the Complaint, see Center for Constitutional Rights online: http://ccrjustice.org/files/Introduction%20to%20the%202006%20German%20Complaint.pdf. On 27 April 2007 the German Federal Prosecutor decided not to proceed with an investigation. See Center for Constitutional Rights online: http://ccrjustice.org/ourcases/current-cases/german-war-crimes-complaint-against-donald-rumsfeld%2C-et-al.

[66] See European Parliament Temporary Committee on the Alleged Use of European Countries by the CIA for the Transport and Illegal Detention of Prisoners, 'Draft Report on the Alleged Use of European Countries by the CIA for the Transport and Illegal Detention of Prisoners' Mr Giovanni Claudio Fava, Rapporteur, Final (2006/2200 (INI)), (PE 382.246v02-00), 30 January 2007; 'Draft Report on the Alleged Use of European Countries by the CIA for the Transport and Illegal Detention of Prisoners' Mr Giovanni Claudio Fava, Rapporteur, Provisional 2006/2200 (INI) 24 November 2006, and Amended Draft Report (PE 382.44v02/00), 8 January 2007.

[67] See, 'Secret Detentions and Illegal Transfers of detainees involving Council of Europe Member States: Second Report', Committee on Legal Affairs and Human Rights, Rapporteur D. Marty (11 June 2007), Council of Europe document 11302 rev; 'Opinion on the International Legal Obligations of Council of Europe Member States in Respect of Secret Detention Facilities and Inter-State Transport of Prisoners', European Commission For Democracy Through Law (Venice Commission), (2006), Council of Europe document CDL-AD(2006)009, and 'Alleged Secret Detentions and Unlawful Inter-state Transfers of Detainees Involving Council of Europe Member States' Report, Committee on Legal Affairs and Human Rights, Rapporteur D. Marty (2006), Council of Europe document 10957.

those of the IRA,[68] but other nationalist elements in the Iraqi insurgency may employ structures and framing processes similar to those of the latter.

This points to a complex, challenging (and pluralist) legal research agenda: what conceptions of law figure in the prognostic framing of Jihadi and other violent groups – divine, domestic, international? To what extent do claimed legal failings by the US and the UK in Iraq and elsewhere figure in their diagnostic framing? To what extent do legal grey zone activities in the 'war on terror' act as resource providers for Jihadi and other groups by promoting radicalisation in those affected by the activities? What are the implications of the extensive litigation strategies engaged in by Guantánamo detainees? As regards the prospects of peacemaking, if a shift from violent activism to political challenge would require changes to challenger groups' framing processes, mobilising structures and the political opportunity structures they face, what legal engineering would be likely to promote such shifts?

This chapter points to the viability of multi-layered legal research on the 'war on terror' involving a variety of legal sub-disciplines. It recognises the importance of a normative approach, but advocates juxtaposing this with grounded socio-legal analysis. This is not to claim that such a multi-layered approach offers the holy grail of a unified theory of law's role in violent conflict, much less a celebratory unified account. Some sub-disciplinary disjunctions are likely to remain and law is always likely to be beset by ambivalences. In part, at least, the analysis may point to law's operating as one potential self-correcting mechanism of the liberal state, with the self-correction springing from the damping effect on conflict of legal claims-making.

[68] See J. Burke, *Al-Qaeda: The True Story of Islam* (London: Penguin, 2004) and P. Sutton and S. Vertigans, 'Islamic "New Social Movements"? Radical Islam, Al-Qa'ida and Social Movement Theory' (2006) 11 *Mobilization* 101–15.

PART FOUR

Prospective constraints on state power

9

Emergency strategies for prescriptive legal positivists: anti-terrorist law and legal theory

TOM CAMPBELL

The measures recently introduced in many jurisdictions in response to the perceived menace of terrorism have sparked controversies not only over civil rights and the limits of toleration, but also over the implications of these measures for legal theory and the relevance of legal theory to the evaluation of such responses to terrorist acts. How should we conceive emergency strategies in legal terms if they appear to abrogate law? What has legal theory to offer by way of principled support for, or criticism of, the rights-restricting policies commonly prompted by such horrendous events as 9/11, the London underground atrocity and the unending suicide bombing in Iraq and elsewhere?

While it cannot be assumed that what we are dealing with here is, as yet, so novel as to mark a distinctive new set of issues for political philosophy and legal theory, neither can it be assumed that we are not faced by a distinctive scenario that calls for radical and controversial measures that do not fit neatly in to our existing legal theories. Current forms of defending and promoting liberal democracy have been fundamentally shaped in a period marked by responses to genocidal and racist states, such as Nazi Germany and apartheid South Africa. These models may not be entirely suitable for dealing with the contemporary concerns about non-state terrorism, where the focus is on preventing freelance or loosely organised terrorism,[1] as much as on the actions of abhorrent states. However, non-state terrorism is not a new phenomenon in human history

Michael Buckingham provided invaluable research assistance with the preparation of this chapter.

[1] A quick glance at Division 102 of the Australian Criminal Code Act 1995 (Cth), which is about 'terrorist organisations' illustrates this point. There, 'terrorist organisation' is defined to mean:

(a) an organisation that is directly or indirectly engaged in, preparing, planning, assisting in or fostering the doing of a terrorist act (whether or not a terrorist act occurs);

and the problem of how to deal with perceived threats to the survival of governments, of states and of peoples, without dismantling liberal democratic institutions, are familiar enough not to catch legal theorists by surprise.[2]

The lessons of history are that suspensions of fundamental civil liberties are commonly the result of the political self-interest of rulers and, even during full-scale war, are usually neither effective nor necessary. It is sensible, therefore, to fully explore the option of dealing with terrorism within states at peace through the application of relatively minor amendment of existing law and legal process. This would be 'business as usual', not because laws and policies would remain unchanged, but because such changes would not trigger measures that present a considerable threat to civil liberties, for it is how to deal with such threats that is, perhaps, the real 'emergency' precipitated by recent terrorist activity, as far as legal theory is concerned.

Overall, this is my preferred strategy and one that can readily be brought within the traditional concerns of legal theory, but there are grounds for adopting a more radical approach, many of which are related to technological development. One such ground is the heightened vulnerability of technologically dependent societies to terrorist attack. Another is the increasing technical capacity of those whose purpose is indiscriminate destruction without regard to their own safety. A third is the inability of highly technologised military forces to eliminate terrorism with the same degree of success as they can defeat armies. These developments give rise to legitimate fears of economic disasters and social disintegration which call, amongst other things, for the aggressive deployment of available communication technologies to anticipate and prevent terrorist acts. The dangers of these techniques being abused is very real, but it is interesting to note that few of those who criticise current anti-terrorist measures, as being

(b) an organisation that is specified by the regulations for the purpose of this paragraph (see subsections (2), (3) and (4)).

To date, the following are just an example of the organisations that have been specified by regulations to be terrorist organisations: Al Qa'ida Islamic Army; Jemaah Islamiyah; Lashkar I Jhangvi; Palestinian Islamic Jihad. A complete list can be found in Part 2 of the Criminal Code Regulations 2002 (Cth).

2 Consider the 'sedition', 'treachery', 'sabotage', 'mutiny' and 'unlawful associations' legislation introduced at the beginning of World War I, e.g., in Australia, the Crimes Act 1914 (Cth), s.24D, s.24AA, s.24AB, s.25, s.30A. For a brief discussion of the placement of state and non-state terrorism in history see L.K. Donohue, 'Terrorism and Counter Terrorism Discourse' in V.V. Ramraj, M. Hor and K. Roach (eds.), *Global Anti-Terrorism Law and Policy* (Cambridge: Cambridge University Press, 2006), pp. 16–18.

disproportionate responses to terrorist events, actually rule out the utilisation of some 'extreme measures' in relation to current norms of privacy and civil liberty. It is also sensible, therefore, to speculate about how legal theory conceives and evaluates such radical political alternatives.

With these caveats, this chapter seeks to contribute to the debate on legal theory and anti-terrorism by exploring the outlines of a legal positivist approach to emergency policies both with respect to the conceptualisation of the issues and regarding how best to deal with the development and abuse of the 'emergency' powers thought to be appropriate for today's security problems. I do this by concentrating on the role that formal 'states of emergency' might play in controlling and directing anti-terrorist measures.[3] The chapter explores, in Part I, the compatibility of such states of emergency with my reading of legal positivism and then considers whether the reasons that underpin support for legal positivism might, in these circumstances, justify certain departures from traditional civil liberties. The competing and complementary roles of parliaments and courts in the process of initiating and controlling states of emergency within a positivist framework are discussed in Part II. In Part III, I take up the Gross–Dyzenhaus debate and discuss whether we should adopt the 'extra-legal' or the 'legality' model to accommodate legitimate anti-terror measures.

My conclusion here is that the Dyzenhaus departures from conventional positivist strict separation of powers (which he calls 'constitutional positivism'[4]) may be justified, but not in quite the same way and not for all, and perhaps not for the major, reasons that Dyzenhaus himself suggests. I accept, for instance, that there may be justification for special court procedures to deal with cases where all the evidence cannot be made public or available to all the parties involved or their lawyers, for security reasons. My rationale for making this compromise and remaining within the bounds of legality differs from that of Dyzenhaus, who is concerned to enable the deployment of a substantive form of the rule of law in order to modify or draw critical political attention to the legislative decisions of parliaments. In contrast, my objective in acceding to special court rules is to give courts the opportunity to decide the cases in point in accordance with formally good positivist law, and to do so in a context where such courts have already accepted that there is a state of emergency legally in existence according to formal standards that satisfy a positivist model of

[3] Much of Part I of this chapter coincides with the approach of K. Roach, 'Ordinary Laws for Emergencies and Democratic Derogation from Rights' (Chapter 10), this volume.

[4] D. Dyzenhaus, *The Constitution of Law: Legality in a Time of Emergency* (Cambridge: Cambridge University Press, 2006), p. 10.

the rule of law rather than a relatively unfettered executive directive. This, I argue, is the best legal (as distinct from political) protection that courts can provide for civil liberties in times of terrorist crisis.

I. Prescriptive legal positivism and the rule of law

In this chapter I adopt a somewhat broader version of what David Dyzenhaus terms 'political positivism'[5] which I call 'prescriptive legal positivism' (PLP). PLP is within the Benthamite tradition which I interpret, in part, as setting forth a conceptual scheme suitable for expressing certain moral views concerning what sort of law and what sort of associated political system, are best suited to sustain human well-being in as fair and democratic way as possible.[6] PLP is the theory that government has the best chance of serving the common good and the interests of the vast majority of individuals when that government is conducted through law and that law is conceived in formal terms as authoritative rules that are expressed in general, clear, specific and prospective terms which can be understood and applied without drawing on controversial moral or speculative judgments. The benefits that derive from such formally good systems of law include efficiency with respect to social outcomes, transparency and accountability with respect to the exercise of authority, decisiveness with respect to definitive resolution of disputes, clarity in the process of political decision-making, the liberty that comes from knowing what is and what is not permitted or required of us, and the political empowerment of citizens in their joint exercise of democratic sovereignty involving the choice of such rules.[7] PLP articulates all this in a legal positivist version of the rule of law, the focus of which is on the instrumental benefits of formally good law and the institutions that go with it, including the separation of powers between lawmaking, executive administration and judicial power, and the

5 *Ibid.*, p. 68: 'Thus positivists wish to avoid any device which will allow judges to claim that they are interpreting the law when they are in fact what they are doing to is substitute their own judgment about the good from the legislative one. I will call this tradition political positivism to distinguish it from it conceptual relation in the work of H. L. A. Hart and Joseph Raz'.

6 T. Campbell, *The Legal Theory of Ethical Positivism* (Aldershot: Ashgate, 1996) and T. Campbell, *Prescriptive Legal Positivism* (London: UCL Press, 2004).

7 This differs significantly from the account of legal positivism presented by D. Dyzenhaus, 'The Compulsion of Legality' (Chapter 2) in this volume. PLP ascribes a prima facie moral justification for political authority that is activated through rule-governance so that some aspects of law's moral authority are not contingently tied to the content of the law. Law does, therefore, have some moral authority that is independent of its content.

intrinsic benefits that such a system brings with respect to the exercise of the right of self and collective determination. For this last reason, PLP is sometimes referred to as 'democratic positivism'.[8]

This quite thin conception of the rule of law, which concentrates on good form rather than good substance, intentionally offers little direct guidance with respect to the proper content of law, which it regards as a matter for civil society, elected parliaments and democratic governments. For those who hope for more from a concept of legality, there is a constant temptation in legal theory and in the practice of politics to expand 'the rule-of-law' concept to contain norms such as substantive equality, material justice and various fundamental rights so that good form can be combined with good substance in a more pervasive constitutional bedrock. This would now appear to be orthodox contemporary 'constitutionalism'. PLP denies that this fatter version of the rule of law, or at least some of its uses, is a desirable ingredient in the model of government through law because it undermines the instrumental benefits of the rule of positive law and leads to the violation of the separation of powers on which many of the institutions and benefits of democracy depend. What the modern natural lawyer views as part of the essence of legality as a moral notion entrusted to courts for its implementation, the legal positivist views as leading to a morally regrettable judicialising of politics and a serious long-term diminution of democratic process.[9]

Enter the 'war on terror'. How does a prescriptive legal positivist respond? If the rule of law is purely formal, has PLP any basis for objecting to formally good laws, democratically endorsed, that diminish, say, the right to a fair trial or the doctrine of habeas corpus? Or, if combating terrorism is obstructed by governance through positive law, should the latter, in some circumstances, give way to the former, giving much greater scope to official discretion in the sphere of civil liberties, so that government may better serve the general interest in security? On the other hand, is the current terrorist 'crisis' perhaps a good example both of the fundamental importance of having a system of formally good positive law, especially in times of turmoil, and of the relative ineffectiveness of moral rights-based judicial review when major rights-threatening emergencies

[8] T. Campbell, *Prescriptive Legal Positivism: Law, Rights and Democracy* (London: UCL Press, 2004), ch. 14.

[9] J. Waldron, *Law and Disagreement* (Oxford: Oxford University Press, 1999); T. Campbell, J. Goldsworthy and A. Stone (eds.), *Protecting Rights Without a Bill of Rights* (Aldershot: Ashgate, 2006).

arise, either because judicial review fails to rein in panicking majorities and opportunistic politicians (its main theoretical justification) and/or because it has to be put to one side because it inhibits effective protection of life and property (as Oren Gross argues in Chapter 3)?

I enter this debate by exploring the extent to which formal 'states of emergency' are compatible with PLP, adopting this point of entry on account of the potential benefits of introducing emergency measures through formal states of emergence. These benefits include (1) the recognition that the measures introduced are exceptional (but not necessarily short term) and subject to periodic review (2) the constraining effects of requiring evidence that a state of emergency exists in terms of pre-existing legislation and (3) the scope that it allows for parliamentary as well as judicial scrutiny of executive action. I argue that PLP has no special problem with the concept of state of emergency per se (or with the concept of wartime regulation, for that matter).[10] In general, alternative laws, no less capable of formally acceptable articulation, can be enacted in advance and applied only when the emergency is declared and legally or politically validated. In general, emergency laws can be framed so as to satisfy the requirements of PLP and its underlying values equally as well as other laws.

The initial problem in reconciling PLP with states of emergency is establishing that the idea of an emergency can be defined in terms that can be applied without recourse to moral or other speculative judgments, thus making it difficult to subject to positivist rule-governance. To meet the norms of PLP, the core concepts deployed in initiating and giving substance to states of emergency and what emergency measures are thereby legitimated must be capable of formulation in a manner that can be understood, followed and applied in an empirically testable and morally neutral manner. In this respect the term 'emergency' alone is grossly inadequate,[11]

[10] By 'state of emergency' I mean a state in which some 'normal' laws are suspended for the duration (short or long) of the 'emergency'. See *The Macquarie Dictionary*, 2nd edn (Sydney: The Macquarie Library, 1991): 'State of emergency: A situation in which a government is granted special powers, by constitutional or legal provision, to deal with a perceived threat to law and order or public safety, as during a time of riot or natural disaster'. 'War' I take to be organised armed conflict.

[11] Lord Dunedin: 'A state of emergency is something that does not permit of any exact definition: it connotes a state of matters calling for drastic action . . .' *Bhagat Singh and Ors* v. *The King Emperor* AIR 1931 PC111; Lord MacDermott: 'Natural meaning of the word itself is capable of covering a very wide range of situations and occurrences, including such diverse events as wars, famines, earthquakes, floods and collapse of civil government'. *Stephen Kalong Ningkan* v. *Government of Malaysia* [1970] AC 379 at 390.

but there is no reason that this cannot be rectified by providing a more detailed and empirical specification of what is to count as an 'emergency' within the legal provisions that enables the declaration of this or that version of a state of emergency.[12]

Similar considerations arise over the criteria for derogation, which serve much the same function as states of emergency within human rights regimes. Thus, the European Convention on Human Rights, in Article 15(1) permits member states to derogate from certain of their rights commitments 'in times of war or public emergency threatening the life of the nation'. Assuming that the first criterion refers to a formally declared war (rather than a rhetorical 'war on crime' or 'war on terror') this would satisfy the expected level of objectivity within the ambit of PLP. However, the alternative criterion, 'threatening the life of the nation', falls far below any acceptable threshold for formally good law, as do most of the vaguely expressed criteria which feature in similar bills, conventions or charters of rights in contrast with many of the examples to be found within emergency legislation.

Here, the analytical habits of legal positivists come into play in detailed conceptualisation of the discourse of emergency. The sort of emergencies that are triggered by the existence or threat of extensive public disorder are distinguished from emergencies that involve the existence or imminence of foreign invasion, or the dangers posed by life-threatening diseases or from the prospect of the illegal overthrow of a government. Variables, such as the nature, degree and extent of harm, the risk of its occurrence and the immediacy of the actual or threatened harm, can all be identified, distinguished and defined in a relatively satisfactory manner.[13]

[12] A typical statutory definition of an emergency in this context is 'a widespread danger to life or property within that state', Emergency and Rescue Management Act 1989 (NSW), s.33. For a characteristic legal definition, see P.E. Nygh and P. Butt (eds.), *Butterworths Australian Legal Dictionary* (Sydney: Butterworths, 1996)*:* 'A sudden state or condition due to an actual or imminent occurrence (such as fire, flood, storm or accident) which endangers the safety or health of persons or which damages property, and which requires a significant and coordinated response . . . The important features of an emergency are a demand as opposed to a desirability, and a sense of danger as opposed to mere apprehension. There must be an urgency which is needed to meet the demand or avoid danger. It is more than an unexpected circumstance which simply suggests a certain course of action as best able to save cost and avoid inconvenience'.

[13] For sample work in this area, see H.P. Lee, *Emergency Powers* (Sydney: Law Book Co, 1984), p. 5, which distinguishes, in the first instance, between wartime, peacetime and civil emergencies.

PLP is difficult to reconcile with a generic, all-encompassing conception of 'emergency' that is used to formulate the conditions for the declaration of a 'state of emergency' involving sweeping changes in which laws are applicable and how they are authorised.[14] Different types of 'emergency' have to be defined in empirical terms and the precise nature of the legal changes that proclaiming such states of emergency involves have to be spelt out in similar detail for each type of emergency. Natural catastrophes need to be distinguished from large-scale industrial accidents, from the use and imminent threat of violence to overthrow governments, from foreign invasion and from virulent outbreaks of deadly diseases. There is no reason to believe that such refinements are not feasible and different categories of 'emergency' identified and overtly linked to specific 'emergency measures'. Examples abound in many jurisdictions.[15] In this regard a 'business-as-usual' model that overlooks or excludes the prior existence of 'emergency measures' or their periodic development, is potentially a null category and something of a straw man as far as classifying responses to the threat of terrorism goes.[16] The analytical work required here is neither particularly sophisticated nor particularly novel, although this is often ignored when

[14] As in State Counter Disaster Organisation Act 1975 (Qld). Section 6A defines 'disaster' in subsection (1) as:

(a) widespread or severe property loss;
(b) widespread or severe human injury or illness;
    (1) loss of human life.
    (2) The event may be natural or caused by human acts or omissions.
    (3) Without limiting subsection (1), the event may be caused by the following –
(a) a flood, earthquake, seismic sea wave, cyclone, tornado, eruption or other natural happening;
(b) an explosion, fire, gas leak, fuel or oil spill or any accident;
(c) an infestation, plague or epidemic;
(d) a failure of, or disruption to, an essential service or infrastructure;
(e) an attack against the state.

Once a state of disaster has been declared, it is open to disaster relief officials to order the surrender of resources to them or placed under their control; to direct the evacuation of persons from, or the refusal of entry to, a disaster area; to take safety measures such as taking possession of vehicles with a view to removing them: see, generally, s.25.

[15] Thus, the Public Order (Protection of Persons and Property) Act 1971 (Cth) relates to the protection of certain Commonwealth and international persons and property from unlawful assemblies. The Environment Protection (Nuclear Codes) Act 1978 (Cth) dealt specifically with nuclear disaster. (Though, it should be noted that this legislation has since been repealed.) Perhaps the most specific example might be the Flour Act 1977 (WA) introduced to ensure the flow of flour to bakeries during strike action.

[16] O. Gross, 'Chaos and Rules: Should Responses to Violent Crises Always be Constitutional?' (2003) 112 *Yale Law Journal* 1011 at 1042–53.

the political argument is engaged over emergency legislation and, indeed, in much theorising on these matters.

It will be objected that these positivist endeavours to cabin the breadth and flexibility of state responses to emergencies by insisting that the elements be articulated prospectively in concrete terms misses a key point about emergencies, namely that they are largely unforeseeable in their details and largely unamenable to rule-governed remedial action.[17] An 'emergency', it is argued, simply is an unpredictable situation that calls for the exercise of flexible discretionary power, a fact that cannot be remedied by any amount of prior analytical effort and scientific investigation.[18]

This is not, however, either a valid analytic point about the very idea of an emergency or descriptive of most actual emergencies. Indeed, the nature and risk of many emergencies can be predicted in scarifying detail, be they bushfires or military coup. Moreover, there are at least some emergencies, including the breakdown of social order, in which the imposition of clear and specific rules, concerning, for instance, emergency drills, is a necessary ingredient of any enduring solution. Evidently, some emergency situations, and not just violent ones, are unpredictable in their timing and may require immediate action, thus sometimes making it difficult to follow standard procedures in combating them effectively. Yet, unpredictability in timing does not mean that we cannot have rules ready when the emergency in question occurs. Lots of emergencies are 'normalised' in this way in that rules are laid down as to what to do when they do occur, even though we may not know when that is likely to be. This is why there is a plethora of 'standby' legislation for different types of emergency.[19] In this context, the only difference here between normalcy and emergency is that the latter trigger a battery of crisis-related laws that have application in the emergency but not otherwise.[20] What an emergency may bring is

[17] Thus Gross associates a system of 'clear rules' with his version of 'business as usual' which he sees as neglectful of the requirements of decisive action in the face of crisis. *Ibid.* at 1021 and 1045.

[18] Thus *Oxford English Dictionary* (Oxford: Oxford University Press, 2000): 'Emergency. A juncture that arises or "turns up", esp. a state of things unexpectedly arising, and urgently demanding immediate action'. Or see *The Macquarie Dictionary*: 'An unforeseen occurrence; a sudden and urgent occasion for action'.

[19] Thus, the Emergencies Act 2004 (ACT) provides in Chapter 7 for emergency management, including the establishment of an emergency management committee in Part 7.1; the formulation and content of an emergency plan in Part 7.2; the management of emergencies in Part 7.3; Commonwealth, State and overseas cooperation in Part 7.4 and emergency relief funds in Part 7.5.

[20] For example, emergency service vehicles are exempted from certain road and motor vehicle provisions, including the regulation of traffic rules, road traffic generally and speed limits on

rule-change not rule-abandonment, or, more commonly, the application of laws that are on the statute book but are not used in normal times because the factual situations to which they apply do not exist. Similarly the frequent instances of 'ad hoc' emergency legislation[21] demonstrates that relatively swift legislative action can be taken in most legal systems to introduce measures to deal with unforeseen emergencies that are not covered by standby legislation. These are fairly banal points of institutional fact, but they are frequently ignored in affirmations about the alleged legal distinctiveness of 'emergency measures', including those pertaining to violent emergencies.

If I am right about the technical possibility of framing the criteria for the existence of an emergency in sufficiently specific and objective terms to satisfy PLP norms of formally good legislation, this opens the way for courts to be admitted as the proper authority to determine whether or not the conditions for a state of emergency are met. Judicial deference to government assurances that these conditions are met is inappropriate on the positivist model of the rule of law. The separation of powers loses most of its point if those who make the laws can adjudicate their application. Hence Lord Hoffman may be seen as affirming a positivist position in the Belmarsh case on the matter of derogation when he held that the derogation was not permitted on the grounds of there being a 'threat to the life of the nation',[22] despite its regrettable imprecision.

Attention then shifts to the nature of the emergency measures themselves. It is these measures, it may be argued, that are typically, perhaps necessarily, open-ended, ill-defined and rule-free in that they specify powers, such as the right of officials to order evacuations, and goals, such as 'the defence of the realm' or 'the maintenance of public order', not the rules that executive government must adopt in pursuing these goals. Emergency measures, it may be argued typically license the use of executive directives and official particularised commands where before properly enacted general laws were required.[23] In a public order emergency governments must

public streets: Road Transport (Safety and Traffic Management) Regulations 2000 (ACT), r.69 (police) and r.70 (ambulance).

21 Thus, Motor Fuel Rationing (Temporary Provisions) Act 1977 (SA): SA enacted this legislation (which essentially provided a rationing scheme based on the issuance of permits to restrict the sale and use of motor fuel) to cope with fuel emergencies. The Act was re-enacted on two further occasions as the Motor Fuel Rationing Act 1980 (SA) and Motor Fuel (Temporary Restrictions) Act 1980 (SA). See Lee, *Emergency Powers*, pp. 183–7 for further examples.

22 *A* v. *Secretary of State for the Home Department* [2005] 2 WLR 87 at 133.

23 Part IIIAAA of the Defence Act 1903 (Cth) provides an example of this. It sets out conditions for the calling out of the Australian Defence Forces to deal with certain civil emergencies,

and may act like military commanders, determine what it is necessary to do to achieve victory, which involves taking charge in a hands-on approach, typically using unchallengeable imperatives to make sure that the objectives are reached.[24] Moreover, the actions of government within these ill-defined boundaries cannot be subject to the normal scrutiny and adjudication of courts without undermining their effectiveness.[25] This is, it is argued, precisely what makes an emergency an emergency.

These points are greatly exaggerated, although they cannot be dismissed a priori. They certainly do not apply to all emergencies. Many governmental powers, not just defence powers and emergency powers, are constitutionally defined in terms of broad purposes, but this does not in itself remove the requirement that policies with respect to these purposes do not require to be implemented through more specific positive laws. And few emergencies are so fast moving as to render normal decision procedures altogether impractical for any sustained period of time. Even when martial law replaces peacetime law, most aspects of rule-governance remain. Indeed, military law is typically characterised by rule books and

including, amongst others, utilising Defence Force personnel to protect Commonwealth interests against domestic violence (s.51A) or to protect the states against domestic violence (s.51B). For a critical commentary on Part IIIAAA, see M. Head, 'Calling Out the Troops – Disturbing Trends and Unanswered Questions' (2005) 28 *University of New South Wales Law Review* 481.

24 Thus, Lord Atkinson said in *R* v. *Halliday* [1917] AC 260 at 281: 'However precious personal liberty of the subject may be, there is something for which it may well be, to some extent, sacrificed by the legal enactment of, namely, success in the war, or an escape from national plunder and enslavement'.

25 For example, Latham C.J. in the *Australian Communist Party* v. *Commonwealth* (1951) 83 CLR 1 at 163, remarked:

> If it is held that it can be determined only by a court, I have difficulty in seeing how a conclusion could be based only upon facts which the Court could properly take judicial notice. A court could not take judicial notice of a 'crisis' before the crisis had happened. A court could not take judicial notice even of widespread espionage and sabotage, most of which would in any case be secretly organized. A court could not determine, by the application of any doctrine of judicial notice, whether a particular interference or a series of interferences with a production in vital industries was really industrial in character (as some would assert) or really political and subversive (as others would allege). The limitation of the principle of judicial notice to facts which are notorious – which are so clear that no evidence is required to establish them – appears so clear that no evidence is required to establish them – appears to me to prevent a court from ever reaching a conclusion based only upon such facts with respect to an issue of actual or potential publish danger calling for the exercise of legislative powers now under consideration.

For other cases in times of an emergency in which the members of the courts have been deferential to the commands of government see, generally, *Ross-Clunis* v. *Papdopoullos* [1958] 1 WLR 546; *Liversidge* v. *Anderson* [1942] AC 206.

standard procedures in an organised system that is in many ways highly positivised.[26] In principle, the emergency measures authorised in a state of emergency ought to be as formally correct as other laws specifying government powers and should be laid down in the particular piece of emergency legislation with justifiable precision, rather than expressed in the broad terms of indeterminate meaning. In these conditions full judicial power of adjudication should apply both with respect to the criteria for declaring an emergency and the provisions that apply within that emergency.

Nevertheless, emergency-style governance may sometimes justifiably include a degree of unaccountable authority which is unlikely to meet with the full approval of PLP, even in its less democratic forms. If the emergencies in question are such that it is necessary to put whole populations on a 'war footing' then the ideals of PLP are at risk, not because the rules are changed but because the domain of rules is crucially curtailed. PLP can continue to insist that decisions to go to war be made in a constitutionally proper manner and that rule governance be retained as far as possible in the conduct of war, but all this does not amount to arguing that a war should be conducted on the same rule basis as a society at peace.[27] Given the sort of rationales that are given for the democratic rule of positive law, particularly the points that are made about the dangers of the abuse of power, the burden of proof falls heavily on those who want to introduce broad powers of executive legislation and wide discretion of minor officials being given the power to issue particular binding commands. Nevertheless, PLP is not a conceptual or a priori theory that is immune from the impact of such arguments as may be put forward in favour of modifying or temporarily abandoning rule-governance. However high the burden of proof, PLP cannot argue that it can never be met, without denying its prescriptive foundations.

This should not, however, be regarded as some sort of intellectual or moral defeat for PLP. The theory is itself founded on a mixture of

[26] The Defence Act 1903 (Cth), Part IIIAAA sets out the powers of Australian Defence Force personnel who have been called out. For example, Division 2 stipulates the powers in relation to the recapture of locations or things, the prevention and ending of acts of violence and protection of persons from acts of violence and Division 3 provides for general security powers.

[27] In Australia, for example, while the Commonwealth is authorised to legislate with respect to things such as the prices of and rationing of goods, rents and the eviction of tenants, the transfer of interests in land, conditions of employment in industry and the proscription of an organisation during times of war, it will not necessarily be justified in doing so during peacetime: *Australian Communist Party* v. *Commonwealth* (1951) 83 CLR 1 at 254–5, *per* Fullagar J.

consequentialist and deontic rationales that terminate in the value of human well-being and the defence of basic human interests, and it is consistent with the theory to acknowledge that there are situations in which these ends are not served by a pure rule-governed polity.[28] The logical possibility of modifying commitment to total PLP follows from the fact that it is morally justified in part by consequentialist considerations. Equally, however, the arguments that PLP deploys to make its case for the rule of positive law assume as a background socio-political fact that states, although necessary for human well-being, are also highly threatening to that well-being, and that the rule of positive law is part of a strategy to obtain the benefits of political organisation while guarding against its abuses. The power that is necessary to benefit those subjected to it is also a power that can be used to inflict grave harm. PLP is therefore primed to be highly sceptical of claims that it is necessary to declare the sort of state of emergency that involves putting a society onto a war footing and resists the assumption that all emergencies are of this sort. The logic of this position requires that it be open to the possibility that positive rule-governance is not socially beneficial or rights-respecting in all circumstances, but it places a very substantial burden of proof on governments when declaring the existence of such circumstances. It also raises fundamental points about the processes that should be adopted to authorise states of emergency and the specific emergency measures to be enforced once a state of emergency is in place.

II. Parliaments and courts in the authorisation of emergency powers

It is a common assumption that all emergencies require us to dispense with adjudicative process for testing the instantiation and use of emergency powers.[29] On such matters, it is often argued, there ought to be almost total deference of courts to the executive who are in the position

[28] Hence John Locke's account of 'prerogative authority' as 'nothing but the Power of doing public good without a Rule' in P. Laslett (ed.), *Two Treatises of Government* (Cambridge: Cambridge University Press, 1988), p. 375.

[29] For instance, in *Dean* v. *Attorney-General of Queensland* [1971] Qd R 391 at 404–5, Stable J. said: '[I]t is not for the court to question the validity of any opinions formed by His Excellency in Council under s 22 [of the State Transport Act 1938–1981 (Qld)]. The Court is concerned with the question of legality and not with fact'. However, this decision might be revisited in light of the High Court of Australia's decision in *Re Toohey (Aboriginal Land Commissioner); Ex parte Northern Land Council* (1981) 151 CLR 170.

to assess the dangers involved and act with the speed and power on the basis of data that cannot be laid before a court of law without endangering the servants of the state and the effectiveness of the emergency measures.

However, a situation in which the executive, elected or not, can simply declare a state of emergency on the basis of its own (honest or dishonest) judgment, and lay down and take the emergency measures involved without being subject to adjudicative challenge, is certainly incompatible with PLP and with democratic government.[30] If such actions were deemed politically inevitable then there would be a fatal deficiency in the PLP capacity to cope with emergencies, since these are, by definition, situations in which, for one reason or another, there cannot readily be recourse to standard political procedures, such as endorsement by legislative assemblies or judicial review of executive declarations.[31]

We have noted that this line is sometimes presented as a conceptual consequence of the term 'emergency' in the everyday sense of a situation where instant forceful action is required to avert imminent catastrophe. This is not, however, to be equated with the terminology of 'emergency' as it features in the broad range of social situations for which emergency responses are called for on the part of the state. The simplistic paradigms that are drawn upon here range from the example of driving a car over the speed limit to take an injured child to hospital to the act of launching a pre-emptive strike on the basis of information that an enemy attack is about to take place. There are, however, many 'crises' and 'emergencies' that call for decisive official action in which there is still plenty of time to observe the relevant procedural protocols and others in which responses can be both delayed and moderate, as could have been the US response to 9/11. Contrary to the explicit assumptions behind Gross's decision to concentrate on problems of violence,[32] there is little reason to think that violent emergencies are that distinctive in the frequency with which they call for executive decision-making that bypass standard procedures due to the unforeseeability and immediacy of acts of violence and conditions of war. (Nor, it might be added, is there any reason to hold that 'emergencies' must be short-lasting rather than long-lasting, whether or not they are emergencies relating to the use of violence.)

[30] See *Australian Communist Party*, at 194–5 per Dixon J.

[31] This was the key issue in the most famous state security civil liberties case in Australian history: *Australian Communist Party* v. *Commonwealth* (1951) 83 CLR 1.

[32] Gross, 'Chaos and Rules'.

In fact, it is clear that the sort of emergency taken as a paradigm in the debates that contend we have a new or particularly difficult problem for legal theory to address, is an emergency that is thought to require a response that involves the suspension of certain fundamental civil rights or democratic procedures, not because there is no time to make decisions and pass laws in the 'normal' way or in the expectation that the danger in question is short-lasting. Rather, the 'emergency' in question is essentially whether or not the occurrence of terrorist acts, that is acts of violence against civilian populations for political or ideological purposes,[33] justifies the adoption or use of existing laws that involve a reduction in certain human rights in order to prevent the violation of the human rights of the victims of terrorist violence. Thus the decision about whether to preventatively detain and/or torture those suspected of having terrorist intentions or associations or to license extensive invasions of privacy are not in themselves particularly urgent either with respect to security practice

[33] Criminal Code Act 1995 (Cth) s.100.1 defines 'terrorist act' as the 'action or threat of action' where:

(a) the action falls within subsection (2) and does not fall within the subsection (3); and
(b) the action is done or the threat is done or threat is made with intention of advancing a political, religious or ideological cause; and
(c) the action is done or the threat is made with the intention of:
  (i) coercing, or influencing by intimidation, the government of the Commonwealth or a State, Territory or foreign country, or of part of a State, Territory or foreign country; or
  (ii) intimidating the public or a section of the public.
    (2) Action falls within this subsection if:
(a) causes serious harm that is physical harm to a person; or
(b) causes serious damage to property; or
(c) causes a person's death; or
(d) endangers a person's life, other than the life of the person taking the action; or
(e) creates a serious risk to the heath or safety of the public or a section of the public; or
(f) serious interferes with, seriously disrupts, or destroys an electronic
  (i) an information system; or
  (ii) a telecommunication system
  (iii) a financial system; or
  (iv) a system used for the delivery of essential government services; or
    (2) a system used for, or by, a transport system.
    (3) Action falls within this subsection if:
(a) is advocacy, protest, dissent or industrial action; and
(b) is not intended:
  (i) to cause serious harm that is physical harm to a person;
  (ii) to cause a person's death; or
  (iii) to endanger the life of a person, other than the person taking the action; or

to create a serious risk to the health or safety of the public or a section of the public or democratic procedures. The rhetoric that rationalises such measures under the discourse of 'emergency' and 'crisis' may draw on the implication of urgency and transience but it is not well founded on such a basis.[34] What is in fact at issue is the departure from prized procedural rights, an 'emergency' here being simply a serious problem that is thought to require such action. If the word 'emergency' gives rise to misunderstanding, here it might be better to speak of 'states of exception'.

PLP regards such civil liberty issues as core political questions, both in the sense that they are substantive matters of governance and in the sense that they are properly decided through the democratic political process. What PLP does have to offer here, in claiming to be a partial but politically justified legal theory, is that the rules of engagement in this 'war on terror' should be spelt out clearly, generally and precisely in order that their efficacy and moral justification may be tested in political debate and decision-making and that, once adopted, they may be followed, applied and subject to adjudication in a rigorous manner that ensures they are properly followed. So, if there is to be preventive detention or torture, and I am not recommending that there should be, then the circumstances in which torture may be employed, and what sort of torture is permitted, should be clear and adjudicatable (a term I use here to identify justiciability through positivist interpretive techniques). In other words, the main PLP critique of anti-terrorist legislation is its (unnecessary) lack of specificity.[35]

This may be seen as much too feeble a defence against major intrusions into the civil liberties of those who are detained without trial and have their liberty restricted without having been convicted of a criminal offence according to the standard procedural norms. And, of course, it would be, if our assumption is that we must look to an ideal of legality administered

[34] See, e.g., N. O'Neill, S. Rice and R. Douglas, *Retreat from Injustice* (Sydney: The Federation Press 2004), pp. 278–80, who critically discuss the decision to amend legislation in some Australian States, e.g. Terrorism (Community Protection) Act 2003 (Vic), to give police extra powers in relation to chemical, biological or radiological disasters occasioned through terrorism rather than from accidents; see, also, J.L. Hiebert, 'Parliamentary Review of Terrorism Measures' (2005) 68 *Modern Law Review* 676 at 677 referring to the Second Report of the Joint Committee on Human Rights, Session 2001–02, Anti-Terrorism, Crime and Security Bill, HL 37/HC 372.

[35] For instance, the original bill that sought to amend the Criminal Code 1995 (Commonwealth) to include terrorism offences would have operated in such a way that nurses who took strike action in support of increased spending on health could have been charged with terrorism if such strike action caused hospital wards to close down: O'Neill, Rice and Douglas, *Retreat from Injustice*, p. 255 citing M. Head, '"Counter Terrorism" Laws: A Threat to Political Freedom, Civil Liberties and Constitutional Rights' (2002) 26 *Melbourne University Law Review* 666 at 673.

by courts to protect civil liberties rather than to the political morality and common decency of our fellow citizens.

That said, PLP need not be regarded as failing to do what law can do by way of protecting civil liberties. Failure with respect to strict adherence to the formal requirements of PLP contributes enormously to the abuse of state power under the guise of dealing with emergencies.[36] It is in the attempts of critics of emergency legislation to insist on clearer specification of the new rules in question that the issues are best clarified, the level of debate improved, the harmful outcome of the legislative process reduced and the rule of law best protected. And it is the insistence of courts on independently scrutinising the application of these formally good laws that the main contribution of courts to the abuse of state power can be made.

The main stress point here is the extent to which it is thought necessary sometimes to defer to executive decision-making as to whether or not an emergency exists and to what it requires.[37] As we have seen, this in turn depends in part on the degree to which positivist standards have been met in the drafting of the emergency laws, as discussed above. That aside, the issue is a matter both of the competence of judiciaries to review executive assessments of security risks and the timescale within which decisions have to been made, assuming the emergency is genuine and the danger imminent.[38] PLP is liable to be pretty hard-line on both matters, placing the burden of proof to be satisfied before a court in both cases firmly on governments.

Further to this, is the adjudicative problem associated with security emergencies, namely a failure to adhere to the strict requirements of procedural justice with respect to the openness of the process and the fair contestability of the evidence involving normal standards of disclosure to the defence where preventive detention and forceful questioning is involved.[39]

[36] Arguably, the failure of Weimar police and lower courts to enforce the basic laws of public order against the initial activities of Nazi thugs contributed more to the triumph of the Nazis than any failures of the higher courts to nullify the unconstitutional conduct of Hitler's later years on natural law grounds and the former was a great deal more feasible than the latter.

[37] See, e.g., J.L. Hiebert, 'Parliamentary Review of Terrorism Measures' (2005) 68 *Modern Law Review* 676, who discusses the relevance of political debate and judicial review in affecting the formulation of terrorism legislation.

[38] *Australian Communist Party*; *A* v. *Secretary of State for Home Affairs* [2004] UKHL 56.

[39] In Australia, some of the matters have been addressed in the National Security Information (Criminal and Civil Proceedings) Act 2004 (Cth). See, also, H.P. Lee, P.J. Lane and V. Morabito, *In the Name of National Security: The Legal Dimensions* (Sydney: LBC Information

On these matters PLP is sensitive to the danger that legitimated departures from normal standards of formal justice is liable to abuse. If and when it does seem justifiable to adopt normally unacceptable methods of interrogation and deprivation of liberty, PLP is more likely to favour such measures as closed courts, limited disclosure to the defence and modification of the standards of proof than interference with the separation of powers.[40] Specialist training of selected members of the judiciary to prepare them for applying rules to complex security situations is less problematic than open uncritical deference to executive judgment or replacing judicial officers with executive functionaries. Adherence to the separation of powers, as between legislative, executive and judicial is not a formalist fetish but a necessary prerequisite of the rule of positive law and the benefits that flow from it. It is vain to require governance through law and allow the executive to make, 'interpret' and apply that law as it chooses.

Nevertheless, there are familiar and sound arguments against having recourse to such compromises and these provide one of the chief reasons for requiring that there be a formal state of emergency before such processes are implemented and that initiating such states of emergency should not be left to the executive, even when such a declaration is subject to judicial scrutiny in terms of formally good existing standby emergency legislation. While there are rule-of-law considerations against asking parliaments to make quasi judicial decisions, it is a desirable element of the process that

Services, 1995), ch. 5–7, for discussion of general issues that arise in relation to government information and judicial scrutiny of national security claims.

40 Some countries have already adopted such similar approaches. In Canada, for instance, the issue of a security certificate is subject to a special judicial review process. There, a single judge may review the reasonableness of the decision to issue the certificate. Where a person challenges the decision to issue the security certificate, the government is permitted to present national security information without that person being present. In some cases, the government is also permitted to proceed without providing a full summary of the information. In *Charkaoui* v. *Canada* 2004 FCA 421, the Federal Court of Appeal upheld the security certificate process. In response to the special judicial review process it found at paragraphs 75 and 84 respectively, although it 'derogates in a significant way from the adversarial process normally adhered to in criminal and civil matters', 'the threat of terrorism or a threat to national security does not represent or reflect a situation of normality, at least not in our country': V.V. Ramraj, M. Hor and K. Roach, 'Postscript: Some Recent Developments' in Ramraj, Hor and Roach (eds.), *Global Anti-Terrorism Law and Policy*, p. 628. This decision was overturned on appeal to the Supreme Court on the grounds that there are 'less intrusive' alternatives which have been developed in Canada and elsewhere, notably the use of special counsel to act on behalf of the named persons: *Charkaoui* v. *Canada* (2007), 2007 SCC 9, 1 SCR 350 at 358.

parliaments as well as courts be required by the emergency legislation to endorse the executive declaration that a state of emergency exists, as Mark Tushnet eloquently suggests.[41]

This is why Bruce Ackerman seeks to modify Supreme Court review of presidential emergency authority by a 'framework statute' which, he predicts, on the basis of constitutional precedent, the Supreme Court is likely to go along with.[42] The advantages that he sees in this arrangement derive from a 'supermajoritarian escalator' according to which, with each passage of a specific period of time, a greater majority in Congress would be required to endorse the continuation of the state of emergency for a further period. An evident disadvantage of such a system is its assumption that emergencies are always short-lived, but the principle of getting the assent of the elected legislatures can be seen as an enhancement of democratic process and a check with respect to those emergency measures whose definition is not amenable to precise specification. This is a division of power solution which has the advantage of drawing on the distinct sources of democratic authority within the US system.

There are separation-of-powers objections to legislatures taking particular decisions rather than general ones, although this can be mitigated if the votes are taken under the rubric of appropriate standby emergency legislation. Another issue arises from the fact that it is difficult to see how an informed decision can be taken as to the satisfaction of conditions laid down for the declaration of an emergency without confidential security information being laid before a large body of people without adequate measures to contain the dissemination of the sensitive security information. Delegating the decision to a specially briefed committee of the legislature is one solution to this problem but it entails significant dilution of the democratic legitimacy of the process. It is, however, an advantage of the formal state of emergency that it makes possible this additional safeguard with respect to the introduction of normally unacceptable emergency measures.

Even with some such parliamentary involvement, the PLP approach to states of emergency may seem inadequate. Parliaments can be swayed by assurances of executive capacity and the alleged availability of secret security information as well as by the panic which terrorist events evoke and the political gains to be got from being seen to stand firm. Perhaps we

[41] 'The Political Constitution of Emergency Powers' (Chapter 6), this volume.

[42] B. Ackerman, *Before the Next Attack: Preserving Civil Liberties in an Age of Terrorism* (New Haven: Yale University Press, 2006).

would be better served by the sort of strong judicial review on the basis of fundamental constitutionalised rights to which PLP is firmly opposed. Is it not precisely in times of emergency that we need inalienable non-derogable rights, such as the right not to be tortured and the right of habeas corpus, that courts may draw upon to override emergency laws that contravene these inviolable human rights? Do we not have here a real-life example of the pressing need for bills of rights in their strongest form, the most evident example of the need for strong judicial review of legislation?[43]

In my view, the current spate of anti-terrorist law demonstrates precisely the opposite. As those engaged in the current debate seem to agree, there is no appreciable difference with respect to the draconian nature of anti-terrorist law and practice between those states that adhere to strong judicial review on the basis of abstract rights and those that favour a weaker form or no such review. Bills of rights and strong judicial review of legislation have little effect on whether basic liberties are whittled down in crises.[44] Those who have insisted that the only real defence against the erosion of fundamental rights is ideological belief, political action and majoritarian democracy seem to have a decisive case in their favour here. This is not to say that the democratic process is a reliable guide as to the correctness of policy outcomes with respect to anti-terrorist measures, only that it is as reliable as more expert and allegedly less partial players. When it comes to such matters, elected politicians, voters and judges tend to agree.[45]

43 See, e.g., G. Williams 'The Rule of Law and the Regulation of Terrorism in Australia and New Zealand' in Ramraj, Hor and Roach (eds.), *Global Anti-Terrorism Law and Policy*; see also, D. Bonner, *Emergency Powers in Peacetime* (London: Sweet & Maxwell, 1985), ch. 6.

44 Gross, 'Chaos and Rules', 1034 : 'In states of emergency, national courts assume a highly deferential attitude when called upon to review government actions and decisions. Both domestic and international judicial bodies share this systematic failure'; and at 1097: 'constitutional arguments have not greatly constrained any government faced with the need to respond to such emergencies'.

45 Interesting questions arise here as to the fallibility of democratic political judgments on such matters. We are told that ordinary voters are poor judges of risk with respect to spectacular harms and always ready to demonise minorities in seeking scapegoats and easy targets for blame and oppressive remedial action. (See Williams in Ramraj, Hor and Roach (ed.), *Global Anti-Terrorism Law and Policy*, p. 536.) Yet it is not clear that incidents of extreme terrorist horror may not stimulate a proper response to preventing future harms in contrast to prior complacency, just as an earthquake or a tsunami may prompt a morally better response to the hardships of others than is manifest in normal times. Vivid imagination may prompt moral improvement. Further it may be the nature of the event rather than the likelihood of it happening and the extent of the damage involved that evokes strong action to prevent its future occurrence.. The deliberate killing of a few thousand people may be judged a worse event than the accidental deaths of many times more than that in

In times of major terrorist crises, such as may be to come, giving the last word to a process of strong judicial review, especially in a system that has become routinised and indeed positivised, in a system of precedent-developed constitutional law may be insufficiently responsive to changed and catastrophic circumstances.[46] Indeed, it may be this worry that leads some theorists to opt for the idea of bypassing constitutional processes when faced with extreme emergencies. Strong executive action in the war on terror, it is felt, must not be hampered by out of touch constitutional courts, therefore legality can, with moral and perhaps even legal propriety, be put to one side in order to get the job done.

We may speculate whether it is a coincidence that models of deliberate illegality (and civil disobedience generally) emanate from theorists working in jurisdictions with strong rights-based judicial review, where there is the prospect that the higher courts will thwart the will of a government that seeks to act in a decisive and effective way. Certainly Gross, in his chapter, focuses almost all of his attention on the particularities of the US polity where popularly elected presidents actually or potentially find themselves in conflict with a Supreme Court that may find their actions unconstitutional on substantive civil liberty grounds. This is a conflict that does not arise to the same extent in a jurisdiction where the constitution does not allow such strong judicial review and in which Parliament is the representative sovereign that may react to any crisis by introducing new laws that cannot be overridden by courts. Constitutional bills of rights with entrenched judicial review, strong or weak, create a special problem for theorists who want to make room for decisive government action in times of crisis. In a parliamentary democracy, governments can obtain legitimately the emergency powers they think they need without the danger of constitutional impropriety, whereas in a mixed system of government where democracy, is tempered by judicial override on moral grounds, declaring a state of emergency may require in effect suspending the constitution.[47] As Bruce Ackerman so eloquently expresses the

car accidents. Prioritising one over the other may not be a calculative error of likelihood so much as a moral judgment of acceptability. Interestingly, even those who focus on the dangers of the collective panic that threatened civil liberties following terrorist atrocities do not go so far as to suggest that such responses are totally irrational.

46 Contrast with *Attorney General of St Christopher, Nevis and Anguilla* v. *Reynolds* [1980] AC 627 and *Teh Cheng Poh* v. *PP* [1980] AC 458.

47 C. Cohloun (ed.), *Dictionary of Social Sciences* (Oxford: Oxford University Press, 2002): 'Emergency powers: The right of the executive to suspend ordinary constitutional procedures and protections in order to respond quickly and effectively to war, civil strife, or other

constitutional constraints on renewal of states of emergency in Poland, the 'current constitution is an invitation to lawlessness',[48] a point that may be generalised to constitutional restraints of other kinds in similar situations.

III. The Gross–Dyzenhaus debate

It is intriguing to consider, in this context, what line PLP might take if required to choose between the Gross and the Dyzenhaus analyses and tactics for dealing with security measures that violate traditional civil rights. In some way the Gross model follows in the path of H.L.A. Hart (who in the relevant parts of his work can be classified as within the PLP camp).[49] When confronted with the claim that legal positivism advocated deference to the laws of evil dictators, Hart points up the moral obligation to disobey morally unjust laws, although it is judges not governments that he has in mind and he does not go on to consider whether such violations could be legitimated by consequent legal or political vindication.[50] In the case of the judiciary, I suspect that he had their resignation in mind. In the case of other participants, perhaps he would go along with Dworkin's thesis on civil disobedience to the effect that the conscientious law violator has to be prepared to take the legal consequences of his acts.[51] Although this is muddied by Dworkin's thesis that civil disobedience may be morally justified on the basis of the person's genuine belief that his apparently disobedient actions are in fact legally justified on the basis of a proper interpretation of constitutional law, at least in the period before the Supreme Court has made a definitive ruling. Accordingly, the disobedient action is not illegal because the relevant legislation is, in the opinion of the dissenter,

crises'. Emergency powers allow the executive to bypass the legislature, to suspend certain rights of citizens and govern by decree – a situation sometimes termed a *constitutional* dictatorship. Most democratic constitutions have some provision for emergency power, typically subject to review by the legislature (in Britain) or the judiciary (in the United States). Their use is considered dangerous to democracy and the rule of law because they can normalise extraordinary police and military powers (as in France during the Algerian crisis of 1961 or in British Northern Ireland after 1973). Over time, they can erode the legitimacy of democratic regimes.

48 Cohloun, *Dictionary of Social Sciences*, p. 88.

49 This applies to H.L.A. Hart, *The Concept of Law* (Oxford: Oxford University Press, 1961) as well as to his more overtly prescriptive writings.

50 H.L.A. Hart, 'The Separation of Law and Morals' (1958) 71 *Harvard Law Review* 593 at 613–16.

51 R.M. Dworkin, *Taking Rights Seriously* (London: Duckworth, 1978).

unconstitutional, a matter that is often a matter of some indeterminacy with constitutionalised bills of rights.

Gross, however, on my reading, takes neither the Hartian line of simply morally legitimating civil disobedience nor the Dworkinian line of acting on a do-it-yourself form of constitutional interpretation. Instead he suggests that governments, including senior officials (so why not all citizens?), should be morally, and in some indirect sense legally, entitled or required to exercise their own judgment on whether to act in an illegal manner, provided they are open about what they are doing and subject their actions to the retrospective assessment of 'the people' either as juries or voters.

Despite its quasi-Hartian credentials, there are many difficulties with this model from the perspective of PLP.[52] The abrogation of the rule of positive law legitimated in a retrospective and quasi-legal manner, as in Gross's model, is an open avenue to abuse of executive power. Gross speaks of the slippery slope from models of accommodation that introduce ostensibly temporary emergency measures that then become normalised, but this underestimates the slippage that occurs when rulers know that there is a tacit, even overt, agreement that they may act illegally if they believe it to be in a vitally important national interest. The awkward halfway house that is involved here is that there is an illegal act that has the prospect of being retrospectively legalised, which is likely to lead to leniency for transgressors unless they can be shown to have acted out of highly questionable motives. There would be perverse incentives for those who take this path to ensure that their tactic is 'successful', by hook or by crook. Nor is it explained why this sort of conduct does not undermine confidence in democratic rulers and the institutions of the rule of law. Overall, Gross has an uphill struggle to convince us that the calculation of the risks of behaving extra-legally by those with the power to set aside the law in extreme circumstances will generally work out better than the path of legality.

Further, the requirement, echoing Rawls[53] in the contention that those engaged in civil disobedience should do so openly and accept the legal consequences of their acts, and that conscientious extra-legal transgressors should be transparent and open about what they are doing, would seem to risk undermining the efficacy of the technique they are adopting, which may well require secrecy and duplicity. The requirement of candour means

52 Dyzenhaus, Chapter 2 and S. Chesterman, 'Deny Everything: Intelligence Activities and the Rule of Law' (Chapter 13), this volume.

53 J. Rawls, *A Theory of Justice* (Oxford: Clarendon Press, 1972), pp. 363–91.

that the official in question is debarred from maintaining the secrecy often required for the success of such Machiavellian actions.[54]

A particularly positivist point against the Gross model is that it seems to require the absence of the opportunity to mount effective legal challenges to ostensibly illegal acts that the official is justified in performing. No legal right should, however, on the PLP approach, be legally inoperative and no illegal act should be permitted with impunity. Indeed if it is, then we empty the notion of so-called legal rights and responsibilities of their legal nature. If, however, the morally/legally permitted illegal act is legally contestable then officials do not have the unfettered power which Gross is intent on giving them. One way or the other, such an arrangement departs from key ingredients of the rule of positive law, particularly the prospectivity and clarity required of formally good law.

Putting the matter another way, PLP is likely to find that the normative status of the Machiavellian ruler blurs the distinction between law and morality. This may be unfair to Gross in that he consistently makes it clear that he is talking about a moral right or duty to commit an illegal act (the Hartian position).[55] Yet there is a certain ambivalence here. Such conduct is described as 'extra-legal' rather than 'illegal', not to say treasonable. The expectation seems to be that presidents should be allowed some leeway on such matters, that courts should be deferential, that juries should be sympathetic to such extra-legalities. Further, there is the clear suggestion that courts (on what democratic authority?) should absolve officials of legal liability where they were genuinely seeking to serve the public in times of crisis, particularly where the illegal acts have been 'ratified' by popular vote.

As a less dramatic departure from the rule of positive law, Dyzenhaus's model seems more congenial to PLP. The courts are still involved and will surely take the relevant legal rules into account when making their decisions. Yet there is a dismissive tone to his analysis of formalistic reasoning that undoubtedly affects Dyzenhaus's willingness to sacrifice what he takes to be the separation of powers to the greater good of efficient security measures that suggests a lesser commitment to formal process than that approved of by strong versions of PLP.[56] This comes out in his

[54] See Chesterman, Chapter 13, pp. 319–20.

[55] Gross, 'Chaos and Rules' at 1097: 'going completely outside the law', not 'within the framework of the legal system', an 'ethic or responsibility'; *ibid.* at 1103: 'the right thing to do'.

[56] D. Dyzenhaus, *The Constitution of Law* (Cambridge: Cambridge University Press, 2006), pp. 66–72.

willingness to countenance judicial deference in security matters, provided there is good reason so to do. Particularly in systems not characterised by the division of power between branches of government, there must be greater emphasis on the separation of powers as a check on the centralised source of political power than Dyzenhaus allows for. PLP is likely, therefore, to look for other ways of dealing with the relatively limited range of factors that affect the standard legal procedures involved where individual liberties are at stake. Evidence in camera, restricted panels of judges and counsel, non-disclosure of the sources of evidence from defendants, lowering of the standard of proof in the case of civil detention on the grounds of dangerousness. These PLP could live with more readily than executivising the adjudicative personnel by including retired judges specially selected and administrators with experience of security practice.

Much depends here on the nature of the judicial review such a modified form of procedural justice would adopt. For PLP its advantage is the prospect of courts deciding whether there is a state of emergency and whether the measures taken under that emergency declaration are lawful, all in terms of pre-enacted emergency legislation which is of reasonable precision and consistency. Dyzenhaus, however, puts more weight on the prospect of such a tribunal acting under the rubric of such human rights principles as are available to it, either through constitutional law, other human rights law or the deep principles of the common law, all of which can be used to turn aside the evident intention of the legislature and the otherwise lawful acts of the executive. His interest in keeping emergency measures firmly within the ambit of the courts is less to bring about the impartial application of such formally good legislation as may be available than to provide an opportunity for judicial review on the grounds of fundamental rights which go far beyond due process. He wants courts to have 'a significant role in evaluating the decision made by other branches of government' and this is to come through the regulative assumption that judges are under a duty to uphold the rule of law and thus maintain 'the integrity of the legal order'.[57] Crucially, the rule of law, on his interpretation, has less to do with pressing for laws that are clear-cut and justiciable in a positivistic sense and refusing to endorse the actions of executives who do not have this sort of authorisation and much more to do with treating subjects, as he says, 'as bearers of human rights', an approach which 'links procedural constraints to substantive values'.[58] This

[57] Dyzenhaus, *The Constitution of Law*, p. 33.

[58] *Ibid.*, p. 13.

is, in coded format, recommendation for prioritising judicial over political judgments as to the content, scope and relative weight of 'human rights'.

Precisely what this involves is none too clear. Thus, in his analysis of the Rehman[59] and Belmarsh cases Dyzenhaus castigates judges who 'lose their nerve' and defer too readily to the executive's judgment that there is an emergency that justifies derogation from the European Convention on Human Rights and praises them when it comes to declaring that certain 'emergency measures' are disproportional and discriminatory, for upholding the 'integrity' of the law.[60] But this is not because he rejects judicial deference in such circumstances, provided it is reasoned, nor because he favours strong judicial review at this point, being apparently satisfied with what he calls the 'weatherman' approach to the UK Human Rights Act 1988, by which he means the process of courts alerting politicians and public opinion concerning the threat to what he counts as legal values.

Against this I would map the PLP position as being tougher with respect to judicial appraisal of executive action under positive law and highly dissatisfied with positive law which is unhelpfully vague and value-laden, as is the case with most human rights provision at the constitutional level. On the PLP model it should be a matter of formally good positive law which determines the criteria for declaring a state of emergency authorising specific emergency measures within that state of emergency. Courts should not resile on grounds of judicial deference to the executive on matters of security. On the other hand, courts should not question the content of emergency measures if they are clearly formulated in the relevant legislation, although, again, they must adjudicate on whether executive action is kept within these defined measures. This is more radical than Dyzenhaus's favoured model of the Special Immigration Appeals Commission (SIAC), which he sees as a bold experiment in bridging the separation of powers or his residual strategy of bringing in substantive common law powers of review that hark back to pre-democratic days. Thus, with respect to Belmarsh, it would not be SIAC or the Appeal Court's duty to second-guess the legislature as to whether, for instance, citizens should be treated differently from non-citizens, but rather to ensure that this is in fact what is done in accordance with positive law.[61]

[59] *Secretary of State for the Home Department* v. *Rehman* [2002] 1 All ER 123.

[60] Dyzenhaus, *The Constitution of Law*, ch. 4.

[61] I am here not offering a legal opinion as to how the UK Human Rights Act 1988 should be interpreted, although I suspect that my disagreement with Dyzenhaus is within the range of feasible alternative readings of the court's duties with respect to that Act, but a political opinion about the preferable constitutional regime within a democratic polity.

Nevertheless, the Dyzenhaus model is not far removed from a PLP approach to emergency measures if we accept that there are (however rarely) sound political justifications for using proactive means that temporarily displace normal legal process and basic liberties. It is, perhaps, and in itself, near enough to 'business as usual' to be tolerable. However the business that PLP sees or wants to see as 'normal' is, as Gross suggests, 'rule-governed', although this does not mean, as he also suggests, inflexible. Rules can and should be changed when necessary, although thereafter, and subject to any later changes, they should be substantively unchallengeable by courts. Perhaps the underlying lesson is that business as usual should not involve court-administered bills of rights that enable courts to draw on broad moral principles to overturn the clear and specific outcomes of democratic process. Both what we accept as normal in a legal system and what we regard as the overriding civil liberties have a significant impact on how these matters are conceptualised and resolved.

Refreshingly, these are not primarily conceptual issues. They relate to the meat of political philosophy as it abuts on what sort of law and legal system we think we ought to have. In this debate, PLP does not provide a total political philosophy, for it leaves most substantive questions to the democratic process and to the deliberations of political discourse generally. This may be considered a welcome feature of a legal theory insofar as it focuses on moral and political issues directly relating to law and orients courts to what ought to be their core business. Dyzenhaus agrees with this political approach to legal theory in general, but his conceptual strategy remains suspect to the extent that, in presenting the issue in terms of what constitutes 'the rule of law', the suppressed assumption is that whatever is declared to fall under the head of 'the rule of law' is a matter for courts, not parliaments. In contrast, I think it important to reframe the debate, accepting openly that we require political constitutional norms to determine what the legal constitution should be.[62]

The type of political constitution favoured by PLP allocates to judiciaries the duty of applying the law (albeit law of a formal sort that meets the legislative standards of PLP) and places the correlative duty of obedience to such rulings on all of us. That does not, however, legitimate judiciaries deciding for themselves how to approach their task. In fact, when judges use their formally ultimate legal power of rule application in other ways

[62] For the concept of a political constitution, see R. Bellamy, *Political Constitutionalism: A Republican Defence of the Constitutionality of Democracy* (Cambridge: Cambridge University Press, 2007).

and for other ends, then they precipitate a legal crisis within PLP which may ultimately legitimate civil disobedience, a fact that would play in to the hands of Oren Gross, especially were he theorising within the context of an old style parliamentary democracy rather than one which accommodates a strong bill of rights regime. The fact that even a functionally weak bill of rights encourages judges to reinterpret the plain meanings of statutory texts, if they deem them to be straying from their view of what is appropriate under a human rights convention, is a negative factor operating within many so-called 'constitutional democracies' that could be used to justify the Grossian 'extra-legal' approach to constitutional crises in times of emergency. Dyzenhaus fears that Gross would leave us in a legal grey hole, that is, a sphere of executive power that is largely without legal constraint. Yet, the alternative he presents is arguably worse in that it creates a political grey hole in which unaccountable judicial power is exercised in a way that undermines political responsibility. Within democratic theory the Gross–Dyzenhaus debate does not present us with an acceptable choice. Perhaps, as both Mark Tushnet and Kent Roach suggest in this volume, a third alternative is required.

10

Ordinary laws for emergencies and democratic derogations from rights

KENT ROACH

I. Introduction

The post-9/11 scholarly debate on emergency powers as represented by the debate between David Dyzenhaus and Oren Gross over legality and extra-legal powers has defined the concept of emergency narrowly in relation to the detention or disruption of suspected terrorists or enemies. This understanding of emergencies is dramatically under-inclusive. It ignores genuine emergencies such as Hurricane Katrina, the Asian tsunami and pandemics, as well as the need for recovery after particularly disruptive acts of terrorism. Although cloaked in the rhetorical urgency of emergencies, the post-9/11 debate about emergencies has been about the treatment of the rights of suspected terrorists, not about how a state will respond to the full range of emergencies that modern society will face.

Although I am sceptical about whether the post-9/11 debate is really about emergencies, I am not sceptical about the fact that modern society will confront genuine emergencies. Such emergencies will require the state to engage in extraordinary measures that may have adverse effects on rights. Modern states have recognised the reality of emergencies and have enacted framework statutes to enable the state to deal with emergencies. To this end, we should be concerned about the ordinary law that governs *all* emergencies. In contrast to the mountains of work that have been devoted to anti-terrorism measures, emergency laws in Canada, the United Kingdom and the United States have attracted comparatively scant scholarly attention. I will suggest that this is unfortunate because emergency laws should provide a principled and creative starting point when societies face a broad range of emergencies.

I thank Victor V. Ramraj, the National University of Singapore's Faculty of Law and the participants at a symposium held in Singapore. I also thank Maxwell Cameron, Yale's University Canadian Studies Program and the participants at a symposium held at Yale in October 2006 where a preliminary version of this chapter was presented.

Emergency laws can be structured either to affirm executive dominance and secrecy or they can be carefully crafted to allow the legislature, the judiciary and the executive to supervise and review the conduct of the state during emergencies. I will suggest that emergency statutes can themselves be seen as a nascent attempt to subject sovereign power in emergencies to the rule of law in a manner similar to that used to subject the administrative state to the rule of law.[1] This difficult task will, as Dyzenhaus suggests, require institutional imagination that will engage courts, the executive, the legislature and creative new hybrid institutions to cooperate in maintenance of the rule-of-law project.[2]

To the extent that either emergency or anti-terrorism measures override rights, we should continue to look to the ordinary law as a starting point. Most modern rights protection instruments allow the state to justify reasonable and proportionate limitations on rights. Some limitations on rights may be justified in the context of anti-terrorism, especially with regard to difficult issues such as preventive detention and secret information.[3] If, however, governments conclude that it is necessary to go beyond reasonable limits on rights and dispense with rights altogether, the ordinary law also provides a vehicle for doing so. The established vehicle for doing away with rights is to invoke provisions that allow for temporary derogations of rights. Although extensive and repeated use of derogations could lead to tyranny, this has not been the post-9/11 experience. Rather, most democratic governments[4] have not been eager to enact temporary democratic derogations from rights, and have instead tried to sell possible derogations from rights as reasonable and permanent limits on rights.

Like Oren Gross's extra-legal model, a derogation model has the virtue of recognising rights even as they are not respected and of not constituting a permanent change to the law. At the same time, however, derogations respect legality and democracy more than the extra-legal model because they are triggered by an *ex ante* legislative act as opposed to the discretionary decisions of officials who decide whether it is necessary to take the risk of violating the law and the rights of suspected terrorists. Derogations are also subject to *ex post* legislative and judicial review which can also

[1] D. Dyzenhaus, 'The State of Emergency in Legal Theory', in V.V. Ramraj, M. Hor and K. Roach (eds.), *Global Anti-Terrorism Law and Policy* (Cambridge: Cambridge University Press, 2005).

[2] D. Dyzenhaus, *The Constitution of Law* (Cambridge: Cambridge University Press, 2006).

[3] K. Roach, 'Must We Trade Rights for Security?' (2006) 27 *Cardozo Law Review* 2151.

[4] In this respect, my chapter only speaks to the approach to emergencies in stable liberal democracies with an active civil society.

occur under the extra-legal measures model, but will not occur if prosecutors decline to prosecute illegal actions or the executive pardons officials who have acted illegally. Derogations will also be subject to sunsets and international supervision.

Professor Gross will argue with some force based on the experience of Northern Ireland, Israel and other states that the derogation model could lead to a permanent emergency.[5] I will suggest, however, that the post-9/11 experience has been quite different and legislatures have been quite reluctant to assume democratic responsibility for derogating from rights. In addition, judges have been able to supervise the few derogations that have been made and to use the possibility of derogation in order to protect the rights of suspected terrorists.

One of the powerful concerns raised by Oren Gross is the problem of the seepage of emergency powers into the regular law. The seepage problem is real for the reasons articulated by Professor Gross. Seepage can, however, be resisted by two strategies that I advocate in this chapter. The first is the use of emergency legislation that has been drafted in advance of particular emergencies and requires legislative reaffirmation of emergencies. A second strategy is to empower courts to require explicit democratic authorisation of derogations from rights. In other words, courts should be especially vigilant about allowing emergency powers to become permanent in those cases in which the exercise of emergency powers result in derogation from rights. I will suggest that the optimal model for democratic derogation from rights, like the optimal model of emergency legislation, will provide a role for judges, bureaucrats and legislators. In addition, derogation measures should also engage civil society and international institutions in reviewing how the state acts during an emergency.[6]

II. Is the debate about emergencies or rights?

Much of the post-9/11 debate about emergency powers focuses on a narrow subset of emergencies that may confront modern society. Oren Gross, for example, noted that emergencies are not limited to war and terrorism and include natural disasters and economic crises, but declared that he will restrict himself to emergencies caused by violence in part because they

[5] O. Gross, 'Chaos and Rules: Should Responses to Violent Crises Always Be Constitutional?' (2003) 112 *Yale Law Journal* 1011; O. Gross and F. Ní Aoláin, *Law in Times of Crisis* (Cambridge: Cambridge University Press, 2006).

[6] J. Lobel, 'Emergency Power and the Decline of Liberalism' (1989) 98 *Yale Law Journal* 1358.

require 'immediate action'[7] and in part because they 'pose the greatest and most sustained danger to constitutional freedoms and principles'.[8] Bruce Ackerman limits his proposal for an emergency constitution to one that will follow another terrorist attack that is the equivalent of the 9/11 attack. It focuses on the detention of terrorist suspects[9] even though similar detentions after 9/11 did not lead to prosecutions.[10] It does not deal with other measures such as quarantines and evacuations that may have to be taken to limit harms after acts of chemical, biological or nuclear terrorism, let alone the broad range of other emergencies. Hurricane Katrina does not even merit a mention in Professor Ackerman's 2006 book.

Claims of emergency powers can be a cloak for the unwarranted detention or harsher treatment of those suspected, perhaps wrongly, of terrorism. Although he rejects the Bush administration's claim that the United States is at war with terrorism. Professor Ackerman has concluded that the crime paradigm is inadequate because of the threats that al Qaeda terrorism presents to the 'effective sovereignty' of the state. He argues that 'it was al Qaeda's success in shaking the public's confidence in the American government's effective sovereignty that gave the attack its overwhelming political resonance. For a while at least, it was perfectly reasonable for ordinary Americans to wonder whether the government was in control of affairs within the nation's borders'.[11] The challenge to the state's effective sovereignty that Professor Ackerman asserts, however, is by no means limited to mass terrorism attacks. Indeed, the broader dimensions of both emergencies and their challenge to the state's effective sovereignty can be seen in the failure of the American state to respond effectively to Hurricane Katrina.

Hurricane Katrina was responsible for 1,836 deaths and revealed serious problems in America's response to emergencies, as well as the organisation and execution of emergency services by the Federal Emergency Management Agency (FEMA) and the Department of Homeland Security. The 2003 SARS outbreak that killed about 800 people around the world also underlines the dangers of pandemics. Although the evil exercise of human agency in acts of terrorism distinguishes terrorism from natural disasters,

[7] Gross, 'Chaos and Rules', 1025–6. [8] Gross and Ní Aoláin, *Law in Times of Crisis*, p. 8.

[9] In B. Ackerman, *Before the Next Attack* (New Haven: Yale University Press, 2006), p. 99. Ackerman argues that 'the emergency constitution should be focused specially on terrorist attacks, and should not be concerned with other crises. It should authorize a declaration of emergency only when a truly devastating attack has occurred . . . '.

[10] D. Cole, *Enemy Aliens* (New York: The New Press, 2003), ch. 2.

[11] Ackerman, *Before the Next Attack*, p. 42.

this distinction is relevant only with respect to the punishment of terrorists and not the preventive or recovery efforts that the state takes to limit harm.

Restricting rights during natural disasters raises the question of equal and collective self-sacrifice as opposed to the sacrifice of the rights of the 'usual suspects'. The random nature of natural disasters serves as a kind of Rawlsian veil of ignorance. We do not know whether we will be the person quarantined because of exposure to SARS or some other disease. In contrast, we do know the likely suspects who will be imprisoned under Professor Ackerman's emergency constitution or dealt with illegally under Professor Gross's extra-legal measures model.

In no small part because it was affected by the 2003 SARS crisis that led to 42 deaths in Toronto, Canada enacted an all-risk national security policy in 2004 that focuses on emergency preparedness and public health as well as the dangers of terrorism. This all-risk approach has the potential to moderate anti-terrorism policy and prevent irrational over-investment in anti-terrorism measures.[12] The failure of the American state to mitigate the harms of Katrina at the same time as it has spent billions of dollars on homeland security, not to mention the war in Iraq, reveals the folly of focusing on terrorism as the prime threat to human security.

The post-9/11 debate about emergency powers has an artificial but telling character in its focus on various harsh measures that some claim may be necessary to prevent acts of terrorism. The debate is not really about emergencies but rights.[13] Even if the emergencies we face are somehow limited to terrorism, it is odd that the emergency powers debate has not extended to what extraordinary measures may be necessary to mitigate the damage of another catastrophic terrorism attack such as requirements that all institutions engage in emergency planning[14] or that cities be evacuated in the wake of a dirty bomb attack. Indeed, the partial focus of the emergency powers debate on harsh measures that attempt to prevent terrorism suggests that the debate may be more about the rights of terrorist suspects than the responsibilities of states in emergencies to protect the

[12] Canada, *Securing an Open Society: The National Security Policy* (Ottawa: Privy Council Office, 2004). See also K. Roach, *September 11: Consequences for Canada* (Montreal: McGill Queens Press, 2003), ch. 7 for a defence of an all-risk approach to national security.

[13] For a similar conclusion see T. Campbell, 'Emergency Strategies for Prescriptive Legal Positivists: Anti-Terrorist Law and Legal Theory' (Chapter 9) in this volume.

[14] The 9/11 Commission found that it took four hours to evacuate the WTC after the 1993 bombings whereas all but 2,152 of the 16,400 to 18,800 people in the twin towers were evacuated in under an hour on 9/11. *The 9/11 Report* (New York: Norton, 2004), ch. 9.4.

lives of their citizens and to re-establish order. One consequence of the skewed and narrow nature of the emergency powers debate is that most commentators have ignored the ordinary laws that govern the broad range of emergencies that may threaten the lives of citizens.[15]

III. The ordinary law of emergencies

Most modern democracies have established laws to deal with emergencies, but these laws have received relatively little attention in the post-9/11 debate about emergency powers. Drawing on Dicey, however, Oren Gross has recognised that emergency legislation provides a means to authorise exceptional powers '*ex ante*, i.e. prior to the exercise of the relevant powers by the executive'[16] and can be contrasted with the *ex post* use of what Dicey described as acts of indemnity and what Gross describes as his extra-legal measures model. Along with Dyzenhaus, I favour the *ex ante* approach because it accords better with legality by authorising and limiting the actions that will be taken in an emergency. It also accords better with democracy by requiring legislatures to act and deliberate before extraordinary powers are exercised.[17] It does not allow unelected members of the executive to act as sovereigns in deciding when an emergency exists and what actions are required to respond to the emergency.[18] The secret and illegal actions of the executive can constitute what Kim Lane Scheppele has criticised as 'stealth emergencies powers'[19] whereas the ordinary law of emergencies can be the subject of democratic and legal deliberation. The *ex ante* approach, however, is not necessarily inconsistent with robust review of what has been done in an emergency. As will be seen, some emergency statutes require both *ex ante* authorisation of state power and *ex post* review of its exercise.

[15] For a notable exception see K.L. Scheppele, 'Small Emergencies' (2006) 40 *Georgia Law Review* 835 at 846 who argues that 'emergencies have been brought into the constitutional order by being normalized' by various emergencies statutes.

[16] Oren Gross, 'Stability and Flexibilty: A Dicey Business', in *Global Anti-Terrorism Law and Policy*, p. 92.

[17] The argument from democracy may explain why Professor Tom Campbell, despite his disagreements with Professor Dyzenhaus over positivism, seems more favourably disposed to Dyzenhaus's legality model than Gross's extra-legal measures model.

[18] Gross acknowledges that as compared to Dicey his 'Extra-Legal Measures model is more open to the possibility of *ex post* ratification taking place outside of the legislature'. *Ibid.*, p. 99.

[19] Scheppele, 'Little Emergencies', 858.

A. American legislation and reform proposals

The National Emergencies Act has not been reformed despite the lessons of 9/11 and Hurricane Katrina. It allows the President to declare emergencies that are then transmitted to Congress and published in the Federal Register.[20] It does not contemplate on its face that the President will attempt to justify the declaration of an emergency or acts taken pursuant to an emergency to Congress.[21] Moreover, it makes no attempt to outline the principles that should govern the President's decision to declare an emergency or to govern the executive response to the emergency or on the rights that may be affected during an emergency. In its single-minded focus on the power of the President to declare an emergency or an exception as opposed to the principles that might govern the declaration and conduct of the emergency, the Act is Schmittian.[22]

The National Emergencies Act allows Congress by a Joint Resolution to end emergencies and requires Congress to consider such a vote every six months.[23] Congress has, however, never ended an emergency and rarely discharges its statutory obligation to consider voting to end an emergency.[24] The routine use of emergency powers in the United States demonstrates that Gross's warnings about permanent emergencies have some relevance in the United States. At the same time, it is ironic that apparent Congressional disobedience to its obligations under the National Emergencies Act and the refusal of courts to order a legal remedy has allowed emergency powers to persist in the United States. Although Gross intends his extra-legal powers model as an antidote to the real problem of permanent emergencies, there is no guarantee that persistent disobedience by officials will not also create a de facto state of permanent and undeclared emergency. Indeed, Gross's model of extra-legal measures may have its greatest power as a description of America's ambiguous attitudes towards legality both generally and in particular with relation to national security.[25]

[20] 50 USC 1621.

[21] On the dangers of Presidential powers during emergencies, see W.E. Scheuerman, 'Presidentialism and Emergency Government' (Chapter 11) in this volume.

[22] C. Schmitt, *Political Theology* (Cambridge: MIT Press, 1985). See also G. Agamben, *State of Exception* (Chicago: University of Chicago Press, 2005).

[23] 50 USC 1622. [24] Ackerman, *Before the Next Attack*, p. 125.

[25] For an account of extra-legal actions such as renditions, torture, secret prisons and unauthorised electronic surveillance, see S. Chesterman, 'Deny Everything: Intelligence Activities and the Rule of Law' (Chapter 13) in this volume. As Gross recognises, this ambivalence may in part be a reaction to the high degree of legalism in the United States. O. Gross, 'Extra-Legality and the Ethic of Political Responsibility' (Chapter 3), this volume. This

A factor in the failure of American emergency legislation to be obeyed or to provide real restraints on the executive may be the fact that the legislation does not engage with rights.[26] As will be seen, comparable British and Canadian legislation attempts to set out some principles and rights to guide conduct during an emergency.

The National Emergencies Act provides that executive orders, rules and regulations 'shall be transmitted to the Congress promptly under means to assure confidentiality where appropriate',[27] but does not provide for means to publish, nullify or amend secret orders or regulations. To his credit, Professor Ackerman has proposed an enhanced accountability system under his emergency constitution that would give members of opposition parties the majority of seats on an oversight committee and the ability to decide whether to make secret information public or to discuss this information in secret sessions of Congress.[28] There is a need for creative responses to the dilemmas proposed by secret information and Ackerman's proposal in this respect is interesting and bold.

The American emergency legislation has been justly criticised from a number of quarters. After concluding that the American system of emergency regulation gives the President powers that are not checked by either the legislature or the judiciary, Jules Lobel suggested increased engagement with international institutions and more local democracy as possible counterweights.[29] Although there has been citizen engagement with the Patriot Act,[30] as well as reactions to media discovery of various abuses of powers by the executive, one shortcoming of relying on local democracy is the secrecy that may surround much emergency action taken for national security reasons. We cannot be assured that everything will come out, especially outside the United States which is exceptional in its approach to media freedom. An urgent priority in the emergency powers debate should

explanation, however, would not seem to explain Congress's failure to respect the bare bone provisions of the National Emergencies Act.

26 Eric Posner and Adrian Vermeule correctly note that American emergency legislation has not been effective, but conclude from this experience that no *ex ante* emergency legislation including the Ackerman proposals can be effective because of the need for executive flexibility to respond to emergencies. Their argument, however, does not consider the consequences of disobeying laws that either prohibit or require certain justifications for the violation of rights. Moreover, it takes a welfarist approach that trades off rights and security as comparable goods. E. Posner and A. Vermeule, *Terror in the Balance: Security, Liberty, and the Courts* (New York: Oxford University Press, 2007), pp. 163–8 and 28.

27 50 USC 1641. 28 Ackerman, *Before the Next Attack*, p. 85.

29 Lobel, 'Emergency Power and the Decline of Liberalism', 1431 ff.

30 M. Sidel, *More Secure? Less Free?* (Ann Arbour: University of Michigan Press, 2004).

be to devise creative means to ensure the maximum exposure of information about what the state is doing during the emergency. Secrecy can act as the handmaiden for unrestrained executive power during emergencies.

Lobel's second proposal for increased international engagement with the exercise of emergency powers is very interesting. As will be suggested in the fourth part of this chapter, one of the significant benefits of formal derogation of rights is that they may engage increased international scrutiny of actions taken at the domestic level. At the same time, however, international scrutiny of how a government exercises emergency powers may be handicapped by the lack of access to information that the government has an interest in classifying as secret, as well as a deferential application of margins of appreciation by international bodies towards domestic action.[31]

Professor Ackerman has rightly concluded that the National Emergencies Act is seriously deficient and he has proposed more robust and meaningful legislative supervision of emergencies through a supermajoritarian escalator that would require legislative ratification of emergences by increasing majorities of the legislature.[32] He argues that 'the escalator expresses a principled presumption in favour of liberty and permits extensions only when there is growing consensus that they are required most obviously, when a massive second-strike attack occurs and the need to prevent another is imperative'.[33] The supermajoritarian escalator is a good idea because it should empower more meaningful debate and deliberation about the exercise of emergency powers. It could also potentially give minorities who are most likely to be harmed by emergency powers more political power.

Although Professors Gross and Ní Aoláin provide an extremely compelling and sensitive account of how discriminatory attitudes can infect anti-terrorism efforts,[34] they fail to propose a means to ensure respect for non-discrimination in the extra-legal measures model and the reality that

[31] Gross and Ní Aoláin, *Law in Times of Crisis*, ch. 5.

[32] Ackerman, *Before the Next Attack*, p. 80. [33] *Ibid.*

[34] They argue that 'targeting outsiders may . . . be seen as bearing relatively little political cost. In fact, it may be considered politically beneficial'. Gross and Ní Aoláin, *Law in Times of Crisis*, p. 221. They use this accurate insight as a reason against models of accommodation, but it applies more strongly against extra-legal measures that are not disciplined by the generalisability of the formal law. For arguments that racial and religious profiling would not be authorised by explicit legislation but that it can thrive when officials have discretionary power see S. Choudhry and K. Roach, 'Racial and Ethnic Profiling: Statutory Discretion, Constitutional Remedies and Democratic Accountability' (2003) 41 *Osgoode Hall Law Journal* 1.

religious, racial and political minorities associated with terrorists will suffer disproportionately from illegal action under the extra-legal measures model. In contrast, Ackerman's supermajoritarian escalator has a minoritarian bias that will not be present when officials or legislatures decide whether to ratify extra-legal measures.[35]

Ackerman proposes that compensation be provided for those detained but not charged. Although it is difficult to argue against compensation, there is a danger that compensation will routinise the detention of suspected terrorists on unjustified grounds. To his credit, Professor Ackerman recognises that those detained as suspected terrorists will require exoneration as well as compensation. This certainly has been the experience in Canada. The Arar Commission's conclusion that after an exhaustive examination it saw no evidence that Maher Arar had violated any laws or was a threat to national security[36] was practically much more important that the $10.5 million in compensation he later received. Exoneration is essential, but may often be impossible because of the secrecy of information and lingering suspicions.[37] There is a danger that compensation could trivialise the rights that are violated by unjustified detention of terrorist suspects. Damages could become a tax on the suspension of habeas corpus and the detention of Muslims who have come to the attention of the authorities.

B United Kingdom legislation

The United Kingdom enacted the Civil Contingencies Act 2004, to replace previous emergency legislation that allowed the executive almost unfettered power. Emergencies are defined broadly in the new law to include not only wars, terrorism and other security threats, but any event or situation that threatens serious damage to human welfare or the environment including contamination of land, water or air with biological, chemical

[35] Ironically, Ackerman's super-majoritarian escalator could have little bite if there was bipartisan consensus on security issues though it could be much more effective in Canada or Europe where there are multiple parties and Muslim minorities are more active in politics than in the United States.

[36] Maher Arar, a Canadian citizen born in Syria, was detained in the United States when in transit back to Canada and was removed to Syria where he was held and tortured as a terrorist suspect before eventually being released after almost a year's imprisonment. Commission of Inquiry into the Actions of Canadian Officials in Relation to Maher Arar, *Analysis and Recommendations* (Ottawa: Public Works and Government Services, 2006) at 9.

[37] Although exonerated in Canada, Mr Arar has not been exonerated in the United States and remains on their watch list.

or radioactive matter.[38] This approach establishes an all-risk approach to emergencies which is based on a realistic assessment of the multiple risks faced in modern society. By imposing obligations on both the private and public sectors, the Act recognises that responsibilities for emergencies are not restricted to governments. This whole society approach to emergencies seems realistic and necessary and it also has the virtue of dispersing power throughout society and not focusing power in the executive.

The Cabinet still has the ability to make a broad range of emergency regulations, but some effort has been made in the law to restrain powers by principles of proportionality. The government defended the law on the basis that it respected a 'Triple Lock' that requires a serious emergency, that existing legislation is inadequate to prevent, control or mitigate the emergency and that the emergency regulation be proportionate to the emergency.[39] Section 20 requires that the person making the regulations certify that they both satisfy legislative restrictions and are compatible with rights in the European Convention. To be sure, these principles could have been improved by clearer statements and explicit reference to the objective requirements of the situation,[40] but they represent an admirable attempt to provide legal principles and limits on the exercise of power. They can be contrasted with the American emergency legislation which leaves the declaration of emergency totally to the discretion of the President without any reference to legal principles that might guide and restrain the exercise of emergency powers.

The new United Kingdom legislation contemplates that emergency regulations enacted by the executive be placed into a richer constitutional environment that includes the legislature and the judiciary. One section of the new Act provides: 'A person making emergency regulations must have regard to the importance of ensuring that Parliament, the High Court and the Court of Session are able to conduct proceedings in connection with the regulations or action taken under the regulations'.[41] The act also requires that regulations be placed before Parliament and lapse if both houses do not pass a resolution approving them within seven days of receiving the regulations.[42] In any event, the regulations lapse after thirty days, but may be renewed.[43] It is assumed that the regulations will be made public and there is no provision for maintaining confidentiality.

38 The Civil Contingencies Act 2004, c.36, s.1. 39 *Ibid.*, s.20–1.

40 See generally C. Walker and J. Broderick, *The Civil Contingencies Act 2004: Risk, Resilience and the Law in the United Kingdom* (Oxford: Oxford University Press, 2006), ch. 5.

41 The Civil Contingencies Act 2004, s.22(5). 42 *Ibid.*, s.27. 43 *Ibid.*, s.26.

The British legislation may be based on an admirable assumption that all law should be public, but both American and Canadian emergency legislation contemplate some secret law. As will be seen, only the Canadian legislation addresses means to ensure scrutiny and repeal of secret laws.

Undoubtedly, the United Kingdom's legislation could be strengthened and made more creative. At the same time, however, it demonstrates an admirable attempt to outline some broad legal principles to govern emergency governance rather than simply consigning these questions to the discretion of the sovereign.

C. Canadian legislation

Canada's Emergencies Act[44] was carefully drafted in light of Canada's unhappy experience with the use of unfettered executive powers under the War Measures Act which was used to intern Japanese–Canadians during World War II and to detain about 500 people associated with Quebec separatism during the October Crisis of 1970 in which two terrorist cells murdered a Cabinet Minister and kidnapped a British diplomat. The War Measures Act provided little in the way of objective restraints on the exercise of executive power and the courts generally deferred to the exercise of executive power. The Supreme Court upheld the denial of habeas corpus under the Act concluding: 'The exercise of legislative functions such as those here in question by the Governor-in-Council rather than by Parliament is no doubt something to be avoided as far as possible. But we are living in extraordinary times which necessitate the taking of extraordinary measures'.[45]

One of the most important and unique features of the Emergencies Act is its pre-commitment to respecting non-discrimination norms during an emergency. Section 4(b) specifically addresses the sad history of discriminatory internment in Canada by providing that '[n]othing in this Act shall be construed or applied so as to confer on the Governor in Council the power to make orders or regulations . . . providing for the detention, imprisonment or internment of Canadian citizens or permanent residents . . . on the basis of race, national or ethnic origin, colour, religion, sex, age or mental or physical disability'.[46] This echoes Article 4 of

[44] SC 1988, c.29. [45] *Re Gray* (1918) 57 SCR 150 at 181–2.

[46] Questions can be raised about the adequacy of this provision especially as it relates to so-called partial profiling in which the state detains a person in part on the basis of race or ethnic and social origin and in part on some other basis. It also does not prevent

the International Covenant on Civil and Political Rights (ICCPR)[47] which provides that emergency measures cannot be inconsistent with international law obligations or 'involve discrimination solely on the ground of race, colour, sex, language, religion or social order'.

Although the Act is designed to apply to all emergencies, it provides for different types and levels of emergency. The most extreme emergency, a war emergency, does not have to be ratified by Parliament for 120 days, a public welfare emergency caused by natural disasters and pandemics has to be ratified within 90 days, an international emergency that affects more than one state by imminent or actual use of force, intimidation or coercion has to be ratified within 60 days, and a public order emergency caused by temporary threats to the security of Canada that cannot be effectively dealt with under other laws within 30 days. Although governments could attempt to manipulate these categories, they would have to justify such attempts to the courts in part because the executive cannot vary the Act by executive decree.[48]

Like section 4(b) with its pre-commitment to non-discrimination, other parts of the Act recognise from past experience that the government may limit rights during an emergency. Section 8 provides that public welfare emergency powers should not be used to end strikes. Section 19 provides that public assemblies may only be restricted during public order emergencies 'when they may reasonably be expected to lead to a breach of the peace'. This provision both enables and restrains the state by incorporating an imminence requirement that has been neglected in modern anti-terrorism legislation. Canada's ordinary law of emergencies attempts to place some prior restraints on executive power. As Kim Lane Scheppele has argued, the modern Canadian approach attempts to restrain executive excesses in emergencies while the relevant American law still follows a pre-World War II tradition of martial law and executive domination.[49]

Executive action in declaring an emergency must under the Act be justified to Parliament at the earliest opportunity. It is not a Schmittian

discrimination against non-citizens. It is also not clear that protections from discriminatory law enforcement should be limited to protection against detention, imprisonment and internment.

[47] This is reenforced by the fact that the ICCPR is specifically referenced in the preamble of the Emergencies Act 'particularly with respect to those fundamental rights that are not to be limited or abridged even in a national emergency'.

[48] Emergencies Act, SC 1988, s.4(a).

[49] K.L. Scheppele, 'North American Emergencies: The Use of Emergency Powers in Canada and the United States' (2006) 4 *International Journal of Constitutional Law* 213.

exercise of unrestrained power. The executive's explanation to Parliament must also include an account of any consultations that it has held with the provinces about the emergency,[50] thus using federalism as a possible restraint on federal executive domination. At the same time, no attempt is made, as in the United Kingdom's legislation, to codify legal principles of proportionality to govern when and how far the executive should invoke emergency powers.

The Emergencies Act provides that motions to discontinue the emergency can be initiated by 20 Members of the House of Commons or ten Members of the Senate. These low numbers represent an attempt to empower minorities in Parliament. In the last decade they would have meant that both leftist and rightist parties and a party dedicated to the separation of Quebec from Canada all could have initiated debate.

One of the largest problems in reviewing state actions during an emergency will be a lack of full information. The speed and confusion of emergencies and emergency responses is one factor, but so is the need or purported need for secrecy as the state responds to various emergencies. This problem is addressed by providing that a special Parliamentary Committee, subject to a secrecy oath that is even included in the legislation, can amend and repeal secret orders and regulations.[51] This Committee is required to have representation from all parties with 12 members in the House of Commons and all parties represented in the Senate. Practically, this would mean that both socialist and separatist parties would be represented on the Committee. This would provide a much more diverse form of review than under Professor Ackerman's proposals for a bipartisan oversight committee controlled by the minority in Congress.

The Parliamentary Committee is required to report on 'the exercise of powers and the performance of duties and functions pursuant to a declaration of emergency'[52] both during and after the emergency. In addition, the government is required to 'cause an inquiry to be held into the circumstances that led to the declaration being issued and the measures taken for dealing with the emergency'[53] within 60 days after the revocation or expiry of the emergency. This requirement should be viewed in the backdrop of the Canadian custom of appointing public inquiries, such as the Arar Commission, headed by a sitting or retired judge. The appointment of a similar judicial inquiry to examine the state's conduct during the emergency should ensure a thorough and impartial examination of

[50] Emergencies Act, SC 1988, s.58(3). [51] *Ibid.*, s.62(5).
[52] *Ibid.*, s.62(1). [53] *Ibid.*, s.63.

the government's conduct. Although such an inquiry would technically be part of the executive, it would enjoy significant de facto independence. The judge heading the inquiry would retain the implicit right to resign and return to his or her regular duties on the bench if the government did not provide full information or attempted to interfere with the Commission's independence. A judicial inquiry into the government's actions during the inquiry could consider governmental actions that would otherwise be secret. As with the Arar Commission, it could challenge and even litigate against the government over the appropriate balance between publicity and secrecy.[54] Legislation that requires review of what happened in an emergency might provide a more reliable means of ensuring review and deliberation about emergency actions than the passage of an act of indemnity or the exercise of prosecutorial discretion or jury nullification that would be used to review illegal action committed during emergencies under Professor Gross's extra-legal measures model.[55]

Canada's Emergencies Act also addresses issues of compensation based on the general principle that individuals are entitled to 'reasonable compensation' from the Crown for 'loss, injury or damage as a result of any thing done, or purported to be done, under the Act'.[56] The Act requires judges of the Federal Court to be used as assessors to determine disputes about compensation. This represents an interesting attempt to bring judges into the process. At the same time, the right to seek judicial review from an assessment is also maintained.[57] Compensation, however, will not address the need to exonerate those who may have been wrongfully identified and detained by the state as security risks.

D. Summary

The best emergencies statutes will, consistent with Dyzenhaus's theory, make creative use of all branches of governments in maintaining the rule of law. The Canadian law demonstrates the potential for legislative review

[54] See *Canada* v. *Commission of Inquiry into the Actions of Canadian Officials in Relation to Maher Arar* [2007] FC 766 deciding that the majority of material that the Arar Commission concluded should be made public could be released over the government's objection that it would excessively harm national security, national defence or international relations.

[55] Gross argues that acts of indemnity 'presents the legislature with a unique opportunity to review the actions of the executive branch and assess them *ex post*, relieved from the pressures of the crisis, before deciding whether to ratify them'. Gross, 'Stability and Flexibility', in *Global Anti-Terrorism Law and Policy*, p. 105.

[56] Emergencies Act, SC 1988, s.48(1). [57] *Ibid.*, s.52(3).

both during and after the emergency.[58] It has procedures somewhat similar to Ackerman's proposed supermajoritarian escalator that are designed to empower legislative minorities during an emergency. It also demonstrates how there can be a creative blurring of all three branches of government that may be particularly helpful to supervise the state during emergencies. Committees that are staffed by a combination of retired judges, retired politicians and retired executive officials may have the combination of the necessary expertise, credibility and public confidence to review the often-secret actions of the state during an emergency.[59] The Canadian Act provides carefully considered *ex ante* restrictions prohibiting internment on the basis of race, national or ethnic origin or religion. The new United Kingdom legislation also sets out legal principles of justification for emergency powers while the comparable American legislation simply recognises the power of the President to declare an emergency while providing Congress a power that has not been used to end emergencies. The American legislation contains no *ex ante* restrictions or legal principles of justification on what can be done in an emergency and no requirements for review of what has been done in an emergency.

IV. The derogation model of emergencies

So far in this chapter I have argued that the post-9/11 debate about emergencies has been more concerned about the rights of terrorist suspects than with the full range of emergencies that may require swift and strong responses from the state. I have also examined some framework statutes that provide for the governance of emergencies and have suggested that they should enable the legislature, the executive, the judiciary and creative hybrid institutions to play a role in applying the rule of law to state conduct during emergencies. In this section, I return to the questions of rights and

[58] As my colleague Lorraine Weinrib has written: 'Bicameral, multi-party examination of government policy, including systemic review of its application in individual cases with access to confidential information and a reporting mechanism can prevent and remedy abuses long before they would come to the attention of the judiciary'. L. Weinrib, 'Terrorism's Challenge to the Constitutional Order', in R.J. Daniels, P. Macklem and K. Roach (eds.), *The Security of Freedom: Essays on Canada's Anti-Terrorism Bill* (Toronto: University of Toronto Press, 2001), p. 105.

[59] K. Roach, 'Review and Oversight of National Security Activities' (2007) 29 *Cardozo Law Review* 53; M. Tushnet, 'Controlling Executive Power in the War Against Terrorism' (2005) 118 *Harvard Law Review* 2673.

examine what should be done when an emergency may require the state to take actions that derogate from rights.

Pointing to the experiences of Northern Ireland and Israel, Oren Gross warns of the danger of a perpetual state of emergency in which powers introduced to deal with the terrorist threat seep into many other parts of the legal system.[60] Gross's warnings are important and historically accurate, but post-9/11 the greatest threat to rights has come not from use of emergency powers, but rather from undeclared emergencies that have attempted to give permanent legislation what my colleague David Dyzenhaus has criticised as a thin veneer of legality. In Dyzenhaus's terms, the problem has been more grey holes than black holes.[61]

To be sure, there have been attempts to create black holes that are states of exception devoid of law such as the attempts to resist all judicial review of the Guantánamo detentions and the warrantless spying by the National Security Agency. Slowly but surely, however, these practices were challenged in court and are now being subject to legislation. Although there has been one officially declared black hole, namely Britain's derogation from the right to liberty to authorise indeterminate detention, it has been repealed after the House of Lords declared it to be disproportionate and discriminatory.[62]

In what follows, I will argue that it is better for courts to push states towards formal black holes that require explicit derogations from rights than to legitimate diluted versions of rights and grey holes. Derogation contemplates official, prospective and legislative declarations of an emergency and a clear desire to reject rights. Derogation is designed to be a temporary measure that comes with considerable political and legal costs, both domestically and internationally. Derogation is a conservative strategy because, like emergency powers, it recognises the baseline set by existing rights, even as it departs from them.[63] Unlike emergency powers, however, the very act of derogation recognises, and in a nation that accepts human rights, stigmatises extraordinary measures as inconsistent with rights. Finally, a derogation from rights is not a blank cheque as the exact extent of the derogation may be subject to domestic judicial review. Some constitutions have standards to justify derogations from rights and some exempt some rights from derogation. Even under more permissive

[60] Gross, 'Chaos and Rules'. [61] Dyzenhaus, *The Constitution of Law*.

[62] *A* v. *Secretary of State* [2004] UKHL 56.

[63] J. Ferejohn and P. Pasquino, 'The Law of the Exception: A Typology of Emergency Powers' (2004) 2 *International Journal of Constitutional Law* 210.

approaches, any derogation will be subject to continuing legislative review and international supervision.

A. Derogation under the American suspension clause

The American suspension clause is restrictive in only allowing one right to be suspended and only for the dire emergencies presented by rebellions and invasions. These restrictions make it possible for judges to take a strong stand in resisting both implicit and explicit suspensions of habeas corpus. In *Hamdi* v. *Rumfeld*, Justice Scalia with the concurrence of Justice Stevens, affirmed the importance of explicit legislative derogations from rights.[64] Like Justice Souter, Justice Scalia refused to find authorisation for detentions of citizens in Congress's authorisation to the President to use all necessary force concluding that 'contrary to the plurality's view, I do not think this statute even authorizes the detention of a citizen with the clarity necessary' to displace various presumptions related to detention. The suspension clause could have considerable value in ensuring that the legislature makes a clear statement of its desire to derogate from rights and in doing so pays the political price for such an act.

Justice Scalia's opinion, however, must be read in light of his subsequent dissent in *Hamdan* v. *Rumsfeld* which held that it was not necessary for Congress to suspend habeas corpus to deprive non-citizens detained at Guantánamo of habeas corpus. There are hints of judicial abdication even in *Hamdi*. In particular, the idea the court should defer to Congress's determination of 'whether the attacks of September 11, 2001 constitute an "invasion" and whether those attacks still justify suspension several years later, are questions for Congress rather than this Court'.[65] This statement is unobjectionable if it simply means that the court will not consider the question because Congress had yet to make a clear statement, but it is more problematic if it means that the court will cede its interpretative authority over the Constitution to Congress on whether there has been a constitutionally sufficient invasion to justify suspension. Although there are eloquent defenders of coordinate construction in which elected legislatures act on their own interpretation of the Constitution even when it

[64] Justice Scalia concluded that 'Although this provision does not state that suspension must be effected by, or authorized by, a legislative act, it has been so understood, consistent with the English practice and the Clause's placement in Article I'. *Hamdi* v. *Rumsfeld* 542 US 507 (2004) at 563.

[65] *Ibid.*, at 579.

differs from that of the independent courts,[66] such an approach is problematic when the legislature acts on behalf of the interests of a permanent majority and takes away the rights of a perpetual minority such as non-citizens or Muslims suspected of terrorism.

Another objectionable feature of Justice Scalia's opinion is the statement that 'when the writ is suspended, the Government is entirely free from judicial oversight'.[67] Although a clear and justified suspension of habeas corpus would deprive courts of that vital device to determine the legality of detention, there should be other mechanisms to challenge detentions for violating other norms. Justice Scalia's approach in allowing a suspension of habeas corpus to create a constitutional void can be contrasted to that taken by Justice Davis in *Ex Parte Milligan* who reasoned that a suspension of habeas corpus only suspends the ability of the courts to require the production of detainees. 'The Constitution goes no further. It does not say, after a writ of habeas corpus is denied a citizen, that he shall be tried otherwise than by the course of the common law . . . [the framers] limited the suspension to one great right, and left the rest to remain forever inviolable'.[68] Justice Scalia was too quick to defer to the legislature on whether derogation has been justified and to view derogation as a completely lawless zone as opposed to a temporary and limited black hole in which habeas corpus and only habeas corpus has been suspended.[69]

One of the values of clear statements that require derogation is that they are democracy forcing. They can force the executive to obtain explicit legislative authorisation and they can play a role in producing what Mark Tushnet in his contribution to this volume calls 'moralised politics'.[70]

[66] M. Tushnet, *Taking the Constitution Away from the Courts* (Princeton: Princeton University Press, 1999).

[67] *Hamdi* v. *Rumsfeld* at 565.

[68] *Ex Parte Milligan* 71 US 2 (1866) at 126. Dyzenhaus similarly argues that 'a derogation from a human rights regime is not a derogation from the rule of law' and he cautions against 'an all or nothing' approach to derogation. D. Dyzenhaus, 'Schmitt v. Dicey: Are States of Emergency Inside or Outside of the Legal Order' (2006) 27 *Cardozo Law Review* 2005 at 2038 and 2040.

[69] This may explain Dyzenhaus's criticism of Scalia on the basis that 'once there is such a clear statement he is prepared to give the stamp of legality to the legal black hole. Blank cheques are fine as long as they are properly certified'. Dyzenhaus, *The Constitution of Law*, pp. 49–50.

[70] M. Tushnet, 'The Political Constitution of Emergency Politics' (Chapter 6), this volume. Professor Tushnet's argument, however, would reject the idea that judicial enforcement or framing the issue as a legal issue of derogation is necessary to achieve a 'moralised politics'. For a related argument that derogation provisions unfairly force legislatures to admit that they are violating human rights when they are only engaging in reasonable disagreements

Justice Scalia effectively criticised the plurality's invention of a diluted version of due process in *Hamdi* when he stated that such an approach 'by repeatedly doing what it thinks the political branches ought to do it encourages the lassitude and saps the vitality of government by the people'.[71] Judicial decisions that force democracy are just one act in a multi-act play. In a society that respects rights, legislatures will be tempted to respond to judicial decisions with new legislation. This legislation will often purport to comply with rights and attempt to create what Dyzenhaus would call grey holes. Courts then have a choice whether to force the issue the second time around by declaring that grey holes cannot be justified, effectively forcing the legislature to confront the more difficult issue of creating explicit black holes that derogate from rights.

Justice Scalia's true colours became apparent in *Hamdan* v. *Rumsfeld* when in dissent he held that the argument that the habeas stripping provisions of the Detainee Treatment Act required legislative suspension of habeas corpus could 'be easily dispatched'.[72] His approach is similar to Professor Ackerman's argument about how his emergency statute would satisfy the requirements of the suspension clause. Ackerman would allow Congress to suspend habeas corpus without paying the political or judicial price for invoking the suspension clause. He admits that his proposed emergency law allowing up to 45 days' detention without full judicial review 'amounts to a partial suspension of the Great Writ'[73] and that 'any restriction of habeas corpus in response to terrorism requires Congress to explore the twilight zone of its constitutional authority' because it is 'a stretch to say that one or two attacks – even very serious ones – amount to an "invasion" or "rebellion"'.[74] Nevertheless, he argues that the court should accept this partial suspension of habeas corpus because the supermajoritarian escalator he proposes 'provides institutional recognition that suspension is a very serious matter'.[75] At the same time, he makes a contradictory argument that 'the easy and extended suspension of the Great Writ by a simple majority in Congress threatens the very foundation of freedom'[76] and should not be accepted. Professor Ackerman's

with the courts over the meaning of rights see J. Waldron, 'Some Models of Dialogue Between Judges and Legislators' (2004) 23 *Supreme Court Law Review* 7. My concern, however, is that without a legal framing of these issues around the question of derogation that the due process rights and equality claims of unpopular groups like suspected terrorists will be trivialised or entirely neglected.

71 *Hamdi* v. *Rumsfeld* at 578.

72 *Hamdan* v. *Rumsfeld* 126 S.Ct. 2749 at 2818 (2006).

73 Ackerman, *Before the Next Attack*, p. 127. 74 *Ibid.*, p. 135.

75 *Ibid.* 76 *Ibid.*, p. 136.

arguments can only be reconciled on the basis that courts should decide cases by making strategic judgments about the relative dangers of suspension of habeas corpus. The courts can ignore a soft and undeclared suspension of habeas, if there is a supermajoritarian escalator, but should enforce the restriction on suspension 'at all cost' should it not be present. Ackerman's approach fudges the suspension of habeas corpus and in doing so attempts to legalise a process of mass detention without judicial review that should only be legal if Congress is prepared to suspend habeas corpus.

B. The Canadian model of derogation

Section 33 of the Canadian Charter is much more permissive than the suspension clause of the American Constitution. It allows federal or provincial legislatures to enact laws notwithstanding fundamental freedoms, legal rights or equality rights for renewable five-year periods. The Charter rights that are not subject to this override, democratic, mobility and minority language rights, are difficult to justify as non-derogable rights on universal standards. The Canadian override would allow Parliament to suspend habeas corpus (one of the legal rights) and even to authorise torture or internment based on race or religion for renewable five-year periods. There is no requirement that there be an emergency or that the measures be strictly necessary in the circumstances.

The Canadian courts have only reviewed the use of the override on one occasion. The Supreme Court upheld Quebec's use of an omnibus override as a protest against the 1982 inclusion of the Charter in the Canadian Constitution over Quebec's dissent. The Court deferred, noting that the legislature might not be able to know what particular Charter right might be relevant in a particular case. A unanimous Court declared 'section 33 lays down requirements of form only, and there is no warrant for importing into it grounds for substantive review of the legislative policy in exercising the override authority in the particular case'.[77]

The Court did not, however, give the legislature an entirely free hand and held that the override could not be used retroactively. The Court's discussion of this matter was quite brief and it justified its decision on the basis that section 33 was ambiguous on this point and the rule of construction against retroactive operation of legislation should be given effect.[78] This decision, however, is perhaps pregnant with meaning. The

[77] *Ford* v. *Quebec* [1988] 2 SCR 712. [78] *Ibid.* at para. 36.

Court's appeal to common law norms governing statutory interpretation suggest that the values of common law constitutionalism may come into play with respect to judicial supervision of the override. Nevertheless, such a reading is in tension with the Court's unequivocal statement that it would not review the substantive merits of the override.

The Canadian requirement that the override can only be used prospectively may support Dyzenhaus's argument that torture is unlegalisable and can only be excused as a violation of law after it has occurred.[79] The Canadian rule against the retroactive use of the override also puts in doubt overrides that function as bills of attainder or criminalise the actions of specific individuals or groups.[80] Once Canadian courts start applying some of the values of the rule of law to the legislature's use of the override, they may end up applying all of its values. This could provide some judicial protections for the rule of law but perhaps at the expense of devaluing an explicit and considered legislative derogation from rights.

Taken by itself and without any rule-of-law restraints, the Canadian override could be an invitation to legislative tyranny. The override has been infrequently employed in Canada. Its major use has been by Quebec in response to a Supreme Court decision that struck down a law that prohibited the use of languages other than French in outdoor commercial signs. The use of the override was controversial and led to Anglophone Ministers resigning from the Cabinet. It also led to Anglophone merchants bringing successful complaints to the then Human Rights Committee of the United Nations under an Optional Protocol to the ICCPR that Canada has signed. As I have suggested elsewhere, this protocol adds an international dimension to dialogues about rights in Canada.[81] Any Canadian exercise of the derogation power can be subject to international review and comment.

[79] Dyzenhaus, *The Constitution of Law*, p. 214. See also Gross, 'Are Torture Warrants Warranted?' (2004) 88 *Minnesota Law Review* 1481 for a similar conclusion. For a contrary argument that torture could only be justified and not excused, see Andrew Simester, 'Necessity, Torture and the Rule of Law' (Chapter 12) in this volume.

[80] For an early rule-of-law argument against declaring specific groups to be illegal under Canada's old War Measures Act see N. Lyon, 'Constitutional Validity of Sections 3 and 4 of the Public Order Regulations' (1971) 18 *McGill Law Journal 136.* But see *Gagnon* v. *Vallieres* (1971) 14 CRNS 350 rejecting this argument.

[81] K. Roach, 'Constitutional, Remedial and International Dialogues About Rights: The Canada Experience' (2005) 40 *Texas International Law Journal* 537. Gross makes a similar point with respect to *ex post* legislative ratifications of illegal acts when he notes that 'even if a particular extra-legal act is domestically ratified *ex post*, it may be subject to a different judgment on the international plane'. Gross, 'Stability and Flexibility', in *Global Anti-Terrorism Law and Policy*, p. 104.

The availability of the override has been used by the Court as justification for making controversial decisions. Derogation provisions may allow courts to be more aggressive on matters affecting national security, precisely because the government retains the option of derogating from rights as interpreted by the courts. The Court's post-9/11 record, however, has been mixed and in one case it held open the very disturbing possibility that it might find deportation to torture to be constitutional in 'exceptional circumstances' without even requiring explicit legislative authorisation or the use of the override.[82] Deportation to torture would always be unjust but the use of the override to authorise it would at least clearly signal to Canadian citizens and the international community what was at stake. I doubt that any Canadian government would use the override to authorise torture. As matters stand now, should courts in the future ever authorise torture, they may do so retroactively by finding it to be a constitutionally exceptional circumstance in a particular case and without full and robust legislative debate. Although the Canadian model of derogation is the most permissive for governments of the models outlined here, it at least requires prospective legislative action. This should ensure advance warnings and an opportunity for national and international debate and condemnation.

C. The European and international model of derogation

To my knowledge the only government that has employed an explicit derogation from rights in response to 9/11 was the United Kingdom, which in 2001 derogated from the right to a fair trial to authorise the indeterminate detention of non-citizens suspected of involvement with international terrorism who could not be deported because of concerns that they would be tortured. Although the decision to derogate received much criticism, it was made in part because of an acceptance of the absolute right against torture. In addition, the derogation was made temporary for 15 months and was subject to special review provisions.[83] Writing in 2003, Conor Gearty warned of the legitimating potential of derogation provisions coupled with the judiciary's traditional deference towards government on matters of national security. He wrote that:

> the override clauses contained in typical human rights charters can, in most states, be actualized without proper democratic accountability. Having been offered a button marked 'self-destruct', it would be surprising if

[82] *Suresh* v. *Canada* [2002] 1 SCR 3 at para. 78.

[83] *Anti-Terrorism, Crime and Security Act 2001*, c.24, ss.28 and 29.

> governments – even non-malicious ones – did not occasionally succumb to the temptation to press it. This is especially so in the atmosphere after 9/11 and has already produced a derogation in the United Kingdom.[84]

I must disagree with Professor Gearty on several accounts. Derogation in the United Kingdom, as well as in Canada and in the United States, all require legislation, which satisfies the ordinary meanings of 'proper democratic accountability'. With the exception of the United Kingdom, countries have not hit the self-destruct button by making formal derogations. People care about their rights and democratic governments have proven not to be eager to make formal derogations. Finally, Professor Gearty, like many others, underestimated the ability of the judiciary in the United Kingdom to supervise derogations.[85] In the first Belmarsh decision, the House of Lords declared the derogation to be disproportionate and discriminatory because there was not a rational connection between preventing terrorism and detaining only non-citizens suspected of terrorism.[86]

Parliament accepted the House of Lords's decision by repealing the derogating provisions, but it also responded with new legislation providing for control orders that could be imposed on both non-citizens and citizens. Requiring the legislature to derogate from the rights of their citizens maximises the potential for full democratic debate and accountability for derogations.

The potential for democratic opposition is, however, only a potential. Parliament responded to the Belmarsh decision with legislation that provided a framework for both non-derogating and derogating control orders. To the extent that it provided for the possibility of derogation, Parliament followed the British pattern of making derogations with respect to anti-terrorism legislation in Northern Ireland. Extensive use of derogations raises Professor Gearty's concerns about legitimising and routinising derogations.

But again, I think these concerns underestimate the reluctance of democratic governments to derogate from the rights of their constituents. The

[84] C. Gearty, 'Reflections on Civil Liberties in an Age of Counterterrorism' (2003) 41 *Osgoode Hall Law Journal* 185 at 203.

[85] On the deference shown by the European Court of Human Rights to derogations, especially from democracies such as Ireland and the United Kingdom, see Gross and Ní Aoláin, *Law in Time of Crisis*, pp. 268–89. For valuable proposals to strengthen the European community's supervision of derogations and to expand the range of non-derogable rights to include non-discrimination norms, see R.St.J. Macdonald, 'Derogations under Article 15 of the European Convention' (1998) 36 *Columbia Journal of Transnational Law* 225.

[86] *A* v. *Secretary of State* [2004] UKHL 56.

British government has so far attempted to avoid derogation by using extremely restrictive control orders in the guise of non-derogating orders. Although the courts should call the government's bluff on the issue of whether the restrictive control orders derogate from liberty, the government's initial use of non-derogating control orders is a testament to its reluctance to pay the political costs of derogation. The fact that the derogation remains an option should also embolden judges. For example, a trial judge who declared that non-derogating control orders were incompatible with rights appealed to the option of derogation as a justification for not adopting a deferential approach to judicial review when he stated:

> The importance of protecting members of the public from the risk of terrorism is not in doubt, but the importance of that objective is not a reason for the court to be less inclined to classify the obligations in these control orders as a deprivation of, rather than a restriction upon, liberty. The Convention makes express provision in Article 15 for there to be a derogation from *(inter alia)* Article 5 'In time of war or other public emergency threatening the life of the nation' . . . In the absence of a derogation under Article 15 of the Convention the respondents are entitled to the full protection of Article 5, and there is no justification for any attempt to water down that protection in response to the threat of terrorism.[87]

A decision that the existing control orders derogate from Article 5 could promote sober second thoughts about whether the government can justify a derogation to the public and the courts. Derogations have both political and legal costs. The derogation option provides judges with a safety net as they negotiate the national security high wire. If the judges err on the side of liberty, they know that the legislature can respond by arguing that security requires derogation.

Derogation, especially after the first Belmarsh decision, is not an instant or final self-destruct button. The government will have to report the derogation to the Council of Europe and under the control order legislation, derogations are limited to 12 months.[88] Even if the legislature decides to use derogating control orders, this will not be the end of the rule of law because the Belmarsh case suggests that the British courts are capable of taking a hard look at whether the government can justify the derogation.

[87] [2006] EWHC 1623 (Admin) at para. 43.

[88] Prevention of Terrorism Act 2005, c.2, s.6. Human Rights Act 1998, s.16. however, follows the more permissive Canadian model of allowing derogations for five-year periods.

D. Summary

The mechanism of derogation resembles common law requirements that the legislature make clear statements if it intends to derogate from rights. For this reason, Dyzenhaus has argued that the idea of a common law constitution 'which controls Parliament does not depend on whether judges will in fact decide they have the authority to resist . . . an explicit override'. Fundamental to common law constitutionalism is the idea that 'when a Parliament has explicitly declared that it does not want the executive to be bound by fundamental legal values, that declaration comes with a political cost'.[89] This is supported by Dyzenhaus's overall conclusion that 'when push comes to shove, all that judges can do is take up the role of weathermen and make real to the people what kind of choice their government is making'.[90] But in a national and international environment that cares about rights, such judicial signals and forcing of legislatures to confront the unhappy prospect of creating black holes will often be enough to make legislatures pull back from the abyss.

Although democratic derogation is part of his model of legality and common law constitutionalism, Professor Dyzenhaus is ambiguous about what judges should do when confronted by a clear derogation and his ambiguity reflects the different models of derogation discussed above. At some junctures, he favours the Canadian model of democratic derogation and suggests that so long as judges force the legislature to clearly state that it wishes to rule without rights and the rule of law, this is the best that the judge can do.[91] The judge is only a weatherman who helps ensure that the public is informed by the legislature that a bad storm has arrived.

At other junctures, Dyzenhaus's judge fights the storm and his vision of derogation is much closer to that found in the European and American models examined above. He criticises the House of Lords's first Belmarsh decision for deferring to the government on the question of whether there was an emergency. This suggests that judges confronted with a derogation should take a hard look both at whether there is an emergency and whether the state's response is justified. This is a robust form of judicial review in the face of a clear legislative invocation of emergency powers and a clear decision to use explicit powers of derogation.

At times, however, my colleague seems to shy away from derogation entirely. He criticises Justice Scalia's dissent in *Hamdi* on the basis that

[89] Dyzenhaus, *The Constitution of Law*, p. 98. [90] *Ibid.*, p. 233.

[91] The judge respects the override not 'merely because it is technically valid' but also because 'it is the product of a properly conducted democratic procedure'. *Ibid.*, p. 211.

Scalia 'is prepared to countenance the government writing itself a blank cheque, as long as it can persuade Congress to certify it'.[92] This seems to suggest little respect for clear legislative decisions to derogate from rights.

Professor Dyzenhaus's theory could be sharpened by greater clarity about his approach to derogation. In earlier work, he drew a distinction between liberal constitutionalism based on judicial supremacy in the American model and a more democratic and dialogic form of constitutionalism.[93] He has built on this point in his work on emergencies by arguing that emergencies require the abandonment of a formal separation of powers and a willingness to allow the executive and the legislature to be a full partner in the rule-of-law project. This is well and good but avoids the critical question of what judges should do when faced with a democratic derogation. Are they simply weatherman? Or should they fight the storm? To my mind, a fuller acceptance of derogation would solidify the democratic credentials of Dyzenhaus's powerful and wide-ranging theory of the rule of law.

Professor Gross has expressed concerns that the executive may be more aggressive when it is supported by *ex ante* legal authorisations.[94] His concerns would be increased in those cases in which the legislature is prepared to make an explicit derogation from rights. Such an argument, however, discounts the ability of judges to interpret the exact ambit of a particular derogation and to apply some rule-of-law values to a derogation even under the permissive Canadian model. The American and European models of derogation provide the judge with additional grounds to review the necessity and proportionality of the derogation. The ability of judges to review the derogation, to fight the storm, could also influence executive conduct during the emergency in a manner not altogether different than that contemplated under the extra-legal measures model. Although Gross places much reliance on the possibility of prosecution as a factor that will

92 Dyzenhaus, 'The State of Emergency in Legal Theory', in *Global Anti-Terrorism Law and Policy*, p. 86.

93 Dyzenhaus, 'Law as Justification' (1998) 14 *South African Journal of Human Rights* 11. See also S. Gardbaum, 'The New Commonwealth Model of Constitutionalism' (2001) 49 *American Journal of Comparative Law* 707; K. Roach, 'Constitutional and Common Law Dialogues' (2001) 80 *Canadian Bar Review* 481.

94 In relation to Governor Eyre's conduct during the Jamaica crisis, Professor Gross questions whether 'the Governor would have been a bit more circumspect and his actions a bit more cautious and less flagrant had the compulsion of legality not been satisfied ex ante, for the imposition of martial law and the measures that followed?' He also cites the anxiety of some within the Bush administration over possible prosecutions as evidence of the restraining effects of the extra-legal approach. Gross, Chapter 3, pp. 78–80.

restrain extra-legal actions, this restraint can be nullified if the executive actor is confident of receiving a pardon or the benefit of prosecutorial discretion. One member of the executive can exempt another member of the executive from the consequence of extra-legal behaviour. Such secret self-dealing is a weakness of the extra-legal model. In contrast, the independent courts will play the dominant role in the derogation model because they will determine the precise ambit and in some cases the necessity and proportionality of the derogation.

V. Conclusion

Most recent commentators writing about emergency powers have focused on the dangers of a repeat of 9/11 or a ticking terrorist bomb while ignoring other real emergencies including Hurricane Katrina and the Asian tsunami. Even within the limited confines of emergencies presented by terrorism, most thinking has been about whether the rights of terrorist suspects should be violated in attempting to prevent terrorism, as opposed to limiting harms and speeding recovery after acts of terrorism.

The skewed nature of the post-9/11 emergency powers debate is unfortunate because little attention has been applied to the ordinary law of emergencies, the laws that govern a wide range of emergencies in many jurisdictions. Such laws provide insights into how the rule of law can be preserved in emergencies. The optimal emergency statute should take up Dyzenhaus's challenge of committing each branch of government, as well as creative hybrids of the different branches, to the maintenance of the rule of law with its emphasis on limited power, non-discrimination and effective review. It should provide legal principles to guide the executive's actions in declaring and acting during emergencies, but it should also provide for effective legislative, executive and judicial review of the state's conduct during the emergency.

To the extent that the post-9/11 emergency powers debate is more about overriding rights in an attempt to prevent terrorism than about how the state should respond to all emergencies, greater attention should be paid to formal and temporary derogations from rights. Derogation measures are already built into most domestic and international rights protection instruments. Since 9/11 we have been too quick to assign ordinary and existing laws to the dustbin of history and to propose novel models that may have unforeseen and harmful consequences.

The optimal derogation provision should be designed to maximise both political and legal deliberation about the justifications for derogation.

Derogations should be based on a deliberate legislative decision that it is necessary to override rights in an emergency. This can be contrasted with Gross's extra-legal measures model which gives each member of the executive a discretion to decide when it is necessary to dispense with rights and laws in order to deal with an emergency. Derogations can also, as the post-9/11 experience in the United Kingdom demonstrates, be subject to robust judicial review. The *ex ante* restraints on derogations will largely be political, but the courts can still play a valuable *ex post* role in interpreting the ambit of particular derogations and in ensuring that derogations are justified and as consistent with the rule of law as possible.

If there is a need for a third way to deal with terrorism not captured by the laws of crime or of war, the derogation model should be considered. Explicit legislative derogation from rights will have significant political costs, ones that most democratic governments have so far been unwilling to pay even in the post-9/11 environment. Moreover, the option of derogation provides judges with a resource to resist legal grey holes that are based on implicit states of permanent emergency and implicit derogations from rights. Derogations honour rights even as they admit that the government is prepared to govern without regard to rights and they force legislatures to be candid about the effects of their actions. Even when they are employed, derogations can offer justiciable questions about ambit of particular derogations, the proportionality of the state's response and the existence of an emergency.

Derogations are a legal and democratic version of Professor Gross's extra-legal measures. They provide an opportunity for both democratic debate about whether a derogation is justified and for reviews of the continued need for and effects of a derogation. Although routine derogations could lead to tyranny, the enactment of permanent grey hole legislation and secret illegalities committed and pardoned by the executive have so far represented a much greater threat to rights and the rule of law in the post-9/11 world than explicit and democratic derogations from rights.

Derogations, like the best emergencies statutes, should be based on explicit legal standards and subject to creative forms of judicial, legislative and administrative review and reconsideration. No model can provide a foolproof guarantee against the real dangers of permanent emergencies that Professor Gross astutely warns against. Nevertheless, wise design of ordinary laws to govern emergencies with the requirement that any derogation from rights be made democratically and subject to review and reconsideration provide the optimal conditions for subjecting all emergencies to the rule of law.

11

Presidentialism and emergency government

WILLIAM E. SCHEUERMAN

Liberal democracy comes in many different shapes and sizes. We find presidents and prime ministers, strong courts outfitted with constitutional review authority as well as weak courts deferential to the legislature, written and unwritten constitutions, bicameralism and unicameralism and a seemingly infinite variety of complex institutional mixtures and compounds. Does this matter for emergency government? Of course it does. Has the post-9/11 debate about emergency power paid proper attention to institutional diversity within contemporary liberal democracy? Probably not. Too many recent attempts to formulate convincing liberal democratic models of emergency law neglect the special challenges posed by *presidentialism*. Especially in presidential systems, the executive possesses strong incentives to exploit, perpetuate and sometimes even manufacture crises. Any plausible model of emergency government not only must acknowledge the fundamental institutional dynamics of presidentialism, but also needs to figure out how to counteract their potentially deleterious consequences for the rule of law (Part I). Unfortunately, the otherwise provocative ideas of two of the most creative contemporary theoreticians of emergency government, Oren Gross and David Dyzenhaus, fail on this score (Parts II and III). Their critical and at times unfairly dismissive responses to those scholars who have at least *begun* to tackle the challenges of presidentialism obscure some of the crucial questions at hand (Part IV).

Let me confess at the outset to at least a certain amount of intellectual and political parochialism. The world's most prominent presidential democracy remains, of course, the United States; my theoretical concerns here derive from deep anxieties about the problematic history of US

I am grateful to all the participants at the Singapore National University symposium in which Gross and Dyzenhaus's ideas were discussed, my colleague, Aurelian Craiutu, for critical comments on an earlier draft, as well as David Dyzenhaus and Oren Gross who greeted my criticisms with their usual generosity. Special thanks, of course, go to Victor V. Ramraj.

emergency government. In recent decades, presidentialism has been subject to devastating criticisms and constitutional architects in the new democracies have in my view rightly hesitated before reproducing it. Only 32 countries, mostly in Latin and South America, have presidential regimes closely resembling the US model.[1] Presidentialism, in fact, has been widely influenced by the US constitutional model. Because of the awesome power advantages enjoyed by the United States, however, the high cost of its version of presidential emergency government is necessarily borne by others as well. If I am right to posit that fundamental institutional mechanisms leave the presidential executive with a pressing political interest in establishing and perpetuating emergency rule, the implications of my argument become anything but parochial. In a historical situation in which the United States continues to exert vast influence at the international level, the victims of its system of presidential emergency government, collateral damage of the institutional irrationalities of an outdated version of liberal democracy desperately in need of overhaul, will be found across the globe.

I. Presidents and their emergencies

Presidentialism can be usefully defined as consisting of four core elements. First, it rests on what Juan Linz aptly describes as *dual democratic legitimacy.* Both the executive and legislature possess independent sources of democratic legitimacy since each is separately elected (either directly or indirectly) by the people. Institutional rivalry is a necessary component of the system since both the President and Parliament can make plausible claims to democratic legitimacy. Of course, conflict is most likely to surface when the executive and legislature are controlled by rival political constituencies. Even when dominated by the same party, however, 'conflict is always latent and sometimes likely to erupt dramatically; there is no democratic principle to resolve it, and the mechanisms that might exist are generally complex, highly technical, legalistic, and therefore of doubtful democratic legitimacy for the electorate'.[2] Typically the President

[1] B. Ackerman, 'The New Separation of Powers' (2000) 113 *Harvard Law Review* 646. See more generally D.V. Verney, 'Parliamentary Government and Presidential Government', in A. Lijphart (ed.), *Parliamentary Versus Presidential Government* (Oxford: Oxford University Press, 1992), pp. 31–77.

[2] J. Linz, 'Presidential or Parliamentary Democracy: Does it Matter', in J. Linz and A. Valenzuela (eds.), *The Failure Of Presidential Democracy* (Baltimore: Johns Hopkins University Press, 1994), p. 6.

proves more successful at advancing this claim to legitimacy. As Karl Marx astutely observed about Napolean Bonaparte's France:

> [w]hile the votes of France are split up among the seven hundred and fifty members of the National Assembly, they are... on the contrary concentrated on a single individual. While each separate representative of the people represents only this or that party, this or that town, or this or that bridgehead, or even only the mere necessity of electing some one of the seven hundred and fifty... he [e.g., the president] is the elect of the nation and the act of his election is the trump that the sovereign people plays once every four years. The elected National Assembly stands in a metaphysical relation, but the elected President in a personal relation, to the nation... As against the Assembly, he possesses a sort of divine right; he is president by the grace of the people.[3]

The personalistic character of presidential legitimacy is deepened when modern technology allows the executive to cultivate a seemingly direct and unmediated relationship to the electorate: via radio and television the President speaks to each of us in the cosy confines of our kitchens and living rooms. Presidential legitimacy takes on increasingly plebiscitary contours, with the President pictured as an immediate and perhaps even intimate embodiment of the popular will. To be sure, similar tendencies towards plebiscitary and personalistic rule are found in parliamentary regimes and constitutional design is by no means their exclusive source, but the institutional structure of presidential democracy makes them especially pervasive there. Institutional tension remains endemic to presidential democracies, however, because Parliament typically has its own reasons for insisting on its superior democratic virtues. Its members may be elected for shorter terms of office, as in the US example, and tout their localism and 'closeness to home'. Even as the President disparages their parochialism while proclaiming his monopoly at advancing the common good, legislators will always understandably remind the electorate of their own competing democratic credentials.

Second, Marx was prescient in pointing out that presidentialism institutionalises '*a sort of divine right*'. Parliamentary regimes tend to separate the roles of partisan political leader and symbolic head of state, whereas presidential government conflates them. This is obvious and perhaps harmless enough as far as the everyday rituals of presidential government go, but it

[3] K. Marx, *The Eighteenth Brumaire Of Louis Bonaparte* (New York: International Publishers, 1963), pp. 32–3.

manifests itself in more controversial ways as well. Our obsession with presidential charisma arguably represents a quest to find a secular replacement for the magical or divine powers once attributed to monarchs. The commonplace association of, especially, the presidential executive with *energy* and *unity* reproduces traditional defences of European kingship, in which only monarchy was envisioned as capable of providing efficient, expeditious and coherent rule.[4] By no means coincidentally, modern presidents are outfitted with vast institutional powers sometimes rivalling those of their royal predecessors. Especially in foreign and military affairs, where royal prerogative remained relatively unchecked even in constitutional monarchies, presidents continue to enjoy stunning discretionary power. Modern presidents not only take over the symbolic functions of traditional monarchy, but they have inherited some of its most striking institutional attributes (e.g. the executive veto). Not surprisingly perhaps, contemporary US defenders of a strong presidency delight in asserting that it holds substantial discretionary power 'not traditionally recognised as belonging to the British King'.[5]

Aspiring presidents regularly try to 'strut high above the political plane inhabited by ordinary mortals' in order both to accentuate the contrast with parliamentary parochialism and justify their own extraordinary political and constitutional authority.[6] How better to buttress their assertion of political and constitutional pre-eminence than by underlining their superiority to the mere 'special interests' of parliamentary politics? Here as well, similar tendencies can be identified in parliamentary regimes, but they remain more common in presidential democracies. A strict separation of powers in which the executive is independently elected, in short, functions to encourage aspirants for executive power to claim possession of traits strikingly reminiscent of their royal forebears, whose claim to authority rested on widespread popular belief in their superhuman talent or charisma.[7] Presidents seek to gain a 'very different aura and self-image' than prime ministers because the plebiscitary character of modern presidentialism demands of them that they appear to stand above or at

[4] W.E. Scheuerman, 'American Kingship? The Monarchical Origins of Modern Presidentialism' (2005) 37 *Polity* 41–6.

[5] M.S. Paulsen, 'The Constitution of Necessity' (2004) 79 *Notre Dame Law Review* 1288. The same basic argument is made though never openly stated in J. Yoo, *The Powers Of War And Peace: The Constitution And Foreign Affairs After 9/11* (Chicago: University of Chicago Press, 2005).

[6] Ackerman, 'The New Separation of Powers'.

[7] Scheuerman, 'American Kingship?', 46–53.

least outside the realm of normal politics and its domination by 'mere' politicians.[8] What better way to garner broad support from a fractured electorate consisting of a stunning array of antagonistic political and social interests?

The history of presidential regimes consists substantially of the rise-and-fall of political outsiders and would-be saviours – the military 'man on horseback', as in Latin and South America, or simply politicians with a local reputation campaigning against Washington-level 'beltway politics', as in the US version – who emerge out of nowhere and sometimes vanish quickly from the political map.[9] In striking contrast to parliamentarism, where ambitious politicians slowly make their way through the ranks of the party machine and Parliament, their peers in presidential regimes succeed by touting a special ability to tackle the great issues of the day, tapping into political dissatisfaction by means of vague rhetoric intended to appeal to the electorate as a whole. Presidentialism creates 'very different popular expectations than those redounding to a prime minister'.[10] As in the monarchical past, widespread political and social anxiety leads many to develop a deep emotional identification with the most immediate personification of the political order, upon whose success so much is thought to depend.[11] Upon election, presidents typically enjoy stunning approval ratings far beyond those of prime ministers, but as soon as they are perceived as having failed to save the electorate from whatever ills plague it, their ratings plummet to levels below those of even the least popular parliamentary leaders.[12] For its fallen gods, the electorate exhibits nothing but disdain.

Third, presidential regimes are characterised by a high level of *temporal rigidity*. Both the President and legislature are elected for fixed terms of office, unalterable even amid political scenarios in which it might seem sensible to do so. Presidents typically face strict term limits, providing the temporal rhythms of political life with a sense of urgency since the executive possesses only a short time in which to advance an agenda.[13] Bruce

[8] Linz, 'Presidential or Parliamentary Democracy', in *Failure of Presidential Democracy*, p. 6.

[9] *Ibid.*, pp. 195–202; also A. Rudalevige, *The New Imperial Presidency: Renewing Presidential Power After Watergate* (Ann Arbor: University of Michigan Press, 2005), p. 55.

[10] Linz, 'Presidential or Parliamentary Democracy', in *Failure of Presidential Democracy*, pp. 6–7.

[11] W.E. Scheuerman, 'Rethinking Crisis Government', in D.J. Sherman and T. Nardin (eds.), *Terror, Culture, Politics: Rethinking 9/11* (Bloomington: Indiana University Press, 2006), p. 299.

[12] Linz, 'Presidential or Parliamentary Democracy', in *Failure of Presidential Democracy*, p. 29.

[13] *Ibid.*, p. 17.

Ackerman aptly notes that presidents are forced to 'race against the constitutional clock': not only are their own terms of office strictly delimited, but they may soon face hostile political opponents in the legislature or courts within a minute span of political time.[14] Of course, even prime ministers have incentives to move forward aggressively with their political agendas, but those incentives are more deeply rooted in presidential systems.

Fourth, the President is elected in a *winner-takes-all* manner, meaning that it necessarily falls into the hands of whatever political constituency happens to gain the most votes in the election. This is arguably an awkward and even perilous situation since the presidency is simultaneously viewed as the symbolic representative of the entire people, as that actor best able to provide energy and unity to the operations of government as a whole and thus legitimately in possession of impressive independent political and constitutional authority. Unfortunately, '[t]he feeling of having independent power, a mandate from the people, of independence for the period of office from others who might withdraw support, including the members of the coalition that elected him, is likely to give a President a sense of power and mission that might be out of proportion to the limited plurality that elected him'.[15] One result of this familiar fact of presidential politics is that the executive tends to exhibit greater enmity towards critics and the political opposition than a prime minister, who faces daily reminders that his political survival depends directly on the continued support of his party and its allies in Parliament. In some contrast to the parliamentary leader, the presidential executive is more likely to be tempted to interpret his authority as constituting nothing less than the real-life expression of the *pouvoir constituent*: even when elected by a mere plurality of votes and the most partisan of political creatures, he and his supporters will prefer to see him as the concrete personification of the unitary popular will. Those who dare challenge his wisdom, especially when wartime or a dire crisis stacks the cards of the political game in his favour, may quickly find themselves branded as political traitors.

Presidentialism generates special problems for any attempt to develop both a normatively acceptable and politically realistic model of emergency legal regulation. In the orthodox view, the unitary executive alone possesses the requisite capacity for 'decision, activity, secrecy, and dispatch' essential for the management of dire or even life-threatening

[14] Ackerman, 'The New Separation of Powers', 651.

[15] Linz, 'Presidential or Parliamentary Democracy', in *Failure of Presidential Democracy*, p. 19.

crises.[16] Political executives everywhere potentially have much to gain politically from emergency or crisis situations, when the electorate is most likely to turn to them for leadership.[17] Yet incentives for declaring and perpetuating emergencies are particularly pronounced in the context of presidential regimes.

First, as in the US where presidents possess sizable 'freedom of unilateral action in a variety of areas, from executive privilege to war powers to covert operations to campaign spending' it is there that the executive typically controls the most impressive arsenal of independent legal and regulatory weapons.[18] No wonder that an anxious electorate regularly turns to the President during a crisis, rushing to forget even long-standing partisan differences in order to 'rally round the flag' and support even legally dubious executive emergency action. Second, the intense institutional rivalry within presidential democracy emboldens the executive to declare, continue and even create crises. In light of the traditional view of the executive as the paradigmatic crisis manager, what better way to force a recalcitrant legislature or judiciary into line? During a crisis situation, the executive can typically expect the legislature and judiciary to kowtow to her preferences, at least as long as she can plausibly argue that the crisis at hand remains genuine. Given the awesome propaganda instruments now typically available to the modern executive, it often proves relatively easy for her to manipulate and sometimes even generate the requisite climate of fear. Even under normal conditions, 'ongoing competition between House, Senate, and Presidency for control over the administrative apparatus has created an excessively politicised style of bureaucratic government, transforming the executive branch into an enemy of the rule of law'.[19] The executive will likely be able to silence political critics while unleashing the full might of the modern state against (real or imagined) enemies to a vastly greater degree in the context of emergency rule.

The strict temporal restraints faced by holders of executive power in presidential regimes exacerbate these structural tendencies. What better

[16] C. Rossiter (ed.), *The Federalist Papers*, No. 70 (New York: New American Library, 1961), p. 424 (Alexander Hamilton).

[17] They also have a great deal to lose, especially if they fail to manage crisis scenarios effectively. In fact, one of the most obvious reasons for the wide swings we see in approval ratings for presidential executives is that they typically fail to perform well in the role of messianic 'saviours' which they may have cultivated in order to gain substantial plebiscitary support in the first place.

[18] Rudalevige, *The New Imperial Presidency*, p. 261.

[19] Ackerman, 'The New Separation of Powers', 641.

way to gain rapid results before the next election[20] than by successfully using crisis situations, real or otherwise, to push for desired political, social and constitutional changes? In an emergency, time is at a premium and since only the executive is presumably suited to fast-moving political action, significant power should legitimately accumulate in his hands. Faced with real or imagined threats, presidents will astutely navigate a climate of fear to pursue controversial public policies and even alterations to the basic constitutional rules of the game. Contemporary history is replete with examples of executive-driven constitutional change undertaken in the shadows of (actual or fictional) crises: De Gaulle's France (1958), Yeltsin's Russia (1993) and even FDR's USA (1933–44), where emergency authority was employed to dismantle a long tradition of constitutionally-based laissez-faire.[21] During a crisis situation, presidents not only take advantage of the traditional view that they alone can combat existential threats in order to beat the constitutional clock, but the commonplace view of them as direct personifications of a unitary popular will conveniently obscures the deeply partisan and highly controversial character of many sought-for changes. The temporal imperatives of the constitutional clock simultaneously incite them to repackage even minor internal and external challenges to the political and social status quo as nothing less than life-or-death crises requiring substantial augmentations of executive prerogative. Recent US political history thus consists to a great extent of presidential declarations of war, metaphorical or otherwise (e.g. the 'war on poverty', 'war on crime', 'war on drugs' and 'war on terror'). Of course, such declarations sometimes amount to nothing more than hyperbolic political rhetoric. As in the ongoing 'war on terror', however, they can result in far-reaching delegations of discretionary power to the President by Congress, as well as muscular employments of what recent US presidents and their academic defenders delight in describing as 'inherent executive power'. To a far greater extent than prime ministers, presidents hold what Andrew Arato describes as a 'material interest' in 'external conflict, and even internal crisis' and this material interest potentially generates abrogations to the normal operations of legality.[22]

[20] For example, an impending congressional midterm election, where the President may face – within two years of his own election, in the US system – heightened legislative opposition or even significant shifts in the composition of the judiciary.

[21] S. Levinson, 'Constitutional Norms in a State of Permanent Emergency' (2006) 40 *Georgia Law Review* 719–35.

[22] A. Arato, 'The Bush Tribunals and the Specter of Dictatorship' (2002) 9 *Constellations* 458.

The tendency for presidents to see themselves as the most immediate embodiments of a unitary popular will, standing above normal politics and in possession of super-mundane talents and a special aura, generates additional perils. In the face of institutional deadlock and stymied by a hostile legislature or courts, presidents may opt to operate outside the boundaries of legal normalcy, enlivened to violate the regular operations of the rule of law. To be sure, this is a permanent danger in any political system. Yet only in presidential democracy do we find structural institutional mechanisms which encourage it. In practical terms this means that the executive is likely to latch onto more-or-less serious challenges to the political community and refashion them into life-or-death threats, or if the crisis at hand is indeed a dire one, milk it for everything it is worth politically even at the cost of undermining the rule of law. Presidents possess an obvious political interest in transforming a low-level crisis into a permanent state of affairs, resisting even modest efforts by competing institutions to rein them in, in order to maintain the exceptional political privileges and prestige they regularly enjoy during an emergency. The fact that so many elected presidents are in fact outsiders to the world of mundane legislative politics, in conjunction with the reality of an electorate which tends to picture them as potential 'saviours' possessing exceptional charismatic powers, exacerbates the anti-legalistic tendencies of presidential government. It is not just that the constitutional clock and fundamental institutional rivalry with the legislature inspire presidential executives to seek convenient but legally dubious end-runs around parliamentary laws; their own political socialisation too often also makes them insufficiently appreciative of parliamentary formalities and legalism. Far too often, establishing emergency government on even the shakiest legal grounds is likely to seem an attractive political option, especially in the face of deep social and partisan divisions which potentially cripple executive action.

Is it any surprise that of the 32 countries that have adopted classical presidential systems, *all but one* have suffered severe breakdowns?[23] Even the United States, the world's oldest and most successful presidential democracy, 'has come close to dictatorship many times in its 225-year history', and it was arguably 'less the foresight of the Constitution's makers than the republican spirit of the leaders that kept the country on the constitutional side of the threshold between emergency government and outright dictatorship'.[24]

23 Ackerman, 'The New Separation of Powers', 646.
24 Arato, 'The Bush Tribunals and the Specter of Dictatorship', 457.

Most ordinary (and too many scholarly) US citizens would likely be taken aback by this assertion, preferring to dismiss it as hyperbole, since we all of course know that the US political system is God's Gift to Man and thus immune to the normal operations of political life. Yet there is no question that the modern US presidential version of emergency government exhibits significant pathologies. During an emergency, the President will simply claim 'inherent presidential authority', while Congress will typically rush to delegate broadly defined powers to the President. At some juncture, a test case reaches the judiciary and the courts are presented with an opportunity to determine whether the President overstepped legal and constitutional boundaries. A sort of gentlemen's agreement works as the necessary cement for the system. The judiciary acts cautiously in challenging presidential authority, especially in the immediate aftermath of the declaration of war or a crisis, allowing for substantial discretionary executive action. In exchange, once the crisis has passed (and a new holder of executive power has perhaps been installed by the electorate), the executive accepts some measure of judicial oversight and maybe even censure. In this model, legislatures have tended to play a subsidiary role in overseeing executive power, as Congress's main function generally consists in doing little more than writing statutory bank cheques. The Patriot Act, which allows for stunning grants of poorly defined emergency power to the executive, is a paradigmatic example.[25] The US presidential system produces an 'emergency regime that puts the fate of our liberties squarely into the hands of an executive that in moments of crisis tends to escape the control of the other branches'.[26] Since emergency-era legislation generally remains on the books long after the initial crisis has passed and future executives regularly build on earlier examples of unilateral executive action as precedents in order to broaden their own discretionary authority, the system tends to generate deleterious long-term consequences for the rule of law: an extensive critical literature demonstrates that it engenders highly discretionary modes of law, blurs any useful distinction between ordinary and emergency law, weakens the protections provided by civil liberties and shifts the focus of decision-making from the legislature to the executive.[27] On the statute books in the United States we find

[25] R. Dworkin, 'The Threat to Patriotism' (2002) 49 *New York Review of Books* 44–9.

[26] Arato, 'The Bush Tribunals and the Specter of Dictatorship', 457.

[27] See generally O. Gross, 'Chaos and Rules: Should Responses to Violent Crises Always Be Constitutional?' (2003) 112 *Yale Law Journal* 1011–1134; J. Lobel, 'Emergency Power and the Decline of Liberalism' (1989) 98 *Yale Law Journal* 1386–1433; C. Rossiter, *Constitutional Dictatorship: Crisis Government In The Modern Democracies* (Transaction, 2002); United

> significant emergency statutes without time limitations delegating to the Executive extensive discretionary powers, ordinarily exercised by the Legislature, which affect the lives of American citizens in a host of all-encompassing ways. This vast range of powers, taken together, confer enough authority to rule this country without reference to normal constitutional processes.[28]

To be sure, presidentialism is by no means the only institutional factor motoring this dynamic in the United States or, for that matter, in other presidential democracies exhibiting similar ills. Yet it undoubtedly remains a major driving force.

II. Oren Gross and the extra-legal model of emergency regulation

Few scholars are as knowledgeable about the pathologies of emergency government as Oren Gross, who has written widely and incisively on them. Legitimate worries about existing emergency regimes have encouraged Gross, in part inspired by an admirable attempt to minimise the executive's worrisome exploitation of the political fruits of emergency rule, to outline an innovative proposal for regulating emergency government. Based on a creative reworking of John Locke's interpretation of emergency prerogative as extra-legal in character, Gross argues that political officials should be permitted to pursue potentially extreme measures in the face of cataclysmic emergencies. We cannot assume that standing legal materials can fully anticipate what the particular dictates of the emergency situation demand of the executive, however.[29] So why not sacrifice the unrealistic idea that emergencies can always be neatly cabined within the rules of law? Even if the law unambiguously bans extreme acts (e.g. torture), it may be necessary to undertake them in the face of major threats.[30] Yet officials should be required to do so while openly underscoring that their actions can claim

States Senate, Special Committee on National Emergencies, *A Brief History of Emergency Powers in the United States* (US Government, 1974).

28 United States Senate, *A Brief History of Emergency Powers*, vi.

29 See generally Gross, 'Chaos and Rules'; also, Gross, 'Providing for the Unexpected: Constitutional Emergency Provisions' (2003) 33 *Israel Handbook on Human Rights* 13. Many of Gross's arguments are brought together in his path-breaking co-authored (with Fionnuala ni Aolain) work, *Law In Times Of Crisis: Emergency Powers In Theory And Practice* (Cambridge: Cambridge University Press, 2006). For Locke's original model of extra-legal or prerogative emergency power, see P. Laslett (ed.), *Second Treatise Of Government* (Cambridge: Cambridge University Press, 1991), pp. 374–80.

30 O. Gross, 'The Prohibition on Torture and the Limits of the Law', in S. Levinson (ed.), *Torture: A Collection* (Oxford: Oxford University Press, 2004), pp. 236–44.

no support from the letter of the law. Since emergency power too often escapes the neat confines of the legal order, officials should stop pretending otherwise. Like Locke, Gross paradoxically argues that the best way to preserve the rule of law is by envisioning executive emergency discretion operating beyond the boundaries of the legal order.[31]

In Gross's account, the refusal to acknowledge the necessary extra-legality of emergency discretion leads precisely to those ills described above: a fusion of ordinary and emergency law, the gradual decay of civil liberties and the decline of the rule of law.[32] Emergency statutes remain on the books well after the crisis which initially justified them fades away; the executive builds on troublesome legal and constitutional precedents from earlier crises in order to amplify his discretionary powers unreasonably. The result inevitably is a ratcheting-down of basic liberties. For Gross, as for Locke before him, we can counteract this trend and maintain the purity of the rule of law only by clearly separating legal normalcy from extra-legal emergency discretion and then reviewing emergency rule publicly and by means of tough retrospective tests.

After pursuing publicly-declared extra-legal emergency action, an official might face criminal or civil charges in court, be forced to resign, suffer impeachment or simply be jettisoned from office by an angry electorate. Alternately, extra-legal executive activities might get indemnified by a legislature or courts or garner endorsement by conventional political mechanisms (e.g. a landslide re-election victory). In this model, stringent conditions for publicity and some clear *ex post facto* determination of the legitimacy of executive emergency action ensure improved popular debate in emergency contexts as well as individual accountability, discouraging the executive from acting unnecessarily or irresponsibly. If the executive must act openly while in full knowledge of the fact that she can claim no basis in law and risks severe *ex post facto* political or legal censure, she will likely avoid unnecessarily repressive measures. Publics will treat emergency rule with deep scepticism, encouraged by the executive's honest

[31] See, generally, Gross, 'Chaos and Rules', and Gross, 'Stability and Flexibility', in V.V. Ramraj, M. Hor and K. Roach (eds.), *Global Anti-Terrorism Law and Policy* (Cambridge: Cambridge University Press, 2005), pp. 98–106; also, in a similar vein, see M. Tushnet, 'Emergencies and the Idea of Constitutionalism', in M. Tushnet (ed.), *The Constitution In Wartime: Beyond Alarmism And Complacency* (Durham: Duke University Press 2005), pp. 39–54.

[32] See generally Gross, 'Chaos and Rules'; also, Gross, 'The Normless and Exceptionless Exception: Carl Schmitt's Theory of Emergency Powers and the "Norm-Exception" Dichotomy' (2000) 21 *Cardozo Law Review* 1825–68; Gross, 'What "Emergency" Regime?' (2006) 13 *Constellations* 74–85.

declaration of both the seriousness of the crisis and the dubious legal basis for her acts to take a careful look at them. This would presumably offer a stark contrast to the present situation, in which executives typically latch onto a dubious precedent or open-ended legal norm in order to legitimise even the most outrageous emergency measures, inevitably obscuring their contested character. If President Bush had openly admitted that the indefinite detention of US citizens was unconstitutional but politically necessary, for example, would not broader segments of the US population soon have been alerted to the controversial nature of his actions? In this view, Mr Bush's dubious appeal to his constitutional powers as 'commander-in-chief', in conjunction with his widely noted preference for executive secrecy,[33] embody some of the most alarming features of modern emergency government.

Despite many criticisms of the extra-legal model,[34] it at first glance appears well adapted to counteracting some of the familiar perils of emergency government both in presidential democracies and elsewhere. Not only might it potentially subject emergency rule to heightened public scrutiny and strict retrospective review, but it also runs directly counter to the commonplace view that effective emergency government necessitates substantial secrecy. The claim that only the unitary executive can maintain the requisite secrecy in emergency contexts has long functioned to justify executive predominance, and by challenging exaggerated assessments of secrecy's virtues, Gross is to be praised for taking aim at a central ideological justification of freewheeling executive emergency discretion.[35] Unfortunately, Gross's proposal ultimately suffers from the same Achilles's heel plaguing most recent legal contributions to the debate about emergency

[33] Think, for example, of the lack of public access to Guantánamo Bay, or the secret manner in which the decision to condone torture was made: see generally M. Danner, *Torture and Truth: America, Abu Ghraib and the War on Terror* (New York: New York Review of Books Press, 2004).

[34] B. Ackerman, *Before The Next Attack: Preserving Civil Liberties In An Age Of Terrorism* (New Haven: Yale University Press, 2006), pp. 88–9; D. Cole, 'Judging the Next Emergency: Judicial Review and Individual Rights in Time of Crisis' (2003) 101 *University of Michigan Law Review* 2587–90; D. Dyzenhaus, 'The State of Emergency in Legal Theory', in *Global Anti-Terrorism Law And Policy*, pp. 65–74; A.Z. Huq, 'Uncertain Law in Uncertain Times: Emergency Powers and Lessons from South Asia' (2006) 13 *Constellations* 89–107; W.E. Scheuerman, 'Emergency Powers and the Rule of Law After 9/11' (2006) 14 *Journal of Political Philosophy* 70–2.

[35] I am not convinced, however, that he thinks through the full implications of this challenge to executive secrecy. As I have tried to suggest elsewhere (see Scheuerman, 'Rethinking Crisis Government'), it potentially raises serious questions about the executive's purported virtues as the predominant emergency actor.

government: it rests on an inadequate appreciation of the institutional dynamics of modern liberal – and especially, presidential – democracy. When those dynamics are considered, it becomes clear why the extra-legal model of emergency rule would at best fail to bring about the attractive changes Gross desires and at worst exacerbate the pathologies he so accurately recounts.

Gross's proposal places special weight on achieving retrospective political and legal checks on emergency government. Especially in the context of presidential democracy, however, this programmatic emphasis seems naive. For reasons outlined above, presidentialism produces a series of special incentives encouraging the executive to manipulate, continue and even manufacture emergency situations in order to bring about political and constitutional changes which not only may be unrelated to the immediate imperatives of the crisis situation at hand, but often remain controversial and deeply unpopular. Emergency government provides unrivalled opportunities for presidential executives in the race against the constitutional clock, opposed by stubborn political opponents in control of the legislature or judiciary. It allows them to mobilise mass support behind both the symbolic and real powers of that institutional actor widely perceived as constituting a direct embodiment of the political community as a whole, or at the very least as best capable of warding off dangerous threats.

Gross forgets that 'as with any first mover in a game where sequence counts, a president's initiative may reshape in his favour the landscape on which political actors move'.[36] Armed with an impressive array of institutional weapons, emergencies provide a ready justification for presidents to seize bank accounts, close down newspapers, clamp down on opposition parties and rapidly deploy the police and military against internal and external foes. A politically astute executive will typically have altered the rules of the political game even before any *ex post facto* tests have to be met. In especially egregious but by no means unusual settings, political opponents will already have been imprisoned, exiled, or, in the extreme case, shot.[37] But even in less polarised crisis contexts, opposition leaders and voices in the media which might once have posed critical questions about the executive's actions will raise only the most cautious questions about emergency measures, worried about seeming out of sync with a nervous public eager to 'rally round the flag'. Faced with an executive outfitted

[36] Rudalevige, *The New Imperial Presidency*, p. 39

[37] The history of presidential government in Latin and South America is littered with such examples.

with awesome symbolic authority and capable of propagating effective daily reminders of the immediate dangers at hand amid an atmosphere of ubiquitous fear, even the most courageous citizens may opt to shut their mouths. *Contra* Gross, the extra-legal model by no means seems destined to enliven public deliberation. If the basic terms of political discourse are determined by an executive with an interest in perpetuating a crisis atmosphere, debate instead is likely to become narrow and astonishingly irrational, with officials soon muttering clichés about 'getting the bad guys' capable of making even the slickest Hollywood producer blush. Even without advancing overt extra-legal acts against the press or opposition, the presidential executive's unparalleled power 'to create facts on the ground' – and by doing so, *redefine the parameters of political debate* – undermines political criticism and subverts freewheeling deliberation.

To be sure, at some juncture the public may tire of the executive's incessant crisis rhetoric and fear-mongering; a comatose media and political opposition suddenly appear to return from the dead. Yet they might re-emerge from the political graveyard only to discover that the political and even constitutional system has undergone salient shifts. The *ex post facto* political and legal checks outlined by Gross might then be mobilised, at least where basic democratic procedures remain intact. However, *those checks will likely be exercised in a new political game whose rules have been substantially redefined in accordance with the executive's partisan preferences.* Should it come as any surprise that recent history offers so many examples of legally dubious executive emergency actions which remain uncensored? Even seemingly cautious attempts to punish legally suspect executive emergency rule often face a hostile reception because they emerge in a novel political universe which the executive has decisively reconfigured.[38]

Gross's preference for extra-legal emergency action risks aggrandising the already troubling tendency in presidential regimes for the executive to act outside or against the law. He can only underplay the dangers of such action by turning a blind eye to the nature of modern executive politics. Whatever its weaknesses, for example, the conventional notion that emergency rule requires some basis in the law at least forces the executive prospectively to provide legal as well as the standard political (e.g. the generic reference to 'national security') justifications for her actions. This familiar attribute of even the most flawed liberal emergency regime plays

[38] Recall, for example, the recent domestic spying scandal in the United States, where even partisan Democrats distanced themselves from Senator Russ Feingold's modest proposal to censure President Bush.

a significant role in constraining the executive. Gross reduces the burden of proof placed on the executive: when pursuing emergency action, she apparently need not offer standard legal or constitutional arguments. He thereby opens the door to controversial forms of emergency action which at least under contemporary liberal models of emergency rule might face careful legal and constitutional scrutiny. Of course, executives universally – but especially in presidential regimes – cynically exploit ambiguous legal and constitutional norms in order to justify her actions. Yet when doing so, they inadvertently prepare the way for a process of legal and constitutional argumentation by means of which those rightly alarmed by the government's measures can begin to respond.

The Bush administration and its academic defenders, for example, have repeatedly offered controversial interpretations of the US Constitution's executive power clause in order to outfit the President with a stunning array of constitutional powers.[39] Though deeply tendentious, those arguments have at least provided political opponents with an opening through which they can begin challenging the Bush administration: opposing legal arguments now widely surface on the web sites of NGOs like Amnesty International and the Center for Constitutional Rights, and even in some – though by no means enough – judicial rulings. Although one should avoid describing this process in overly Pollyanna-ish terms, only the most dogmatic legal scepticism can consistently discount the virtues of such argumentation, seeing in it nothing more than a series of normatively meaningless strategic games. Even if such debates often fail to put an immediate stop to the executive's actions, they create an indispensable discursive and argumentative field on which any effective political opposition will soon find itself operating.

III. David Dyzenhaus and the common law model

Inspired by a rich tradition of common law models of emergency government, David Dyzenhaus rejects Gross's extra-legal model and proposes that emergency rule be directly subordinated to the rule of law, interpreted as embodying an ambitious collection of substantive moral and legal values, including ideals of fairness, reasonableness and equality before the law. Like Gross and many others, he concedes that emergencies sometimes

[39] See generally H.C. Mansfield, 'The Law and the President: In a National Emergency, Who You Gonna Call?', *Weekly Standard* (16 January 2006), p. 12; Paulsen, 'The Constitution of Necessity'; Yoo, *The Powers Of War And Peace.*

require novel legal and regulatory innovations. However, institutional experiments with emergency government must maintain strict fidelity to core elements of the rule of law. Every institution of government is expected to cooperate in realising the law's underlying commitment to 'important moral values' and especially respect for the 'fundamental interests of the individual', but judges have a special role to play as guardians of the rule of law during emergencies.[40] Because both parliament and the executive then risk pursuing measures inconsistent with the rule of law, the task of preserving its core values will likely fall to the courts. In practical terms this means that judges should rigorously scrutinise emergency measures, always keeping in mind that 'the law that rules is not just positive law; the law includes values and principles to do with human dignity and freedom'.[41] This substantive – and by no means uncontroversial – interpretation of the rule of law generates a more-or-less pre-eminent role for the judiciary in supervising emergency government. Even if the judiciary lacks formal authority to overturn onerous emergency legislation, Dyzenhaus wants the courts at least to underscore its inconsistency with rule-of-law values and thereby hopefully force its reconsideration. In his view, the real culprit behind the pathologies of modern emergency government are legal positivism and the traditional or 'formal separation of powers', which he tends to interpret as working in unison to bring about an inappropriate judicial deference to Parliament and the executive.[42] In opposition to those who preach the supremacy of legislative rule making, Dyzenhaus insists that the traditional separation of powers doctrine should be seen as instrumental to the broader aim of achieving fundamental moral values in the law. Since legislatures typically delegate extensive power to the executive during emergencies, Parliament too often serves as little more than a rubber stamp for problematic forms of executive discretion inconsistent with the rule of law. Positivism and a misleading conception of the separation of powers lead judges to defer to the legislature in the name of democracy, but in reality they are merely selling the rule of law down the river.[43]

[40] D. Dyzenhaus, 'Intimations of Legality and the Clash of Arms' (2004) 2 *International Journal of Constitutional Law* 248. The most recent statement of Dyzenhaus's views is found in *The Constitution Of Liberty: Legality In A Time Of Emergency* (Cambridge: Cambridge University Press, 2006).

[41] D. Dyzenhaus, 'Humpty Dumpty Rules or the Rule of Law: Legal Theory and the Adjudication of National Security' (2003) 28 *Australian Journal of Legal Philosophy* 13.

[42] In this model, 'the legislature makes policy decisions, public officials implement those decisions, and judges make sure [they] are limited by constitutional principle'. (Dyzenhaus, 'The State of Emergency in Legal Theory', in *Global Anti-Terrorism Law and Policy*, p. 78).

[43] See generally Dyzenhaus, above, notes 34, 40 and 41.

A great deal can be said in favour of this position. While seeking to contain emergency government by the proven methods of a judiciary schooled in the common law mindset, Dyzenhaus concedes the necessity of institutional creativity. Perhaps in some tension with his strong common law preferences, he occasionally concedes the virtues of outfitting administrative tribunals, conceived along the lines of hybrid executive–judicial bodies, with significant authority in order to counteract the familiar dangers of emergency government.[44] Yet I doubt that Dyzenhaus's recognition of the need for institutional reform goes far enough. Moreover, good reasons remain for wondering whether his approach would not tend to produce a political system in which 'judges are the ultimate decision-makers with respect to the specification and enforcement of fundamental values', especially in light of his broad reading of the rule of law as consisting of a number of unavoidably abstract political and moral ideals.[45] If so, Dyzenhaus has perhaps salvaged the rule of law, but only at the cost of sacrificing self-government: his attempt to update the common law position would simply end up reproducing its familiar anti-democratic preference for (wise) judges over (purportedly irrational) popular majorities. Although supposedly stimulated by Lon Fuller, Dyzenhaus's reading of the rule of law ends up looking vastly more ambitious – and controversial – than Fuller's 'inner morality of law'.[46] Whether or not a resurrected model of the common law can do justice to either modern pluralism or modern democracy, in short, remain legitimate critical concerns. Last but by no means least, one would do well to recall a substantial historical literature directly undermining Dyzenhaus's tendency to pin the blame for the ills of contemporary emergency government on legal positivism. Empirical evidence suggests that the cautious mindset of the common law jurist and by no means the bogeyman of legal positivism, has played more than its fair share in the great injustices of modern emergency rule.[47]

[44] I am referring to his fascinating comments on the UK's Special Immigration Appeals Court (SIAC). I am grateful to Victor V. Ramraj for bringing the potential significance of this aspect of Dyzenhaus's position to my attention. Nonetheless, I remain doubtful that Dyzenhaus's common law (and Dworkinian) tendencies mesh as easily with the possibility of far-reaching institutional reform, in which (modified) administrative bodies play a decisive role in overseeing emergency government, than he himself apparently believes.

[45] T. Campbell, 'Blaming Legal Positivism: A Reply to David Dyzenhaus' (2003) 28 *Australian Journal of Legal Philosophy* 33.

[46] L. Fuller, *The Morality Of Law* (New Haven: Yale University Press, 1964).

[47] See generally, Campbell, 'Blaming Legal Positivism'; S. Ellman, *In A Time Of Troubles: Law And Liberty In South Africa's State Of Emergency* (Oxford: Oxford University Press, 1992);

Dyzenhaus's dependence on the worn-out lens of the positivism/natural law debate tends to distort his analysis. Like Gross, Dyzenhaus shows little appreciation for the special challenges posed by institutional diversity in general and presidentialism in particular. Common law systems long ago abandoned the so-called formal separation of powers which he holds responsible for the ills of emergency government: presidential and semi-presidential regimes expressly outfit the unitary executive with impressive legislative power and courts there often defer to the executive for legitimate constitutional reasons. So we probably cannot hold it culpable for the pathologies of emergency government especially in presidential democracy. At a minimum, it would be helpful to consider the possibility that common law mechanisms operate differently in presidential than in parliamentary versions of liberal democracy. Especially in presidential regimes, where institutional rivalry between the executive and legislature emboldens the executive to declare and perpetuate crises, real or otherwise, the slow-moving common law judiciary may find itself unable to respond coherently to the dynamic of executive-driven emergency government. As in Gross's extra-legal model, the common law approach necessarily depends, despite Dyzenhaus's occasional comments to the contrary, chiefly on retrospective supervision of state action. But as we saw above, this becomes problematic when the presidential executive exploits his advantages as a 'first mover in a game where sequence counts' and executive initiative 'may reshape in his favor the landscape on which political actors move'.[48] After the executive has acted, the courts oftentimes do weigh in, but they do so in the context of a novel political environment in which executive initiative has already potentially reshuffled the rules of the game. The courts not only find themselves operating in a political universe in which the cards have perhaps been stacked against critics (as well as victims) of emergency government, but they necessarily tend to focus on individual cases, meaning that they necessarily confront egregious but by no means typical violations of basic liberties. Not surprisingly, if we take a careful look at political systems which institutionalise presidentialism in the context of a strong common law tradition (e.g. the United States), the judiciary only manages useful but necessarily limited corrections

K.D. Ewing and C.A. Gearty, *The Struggle for Civil Liberties: Political Freedom and the Rule of Law in Britain* (Oxford: Oxford University Press, 2001), pp. 1914–15; K.L. Scheppele, 'North American Emergencies: The Use of Emergency Powers in Canada and the United States' (2006) 4 *International Journal of Constitutional Law* 213.

[48] Rudalevige, *The New Imperial Presidency*, p. 39.

to the most extreme government emergency measures long after their enforcement. As Arato has accurately observed, the 'constitutional under-regulation of emergencies' in the context of a legal system with a strong common law orientation, in conjunction with the poorly defined constitutional powers of a plebiscitary president, may tend to increase the likelihood of illegal and unconstitutional emergency government.[49] Congenital structural tendencies which drive the President incessantly to expand emergency discretion mean that the courts always lag behind, its review powers outpaced in an institutional competition which the courts cannot possibly win: before our cautious common law judges have even begun to grapple with the ramifications of the last round of presidential emergency decrees, the executive has already undertaken new ones. Especially in presidential regimes, where the executive is driven to exploit crisis situations in order to demonstrate her capacity for effective leadership and gain political leverage, common law emergency oversight seems rather fragile.

No wonder that so much of Dyzenhaus's writings on emergency rule take on hortatory tones, as he repeatedly scolds the courts for abandoning the critical resources of the common law tradition. But the real problem he misidentifies is that fundamental institutional mechanisms too often discourage them from doing so. In addition, when widely viewed as the most direct real-life embodiment of the popular will or as a charismatic saviour who alone can protect the polity from severe external threats, the ideological appeal of presidential power is likely to prove just as influential among judges as among other institutional and even extra-institutional political actors. Judges in common law jurisdictions arguably prove no more immune to presidential pomp and what Marx called a 'a sort of divine right' than the rest of us: the history of common law jurisdictions is littered with the wreckage of bad legal rulings. In some settings, common law judges may have less to fear from draconian emergency measures, for example, than grassroots political movements, their parliamentary representatives or political organisations sympathetic to their cause. Such constituencies are likely to respond to emergency measures with outrage and quickly seek to alter them by means of political and ultimately parliamentary mobilisation, whereas tenured judges may simply respond with nothing more than shockingly quiescent and legally smug rulings: a recent string of US federal and supreme court rulings, for example, 'has invoked repressive precedents from the gravest wars of the past as if they were

[49] Arato, 'The Bush Tribunals and the Specter of Dictatorship', 457 and 463.

applicable to our present predicament', despite fundamental differences between the so-called 'war on terror' and previous US military engagements.[50] Is it any surprise that the real-life history of common law systems offers at best a mixed record at circumventing the excesses of emergency executive rule? Or that judges too often fail to counteract the excesses of emergency executive rule?

In the final analysis, judges fail to perform the Herculean tasks of emergency oversight Dyzenhaus ascribes to them not chiefly because of a lack of political will or their susceptibility to the alleged sins of positivism, but because of built-in institutional components of especially the presidential version of liberal democracy.

IV. A way out?

If we are to minimise the pathologies of emergency government, we need to pay closer attention than either Gross or Dyzenhaus to questions of fundamental institutional design. As I have tried to argue, both authors are blind to the structural dangers posed by presidentialism. To be sure, it would be naive to deny that alternative institutional varieties of liberal democracy pose distinct challenges for emergency legal regulation or to conclude these reflections with a naive endorsement of presidentialism's chief institutional rival, parliamentarism, as a ready-made solution to the dilemmas diagnosed by Gross and Dyzenhaus. If we are to determine which institutional model best counteracts the ills of emergency rule, we will need to move beyond the simplistic dichotomy of presidentialism versus parliamentarism that continues to plague scholarly reflection on institutional design and consider the possibility of new and more fruitful institutional compounds.[51]

For better or worse, each generation does not typically get to choose the institutional variety of liberal democracy under which it must live, especially if its historical predecessors, as in the US model, bequeathed to it an especially rigid constitutional system.[52] So how might those of us stuck with presidentialism best navigate the murky waters of emergency government? Might we at least mitigate the problems described in the first section of this essay?

[50] Ackerman, *Before the Next Attack*, p. 20.

[51] See generally Ackerman, 'The New Separation of Powers'.

[52] I am thinking, of course, of the arduous formal amendment procedures found in the US Constitution.

In my view, the best answer thus far to this tough question comes from a group of scholars who have tried to learn from the new and recent democracies and their quest to come up with a workable system of formal constitutionally-based emergency power.[53] A major strength of this approach is that it begins with a hard-headed analysis of what Ackerman describes as the 'presidentialist war dynamic' according to which the President is most likely to dominate the political game by effectively exploiting crisis situations.[54] In this view, properly designed constitutional mechanisms alone establish useful prospective legal guidelines for emergency authority, help create a clear separation between ordinary and emergency law and provide standards by which we can delineate legal from illegal emergency government. Powers 'that can be called up during an emergency are fixed in advance of the emergency itself' by constitutional devices that establish basic rules for their exercise.[55] Constitutional provisions alone determine when and how emergency power is to be put into effect. No emergency action is allowed to take on a permanent legal character and thereby blur the boundary between ordinary and exceptional law. Legally codified time restrictions should always be placed on its exercise. Formal constitutional devices also 'enumerate a formidable set of fundamental rights that must be respected during crises', though allowing for some diversions from legal normalcy.[56]

Especially important for our purposes here, strict *ex ante* legal devices counter the familiar institutional dynamic by which the executive unilaterally defines, declares and potentially gains from crisis situations. Prospective standing constitutional rules specify how and when emergencies can be declared and the executive is forced to rely on other decision-making organs (chiefly the legislature) in order to set up emergency government. Of course, executives inevitably will manipulate even the strictest system of constitutional norms, seeking to use it to their political advantage. Yet this approach suggests that we might at least reduce this problem by developing

[53] See generally Ackerman, see above notes 34 and 23; G. Negretto and J. Rivera, 'Liberalism and Emergency Powers in Latin America: Reflections on Carl Schmitt and the Theory of Constitutional Dictatorship' (2000) 21 *Cardozo Law Review* 1797–1824; Rossiter, *Constitutional Dictatorship*; K. Scheppele, 'Law in a Time of Emergency: States of Exceptions and the Temptations of 9/11' (2004) 6 *University of Pennsylvania Journal of Constitutional Law* 1001–80; Scheuerman, 'Emergency Powers and the Rule of Law'.

[54] Ackerman, *Before The Next Attack*, p. 7.

[55] J. Ferejohn and P. Pasquino, 'The Law of Exception: A Typology of Emergency Powers' (2004) 2 *International Journal of Constitutional Law* 210 at 235.

[56] Ackerman, *Before The Next Attack*, p. 68.

an effective system of institutional checks and balances. In order to exercise emergency power, the executive needs the support of the legislature. By itself, this offers few impediments to a politically astute occupant of executive power. In a parliamentary system, the executive is likely to have been chosen by the legislature and probably exercises de facto political control of his party and its elected representatives. In a presidential system with a strict separation of powers, even members of hostile political parties tend to turn to the executive for political guidance during crises. So how can the mere fact that executive action requires legislative endorsement function as more than a rubber stamp for executive prerogative?

Ackerman offers two clever proposals to help ward off this familiar hazard. Inspired by the example of the South African Constitution,[57] he advocates a *supermajoritarian escalator* according to which every (temporally limited) extension of emergency power would require more *extensive* legislative support than previous promulgations. The aim of this proposal is to ensure that emergency government is no partisan weapon of an incumbent executive and instead remains 'representative of every part of the citizenry interested in the defense of the existing constitutional order'.[58] Second, during an emergency situation, 'members of opposition political parties should be guaranteed the majority of seats on the [legislative] oversight committees' so as further to reduce the perils of partisan manipulation of executive emergency power.[59]

Now much more surely needs to be said about this approach to emergency regulation – elsewhere I describe it (favourably) as the formalist model[60] – in order to render it plausible to those legitimately sceptical of what might appear as yet another (illusory) institutional 'easy fix'. For now, I would like to conclude by merely responding to serious criticisms of this approach recently expressed or at least implied by Gross and Dyzenhaus.

At one juncture, Gross asserts that his extra-legal model 'does not seek to exclude the constitutional models of emergency power' since it apparently only applies to truly cataclysmic crises.[61] Elsewhere, however, he generally expresses more scepticism, pointing out that real-life attempts to constitutionalise the emergency tend to be contradictory and internally

[57] After 21 days, extensions of emergency power have to be approved by 60 per cent of the National Assembly and a state of emergency can never be extended for more than three months.

[58] Rossiter, 'Constitutional Dictatorship', xiii.

[59] Ackerman, *Before The Next Attack*, p. 85.

[60] W.E. Scheuerman, 'Emergency Powers' (2006) 2 *Annual Review of Law and Social Science* 270–3.

[61] Gross, 'Chaos and Rules', 1134.

inconsistent, with existing constitutional materials exhibiting no clear agreement on how we might best define and subsequently codify the disparate faces of emergency rule. In this second (and, I think, more pervasive) line of argumentation, he seems to endorse a form of *legal scepticism* according to which it is simply impossible prospectively to codify a *substantive* definition of what constitutes an emergency situation.[62] If generations of constitutional architects have failed at this task, why naively assume that we might prove more adept at accomplishing it? From this perspective, a pivotal dilemma facing formal constitutional emergency power is that it exaggerates the capacity of formal law to anticipate and thus tackle the specific exigencies of the crisis at hand. Since emergencies easily represent novel scenarios which constitutional definitions of the emergency fail to capture, by implication, the quest to tame emergency power by constitutional means is necessarily truncated as well.

Yet perhaps we can counter this argument by interpreting formal constitutional mechanisms in an overtly *proceduralist* vein.[63] Many present-day constitutional emergency clauses rightly tend to de-emphasise the importance of some legally pre-given *substantive definition* of what specific events or occurrences deserve to be described as emergencies in favour of underlining the importance of a legally regulated *process* of political and institutional give-and-take in which special powers are delegated to some actors (typically, the executive) while being made accountable to others (judges and legislators). This approach relies less on trying prospectively to define the particular contours of all conceivable emergencies. Instead, it establishes procedural mechanisms whereby political actors themselves can determine whether or not a particular development at hand constitutes an emergency. Of course, one might respond that any attempt to separate the substantive definition of the emergency from the procedural rules determining the exercise of emergency powers is counterintuitive at best and theoretically incoherent at worst.[64] Yet recall that in *any* existing liberal democracy, a rich diversity of competing and even antagonistic substantive views can be found, for example, about the proper scope and substance of ordinary legislative power: we continue to disagree about its

62 See generally Gross, 'Providing for the Unexpected'. In his excellent piece in this volume, Tom Campbell, 'Emergency Strategies for Prescriptive Legal Positivists: Anti-Terrorist Law and Legal Theory' (Chapter 9), suggests some plausible reasons we might question this view.

63 See Arato, 'The Bush Tribunals and the Specter of Dictatorship', 470.

64 Tushnet, 'Emergencies and the Idea of Constitutionalism', in *The Constitution in Wartime*, p. 47.

appropriate extent (in debates about privacy and economic regulation, for example) as well as its purposes and ends. This disagreement need not undermine the effective exercise of legitimate legislative power, however. We accept or at least accede to various constitutionally-based procedural devices (e.g. voting procedures, various institutional rules) which produce more-or-less successful exercises of legislative power, even if we disagree fundamentally about its proper character or scope.

In a recent *Cardozo Law Review* article, Dyzenhaus offers an equally incisive challenge to the formalist approach. He accuses Ackerman (and, if I understand him correctly, also Clinton Rossiter) of covertly endorsing emergency government along the lines of 'a legal black hole because the rule of law, as policed by judges, has no or little purchase'.[65] What makes Dyzenhaus understandably nervous is Ackerman's controversial proposal that emergency government be allowed to detain suspected terrorists for a predetermined period according to legal standards less strict than those normally operating in the law: when suspected terrorists are brought into court, judges should rely on a 'reasonable suspicion' standard, less demanding than the traditional 'probable cause' required by the ordinary criminal law, to decide whether they can be detained.[66] Officials will then have 45 days in which they must prepare their case against the accused, at which point all cases will be heard in courts governed by normal criminal procedures. If the security officials then fail to press charges or convince a judge that the test of probable cause has been met, detainees are immediately freed. The state security services are required to pay $500 for every day to those never charged or subsequently acquitted in a criminal court.

I share Dyzenhaus's anxieties about some of the details of this proposal.[67] Yet by focusing on the most controversial element of Ackerman's specific proposals, Dyzenhaus loses sight of the forest through the trees. To describe Ackerman's model as condoning 'sheer lawlessness' and thus as preliminary evidence for the bankruptcy of formalised constitutional emergency power, seems tendentious. One reason for both the supermajoritarian escalator and the requirement of just compensation is to provide state officials with pressing incentives to 'push them to begin serious work

[65] Dyzenhaus, 'Schmitt v. Dicey: Are States of Emergency Inside or Outside the Legal Order' (2006) 27 *Cardozo Law Review* 113. In his piece in the present volume, 'The Compulsion of Legality' (Chapter 2), he seems to have at least toned down some of his polemics against Ackerman.

[66] Ackerman, *Before the Next Attack*, p. 46.

[67] D. Cole, 'In Case of Emergency' (2006) 43 *New York Review of Books* 40–3.

at once: with hundreds or thousands in custody, they will try to clear out those who have been arrested by mistake' as expeditiously as possible.[68] Dyzenhaus refers too dismissively to Ackerman's 'political economy' of 'political incentives and disincentives', when in fact Ackerman, to his credit, is tackling difficult questions of institutional design in order to determine how to minimise the number of detainees who might be subjected to the reduced standard of 'reasonable suspicion' in the first place.[69] More significantly, 'reasonable suspicion' remains a legal standard and detainees will have their day, though at first admittedly only a short one, in court when initially arrested. Security agencies are forced to justify the reasonable character of their acts to judges, torture is banned and detainees are provided independent legal counsel so as to prepare complaints and get ready for a not-so-distant day when they will enjoy the full protections of the ordinary criminal law. We can of course quite legitimately debate whether Ackerman's suggestion compromises too many features of the rule of law as conventionally understood. Yet to describe this scenario as a 'legal black hole' or 'sheer lawlessness' fails to do justice to his proposal. This is no mere semantic distinction, since the Bush administration in fact does envision its activities in the 'war on terror' along the lines of a 'legal black hole' in which presidential power is effectively unlimited.[70] Not surprisingly, it denies accused terrorists many of the rights described by Ackerman in his proposal.

Dyzenhaus seems to think that a basic flaw with all proposals for constitutionalised emergency power is that they ignore 'the fact that judgments about necessity are for the dictator [e.g., emergency executive] to make, which means that these criteria are not limits or constraints but mere factors about which the dictator will have to decide'.[71] But this obscures the crucial point that the formalist model provides for demanding institutional tests by means of which the polity can at least minimise the executive's tendency to try to monopolise such judgments: emergency rulers are made strictly dependent on other institutional actors and their potentially competing conceptions of necessity. In Ackerman's proposal, for example, the President might seek to continue emergency rule, but if she fails to convince an ever expanding supermajority of legislators of the basic soundness of her views or if the courts determine that the executive

[68] Ackerman, *Before the Next Attack*, pp. 106–7. [69] Dyzenhaus, 'Schmitt v. Dicey', 112.

[70] W.E. Scheuerman, 'Carl Schmitt and the Road to Abu Ghraib' (2006) 13 *Constellations* 109–24.

[71] Dyzenhaus, 'Schmitt v. Dicey', 109.

has violated the emergency power procedures outlined by constitutional law, she is acting outside the law. Obviously, this model offers no perfect guarantee that officials will always respect the law, though it does provide far more impressive institutional weapons to those worried by the spectre of executive illegality than typically possessed by them in existing emergency legal regimes. To conclude that constitutional emergency power is necessarily flawed because what prevents its abuse is in the final instance nothing more than the executive's 'honest and steadfast intention to return to the ordinary way of doing things' again fails to do justice to the argument at hand.[72] At the very least, Dyzenhaus downplays the many ways in which strict institutional checks and balances operate here so as not only to establish binding legal and constitutional checks on the executive, but also to provide her with every imaginable incentive to minimise emergency executive discretion and quickly return to the sphere of normal legality.

What ultimately drives Dyzenhaus's deep animosity, as he himself admits, is that Ackerman fails to endorse a 'fairly substantive or thick conception of the rule of law' in which the judiciary tends to play a pre-eminent role.[73] In other words, by apparently demoting judicial supervision of accused terrorists, while supposedly reducing the rule of law to nothing but formal 'external legal constraints' (e.g., the supermajoritarian escalator and other constitutional mechanisms), Ackerman betrays the critical resources of the common law tradition and helps subvert the rule of law.

This criticism ultimately relies on issues of fundamental jurisprudential philosophy that I can only touch on here. Nonetheless, it is troubling that Dyzenhaus focuses on the most controversial details of Ackerman's proposal in order to discount the general project of constitutionalising extraordinary emergency power. This leads him not only ultimately to downplay the potential value of far-reaching institutional innovations in the context of emergency rule, but also to neglect many ways in which the competing approach arguably does a better job than his own at upholding classical rule-of-law values. It is Dyzenhaus, and not Ackerman, who arguably offers a truncated understanding of the rule of law. The basic premise of the formalist model, of course, is that emergency power can be subjected to constitutional legal devices embodying the traditional legal virtues of clarity, prospectiveness, publicity, generality and stability. The 'external constraints' endorsed by Ackerman – including the

[72] *Ibid.* at 110. [73] *Ibid.* at 113.

supermajoritarian escalator, strict predetermined temporal restraints on the exercise of emergency discretion, stringent compensation rules, formal oversight rights for the opposition in parliament – all represent potentially practical institutional attempts to flesh out and buttress traditional rule-of-law virtues by making sure that government action, even during emergencies, remains relatively *prospective, transparent, predictable and general in scope.* In this approach, as in the common law model, judicial supervision plays a significant role in preserving basic rule-of-law virtues, notwithstanding the specific idiosyncrasies of Ackerman's ideas about preventive detention. Yet in some contrast to the common law model, Ackerman and others recognise that *ex post facto* judicial supervision needs to be complemented by clear prospective or *ex ante* emergency legal devices. The rule of law, after all, demands not only judicial review, but also relatively stable and clear general legal norms on which state action is based. It demands an institutionally astute 'political economy' of government which requires that both the legislature and executive act according to clear, relatively predictable, general rules and procedures. By necessity, constitutional norms should have been set up *prior* to the occurrence of any crisis. We can reasonably expect that they will achieve greater impartiality and even-handedness than even the most impressive judicial rulings delivered in the aftermath of a state of emergency; like every form of general prospective rule making, emergency constitutional clauses will be promulgated without advanced knowledge of the specific political interests or constituencies likely to gain from their employment.

This is also why it is misleading to claim that the position outlined in this chapter represents a form of cynical realism which somehow 'denies the worth of legal theory altogether' and seeks to 'debunk normative conceptions of law'.[74] My thesis is not that the institutional realities of presidential democracy preclude the achievement of the rule of law, but rather that Dyzenhaus's overly court-centred vision of the rule of law is likely to fail at effectively countering the pathologies of emergency government in the context of presidential democracy. Only if we understand the rule of law correctly – and I worry that Dyzenhaus does *not* – can we begin to

[74] See Dyzenhaus, Chapter 2, p. 39. I am rather surprised to find myself placed by Dyzenhaus in the company of legal sceptics like Tushnet and Lazar (see respectively 'The Political Constitution of Emergency Powers' (Chapter 6) and 'A Topography of Emergency Powers' (Chapter 7) in this volume). As he knows, I have always criticised legal scepticism. The implicit suggestion, also in Tushnet's piece, that a 'political' (e.g. power-oriented, institutionally-sensitive) approach to understanding emergency government is somehow anti-legal strikes me as incorrect.

challenge the pathologies of presidential emergency rule. Nor do I succumb to what he describes as a 'cult of the given'. On the contrary, I strongly recommend that constitutional architects avoid presidentialism, but when (like contemporary US citizens) we are stuck with it, we need to rely on numerous institutional devices instantiating rule-of-law virtues in order to circumvent its dangers. If anyone here succumbs to the 'cult of the given' it is Dyzenhaus, who simply refuses, in a manner far too commonplace in the common law tradition, to concede sufficiently that 'judges have a dismal record of deference to the executive in times of emergency' for structural reasons and not chiefly because they have failed to follow his particular rendition of jurisprudence. Arguably, it is the position I have tried to defend that takes Dyzenhaus's declared view that the rule of law requires cooperation between and among institutions more seriously than he himself has.[75]

Can we be so sure that Dyzenhaus's alternative rule of law, likely dominated by judges outfitted with substantial authority to interpret abstract, controversial and unavoidably vague notions of fairness, reasonableness, 'important moral values' and respect for the 'fundamental interests of the individual' would do a superior job maintaining basic rule-of-law values? As I have tried to argue in this essay, there are many pressing reasons for concluding that especially in presidentialist democracy our scepticism would be fully justified.

[75] In a helpful written communication, Rueben Balasubramaniam similarly wrote that 'both of you seem to share in a very similar vision of the rule of law as a joint project'. I think this correct.

PART FIVE

Judicial responses to official disobedience

12

Necessity, torture and the rule of law

A.P. SIMESTER

Not every aspect of the debate over regulating states of emergency is especially controversial. There is widespread agreement, for example, that the scope of executive power has grown in recent years, most notably in the United States of America. Constitutional scholars also generally concur that, at least in ordinary times, this trend is undesirable. The debate becomes more heated in the context of emergencies. Even here, however, many commentators accept that officials will sometimes need to do acts that are not permitted under the 'ordinary' law. What they disagree about is how to allow for them.

Various solutions have been advocated. In what follows, I will note just four. The first, and most extreme, possibility is for the legislature to create a legal 'black hole', within which officials have unfettered power to act. At the opposite end of the spectrum is to do nothing, leaving the actions of each official to be governed and judged according to the resources of the ordinary law. Third, somewhere between these options, one might not change the operative law but instead create a mechanism by which a retrospective indemnity or validation, may be conferred upon officials who perform otherwise unlawful actions in an emergency: one version of this proposal is the extra-legal measures (ELM) model advocated by Oren Gross.[1] The fourth alternative is to create a specialist regime of administrative law, operative during a state of emergency, which governs

This paper was presented at NUS, Auckland and Cambridge, and I am very grateful to all who participated in the ensuing discussions; also to David Dyzenhaus, Alon Harel, Andrew von Hirsch, Antje Pedain, Tom Poole, Bob Sullivan and the editor for helpful comments on earlier drafts; and to the Ministry of Education for Academic Research Fund support.

[1] O. Gross, 'Chaos and Rules: Should Responses to Violent Crises Always be Constitutional?' (2003) 112 *Yale Law Journal* 1011. See also O. Gross and F. Ní Aoláin, *Law in Times of Crisis: Emergency Powers in Theory and Practice* (Cambridge: Cambridge University Press, 2006), especially pp. 110–72.

actions taken by officials within the scope of the regime. This prospect has been explored by David Dyzenhaus.[2]

I.

An advantage of the fourth model is that it does not require us to suspend legal control of officials even during emergencies. In rejecting the Gross model of extra-legal responses to state emergencies, Dyzenhaus suggests that it is possible to give officials, *ex ante*, specific legal resources with which to treat emergencies, so that their responses comply with the rule of law. Legal solutions of this sort can work by creating a quasi-administrative framework within which discretionary power is delegated to officials in a manner that is susceptible of guidance and trammelling by the law: I shall call this a 'Controlled Delegation' (CD) model. Actions taken within the terms of the emergency framework would not, then, be taken inside a legal vacuum but may be reviewed judicially.

This solution will not always work. There are at least three types of scenario where the legal resources made available to officials might nonetheless run out. First, the background situation may not constitute a state of 'emergency', wherefore the conditions triggering the discretionary framework are not established. Second, the guiding content of the emergency regime may not extend to the particular case at hand. Third, the emergency regime may determine that the contemplated response by officials is illegitimate; indeed, Dyzenhaus suggests that this is systemically true of certain types of response, such as torture – that such actions are 'unlegalisable'. Optionally, other responses too may be precluded. In each of these scenarios, there may be a need for officials to take urgent action that is not sanctioned *ex ante* by legislation. Where this occurs,[3] we must confront again the worry that so concerns Gross and others.

The main advantage of the ELM model for dealing with these cases is strategic, in so far as it turns upon future consequences for the rule of law. Gross urges that his model, which requires acknowledgement that an official's acts are unlawful, is more likely to resist the (undesirable) seepage

[2] D. Dyzenhaus, 'The State of Emergency in Legal Theory', in V.V. Ramraj, M. Hor and K. Roach (eds.), *Global Anti-Terrorism Law and Policy* (Cambridge: Cambridge University Press, 2005), p. 65.

[3] Importantly, however, the *demesne* of such cases will be smaller if Dyzenhaus's proposal is implemented, a point that generates important benefits for the rule of law. See further the discussion of necessity below, Part II.

of emergency executive powers into the 'ordinary' legal system. Unlike Dyzenhaus's suggestion, which requires extensive institutional modifications, implementation of the ELM model is fairly straightforward, in that there is no requirement to alter the substantive ordinary law; the model requires only the addition of a complex procedural mechanism to apply in emergencies. Admittedly, its implementation depends on whether a workable distinction can be drawn between the ordinary and the emergency – a distinction rejected by Dyzenhaus[4] – but, provided the context is sufficiently elaborated, it seems to me at least arguable that some such dichotomy could be stipulated; it may be susceptible of vagueness and potential manipulation, no doubt, but most cases would fall on one side or other of its blurred boundary.

On the other hand, the model has potential disadvantages. *Any* model that depends on the existence of emergency rather than ordinary conditions risks 'seepage' at least in situations on or near the borderline. It may not work well in a culture of secrecy;[5] indeed, it may help to generate such a culture, since, if otherwise unlawful actions have an effective interim permission,[6] there are likely to be incentives to suppress the future reckoning.[7] Perhaps even more worryingly, by deferring the adjudication procedure, the ELM model offers officials the hope that they may be exonerated later rather than the certainty of unlawfulness now, thus loosening the stringency of prohibitions. In turn, this may lead to a worsening of respect for the rule of law and for the law's substantive values; in the nightmare scenario, Dyzenhaus worries, we may end up living in a discretionary world where state officials routinely perpetrate torture, indefinite detention and the like.

I cannot assess the likelihood of these risks here. It is enough for now to observe that, like its strengths, many of these objections are also strategic.

[4] Who describes it as 'false': Dyzenhaus, 'The State of Emergency', in *Global Anti-Terrorism Law and Policy*, pp. 69 and 73; see too Gross, 'Chaos and Rules', Part IV. Note, however, that the CD model will also require determinations whether a matter is appropriately subject to the delegated regime.

[5] For discussion of this issue, see S. Chesterman, 'Deny Everything: Intelligence Activities and the Rule of Law' (Chapter 13), this volume.

[6] Strictly, on the ELM model, non-disclosure would mean that the actions are not *entitled* to interim permission. Gross stipulates that the official must 'openly and publicly acknowledge the nature of their actions' in order to be eligible for *ex post* ratification: Gross, 'Chaos and Rules', p. 1023.

[7] Which, in any event, may amount to rubber-stamping in a suitably panicked political atmosphere: Dyzenhaus, 'The State of Emergency', in *Global Anti-Terrorism Law and Policy*, p. 73.

This should be no surprise, since the arguments share a common perception that something needs to be done in the face of terrorism: we cannot avoid changes to the legal system, but we want to limit the damage. Indeed, while Dyzenhaus clearly would not welcome the prospect, his own proposal is, strictly speaking, compatible with the Gross model.[8] One might have an ELM mechanism in place to deal with cases not anticipated by the emergency CD regime.

Their models are compatible, in part, because both writers accept that in some emergency situations the resources of the law run out. Faced with the need to perform a prohibited act, the official is on her own. She must φ,[*] but cannot. Through no fault of her own, she is caught in a moral disaster. It is a moral disaster because neither option is right: it is wrong to φ, but terrible consequences await if she does not.

Moreover, the disaster seemingly belongs to the state. The reason to φ arises not from the official's personal needs, but out of the interests of the state, interests the official may have a duty to serve.[9] At the same time, the state is the very source of the prohibition. Yet, rather than assume responsibility for the official's dilemma, the state has abandoned her. At the crucial moment when nuanced guidance is most needed, she is cut off. Thus there are not one but two reasons why the legal system needs to respond. The first and obvious reason is that it is in the state's interests for the official to φ. The second reason, however, arises because the official, qua citizen, needs to be freed from the grip of a moral disaster. The law should place no one, official or otherwise, in an impossible position.[10] When they face the prospect of illegality and prosecution, officials need guidance too.

[8] Their potential for compatible implementation does not imply that they have similar normative bases, as Dyzenhaus makes clear in his contribution to this volume: 'The Compulsion of Legality', Chapter 2.

[*] The Greek symbol, *phi*, used here to designate some (typically, prohibited) act. – Ed.

[9] I cannot develop the point here, but it strikes me that one can have duties that subsist and which one breaches by failing to discharge, notwithstanding that their discharge is impossible or even unjustified. For insightful discussion, see J. Gardner, 'Wrongs and Faults', in A.P. Simester (ed.), *Appraising Strict Liability* (Oxford: Oxford University Press, 2006) p. 51, § 2.

[10] Admittedly, this is not to suggest the official is trapped inside a *legal* contradiction. If φing really is prohibited in the circumstances at hand, it follows that she is legally permitted not to φ. The difficulties lie in knowing whether the prohibition extends to these circumstances and, if it does, in the conflict between the law's prohibition and the official's extra-legal mandate to φ.

II.

There is something in this argument.[11] Other things equal, it is better for the law to offer more rather than less detailed guidance to its citizens, official and otherwise. This is a reason to support the CD model. But in my view, the existing debate understates the resources of the ordinary law. In emergency situations, there will sometimes be a need for officials to take urgent action that cannot be sanctioned *ex ante* by legislation; and this may occur even within the more detailed emergency provisions in a CD regime. Yet in these cases, the law does not simply run out. It does not follow that the action, if taken, is necessarily extra-legal. The common law knows a range of general defences, according to which otherwise unlawful acts may be permissible, or at least forgivable, in certain circumstances. In particular, the defence of *necessity* might be thought of as a last resort for legality; as a fall-back, catch-all, principle of ordinary law which acknowledges that exceptional situations arise and subjects them to legal review.

By articulating defences such as necessity, the legal system adds the interstitial nuance that its prohibitions require. Yet in order to do so, the law must import supplementary resources from the moral system. This raises the question: does the availability of necessity itself dilute the rule of law, proffering the very evils that Gross wants to avert?[12] Fortunately, the answer is no. Once we dispel certain misconceptions about the defence, a principled account of necessity can be given, in which its existence is both justified and exceptional.

Necessity falls within the class of what may be termed *rationale-based* defences. To take a simple case, suppose that V is a terrorist who is about to detonate an explosive in a crowded shopping mall. D, a police officer, recognises what V is about to do and shoots him dead. D has committed a *prima facie crime*: she has fulfilled both the conduct and mental elements of

[11] I emphasise that Dyzenhaus and Gross do not themselves make the argument sketched above. I have sought only to suggest a line of reasoning that they may find congenial.

[12] Such a concern lay behind the rejection of necessity as a justification in Canada: '[t]he Criminal Code has specified a number of identifiable situations in which an actor is justified in committing what would otherwise be a criminal offence. To go beyond that and hold that ostensibly illegal acts can be validated on the basis of their expediency, would import an undue subjectivity into the criminal law. It would invite the courts to second guess the legislature and to assess the relative merits of social policies underlying criminal prohibitions. Neither is a role which fits well with the judicial function'. *Perka* v. *R* [1985] 13 DLR (4th) 1, 14 (Dickson J.). The same concern did not persuade the English Court of Appeal in *Pommell* [1995] 2 Cr App R 607.

a crime of intentional homicide. The offence definition is satisfied. But the law does not stop there. Even though intentional homicide is prohibited, on this occasion its commission will not lead to D's conviction, because D has a supervening,[13] rationale-based defence. A defence of this sort denies neither the conduct nor mental element of the prima facie crime; rather, it avers D's responsibility for her action and explains the further reasons why she did it. For the defence to be successful, those reasons must justify or at least excuse what she did. In effect, when D claims a rationale-based defence she asserts: yes, I did the prohibited act, I did it deliberately, and here's *why*.

In the case of the police officer, her claim is one of justification. We might say – and criminal theorists often do say – that her action was a proportionate and necessary response to the emergency situation. More accurately, we can say that D's action was an *appropriate* response and, for that reason, permissible.[14]

The refinement may seem like a small move. Actually, however, it is crucial, for reasons so far unrecognised in the literature; reasons that are crucial to the acceptability of justifications within the moral and legal systems. Standard formulations of necessity run along the lines that conduct is justified whenever, after weighing up all the alternatives, φing is a proportionate or 'lesser' evil than not-φing.[15] According to the Model Penal Code (MPC), 'Conduct that the actor believes to be necessary to avoid a harm or evil to himself or to another is justifiable, provided that: (a) the harm or evil sought to be avoided by such conduct is greater than that sought to be prevented by the law defining the offense charged . . .'[16]

13 Cf. A.P. Simester, 'Mistakes in Defence' (1992) 12 *Oxford Journal of Legal Studies* 295 at 295–6: a supervening defence is one that denies neither *actus reus* nor *mens rea* but, rather, seeks to avoid liability by reference to accompanying considerations not contemplated in those elements of the offence definition. Not all supervening defences are rationale-based. Rather than assert and explain D's responsibility, for example, insanity and infancy deny D's moral responsibility for the conduct altogether, thereby taking D out of the realm of moral agents. For discussion of the distinction, see J. Gardner, 'The Gist of Excuses' (1998) 1 *Buffalo Criminal Law Review* 575.

14 Specifically, her response was an appropriate act of self-defence, on behalf of herself or others. I return to this below.

15 Compare C.M.V. Clarkson, 'Necessary Action: A New Defence' [2004] *Criminal Law Review* 81, who would generalise this approach to other rationale-based defences. Some of the discussion in this section is drawn from the reply to Clarkson by W. Chan and A.P. Simester, 'Duress, Necessity: How Many Defences?' (2005) 16 *King's College Law Journal* 121.

16 § 3.02(1).

A similar, common law formulation finds favour in the English Court of Appeal:[17]

> The claim is that [D's] conduct was not harmful because on a choice of two evils the choice of avoiding the greater harm was justified. . . . According to Sir James Stephen there are three necessary requirements for the application of the doctrine of necessity: (i) the act is needed to avoid inevitable and irreparable evil; (ii) no more should be done than is reasonably necessary for the purpose to be achieved; (iii) the evil inflicted must not be disproportionate to the evil avoided.

These standard accounts suggest an approach in which the reasons for and against φing are stacked up against each other in order to determine which pile has the greater weight. I can break into a cabin during a snowstorm because saving a life is more important than respecting property rights. Firefighters can raze V's house to create a firebreak because losing the village outweighs the evil of losing the one home. In Judith Thomson's famous Trolley Problem,[18] D can throw a switch to divert the trolley because five deaths constitute a proportionately greater harm than just one. And so on.

Now if that really were the right way to think about necessity, the relationship of necessity to the rule of law would present serious difficulties. In particular, a general 'lesser-evils' defence might weaken the rule of law through its capacity for expansive interpretation and application, something that might be used in times of crisis to lend the garb of legitimacy to otherwise extra-legal measures. Even in ordinary times, its availability would risk undermining legislative prohibitions. In effect, the defence would threaten to revise every prima facie offence into an ad hoc exhortation not to inflict harm save reasonably. Determining what actions were permissible would then become a matter of case-by-case discretion, notwithstanding legislative efforts to lay down general rules.[19]

[17] *In re A (Children) (Conjoined Twins: Surgical Separation)* [2001] Fam 147 at 236 and 240 (Brooke L.J.). The reference is to Stephens, *Digest of the Criminal Law*, 4th ed. (London: Macmillan, 1887), pp. 24–5.

[18] D is the driver of a runaway rail trolley that is about to strike and kill five workmen on the track ahead. If he diverts the trolley to a siding, the five will be saved but the trolley will instead strike and kill a lone worker who is on the siding. J.J. Thomson, 'The Trolley Problem' (1985) 94 *Yale Law Journal* 1395. Although the case is commonly described as Thomson's, she herself derives it from P. Foot: 'The Problem of Abortion and the Doctrine of the Double Effect' (1967) *Oxford Review* 5.

[19] This possibility is sometimes avoided where the legislature has enumerated the permissible exceptions with sufficient specificity to exclude a justification based on the facts at hand:

Clearly, it is inappropriate for individuals or even courts to substitute their ad hoc judgments of the balance of interests, Robin Hood-like, for the general determination of social priorities that is properly made by parliament.[20] But there are two factors that mean necessity, properly understood, does not do this. The first is the circumstance of urgency, a standard feature of φing in emergency situations. Supervening justificatory defences are available only when an individual is faced with having to violate the law in situations where recourse to legitimate state authorisation is impossible. In such cases, the rule of law is not so much by-passed as unavailable. The individual does not usurp the determinative role of the legal system. Conversely, if the situation is not urgent, so that recourse to lawful authorisation is possible, neither official nor private citizen may take the situation into her own hands.

The second factor is that justifications are not simply a matter of weighing up the strength of various reasons. For a reason to justify committing a prima facie wrong, not only must it possess the requisite strength, but it must also stand in the right relationship to that wrong. In particular, some reasons for committing the wrong may be *excluded*,[21] under certain or even all circumstances, from consideration. This point implies a key deficiency in the standard common law and MPC analyses, since the possibility of excluded reasons is not addressed by a generic criterion of proportionality or of 'lesser' evil. A justification cannot be established merely by piling up the assorted desirable features of an action and balancing them against all the various disadvantages, because the matter is not simply a weighting exercise. Justificatory reasons are a matter of category as well as degree.

cf. MPC, § 3.02(1)(b)-(c); *Quayle* [2005] EWCA Crim 1415, [2005] 1 WLR 3642 (permissibility of privately using cannabis for pain relief held to be excluded by the comprehensive nature of the legislative scheme). Compare the express provision that the right against torture is non-derogable in the European Convention on Human Rights, Arts. 3 and 15. Inevitably, explicit provision of this sort is not the norm.

20 See, e.g. *Southwark London Borough* v. *Williams* [1971] Ch 734 at 740 (Edmund Davies L.J.): 'The law regards with the deepest suspicion any remedies of self help, and permits these remedies to be resorted to only in very special circumstances. The reason for such circumspection is clear – necessity can very easily become simply a mask for anarchy'. The point is that the legal system cannot operate if its authority is optional. Thus the use of vacant council properties, as in Southwark, is best resolved by political decision-making processes, implemented by consistent administration, rather than by ad hoc self-help actions such as squatting.

21 I adopt the terminology from Raz, *Practical Reason and Norms*, 2nd ed. (Princeton: Princeton University Press, 1990), § 1.2. I have in mind here the exclusion of reasons over and above those excluded by legislative provision: above, n. 19.

Indeed, these differences of category are built into the very classification of rationale-based defences. The most straightforward type of necessitous action is self-defence, unequivocally a justification, which is available where D acts against V in order to ward off a threat that V himself poses. In these cases the driving normative force behind the defence is D's right to protect herself (or another person) against unlawful attacks, a right grounded, in turn, in the interests that D (or another) has in personal autonomy and physical integrity. That right, which allows for limited self-preference, defeats V's interests and carves a partial liberty out of D's general duty not to cause harm to others. As with all justifications, the extent of the liberty remains dependent on norms of proportionality, and its recognition by the legal system is constrained by rule-of-law considerations – in particular, the requirement of urgency.[22] Thus the moral and legal character of D's conduct here is distinctively righteous.[23] D acts to preserve a moral and legal, entitlement; and her reason for harming V is, in principle, an eligible reason for acting and not one excluded *tout court*. It is no accident that self-defence overlaps with prevention of crime defences. D has a right not to be attacked. In situations where it is impracticable for the state to assert that right on her behalf, she upholds that right by acting in self-defence.

In other cases of justifying necessity, by contrast, D's conduct is not consonant with the legal regime. D wrongs V, but the wrong is morally and legally permitted, as when D enters V's house in order to call an ambulance on behalf of E, a person urgently in need of medical treatment. Here, 'lesser-evils' necessity comes into its own. Its advantage – and its weakness, as well as its challenge to the rule of law – lies in the fact that the defence lacks the narrow, right-defending focus of self-defence. Even though neither D nor E is wronged, D can cite her life-saving reason in order to defeat the duty she owes not to violate V's property rights. But she can do so only because a reason of this sort is not excluded by V's proprietary rights.[24] It can be stacked up against the reasons not to damage V's property when determining whether, all things considered, it

[22] Hence an objection to *Kelly* [1989] NI 341, where D was held justified in fatally shooting someone believed by D to be a terrorist who, if allowed to escape, would go on to commit terrorist offences at some point in the future. In the absence of urgency, it should not be open to D to bypass normal state mechanisms for regulating potential wrongdoing by others. For criticism, see Simester and Sullivan, *Criminal Law: Theory and Doctrine*, 3rd ed. (United Kingdom: Hart Publishing, 2007), § 21.2(v).

[23] Distinctively, but not uniquely: compare, e.g., the sibling justification of defence of property.

[24] Cf. Raz, above n. 21. In this case, the fact that V has a property right supplies what Raz would call a protected reason: a first-order reason to respect V's property coupled with a

is permissible (i.e. justified) for one to act as does D. This does not mean the wrong goes away: there may, for example, be a duty to pay damages for any loss that V suffers.[25] Yet it is a permitted wrong, and we can conclude that D does not act badly all things considered – she does not act badly overall – when she does that wrong. Her reasons for acting are sufficient (eligible and proportionate) to render her conduct morally permissible and, in turn, lawful.

Yet that conclusion is not always open. The reasons not to violate V's person are not like those concerning V's property and exclude a much wider range of counter-considerations. Thus, in the absence of V's consent, it supplies *no reason at all* in favour of removing one of V's kidneys that transplanting the kidney into T's body will save T's life.[26] The 'reason' is excluded from consideration; indeed, its exclusion is part and parcel of the very importance of our rights to personal autonomy and integrity – that they are not amenable to this kind of algebra. T's need for the kidney cannot be stacked up against the reasons not to harm V when deciding, all things considered, what to do. Absent some further non-excluded reason, we can conclude that, all things considered, D should not remove V's kidney. Were D to proceed with the operation, she would both wrong V and, in so doing, act badly overall. Her reasons for acting are insufficient (because ineligible) to render her conduct lawful.

There is more to be said about necessity,[27] and some of the pay-off will be seen in Part IV. But for present purposes the important point is

second order, exclusionary reason to disregard certain sorts of reasons for overriding that first-order reason. Hence, self-aggrandisement is excluded as a reason for overriding V's property right, but preservation of life is not.

[25] While remaining a civil (tortious) wrong, however, it does cease to be a criminal wrong. Cf. Simester and Sullivan, *Criminal Law: Theory and Doctrine*, § 21.3(ii)(d); Gardner, n. 9 above.

[26] Compare Judith Thomson's discussion of the surgeon example in 'The Trolley Problem' (1985) 94 *Yale Law Journal* 1395 at 1396. This way of expressing the matter is pragmatic. Strictly speaking, a reason exists but has no practical force, since it should not be acted upon.

[27] It may be tempting to read these examples as showing no more than that the exclusion of reasons is a matter of hierarchy, so that necessity is available only where the interest saved is of a higher order than the victim's. Not so, as the Trolley Problem illustrates. Notwithstanding that the interests at stake are of similar order, diverting the trolley to save five at the expense of one (P) is permissible, even though it would be impermissible for a surgeon to harvest V's organs in order to make life-saving transplants into five other patients. Compare, too, the famous case of *Dudley* v. *Stephens* (1884) 14 QBD 273, where survivors of a shipwreck, adrift in the South Atlantic, killed and consumed the youngest and weakest member of their party. Had they not done so, they would probably have died; but they were convicted of murder and their claim of necessity was – rightly – refused.

These examples illustrate a further wrinkle to the necessity defence, one that I cannot explore here. They show that the exclusion of reasons is itself contextual. It turns in part that the defence, if properly understood and applied, is no malleable tool with which to negotiate the rule of law. To the contrary: it offers a mechanism by which the conduct of officials falls to be normatively regulated, by the courts, *within* the legal system. In this it differs fundamentally from the ELM model, which, depending on the ratifying procedure, would gift the ratifier with a prerogative of arbitrary mercy.

III.

Not all rationale-based defences are justifications. In cases where D both commits a prima facie wrong and, all things considered, acts badly, normally the secondary possibility will arise that D has a rationale-based *excuse.*[28] Suppose, for example, that D attacks and seriously injures V because T threatens otherwise to kill her. Notwithstanding that it was impermissible for D to act as she did, in the sense that there were insufficient valid reasons for her conduct, we may be reluctant to fault D. Our reluctance is because, although D's reason for acting was (objectively speaking) inadequate, we can quite understand that it was good enough for D. She feared for her life. Any reasonable person might have been impelled by such a fear; where this is so, we cannot make the inference of culpability that would normally entitle us to blame D for her actions. In such cases, we may allow an excuse. For the sake of clarity, I shall call this excuse *duress.*

Even though one may say in duress cases that, like necessity and self-defence, the individual acts under great pressure, the role of the pressure differs. In duress, the pressure directly explains D's motivation. D is right to fear for her life: her only mistake is to treat that as a reason for injuring V.[29] But that mistake merely discloses an imperfect virtue – a limitation – not a fault. We do not count, among the qualities reasonably expected

on the relationship of the reasons, excluded and excluding, within an agent's practical deliberation. Sometimes reasons are excluded *as ends*, without always being excluded in other roles. In the trolley example, it matters crucially that the harm to P is a concomitant or side effect of the driver's intended action. By contrast, the harm to V is directly intended by the surgeon as a means to an end. In *Dudley* v. *Stephens* the victim's death was similarly intended as a means to an (excluded) end and was, as such, unjustified. For further discussion of the importance of this distinction to justifications, see A.P. Simester, 'Why Distinguish Intention from Foresight', in A.P. Simester and A.T.H. Smith (eds.), *Harm and Culpability* (Oxford: Clarendon Press, 1996), pp. 71–102.

28 Rationale-based excuses are a subset of the defences that are commonly described as excuses. See n. 13 above.

29 That is to say, her only – and understandable – mistake is to treat the reason as non-excluded; since, but for its exclusion, it would have sufficed to justify her action.

of D, the levels of self-control and altruism that would be needed for D to refrain from acting. In this sense, it is apt to describe the defence as a 'concession to human frailty'.[30] It reflects an imperfection characteristic of humans in general and not one peculiar to D.

In necessity, the importance of the emergency situation is different. Like all justifications, it is a concession to the rule of law. It explains, as I said earlier, why D is not usurping the proper role of the state. One cannot raze V's house in order to create a firebreak, and thereby preserve the village, without official authority unless the fire is at hand.[31] Thus necessity is like self-defence rather than an excuse, in that D's motivation constitutes, objectively speaking, a legitimate and not excluded reason for acting.

Why does this matter to officials? In the public context, the divide between justification and excuse is crucial. Dyzenhaus crosses that divide when he contemplates that officials who act outside the law may sometimes claim a rationale-based excuse.[32] But the line is not for crossing. Except for epistemic mistake (a quite different type of case), it is not open for the state or any individual acting qua official to claim an excuse. Official action constituting a prima facie crime can only be justified. If the action is justified, it is permissible – i.e., lawful. There is good reason to do it. Otherwise, the action is unlawful. For the state, there is no middle ground. Individual persons may be excused for acting unlawfully, on the grounds that their impermissible choice was blameless.[33] But excuses, which reflect profoundly human characteristics, are simply inapplicable to artificial actors such as the state. The pressure to which an excused person bows is personal. Thus official torture is inexcusable, although – conceptually speaking – torture by individuals *in extremis* might not be.

This may seem counter-intuitive. Surely one can be excused when acting on behalf of others? It is uncontroversial law that duress can sometimes

[30] E.g. *Howe* [1987] 1 AC 417 at 432–5.

[31] Cf. *Shayler* [2001] 1 WLR 2206. D, a civil servant employed in MI5, was held to be in breach of the Official Secrets Act 1989 (UK) after he shared secret information with a newspaper, notwithstanding that he believed the actions of MI5's threatened rather than enhanced public security. D was not attempting to avert some crystallised, imminent catastrophe – there was no forthcoming incident his actions were intended to avert, merely a fear that the covert operations of MI5 threatened public security generally.

[32] Dyzenhaus, 'The State of Emergency', in *Global Anti-Terrorism Law and Policy*, p. 84.

[33] There is no reason, of course, why those persons cannot themselves be officials. They cannot be excused qua officials and their official actions would remain unlawful, but from the perspective of the criminal law they are charged as individuals and, as such, are entitled to claim the same range of excuses as anyone else; provided, as with any excuse, it applies to them personally – as to which, see below in the text.

be levied through a third party, as when T's threat is directed at D's child. In such cases, it seems entirely understandable for D to be moved by concern for his family into committing the wrong that T demands. Yet if D may claim an excuse, then perhaps the state may, analogously, succeed to an excuse when acting on behalf of those threatened by a predicted attack? If it would be excusable for D to μ, why can't the state μ in D's place?

I think there are two responses to this argument. First, the analogy to third-party threats does not refute the point that a rationale-based excuse like duress must apply personally to D. Duress is not vicarious: what counts is the effective pressure that the threat exerts *on D*. Thus, in the example, it is of central importance that the threat is to D's child. The excused father acts neither impersonally nor impartially, but because the threat directly engages his own, most cherished values. He intervenes not from sympathetic concern for the child's predicament, but out of personally experienced fear. Recognising this aspect of duress helps us to make sense of the common law restriction that the threat must be directed against either the defendant himself or someone close to him.[34] Each and every life is valuable and, as human life, valuable equally. Without more, a stranger cannot adjudicate between them. But we can quite understand, indeed hope, that a father does not think that way. A father who sacrifices another's interests to save the life of his child may be a wrongdoer. Yet in doing wrong he exhibits a very human quality, a quality of being a good father.[35]

The first response, then, involves a claim about the manner in which duress is experienced. It implies that agents can only be excused personally. Vicarious motivation will not do. There is, however, a limitation to this response. While the same logic excludes vicarious excuses for other artificial actors, such as corporations, it does not exclude the attribution of an excuse in tandem with the prima facie offence under doctrines of

[34] *Hasan* [2005] UKHL 22, [2005] 2 AC 467. Make sense of, but not necessarily justify. One can imagine scenarios in which a person's concern for the welfare of others is sufficient, depending on the nature of threat, to lead that person into compliance even though the threat is against a stranger. (Cf. Horder, 'Self-Defence, Necessity and Duress: Understanding the Relationship' (1998) 11 *Canadian Journal of Law and Jurisprudence* 143 at 163.) The exclusion of such cases would have to be justified, if at all, by reference to institutional concerns.

[35] The example illustrates a more general point: that even one who acts blamelessly may be damaged, morally speaking, by the position in which he finds himself. Similarly, a state threatened with terrorist attacks cannot hope to escape morally unscathed, no matter what its response.

identification.[36] There the logic is different: the corporation is imputed with a package comprising some designated (senior) individual's conduct and culpability. At least at international law, analogous doctrines of identification are required to recognise the state as an agent, and in principle such doctrines could also impute excuses. More generally, there seems no reason to exclude the possibility of excuses within any legal system where the state is itself a subject.[37]

The second reply is, therefore, specific to domestic law. Besides being artificial, the state is a special type of actor. The relationship of a state to its citizens is nothing like that of father to children, or indeed any form of inter-human relation, because the state is a purely instrumental creation without personal values. Moreover, in accordance with the state's claim to authority, that relationship is constituted by rules, including those rules which grant powers to the state and its officials. The requirement of lawfulness binds the state to act according to those rules. This is a central requirement of the rule of law. Part of the very point of being an official is impersonality. It is not open for the state or its officials to prefer the interests of one person to another, since the state is not entitled to be closer to one person than another. It is equidistant, impartial to all.

Yet, for all that, doubt may persist. Surely, one may ask, the state is entitled to be moved by the plight of its citizens? Consider, for example, the controversial case of Wolfgang Daschner, vice-president of Frankfurt am Main police. Daschner led investigations into the kidnap of 11-year-old Jakob von Metzler, son of a prominent banker. The kidnapper, Magnus Gaefgen, was arrested after collecting the ransom payment but refused to disclose Metzler's whereabouts despite lengthy questioning. Hoping to save the boy, Daschner eventually instructed that Gaefgen should be threatened with torture, at which point Gaefgen confessed that Metzler was already dead and revealed the location of his body. Daschner was subsequently found guilty of coercion. Yet the charge was a misdemeanour – more serious charges were not pressed – and the conviction suspended,[38]

[36] As to which see Simester and Sullivan, *Criminal Law: Theory and Doctrine*, § 8.2(iii).

[37] Such as international law or, conceptually, inter-planetary law. I am grateful to Eleanor Wong for convincing me of this point.

[38] This may need explanation to common lawyers unfamiliar with the German penal system (and I am grateful to Antje du Bois-Pedain for her help with this). Although found guilty, Daschner was not sentenced but rather 'warned' that a fine of €10,800 would be imposed should he reoffend within one year. Under German law, the effect is that the finding of guilty does not count as a criminal conviction. This disposition of a criminal case is highly unusual and should be distinguished from a 'suspended sentence', in which execution of the sentence is merely held pending. A trial court can only dispose of a case with a 'warning' instead of punishment if (1) the court expects that the defendant will not reoffend; (2) special

reflecting the considerable support that his case attracted. It seems that many regarded Daschner as akin to Gross's moral hero, one who chose to disobey the law for the sake of a moral imperative.

Perhaps this is a borderline case. I do not deny that it has a complex moral pull. But it is a mistake to think the pull is *excusatory*. 'Moral heroes' are not excused. They are heroes because, despite the impediments, they do what is morally right.[39] If there is hesitation over the assessment of Daschner's case, it is because of uncertainty about whether his conduct was *justified*: morally speaking, might it have been permissible? Or did he act for an excluded reason, like so many – perhaps all – putative reasons for threatening or perpetrating torture?

I shall say something further about this last question in Part IV. For the moment, what counts is that an uncertain justification is not in itself a ground to find an excuse. Whether someone is justified in perpetrating a wrong is an all or nothing question. If, all things considered, there is sufficient reason to φ, one crosses the threshold into permissible action; otherwise, one remains outside, consigned to the world of acting badly. Determining that question may involve borderline judgments about the balance and eligibility of reasons,[40] but the conclusion is discrete: between the competing reasons, it is winner-takes-all. Unlike excuses, justification does not come in degrees. If justified, the actor needs no excuse; but if unjustified, whatever reasons there were in favour of φing are defeated and have nothing more to offer. Thus the possibility of justification supplies no direct foundation for excuse.[41] The case for each must be built separately.[42]

IV.

On the other hand, is torture ever justifiable? I take this question to be at the heart of the inquiry whether, morally speaking, torture is ever legalisable.

circumstances of the case exceptionally make the imposition of punishment unnecessary; and (3) non-imposition of punishment in the case does not undermine the rule of law.

39 Especially, where the impediments make it permissible or, at least, excusable *not* to do so.

40 This is one reason why, in determining whether an actor was justified, the law does not require her to weigh the reasons with 'jeweller's scales': *Reed* v. *Wastie* [1972] Crim LR 221 (DC).

41 This is not to deny that the *underlying* reasons in favour of an action can – whether or not defeated – be pertinent to an excuse, in so far as it is understandable why D treated those reasons as sufficient. By not requiring 'jeweller's scales' (*Reed* v. *Wastie*, *Ibid.*), the law neatly sidesteps having to consider an excuse of borderline moral error; instead piggybacking such cases on the relevant justification.

42 Indeed, in law, there is no reason why the two cannot overlap.

It is a central question, but not necessarily decisive, because there are also practical and institutional arguments to consider. For instance, there is a risk that officials might stretch the boundaries of legal torture, exploiting its selective permission to brutalise and abuse the powerless.[43] Moreover, torturing people in the name of the state may be thought to betray the very nature of law. As Jeremy Waldron puts it, law is not savage:[44] its rule may be mandatory, but not brute. At the core of any decent legal system is a commitment to respect the dignity of those it governs, and not to trample all over them – to treat them as reasoning human beings rather than drones. To license torture would violate that commitment, corrupting the entire legal system and bridging the divide between rule of law and rule by power.

These kinds of argument supply reasons for thinking that torture should be prohibited absolutely, without possibility of derogation. But they have been well made by others and I shall not pursue them here. Instead, my concern is with the question whether torture may sometimes be morally permissible, and with the intersection of torture and justification. My remarks in this section are intended only to sketch the structural issues and not to enter the debate in detail. I want to highlight what I think is a mistaken approach and to suggest another direction for the debate.

The mistake is made when writers view the justification of torture through the lens of necessity and it is compounded when they apply a metric of lesser evils. Since torture is abhorrent, something pretty extreme is required to justify it and, in practice, such cases may be unlikely. But implicit in this way of thinking is that, in principle, it is just a matter of finding a sufficiently serious case. Unless evils are treated as infinite, the moral prohibition is not, indeed cannot be, absolute: 'The use of torture is so profound a violation of a human right that almost nothing can redeem it – almost, because one can not rule out a case in which the lives of

[43] See, e.g., O. Gross, 'Are Torture Warrants Warranted? Pragmatic Absolutism and Official Disobedience' (2004) 88 *Minnesota Law Review* 1481, § I; S.F. Kreimer, 'Too Close to the Rack and the Screw: Constitutional Constraints on Torture in the War on Terror' (2003) 6 *University of Pennsylvania Journal of Constitutional Law* 278 at 322.

[44] J. Waldron, 'Torture and Positive Law: Jurisprudence for the White House' (2005) 105 *Columbia Law Review* 1681 at 1726–7: 'People may fear and be deterred by legal sanctions; they may dread lawsuits; they may even on occasion be forced by legal means or legally empowered officials to do things or go places against their will. But even when this happens, they will not be herded like cattle or broken like horses; they will not be beaten like dumb animals or treated as bodies to be manipulated'.

many innocent persons will surely be saved by its use against a single person'.[45]

The difficulty with this analysis is that, provided the stakes are high enough, potentially anything goes.[46] For those who advocate official torture, an extreme case can be generated as a kind of high-water mark. Once a single case is accepted on the weight of numbers, algebra can take over. Indeed, there is no principled ground to limit official torture to the infliction of harmless but unbearable pain.[47] Why not mutilate the suspect – or the suspect's family – to get her to talk? (If that's worse, its justification merely requires that more lives depend on it.) The conclusion of this approach is that, at the very point when its bite is most needed, the 'right' not to be tortured loses its teeth. It becomes a right not to be tortured *until we really need to.* Anyone who subscribes to the simple view of necessity as a 'lesser evils' defence necessarily buys into this analysis. The game is lost: not so much because they have underestimated the evil of torture, but because they have misunderstood its justification.

The better view is that torture can never be justified by necessity. But it does not follow that torture can never be justified.

An analogy may be helpful to the more familiar context of homicide. In *Dudley and Stephens* it was said that, though their lives were at stake, three shipwrecked mariners were not entitled to kill and eat the cabin boy. Rightly, necessity did not justify his murder. But perhaps we can generate a high water mark? Would it make a difference if a hundred or a thousand lives depended on the homicide? No. Dudley had no unexcluded reason in the circumstances to kill Parker, because the need to save his life or the lives of the others was incapable of generating one. Multiply the numbers and you still get zero. So it is with torture. For a parallel example, imagine the state is confronted with an ultimatum. A credible threat is received from terrorists that, unless V – a randomly selected, innocent person who happens to be of a different religion – is tortured publicly, the terrorists

45 S.H. Kadish, 'Torture, the State and the Individual' (1989) 23 *Israel Law Review* 345 at 346. In a footnote, Kadish seeks to safeguard his position by suggesting that the imbalance in the weighting of evils must be 'extremely great'.

46 This point is made by Kreimer, above n. 43 at 306.

47 Alan Dershowitz advocates judicial torture warrants with such a restriction: *Why Terrorism Works: Understanding the Threat, Responding to the Challenge* (New Haven: Yale University Press, 2002), ch. 4. He does, however, recognise the ad hoc nature of the limitation at p. 146. Dershowitz's argument rests on values of transparency and accountability, given his prediction that officials will practise torture even if prohibited. I cannot address that argument here.

will detonate a bomb and thereby kill a thousand people. On these facts, it seems to me that the state is not morally entitled to torture V.[48] The threat cannot justify torture because the putative reason it generates is excluded.

Yet that leaves a puzzle. If it makes no difference when excluded reasons are multiplied, why do some cases seem more difficult, more borderline, than others? An excluded-reasons analysis seemingly admits of no middle ground and therefore of no hard cases. And if there are genuinely hard cases for the justification of torture, that would seem a reason for doubting the validity of an excluded-reasons analysis.

Part of the explanation is that the question, whether a particular reason for φing is excluded, may itself be borderline. Once a given reason is excluded, multiplying the numbers makes no difference; but are we always convinced of its exclusion? That depends, in part, on how important the underlying interests are and on why we value them. In the case of torture, our interests as human beings in dignity and integrity are profound and it seems to me that they exclude general reasons of necessity pretty clearly. Others may think the matter a closer call, which would help to explain why they perceive at least some cases as hard. But in my view, the truly borderline cases, where the putative justification is perhaps not excluded, lie elsewhere. Their appeal arises because they go beyond a claim of necessity.

Consider again the case of Wolfgang Daschner. Even though only one life is at stake, it seems a more plausible case for justification than many multi-person hypotheticals. Daschner's case, like some of the standard terrorist examples, involves a key feature that differentiates them from the Ultimatum case. They involve torturing the would-be wrongdoers themselves – those responsible for planting the bomb, hijacking the plane, abducting the child, etc. – in order to forestall their wrong.

This additional ingredient starts to reorient the justification away from necessity and toward self-defence. We can see this, too, in the analogy to homicide. *Dudley* v. *Stephens* illustrates the exclusionary rule that, just as the surgeon may not harvest a patient's kidneys, one may not take V's life in order to preserve the life of others. Yet, notwithstanding the interdiction, one may do that very thing when acting in self-defence. *One may do so when V is the source of the threat.* This is a crucial difference between self-defence and necessity, the additional feature that prevents self-defence

[48] This conclusion holds, it seems to me, without the need to invoke whatever reasons may exist not to bow to terrorist threats generally.

from collapsing into the general, residual justification of necessity. In self-defence, one responds to a threat from V by attacking V, the source of that threat.[49] In necessity, one responds to a threat by attacking *someone else.*

The possibility of self-defence shows that even fundamental rights can have limits. V's right to life does not exclude self-protection as a reason for action, even lethal action, on behalf of those whose lives V threatens. But the response must be addressed to V. Otherwise, one is on the wrong side of Thomas Nagel's distinction between fighting 'clean' and fighting 'dirty': 'To fight dirty is to direct one's hostility or aggression not at its proper object, but at a peripheral target which may be more vulnerable, and through which the proper object can be attacked indirectly'.[50] V is 'the proper target' because V is responsible for the threat. One cannot target a peripheral victim, T, because T's right to life excludes that move. Vis-à-vis T, the justification is one of necessity and excluded.[51]

Although I cannot pursue the possibility here, perhaps that conclusion can be generalised for all fundamental rights. It may be that directly intended violations of a fundamental right can *never* be justified; and this is part of what it means for a right to be fundamental. (If that is correct, the corollary is that necessity is always unavailable in such cases, because necessity is the residual defence of a justified wrong.) But fundamental does not mean exhaustive. Sometimes the underlying interest is not absolutely protected by the right, so that harm to the interest is not always a wrong. Unlike necessity, the core justifications (like self-defence, prevention of crime, lawful arrest and punishment) operate to justify *harmful* actions by showing that the action was not a wrong at all. They deny that V's right was breached.[52]

For the action not to be a wrong, however, the harm must be inflicted in response to an event *for which V is responsible.* This is why it is objectionable, for instance, to punish (or torture) innocent persons, such as

[49] I assume here that the threat is an unjust or unjustified one. For lengthy exploration of this type of condition, see S. Uniacke, *Permissible Killing: The Self-Defence Justification of Homicide* (Cambridge: Cambridge University Press, 1994).

[50] T. Nagel, 'War and Massacre' (1972) 1 *Philosophy and Public Affairs* 123 at 134. Nagel uses the example (at 138) of distracting, and thereby capturing, an enemy throwing hand grenades at you by machine-gunning his nearby wife and children.

[51] I think this point helps significantly in the explanation of Jonathan Bennett's Terror Bomber example: 'Morality and Consequences' in McMurrin (ed.), *The Tanner Lectures on Human Values* (Cambridge: Cambridge University Press, 1980), pp. 45–116 at p. 95.

[52] For the avoidance of doubt, this is not a claim that any of V's rights are forfeited. V would be wronged, for instance, when attacked by someone unaware of the threat V posed. See, e.g., Simester, above n. 27.

the family members of a defector or a suicide bomber, in order to deter wrongdoing. It is punishing 'dirty'. Conversely, it is part of the appeal of Wolfgang Daschner's case that the policeman's threat to torture Gaefgen is made in order to prevent wrongdoing *by Gaefgen himself*; to uphold the child's right to life against the unjust threat that Gaefgen has posed.

Even armed with these distinctions, however, two kinds of difficulty remain. Between them, they contrive to leave even the more plausible cases for torture on a moral borderline. The first is a problem of collective responsibility. Typically, the kinds of cases that motivate Alan Dershowitz and other proponents of official torture differ slightly from Daschner's.[53] Officials have, say, captured one member (V) of a terrorist group while the remaining members, having eluded arrest, are now embarked on the group's mission to destroy an occupied building. Is it permissible for the officials to use a degree of torture in order to identify and then evacuate the target? The putative justification looks somewhat like self-defence, in that the officials are seeking to prevent a wrong; but its application to V requires us to broaden the scope of V's responsibility, extending it beyond threats that V has personally authored. V is certainly not an innocent third party. Doubtless he is a complicitous wrongdoer and a co-conspirator. But he does not seem to be doing the very wrong that the officials seek to prevent.

Collective responsibility is a natural source of borderline cases. However, it is not specific to torture. A similar issue arises in other contexts, such as homicide. For instance, any proposal that the bombing of Hiroshima was a justified act of self-defence involves, implicitly, a claim that the citizens of that city were responsible for the aggressive actions of their Government. Whether that claim is plausible (and it has been rejected in international law), the broadening of responsibility doctrines beyond direct authorship is clearly problematic for justification in general.

Fortunately, this complex issue is not raised, at least, by Herr Daschner. He has in his hands the very perpetrator.[54] Why, then, do we hesitate even over this case? The reason, I think, is uncertainty whether there is *any* non-excluded reason for perpetrating torture, even self-defence. Perhaps torture is unjustifiable, *tout court*. Perhaps, at the last, the analogy between homicide and torture runs out? While self-defence may not be an excluded reason for homicide, perhaps it is an excluded reason for torture?

[53] See, e.g., Alan Dershowitz, above n. 47, pp. 143–4.

[54] I leave aside the obvious difficulties that one might be mistaken about a suspect's identity or responsibility for the threat or that the information gained may not be reliable.

I cannot resolve these questions here. Again, my remarks are directed primarily at the structure of the debate. Homicide and torture are certainly disanalogous in some respects. Homicide is a harm-based wrong – what criminal lawyers sometimes call a result crime. At root, homicide is wrong because it involves bringing about the deaths of other people and not because of the manner in which it is done. Torture, however, is a conduct-wrong, a wrong independently of any harmful consequences it may generate. Even supposing that it is possible to inflict non-injurious torture,[55] doing so is not just a wrong; it is *the very* wrong of torture, notwithstanding that no harm may result. It is a wrong primarily because of how the torturer treats other people.

Torture dehumanises. It is just about as radical an attack on human dignity as can be mounted.[56] By contrast, it seems to me possible to *harm* another person without violating their right to dignity. This is part of the point of requiring that self-defence be directed at the source of the threat: one thereby acknowledges the victim as a responsible, autonomous human being. When D takes action against V in justified self-defence, D responds to and addresses V's conduct. D's action recognises V as the author of a wrong[57] and thus it treats V with the respect due to an autonomous agent in V's position. In this sense, one person can harm another person respectfully, without denying their shared humanity. But that is not what torture does. Quite the opposite. Whatever the motivation, torture aims to degrade. Its purpose is to reduce V to something less than fully human, to 'break' V into a person who cannot make rational or reflective choices. This is, I think, what makes torture problematic even in hypotheticals where the victim is the very source of the threat. In a sense, its aim is not to restrict the exercise of agency but to attack agency itself. Justifications like

[55] Cf. the kind of torture advocated by Alan Dershowitz's hypothetical FBI agent, involving the infliction of pain *simpliciter* without risk to health: above n. 47, p. 144. Even if non-injurious torture was possible, however, there remains the risk of psychological harm.

[56] One might think that homicide also dehumanises its victims and there is a literal sense in which that is true. But it is a different sense. The value attacked in homicide – life – is a *precondition* of those values, such as human dignity, which are bound up with how that life is lived. It does not incorporate them. Hence to attack the one is not necessarily to attack the latter. This is why we can make sense of some arguments for voluntary euthanasia, e.g. that there are things worse than death, and that there is a right to 'death with dignity'. Such claims may be controversial, but they do not seem incoherent.

[57] For this reason, self-defence against the insane may seem a borderline case, in so far as insane aggressors are not morally responsible for their actions. The point here, though, is that in such cases one still *treats* the victim as a responsible agent, i.e. respectfully and without violating the victim's claim to human dignity.

self-defence operate as a kind of mediator in human interaction. They enable us to negotiate the mutual enterprise of human coexistence, an enterprise in which V participates. They help construct the dialogue of conflict and reconciliation, the give and take of human interaction. But torturing someone does not seem to fit within any *shared* human enterprise. There is no social dialogue in torture, no give and take. It thrusts the victim outside the realm of human experience, outside the human community. As such, it is a wrong seemingly beyond the characteristic range of self-defence. Even the strongest cases seem irredeemably borderline.

V.

But what of the argument that, as Dyzenhaus suggests, the rule of law may sometimes be sacrificed for the sake of the rule of law?[58] Or, more generally, that it may be legitimate to suspend a constitution in order to preserve the constitutional order?[59] Surely we can breach the rule of law to save it? And if the state's very existence is under threat, do we really have to worry about the niceties of constitutional rights? Reasoning of this sort suggests the possibility of content-neutral justifications: *any* action is permissible, provided it is taken for the sake of the constitutional order. This is the logic of the black hole model.

It seems to me that this move is too coarse-grained. Justification is always a bilateral relation, between action and need. The emergency powers debate is not a single-faceted dispute about the extent of the emergency: it is a debate about permitting wrongs. Whether emergency action is legitimate thus depends both on the content of the action and on the nature of the need. That does not mean a black hole is unjustified. But it does mean that its content calls, specifically, for justification. Neither can one appeal to our interest in the rule of law to justify any violation of the rule of law. It depends on *which* rule-of-law violation is being perpetrated, and which rule-of-law interest is thereby advanced. Consequently, the association needs to be unpicked between derogation from a fundamental right, such as that interdicting torture, and violation of the rule of law. The debate requires greater specificity.

[58] Dyzenhaus, Chapter 2, p. 48: 'In a democracy, the rule of law should only be sacrificed for the sake of the rule of law and that condition imposes its own constraints on the sacrifice'.

[59] See, e.g., C. Rossiter, *Constitutional Dictatorship: Crisis Government in the Modern Democracies* (Princeton: Princeton University Press, 1948), p. 298.

It may be helpful here to distinguish delegation from remaindering. When powers are *delegated* to officials, the officials are given a discretion to change the normative position of others. But the exercise of that discretion is not unfettered. The delegation is subject to authoritative guidance and may be reviewed in terms of that guidance. (Hence the CD model contemplated by Dyzenhaus involves a form of delegation.) By contrast, when power is *remaindered*, the officials receive an unfettered discretion. Within the scope of the remaindered power, they can do what they like. This time, the law really has run out. It has made its way to the edge of a black hole.

The objection to black holes is often framed in terms of the rule of law, which is rightly thought to be threatened when powers to set the legal rights, duties and liberties of individuals are remaindered to officials and not regulated by law. But even this objection needs to be refined, because not every aspect of the rule of law need be infringed. For example, bearing in mind that the perimeters of the 'black hole' must themselves be defined by the legal system, suppose that those boundary conditions are clearly specified in advance and require some defined conduct by individuals before they are deemed to have entered its domain. Then there would at least be prospectivity: individuals have an opportunity to avoid falling within its scope and cannot complain about lack of notice when they deliberately jump.[60]

More pertinently, black holes are significantly different from indefinite detention, another candidate for rule-of-law objections. The legal situation in a black hole is in one sense clearly delineated: the official is legally permitted to do things that otherwise would be unlawful. Inside a black hole, *the law* has determined that its denizens have no legal rights. Further, the conditions of entry into and exit from a black hole may be clearly specified by law and not at the discretion of the officials. The objection is to the content of the regime, not the perimeter. By contrast, the objection to indefinite detention lies at the perimeter.

Indefinite detention need not deprive an individual of all rights, but only of freedom. Torture and other mistreatment can remain illegal. Moreover, the quarantine of infectious citizens and detention of enemy soldiers seems, on occasion, to be justified. The real problem, then, is not the content of the applicable legal regime but the specification of its boundaries.

[60] A further worry would arise here if the criteria were linked not to the particular conduct of a person caught within the black hole, but to conduct by others that triggers a state of emergency.

A permissible detention has originating and terminating conditions (e.g. based on the ongoing health risk) that are intrinsically bound to the reasons why that detention is justified and which are not at the discretion of the officials who administer it. By contrast, where the terminating conditions of indefinite detention are at the unregulated discretion of officials, such an institution is unjustified (because its rationale does not shape its boundaries) and may be unlegalisable.[61] Yet this particular concern need not apply to black holes. Neither does it affect official torture warrants, provided they are closely and carefully regulated. All these things are problematic. But not in the same way.

One should certainly object to black holes. The core of the objection needs no 'rule-of-law' label. It is simple and direct. Suppose that D's φing would violate a fundamental moral right held by V. If it would be unjustified to φ, it follows that D should not φ. Moreover, *the State should not permit D to* φ. When it does, the state becomes complicit in D's wrong. If it is wrong to torture people, it is wrong to empower people to torture.

Let us call this the permission objection. It is general in nature and applies to any legislative attempt to derogate from fundamental rights. One might think that it can also be generalised – collapsed – into a legality objection, that officials are permitted to act untrammelled, unregulated by law: that law has abdicated its regulatory role and arbitrary power reigns. But that would be a conflation, not a generalisation. The objections are different. To see this, consider a narrower, more tightly focused scenario, in which there is a partial 'black hole'. Suppose that qualifying inmates are relocated to a defined region, in which they are subject to rules specifying that they may be freely assaulted or tortured by designated officials, provided they do not suffer grievous bodily harm. The region is otherwise governed by ordinary law – they may not be raped, killed or subjected to any other generally proscribed wrong. Within this region the law has not abandoned the oversight of state officials. Yet the regime is profoundly wrong, because its inmates lack certain fundamental rights. It contravenes the permission objection.

A full-scale black hole precisely comprises the comprehensive set of partial black holes. It does not so much say 'anything goes', as '*everything* goes'. Thought of in this way, it is not clear that the legality objection adds much of importance to the collection of permission objections that a black

[61] As Dyzenhaus suggests: Chapter 2, text at n. 39.

hole generates. It seems secondary in nature. This is not to say that the ability to plan a life is unimportant, even in a regime where fundamental wrongs are permitted. But it is not the core value. Moreover, it is not entirely violated. Even a black hole has legal boundaries which the official must observe. Provided those boundaries are clearly articulated, one can arrange not to become an inmate.

Nonetheless, it seems to me that there is something special about black holes or at least black holes of this sort. They are, I think, inconsistent with democracy. Among the fundamental requirements of a democratic legal system, apart from its public character, is the principle that those it governs have the opportunity to participate in the law-making process as equals.[62] The rules and the rule-making process are the same for all.

I will outline rather than defend the point here. Apart from certain categorical exceptions, such as children,[63] the members of a modern democracy are – and have a right to be – treated as having equal standing in the community. We no longer segregate citizens into distinct legal and political classes (women, serfs, slaves, etc.), but recognise that everyone is equal before the law.[64] This means both that each person has an equal right to participate in the democratic process and, conversely, that the law does not discriminate between individuals. Individuals thereby have a shared responsibility for the law: they are both its authors, through representatives answerable to them, and the joint subjects of its governance. In turn, laws are and should be, rules of general application, that govern everyone – or, as a minimum, everyone falling within the relevant class affected by the rationale behind the rule. It is, in short, a constitutional principle of any democracy that everyone is equal before the law. A black hole utterly violates this principle. Those within its grasp have a different status from the rest of us.

[62] Formulated in this way, the democracy objection applies only to nation's citizens and not to aliens, who do not participate in the collective activity of self-government. Nonetheless, the core objection stated in the previous paragraph would remain applicable.

[63] Even then, the distinction is drawn contextually and not for all purposes; and members of such categories are to be treated even-handedly within the category.

[64] This can, of course, itself be analysed as an aspect of the rule of law. See, e.g., A.V. Dicey, *Introduction to the Study of the Law of the Constitution*, 10th ed. (London: Macmillan, 1959), p. 193.

13

Deny everything: intelligence activities and the rule of law

SIMON CHESTERMAN

In the opening scene of *The History Boys*, Alan Bennett's recent play about education and childhood, a schoolteacher who has become a celebrity through populist iconoclasm advises a group of elected officials on the best way to sell a distasteful piece of legislation curtailing civil liberties to a sceptical electorate: 'I would try not to be shrill or earnest. An amused tolerance always comes over best, particularly on television. Paradox works well and mists up the windows, which is handy. "The loss of liberty is the price we pay for freedom" type thing'.[1]

Debates about the appropriate legal response to emergency frequently invoke paradox, with Carl Schmitt at the perilous extreme arguing that the exercise of sovereign power reveals a foundational problem in legal liberalism itself.[2] For the purposes of this volume, the debate is framed as a call for pragmatic recognition that, *in extremis*, public officials may be required to act outside the law and that after-the-fact ratification recognises this and limits the possibility of abuse;[3] on the opposing side, the response is that the embrace of 'extra-legal measures' misconceives the rule of law,

I am grateful to R. Rueban Balasubramaniam, David A. Jordan, Andrew Simester, Victor V. Ramraj and participants in the workshop convened at the National University of Singapore in January 2007 for their comments on earlier drafts of this text. The chapter is part of a larger research project on intelligence and international law. See further S. Chesterman, *Shared Secrets: Intelligence and Collective Security* (Sydney: Lowy Institute for International Policy, 2006); 'The Spy Who Came In from the Cold War: Intelligence and International Law' (2006) 27 *Michigan Journal of International Law* 1077.

1 A. Bennett, *The History Boys* (London: Faber and Faber, 2004).

2 D. Dyzenhaus, 'The State of Emergency in Legal Theory', in V.V. Ramraj, M. Hor and K. Roach (eds.), *Global Anti-Terrorism Law and Policy* (Cambridge: Cambridge University Press, 2005), p. 73. See, e.g. C. Schmitt, *Political Theology: Four Chapters on the Concept of Sovereignty*, G. Schwab (trans.), (Cambridge, MA: MIT Press, 1985), p. 13.

3 O. Gross, 'Chaos and Rules: Should Responses to Violent Crises Always be Constitutional?' (2003) 112 *Yale Law Journal* 1011. See also Gross, 'Extra-Legality and the Ethic of Political Responsibility' (Chapter 3), this volume.

underestimates the capacity of constitutional orders to deal with crisis and overestimates the ability and willingness of skittish publics to reign in officials.[4] The two positions thus caricatured are identified in this volume with the work of Oren Gross and David Dyzenhaus, though the debate is, of course, far older than these agonists of post-9/11 constitutionalism. As Dyzenhaus acknowledges, the question of whether the response of the executive in an emergency is constrained by law was an argument Dicey had with himself a century ago;[5] Gross first traced the essence of his own argument back two centuries further to John Locke's theory of prerogative power[6] and in his chapter for this volume extends the pedigree back to Rome.[7]

What the two approaches have in common is that they presume a measure of public deliberation on the appropriate response to crisis: Gross calls explicitly for a process of ratification of extra-legal measures; Dyzenhaus prefers to encourage experiments in institutional design subject to the rule of law. The problem with both accounts is that the various activities contemplated in this discussion – assassination, torture, unregulated detention, surveillance unfettered by civil liberties – are typically conducted on a covert basis. Covertness may be deemed necessary for reasons of effectiveness, but also for political expediency: the damage to a nation that admits that it tortures may be more lasting than the harm torture is intended to avert.

This chapter in Part I revisits the debate over exceptionalism, focusing on the question of whether *ex post* ratification could ever be a practical constraint on otherwise unlawful behaviour that is normally intended to be shielded from public scrutiny.[8] It then turns, in Part II, to the question of whether public deliberation is a realistic prospect, drawing on three cases in which something approaching Gross's extra-legal measures model has been adopted by the United States: the use of aggressive interrogation techniques that push the limits of torture, secret detention and extraordinary rendition of suspects, and warrantless electronic surveillance.

[4] Dyzenhaus, 'State of Emergency'.

[5] *Ibid.*, pp. 65–6. See A.V. Dicey, *Lectures Introductory to the Study of the Law of the Constitution* (London: Macmillan, 1885), pp. 291–301.

[6] Gross, 'Chaos and Rules', 1102. See John Locke, *Two Treatises of Government* (Cambridge: Cambridge University Press, 1988), p. 166.

[7] Gross, Chapter 3.

[8] The chapter thus focuses on what Terry Nardin refers to as prudential rather than moral issues. See further Nardin, 'Emergency Logic: Prudence, Morality and the Rule of Law' (Chapter 4), this volume.

Part III presents an alternative lens through which to view assertions – whether publicly debated or not – that illegal conduct was justified: not as calls for *ex post* ratification of the conduct but for mitigation in the imposition of penalties. The conclusion is broadly consistent with Dyzenhaus's critique of Gross, but points to further challenges for the rule of law given apparent incentives in extreme situations not merely to circumvent the law but to remain silent about it.

I. Ratification

Oren Gross's extra-legal measures model proposes to inform public officials that

> they may act extralegally when they believe that such action is necessary for protecting the nation and the public in the face of calamity, provided that they openly and publicly acknowledge the nature of their actions. It is then up to the people to decide, either directly or indirectly (e.g., through their elected representatives in the legislature), how to respond to such actions. The people may decide to hold the actor to the wrongfulness of her actions, demonstrating commitment to the violated principles and values. The acting official may be called to answer, and make legal and political reparations, for her actions. Alternatively, the people may act to approve, ex post, the extralegal actions of the public official.[9]

A central requirement of such an approach is candour: 'To be implemented properly, the model calls for candor on the part of government agents, who must disclose the nature of their counter-emergency activities'.[10]

Indeed, candour is seen as one of the virtues of the model. Gross refers in passing to the use of illegal interrogation techniques – *sc.* torture – by Israel's General Security Service (GSS) during the 1980s. The example is used to show the hypocrisy of legal systems that are aware of a pattern of conduct but unwilling to acknowledge its normative implications.[11] The example he gives of the Landau Commission, whose investigating of these techniques struck a determinedly ambiguous position, might appear to support Gross's analysis that some societies countenance extra-legal activity. But it ignores the fact that in 1999 the Israeli Supreme Court struck down the procedures, specifically holding that detainees could not

[9] Gross, 'Chaos and Rules', 1023. [10] *Ibid.*, at 1024.

[11] *Ibid.*, at 1045, citing 'Commission of Inquiry into the Methods of Investigation of the GSS Regarding Hostile Terrorist Activities, October 1987 (Landau Commission)' (1989) 23 *Israel Law Review* 146.

be tortured.[12] The President of the Court issued an unusual and eloquent coda to a judgment that sought to reaffirm the rule of law and certainty:

> This is the destiny of a democracy – it does not see all means as acceptable, and the ways of its enemies are not always open before it. A democracy must sometimes fight with one arm tied behind her back. Even so, a democracy has the upper hand. The rule of law and individual liberties constitute an important aspect of her security stance. At the end of the day, they strengthen its spirit and this strength allows it to overcome difficulties.[13]

The Court left open the possibility that an individual might nevertheless claim a defence of necessity, but this is a legal regime in its own right quite different from the argument that such an official be given an opportunity to act outside the law in the hope that the law might be changed or the wrong ignored.[14]

Gross might respond that this is precisely an example of his model working – the Court refused to provide the sort of de facto ratification embraced by the Landau Commission – but it is also suggestive of deep problems in the role he ascribes to ratification. The precise manner of ratification is presented as an open list of possibilities, ranging from bills of indemnity to re-election of a president who has run on a policy justifying selective use of torture.[15] In the most concrete example given, the police officer who tortured a suspect in order to locate the ticking bomb – an ideal-type hypothetical that has no precedent except in fiction (notably the 'real-time' television series *24*[16]) and its repeated invocation to justify more general use of torture – may be sacked, prosecuted, sued or impeached.[17] For the model to be coherent, a formal choice *not* to pursue any of these avenues should be ratified by 'the people'. The clearest example of how this might happen is through legislation intended to immunise 'public officials from any potential civil or criminal liability',[18] though the extraordinary case of *Little* v. *Barreme*[19] (in which the captain of a US

12 *Public Committee Against Torture* v. *Israel* (Supreme Court of Israel, 26 May 1999) HCJ 5100/94 1, available at http://elyon1.court.gov.il/files_eng/94/000/051/a09/94051000.a09.pdf at 23. Gross makes a passing reference to the case but only to cite the difficult role of judges in a society like Israel: Gross, 'Chaos and Rules', 1122 at n. 478.

13 *Public Committee Against Torture v. Israel*, 37.

14 Necessity is discussed in Part III, below. See also A.P. Simester, 'Necessity, Torture and the Rule of Law' (Chapter 12), this volume.

15 Gross, 'Chaos and Rules', 1099. Gross's chapter in this volume expands the list slightly.

16 J. Mayer, 'Whatever It Takes: The Politics of the Man Behind "24"' *New Yorker* (19 February 2007), p. 66.

17 Gross, 'Chaos and Rules', 1099. 18 *Ibid.* 19 6 U.S. (2 Cranch) 170 (1804).

vessel was found guilty, lost an appeal to the Supreme Court, but was reimbursed by Congress for his fines and expenses with interest), is surely the exception that proves the rule.[20] More importantly, Gross's switch from singular ('the actor') to plural ('public officials') – presumably necessary in order to avoid the requirement for individualised legislation – defines the contours of the slippery slope down which we have begun to descend.

Political ratification is no more stable as the foundation for a model. The fact that a majority of Americans voted Republican in 2004 cannot sensibly be understood as ratifying widely reported abuses of power, any more than the fact that they voted Democrat in 2006 and thereby evinced a change of heart and desire for prosecutions. Much as a victorious political party is wont to claim a mandate, it is inconceivable that an election would be fought on issues defined clearly enough or won by a margin sufficient to warrant the conclusion that otherwise illegal conduct has been ratified.[21]

Other possibilities such as prosecutorial discretion, recalcitrant juries and executive pardons are dealt with in a couple of sentences.[22] Of these, discretion and pardons seem the most likely, though both are exercised by the executive branch that is also most likely to be the author of impugned conduct. Prosecutorial discretion in particular begs the question of what impact an explicit policy of encouraging vigilantism, on the basis that well-justified acts will be exonerated, will have on more general police investigative practices.

II. Deliberation

Whatever form of ratification is contemplated, a central claim of the extra-legal measures model is the idea that all of this can be acknowledged openly.[23] Indeed, Gross suggests that this open ratification, activating a kind of public responsibility, is the main contribution of the model to analogous discussions in Weber and Walzer.[24] An act that would normally be illegal

[20] See Gross, 'Chaos and Rules', 1109–10.

[21] *Cf.* Gross's discussion in the present volume of John Yoo's claims that the 2004 election was a referendum on torture.

[22] *Ibid.*, at 1115. See now O. Gross and F. Ni Aoláin, *Law in Times of Crisis: Emergency Powers in Theory and Practice* (Cambridge: Cambridge University Press, 2006).

[23] Gross, 'Chaos and Rules', 1099–1100. [24] *Ibid.*, at 1105.

> must be aimed at the advancement of the public good and must be openly, candidly, and fully disclosed to the public. Once disclosed, it is a matter for the general public, either directly or through its elected representatives, to ratify, ex post, those actions that have been taken on its behalf and in its name, or to denounce them.[25]

Quite apart from the challenge posed to the rule of law by public officials 'openly' and 'candidly' violating the law, '[o]pen and candid acknowledgment by the authorities of the need to resort to extralegal measures'[26] would amount to an admission of guilt for the purposes of any punitive proceedings. Though some actors might take the risk in order to receive absolution, in the absence of some pre-existing guarantee that *ex post* ratification is more than a mere possibility there is little incentive to do so.

As Dyzenhaus observes, the atmosphere of fear presumed by the model makes it highly likely that an expectation of after-the-fact validation of illegal official acts may arise and that it would be met easily.[27] In a limited number of high-profile crises this may be true, but in operational terms it is more probable that precisely the same logic that allows officials to violate existing laws will encourage them to keep those actions secret. This may be for pragmatic reasons of effectiveness, reflected in the reluctance of officials to discuss precise interrogation practices that would forewarn enemies and frustrate the purpose of the methods or to acknowledge surveillance methods that might alert targets of investigation. A second set of concerns encouraging secrecy are the broader ramifications of a government openly acknowledging that it violates norms that are not merely domestic but international. Damage to the moral standing of the United States caused by revelations of abuse at Abu Ghraib, Guantánamo Bay and secret CIA detention facilities was not reduced even in cases where it was claimed that interrogation had enabled authorities to avert terror plots. Indeed, periodic assertions that a new plot had been discovered – in at least some cases years old and not beyond the planning stages – appeared to be invoked opportunistically precisely to deflect criticism.[28] A

[25] *Ibid.*, at 1111–12. [26] *Ibid.*, at 1127.

[27] Dyzenhaus, 'State of Emergency', in *Global Anti-Terrorism Law and Policy*, pp. 72–3.

[28] For example, when defending the use of warrantless wiretaps within the United States by the National Security Agency, the Bush administration offered the example of Iyman Faris – a truck driver with a fanciful plot to destroy the Brooklyn Bridge with a blowtorch – as evidence of the value provided by the extra-legal measures employed under the controversial 'Terrorist Surveillance Program'. See M. Hosenball and E. Thomas, 'Hold the Phone; Big Brother Knows Whom You Call: Is That Legal, and Will It Help Catch the Bad Guys?' *Newsweek* (22 May 2006), p. 22.

third reason to be hesitant about embracing a public deliberative model to limit extra-legal adventures is that it is not typically elected officials who engage in the relevant investigative or intelligence activities. Such actors – the police, intelligence operatives, special forces – are unlikely to be responsive to the political pressures that the extra-legal measures model would have serve as the primary check on their behaviour.

This section briefly discusses three areas in which the United States has pushed at the limits of domestic and international legality as part of an effort to respond to security threats. The three areas – torture, secret detention and extraordinary rendition, and unlawful surveillance – do not correspond directly to the three reasons for secrecy outlined above, but illustrate the manner in which such decisions are made and justified.

The general tenor was outlined by Vice President Dick Cheney five days after 11 September 2001, when he suggested a broad but undisclosed agenda for combatting future terrorist attacks in an interview on NBC's 'Meet the Press':

> We also have to work, though, sort of the dark side, if you will. We've got to spend time in the shadows in the intelligence world. A lot of what needs to be done here will have to be done quietly, without any discussion, using sources and methods that are available to our intelligence agencies, if we're going to be successful. That's the world these folks operate in, and so it's going to be vital for us to use any means at our disposal, basically, to achieve our objective.[29]

Much, in the end, was debated publicly though this tended to be the result of investigative journalism or disclosures in legal action on behalf of affected individuals. There was little evidence of a willingness on the part of the executive to have arguments over legality 'openly, candidly, and fully disclosed'. On the contrary, questionable conduct was asserted – at times improbably – to fall within the law. The most troubling conduct was simply denied.

In the case of torture, for example, the Bush administration maintains the official position that it neither uses nor condones torture. Since 2001, however, it has authorised interrogation techniques widely regarded as torture, including by its own Department of State in annual human rights

[29] Quoted in Human Rights Watch, 'Getting Away with Torture? Command Responsibility for the US Abuse of Detainees' (Human Rights Watch, New York, April 2005), available at http://hrw.org/reports/2005/us0405.

reports on the practice of other countries.[30] The United States is a party to the Convention Against Torture and torture is prohibited under US law whether it occurs within the jurisdiction of the United States or not.[31] Nevertheless, in an August 2002 memorandum, the Department of Justice Office of Legal Counsel prepared a memorandum on the standards of conduct permitted under the US law implementing the Convention Against Torture. Among other things, this memorandum adopted an exceptionally narrow definition of torture, which was limited to physical pain 'equivalent in intensity to the pain accompanying serious physical injury, such as organ failure, impairment of bodily function, or even death' or mental suffering that results in 'significant psychological harm of significant duration, e.g., lasting for months or even years'.[32] The memorandum was one of a series of legal manoeuvres adopted in the context of the 'war on terror' that included, among other things, attempts to limit application of the Geneva Conventions.[33]

None of this analysis was intended to be made public. Following a seminal article in the *Washington Post* in December 2002 the growing allegations of mistreatment by US officials were harder to ignore,[34] but it was only after photographic evidence of abuse leaked from the Abu Ghraib prison in April 2004 that the issue came to be publicly debated. Even then, most of the discussion was driven by the response to unauthorised leaks of information, including the August 2002 memorandum and other documents.

[30] Descriptions of Techniques Allegedly Authorised by the CIA (Human Rights Watch, New York, 21 November 2005), available at http://hrw.org/english/docs/2005/11/21/usdom12071.htm.

[31] 18 U.S.C. §§ 2340 at 2340A.

[32] J.C. Bybee, Memorandum for Alberto R. Gonzales, Counsel to the President, Re. Standards of Conduct for Interrogation under 18 U.S.C. §§ 2340–2340A (Department of Justice Office of the Legal Counsel, Washington, DC, 1 August 2002), available at http://www.tomjoad.org/bybeememo.htm.

[33] The Bush administration refused to apply the Geneva Conventions to captured al Qaeda or Taliban fighters during the US war in Afghanistan. On 13 November 2001, President Bush issued a military order governing the 'Detention, Treatment, and Trial of Certain Non-Citizens in the War Against Terrorism'. 66 Fed. Reg. 57833. This order allowed the trial of Taliban or al Qaeda combatants by military commissions, arguably in violation of the Geneva Conventions. Although this action was eventually struck down by the US Supreme Court in *Hamdan* v. *Rumsfeld*, 126 S.Ct 2749 (2006), it was largely reinstated by the US Congress with the passage of the Military Commissions Act of 2006, Pub. L. No. 109–366, 120 Stat. 2600 (17 October 2006).

[34] D. Priest and B. Gellman, 'US Decries Abuse but Defends Interrogations: "Stress and Duress" Tactics Used on Terrorism Suspects Held in Secret Overseas Facilities' *Washington Post* (26 December 2002).

The legal position of the August 2002 memorandum was repudiated by the United States on 30 December 2004, though no definition of torture has been provided in its place.[35] Among other contradictory signals, the Bush administration later opposed efforts led by Senator John McCain to strengthen the legal prohibition of torture.[36] A particular controversy continues on the question of 'waterboarding' – a technique whereby a detainee is bound to a board slanted at a decline, cellophane is placed over his face and water is then poured on his head resulting in a physiological response similar to drowning. In March 2005, Porter J. Goss, then Director of the CIA, described waterboarding as a 'professional interrogation technique'.[37] In October 2006, Vice President Dick Cheney appeared to agree with the use of waterboarding, specifically for Khalid Sheikh Mohammed, concurring with the statement that a 'dunk in water' for such an individual is a 'no-brainer' if it saves American lives.[38] White House Press Secretary Tony Snow later attempted to clarify that Cheney had not been referring to waterboarding but merely to a literal 'dunk in the water', prompting a reporter to ask 'so "dunk in the water" means what, we have a pool now at Guantánamo, and they go swimming?'[39]

A similar dynamic was evident in the US practice of secret detention and extraordinary rendition. Following occasional reports of secret detention centres – black sites – at Bagram Air Force Base in Afghanistan[40]

35 Although no specific definition has been provided for torture, the US Defense Department has responded to the detainee abuse scandals by issuing a revised and comprehensive set of guidelines governing all military interrogations. On 6 September 2006, the US Army issued a new field manual on interrogations to replace the former Field Manual (FM) 34–52 which had been published in 1992. The new manual, FM 2–22.3 'Human Intelligence Collector Operations' details the 19 techniques which may be used during the interrogation of detainees by US military personnel. The list is exhaustive and the techniques listed represent the only methods that may ever be used. This manual, however, does not apply to intelligence agencies outside of the military. The US Central Intelligence Agency, for example, is not bound by the manual and the specifics methods of its interrogations remain unknown to the general public. C. Graveline, 'The Unlearned Lessons of Abu Ghraib' *Washington Post* (19 October 2006).

36 See, e.g. K. Zernike, 'Senate Approves Broad New Rules to Try Detainees' *New York Times* (29 September 2006).

37 M. Mazzetti, 'CIA Worker Says Message on Torture Got Her Fired' *New York Times* (22 July 2006).

38 Interview of the Vice President by Scott Hennen, WDAY at Radio Day at the White House, 24 October 2006, available at www.whitehouse.gov/news/releases/2006/10/20061024-7.html.

39 Press Briefing by Tony Snow, 27 October 2006, available at www.whitehouse.gov/news/releases/2006/10/20061027-1.html.

40 Priest and Gellman, 'US Decries Abuse'.

and Guantánamo Bay's Camp Echo,[41] it was another *Washington Post* article in November 2005 that revealed the scale of the programme and growing debates within the CIA about its legality and morality.[42] At the request of senior officials, the *Post* did not publish the name of Eastern European countries – believed to be Poland and Romania – involved in the programme, but stated that sites in the programme also included Afghanistan, Guantánamo Bay and Thailand. The reason given for the overseas location of the black sites was that it avoided US domestic law that would prohibit such secret detention, with the CIA operating on the authority of an order issued by President Bush on 17 September 2001.[43]

Secrecy was needed, however, in order not to raise legal questions in the foreign jurisdictions concerned. When published reports in June 2003 revealed the existence of the site in Thailand, Thai officials insisted that it be closed. The CIA abandoned plans to develop its facility in Guantánamo Bay when US courts began to exercise greater authority over military detainees in the main part of the facility.[44] The response from the CIA to the *Post* report was to request the Justice Department to open a criminal investigation to determine the source of the information.[45] A senior intelligence officer, Mary O. McCarthy, was later fired from the CIA, apparently in connection with the earlier story.[46] President Bush first acknowledged the use of secret prisons in September 2006, shortly before moving 14 suspects from CIA detention to the military detention camp at Guantánamo Bay, in theory ending the programme.[47]

Estimates of the total number of detainees in black sites are about one hundred. A further hundred are believed to have been involved in the programme of extraordinary rendition, the transfer of untried persons to other countries for imprisonment and interrogation – in particular to

41 D. Rose, 'Revealed: The Full Story of the Guantánamo Britons' *Observer* (London) (14 March 2004).

42 D. Priest, 'CIA Holds Terror Suspects in Secret Prisons: Debate Is Growing Within Agency About Legality and Morality of Overseas System Set Up After 9/11' *Washington Post* (2 November 2005).

43 D. Johnston, 'CIA Tells of Bush's Directive on the Handling of Detainees' *New York Times* (15 November 2006).

44 Priest, 'CIA Holds Terror Suspects'.

45 D. Johnston and C. Hulse, 'CIA Asks for Criminal Inquiry over Secret-Prison Article' *New York Times* (9 November 2005).

46 D.S. Cloud, 'Colleagues Say CIA Analyst Played by Rules' *New York Times* (23 April 2006).

47 S. Shane, 'Detainees' Access to Lawyers Is Security Risk, CIA Says' *New York Times* (5 November 2006).

countries with records of abuse and torture of detainees, such as Egypt, Jordan, Morocco, Pakistan and Uzbekistan. An official directly involved in the process described it in the following way to the *Washington Post*: 'We don't kick the [expletive] out of them. We send them to other countries so *they* can kick the [expletive] out of them'.[48] Authority for such forcible transfers is apparently outlined in a 13 March 2002 memorandum entitled 'The President's Power as Commander in Chief to Transfer Captive Terrorists to the Control and Custody of Foreign Nations'. The Bush Administration has refused to release or describe this memorandum, but it is referred to in the August 2002 memorandum on interrogation methods.[49]

Prominent examples of extraordinary rendition include the Syrian-born Canadian citizen Maher Arar, who was detained in the United States in September 2002 before being flown to Jordan and then Syria, where he was interrogated and tortured by Syrian authorities. A year later he was released without charge and returned to Canada, where a public inquiry cleared him of any suspicion, sharply criticised the Royal Canadian Mounted Police and other government departments and led to a formal protest over US treatment of Arar.[50]

Another relatively well-documented case concerns Hassan Mustafa Osama Nasr, also known as Abu Omar, an Egyptian cleric apparently abducted by the CIA from Milan in February 2003. He was taken to an American base in Aviano and then flown to Egypt, where he was taken into custody. In April 2004 he was released and telephoned his wife, informing her among other things that he had been tortured with electric shocks, had lost hearing in one ear and could barely walk. Shortly after this call he appears to have been rearrested by Egyptian authorities and has not been heard from since. In June 2005 an Italian judge issued a warrant for the arrest of 13 US citizens said to be agents or operatives of the CIA.[51] Of the 13 names, investigations by the *New York Times* indicated that eleven were

[48] Priest and Gellman, 'US Decries Abuse'.

[49] Bybee, Torture Memorandum, p. 38. See D. Priest and D. Eggen, 'Terror Suspect Alleges Torture: Detainee Says US Sent Him to Egypt Before Guantanamo' *Washington Post* (6 January 2005).

[50] See the Arar Commission report at www.ararcommission.ca. Among the criticisms of the RCMP were allegations that it had tried to silence a reporter covering the case by raiding her home and office. See I. Austen, 'Canada's Police Commissioner Resigns over Deportation Case' *New York Times* (7 December 2006).

[51] S. Grey and D. van Natta, '13 with the CIA Sought by Italy in a Kidnapping' *New York Times* (25 June 2005).

probably aliases: public records showed that some names received Social Security numbers less than ten years earlier, and that some had addresses that were post office boxes in Virginia known to be used by the CIA.[52] In April 2006, shortly after the Italian general election, the outgoing Justice Minister announced that he would not seek extradition of an expanded list of 22 CIA officers,[53] but two high-ranking Italian intelligence officers were later arrested for alleged complicity in the kidnapping.[54]

A third area where US government activity clearly went beyond established law is in the area of electronic surveillance. Interception of telephone calls by the National Security Agency (NSA) between a party in the United States and a party in a foreign country is governed by the Foreign Intelligence Surveillance Act (FISA), allowing for interception when a warrant is procured in advance or, in some circumstances, within 72 hours of beginning the intercept. A warrant may be issued if 'there is probable cause to believe that . . . the target of the electronic surveillance is a foreign power or an agent of a foreign power'.[55] The law was passed in 1978 following intelligence scandals; in the following years the court rejected just five of almost 19,000 requests for wiretaps and search warrants. Under the programme in question, this check on the NSA's activities was removed in cases where it was suspected that one party to a phone conversation had links to a terrorist organisation such as al Qaeda. The presidential authorisation creating the programme is classified and it appears that even congressional intelligence committees were only partially briefed on its scope, though President Bush has said the authorisation is renewed 'approximately every 45 days'.[56] Administration lawyers defended the programme variously on the basis that congressional authorisation was implied in the 18 September 2001 Congressional Joint Authorisation for the Use of Military Force or that the President enjoys the inherent power to authorise such activities in his constitutional role as Commander-in-Chief.[57] These arguments have been largely rejected by legal academics and the programme was

[52] A. Liptak, 'Experts Doubt Accused CIA Operatives Will Stand Trial in Italy' *New York Times* (27 June 2005).

[53] P. Kiefer, 'Italian Minister Declines to Seek Extradition of CIA Operatives' *New York Times* (13 April 2006).

[54] I. Fisher and E. Povoledo, 'Italy's Top Spy Is Expected to Be Indicted in Abduction Case' *New York Times* (24 October 2006).

[55] 50 U.S.C. §1803(a)(3).

[56] President's Radio Address, 17 December 2005, available at www.whitehouse.gov/news/releases/2005/12/20051217.html.

[57] For a discussion of presidentialism in the present context, see W.E. Scheuerman, 'Presidentialism and Emergency Government' (Chapter 11), this volume.

declared unconstitutional by a District Court judge, though her decision has been stayed pending appeal to the 6th Circuit Court of Appeals.[58] A series of legislative proposals to deal with the controversy are at various stages in Congress, ranging from a proposal to grant retroactive amnesty for warrantless surveillance conducted under presidential authority to reassertions of FISA as the exclusive means of authorising foreign surveillance.[59]

Once again, however, open discussion of the programme and remedies for apparent violation of the law was involuntary. The *New York Times* learned of the programme in 2004 but was persuaded by the Bush administration not to publish the story for more than a year.[60] Only when the story was published – in part, it seems, because the information was shortly to be disclosed in a book by one of the journalists involved[61] – did congressional leaders begin to challenge the legality of the programme. In a press conference Attorney General Alberto Gonzales said that the administration had 'discussions with Congress in the past – certain members of Congress – as to whether or not FISA could be amended to allow us to adequately deal with this kind of threat, and we were advised that that would be difficult, if not impossible'.[62] He later clarified that he had intended to say that it would have been difficult, if not impossible, to obtain legislation without compromising the programme. For his part, President Bush declared that leaks to the press concerning the programme were 'a shameful act' that was 'helping the enemy'. He added that he assumed a Justice Department investigation into the leak was moving forward, though there appears to have been no effort on the part of investigators to contact the journalists involved.[63]

In each of these cases – torture, extra-judicial detention and warrantless surveillance – public deliberation on the legality of the practice clearly was never intended by the relevant officials. The reasons for embracing

[58] *ACLU* v. *NSA* (US District Court-E.D. Mich., No. 06-CV-10204, 17 August 2006).

[59] W. Pincus, 'Specter Offers Compromise on NSA Surveillance' *Washington Post* (9 June 2006).

[60] J. Risen and E. Lichtblau, 'Bush Lets US Spy on Callers Without Courts' *New York Times* (16 December 2005).

[61] J. Risen, *State of War: The Secret History of the CIA and the Bush administration* (New York: Free Press, 2006).

[62] Press Briefing by Attorney General Alberto Gonzales and General Michael Hayden, Principal Deputy Director for National Intelligence, 19 December 2005, available at www.whitehouse.gov/news/releases/2005/12/20051219-1.html.

[63] Press Conference of the President, 19 December 2005, available at www.whitehouse.gov/news/releases/2005/12/20051219-2.html; D. Eggen, 'White House Trains Efforts on Media Leaks: Sources, Reporters Could Be Prosecuted' *Washington Post* (5 March 2006).

secrecy in counter-terrorism operations may be well-founded. In 1998, for example, the *Washington Times* reported that the NSA was able to monitor Osama bin Laden's satellite phone.[64] Soon after the story was published, bin Laden ceased using the phone and largely disappeared from the reach of US intelligence. A CIA agent who ran the bin Laden desk at the time has suggested that a direct causal link can be made between publication of the article and the 11 September 2001 attacks on the United States.[65] Nevertheless, once embraced, a culture of tolerating secrecy in pushing the limits of law is difficult to contain. As the Church Committee found in the 1970s – part of the process that led to the adoption of FISA – the doctrine of 'plausible deniability' was developed in order to avoid attribution of illegal conduct to the United States for covert operations. Evidence before the Committee, however, clearly demonstrated that the concept, initially intended to protect the United States and its operatives from the consequences of disclosures, soon expanded to mask decisions of the President and his senior staff.[66]

It appears unrealistic, therefore, to put much hope in the prospect that such decisions will ever be made either openly or candidly. Gross's chapter in this volume argues that the analysis presented here is itself unrealistic, though predicating a model for protecting the rule of law on the existence of a 'robust and engaged civil society' supported by relentless journalists and fearless bloggers narrows the application of extra-legal measures to the United States and a handful of other countries. Such a conclusion should change the calculus for responding to conduct that may violate the law, in particular, challenging the assumption that illegal conduct will be closely examined and in appropriate circumstances ratified. On the contrary, the cases examined here suggest the need to adopt a precautionary approach that does not assume the good faith of interested officials serving as judges in their own cause.

III. Mitigation

How, then, should a legal system deal with rare circumstances in which violation of the law may be perceived as justified or even necessary?

64 M. Sieff, 'Terrorist Driven by Hatred for US, Israel' *Washington Times* (21 August 1998).

65 P.R. Keefe, 'Cat-and-Mouse Games' *New York Review* (26 May 2005), p. 41.

66 Church Committee Reports, United States Senate Select Committee to Study Governmental Operations with Respect to Intelligence Activities, Senate, 20 November, 1975, II, Section B: 'Covert Action as a Vehicle for Foreign Policy Implementation', p. 11.

Necessity, discussed in more detail by Andrew Simester in this volume, provides a partial remedy – though the examples discussed in this chapter would not all fall within its relatively narrow framework. To be successful, a necessity defence must typically demonstrate that the harm sought to be avoided was greater than the harm caused, that there was no reasonable alternative to the action taken and that the actor did not create the danger he or she sought to avoid. A key question is whether the honest belief of the accused is sufficient to justify the defence: in Gross's hypothetical, it is highly likely that the decision whether to ratify torture or not would depend on whether the tortured person did in fact know where the ticking bomb was located.

The American Law Institute adopted a belief-based 'choice of evils' approach to the question in its Model Penal Code:

> Conduct that the actor believes to be necessary to avoid a harm or evil to himself or to another is justifiable, provided that: (a) the harm or evil sought to be avoided by such conduct is greater than that sought to be prevented by the law defining the offense charged; and (b) neither the Code nor other law defining the offense provides exceptions or defenses dealing with the specific situation involved; and (c) a legislative purpose to exclude the justification claimed does not otherwise plainly appear.[67]

This definition of necessity was cited in the August 2002 memorandum prepared by the Department of Justice Office of Legal Counsel that purported to authorise torture outside the United States as 'especially relevant in the current circumstances'.[68] Assuming the existence of al Qaeda sleeper cells plotting against the United States on a scale equal to or greater than the 11 September 2001 attacks, the memorandum argued that 'any harm that might occur during an interrogation would pale to insignificance compared to the harm avoided by preventing such an attack, which could take hundreds or thousands of lives'.[69] Two factors were said to shape the contours of a necessity defence to torture: the degree of certainty that an individual has information needed to prevent an attack and the likelihood and scale of that attack.[70]

67 US Model Penal Code, s. 3.02.

68 Bybee, Torture Memorandum, pp. 39–40.

69 *Ibid.*, p. 41.

70 *Ibid.* Departures from the Convention Against Torture in the US implementing legislation were interpreted as supporting this view. Torture was not defined as the intentional infliction of severe pain or suffering 'for such purpose[ ] as obtaining from him or a third person information or a confession'; by removing this purpose element, 'Congress allowed the necessity defense to apply when appropriate'. In addition the Convention Against Torture's provision that 'no exceptional circumstances whatsoever, whether a state of war or a threat of war, internal political instability or any other pubic emergency, may be invoked as a

This opportunistic reading of the prohibition of torture – ignoring, among other things, the explicit intention at international law that torture be non-derogable – adopts a logic similar to Gross: one constructs an ideal-type situation in which a reasonable person would countenance torture and then extends this reasoning to assert that the prohibition on torture is inherently qualified.[71] The flaw in this approach is that the ticking time bomb scenario is both highly seductive and wildly implausible. Henry Shue's critique is dated but worth quoting at length:

> The proposed victim of our torture is not someone we suspect of planting the device: he is the perpetrator. He is not some pitiful psychotic making one last play for attention: he did plant the device. The wiring is not backwards, the mechanism is not jammed: the device will destroy the city if not deactivated.
>
> . . . The torture will not be conducted in the basement of some small-town jail in the provinces by local thugs popping pills; the prime minister and chief justice are being kept informed; and a priest and doctor are present. The victim will not be raped or forced to eat excrement and will not collapse with a heart attack or become deranged before talking; while avoiding irreparable damage, the antiseptic pain will carefully be increased only up to the point at which the necessary information is divulged, and the doctor will then immediately administer an antibiotic and a tranquilizer.[72]

Even Shue concludes, however, that if the precise facts of the ticking bomb scenario were satisfied, it would not be possible to deny the permissibility of torture.[73] But the implausibility of the perfect scenario is precisely why there is a rule against torture without the possibility of derogation.

For similar reasons, necessity as a defence in criminal law is circumscribed extremely narrowly. In the paradigmatic case of *R* v. *Dudley and Stephens*, two men were shipwrecked at sea for almost three weeks before killing and eating their cabin boy. Even so, they were convicted and sentenced to death:

> It is not needful to point out the awful danger of admitting the principle which has been contended for. Who is to be the judge of this sort of necessity? By what measure is the comparative value of lives to be measured? Is it to be strength, or intellect, or what? It is plain that the principle leaves to him

justification of torture' was not incorporated in the text of Section 2340. Bybee, Torture Memorandum, p. 41, n.23.

71 Cf. W.B. Wendel, 'Legal Ethics and the Separation of Law and Morals' (2005) 91 *Cornell Law Review* 82–4.

72 H. Shue, 'Torture' (1978) 7 *Philosophy and Public Affairs* 124 at 142.

73 *Ibid.*, at 141.

> who is to profit by it to determine the necessity which will justify him in deliberately taking another's life to save his own. In this case the weakest, the youngest, the most unresisting, was chosen. Was it more necessary to kill him than one of the grown men? The answer must be 'No'
>
> 'So spake the Fiend, and with necessity, The tyrant's plea, excused his devilish deeds.'
>
> It is not suggested that in this particular case the deeds were 'devilish' but it is quite plain that such a principle once admitted might be made the legal cloak for unbridled passion and atrocious crime. There is no safe path for judges to tread but to ascertain the law to the best of their ability and to declare it according to their judgement; and if in any case the law appears to be too severe on individuals, to leave it to the sovereign to exercise that prerogative of mercy which the Constitution has intrusted to the hands fittest to dispense it.[74]

The sentence was later commuted to six months' imprisonment by Queen Victoria.

Taking seriously the argument that certain forms of *ex post* ratification may encourage (or at least not discourage) official acts necessary for security while maintaining a degree of uncertainty appropriate to discourage abuse, it is possible to distinguish at least four ways in which ratification might operate. First, it might assert the absence of a wrong through a general amnesty. Second, it could acknowledge a wrong but absolve it, through some form of indemnification. Third, an act might attract formal legal sanction but with a minimal penalty being imposed. Fourth, through the exercise of discretion no action might be taken to investigate an alleged wrong. Of these, only the third approach would appear to maintain the uncertainty that is at the heart of Gross's model, yet this is more properly seen not as a call for ratification of an act but mitigation in punishment for a wrong.[75]

A better view, then, may be not to think in terms of ratifying the wrong but mitigating the penalty. This is distinct from legal absolution – if prosecuted an individual would still have a conviction entered against his or her name – but in extraordinary circumstances discretion may be exercised at the imposition of penalties. Such an approach has the virtue of reaffirming the legal norm and imposing at least nominal sanction, while recognising that further punishment may serve no social purpose.

[74] *R.* v. *Dudley and Stephens* (1884) 14 Q.B.D. 273.

[75] *Cf.* Terry Nardin's distinction between excuse and justification in Chapter 4, this volume.

An analogy may be made with the legal status of euthanasia. Though legalised in a few jurisdictions, euthanasia is regarded generally as a grave challenge to the legal system. Arguments in favour of patient autonomy and the reality of medical practice must be weighed against the danger of eroding the bright line rule that prohibits intentional killing.[76] The ethical and religious response has been to qualify the intent component of this prohibition, relying on somewhat artificial doctrines such as double effect (an overdose of morphine is intended to relieve pain, rather than to kill) and act–omission (withholding food or hydration that leads to death is distinct from administering poison).[77] The legal response, in a number of cases, has been to affirm the bright line rule but impose no penalty.[78]

Obviously, as the demand for any such violation of an established norm increases, so the need for legal regulation of the 'exception' becomes more important. This seems to be occurring in the case of euthanasia, as medical advances have increased the discretion of doctors in making end of life decisions. In many jurisdictions, continued reliance on the possibility of a homicide charge is now seen as an inadequate legal response to the ethical challenges posed by euthanasia.[79] In relation to the various forms of criminal conduct contemplated in this discussion, there appears to be no such groundswell of support for a change in the law.

It might be argued that the approach here is similar to *ex post* ratification. Indeed, the exercise of discretion in the mitigation of penalty might take place either in a judicial process, such as imposing a token penalty or as part of an executive pardon in the manner of Queen Victoria's commutation of the cannibals' sentences. But by requiring a judicial process first

[76] See, e.g. Report of the House of Lords Select Committee on Medical Ethics (1993–94 HL 260) ('Walton Report').

[77] See generally J. Keown (ed.), *Euthanasia Examined: Ethical, Clinical and Legal Perspectives* (Cambridge: Cambridge University Press, 1995).

[78] See, e.g. *R* v. *Cox* (1992) 12 *Butterworths' Medico Legal Reports* 38. Dr Nigel Cox was unable to control the pain of a patient suffering from rheumatoid arthritis who repeatedly begged him to kill her. Making no attempt to conceal what he was doing, he gave her a lethal injection of the poison potassium chloride. A nurse reported the action and he was charged with attempted murder (by this time the body had been cremated and there was no evidence that the injection was the operative cause of death). He was convicted of attempted murder, but given a one year suspended sentence; the General Medical Council reprimanded him but permitted him to remain a practising doctor: J. Harris, 'Euthanasia and the Value of Life', in J. Keown (ed.), *Euthanasia Examined: Ethical, Clinical and Legal Perspectives* (Cambridge: Cambridge University Press, 1995), p. 7.

[79] See S. Chesterman, 'Last Rights: Euthanasia, the Sanctity of Life and the Law in the Netherlands and the Northern Territory of Australia' (1998) 47 *International and Comparative Law Quarterly* and sources there cited.

to determine the existence of the wrong, mitigation reduces the danger of an executive asserting for itself the right to approve conduct that is never scrutinised. The key difference is trust: as the cases discussed in this chapter show, there is little reason to trust the candour of an executive to openly disclose alleged wrongs perpetrated in the name of national security. In the absence of investigative journalists at newspapers such as the *New York Times* and *Washington Post*, few, if any, of the questionable actions discussed here would have been exposed to any form of public scrutiny. This is not to suggest that a mitigation approach would encourage any more candour – on the contrary, it assumes that political and legal incentives will always encourage secrecy. Nevertheless, the possibility of prosecution and punishment will do more to improve behaviour than formalised endorsement of wrongdoing asserted to be in the national interest.

IV. Conclusion

Hard cases make bad law, as Oliver Wendell Holmes, Jr, famously warned a century ago.[80] Justice Holmes's observation seems especially apt here. But the context from which the cliché is typically lifted also bears examination. As Holmes noted, the hard cases are frequently the great ones:

> Great cases like hard cases make bad law. For great cases are called great, not by reason of their real importance in shaping the law of the future, but because of some accident of immediate overwhelming interest which appeals to the feelings and distorts the judgment. These immediate interests exercise a kind of hydraulic pressure which makes what previously was clear seem doubtful, and before which even well settled principles of law will bend.[81]

How the current historical period will be viewed, what effects the war on terror will have on norms that had until very recently been regarded as well settled and what role lawyers and academics will play in shaping those norms depends very much on the consequences of the hydraulic pressure currently at work on the international system.

'Americans will always do the right thing', Winston Churchill once observed, 'after they've exhausted all the alternatives'. There is, in the wake of the repudiation of the torture memorandum, renewed vigilance on

[80] *Northern Sec. Co.* v. *United States*, 193 US 197 at 400 (1904). Cf. Gross, 'Chaos and Rules', 1132.

[81] *Northern Sec. Co.* v. *United States* at 400–1. Holmes, of course, was writing a dissent.

the part of the judiciary[82] and the falling of scales from the eyes of the American public, some reason to hope that this cliché will be borne out and that the considered outcome of public deliberation within the United States will be a reaffirmation of the rule of law even in times of crisis.

[82] See, e.g. *Hamdi* v. *Rumsfeld*, 542 US 507 at 578–9 (2004), where Justice Scalia in dissent wrote: 'The Founders well understood the difficult tradeoff between safety and freedom. "Safety from external danger," Hamilton declared, "is the most powerful director of national conduct. Even the ardent love of liberty will, after a time, give way to its dictates. The violent destruction of life and property incident to war; the continual effort and alarm attendant on a state of continual danger, will compel nations the most attached to liberty, to resort for repose and security to institutions which have a tendency to destroy their civil and political rights. To be more safe, they, at length, become willing to run the risk of being less free." The Federalist No. 8, p. 33.

The Founders warned us about the risk, and equipped us with a Constitution designed to deal with it. Many think it not only inevitable but entirely proper that liberty give way to security in times of national crisis that, at the extremes of military exigency, *inter arma silent leges*. Whatever the general merits of the view that war silences law or modulates its voice, that view has no place in the interpretation and application of a Constitution designed precisely to confront war and, in a manner that accords with democratic principles, to accommodate it'.

PART SIX

Post-colonial and international perspectives

14

Exceptions, bare life and colonialism

JOHAN GEERTSEMA

I follow the strange caravan of soldiers, women and children till they reach the mountain. At the top the leader of the soldiers plants a flag between two slabs of rock and proclaims Martial Law. He sings a song which, he boasts to the women and children, is his 'national anthem'. 'God save the Queen', the soldiers all say in unison .... To my horror I find the women and children on their knees, licking the rocks around the flag, the leader of the soldiers egging them on with mad glee. 'Clean it up!' he shouts dementedly, waving his bayonet near their terrified faces. The other soldiers stand by and threaten the ones who refuse to lick. A woman gets shot. Another suddenly stands up and rushes towards the cliff. She plunges to her death. 'This is what will happen to you if you don't clean the rocks', the leader says, his complexion pink and slightly sunburnt.[1]

Terror becomes total when it becomes independent of all opposition; it rules supreme when nobody any longer stands in its way. If lawfulness is the essence of non-tyrannical government and lawlessness is the essence of tyranny, then terror is the essence of totalitarian domination.[2]

I. Introduction

According to Carl Schmitt, the exception constitutes a norm-less – or nearly norm-less – space. In the state of exception, 'the state remains, whereas law recedes ... the norm is destroyed in the exception'.[3] In order to

I would like to thank all the participants in the symposium *Terrorism and the Rule of Law: Legal Theory in Times of Crisis* for their comments and criticisms and especially Kanishka Jayasuriya and David Dyzenhaus for very helpful discussions. Most particularly I would like to thank Victor V. Ramraj for his feedback on various drafts and for having invited me to the symposium.

[1] K.S. Duiker, *The Quiet Violence of Dreams* (Cape Town: Kwela Books, 2001), pp. 367–8.

[2] H. Arendt, *The Origins of Totalitarianism* (San Diego: Harcourt, 1966), p. 464.

[3] C. Schmitt, *Political Theology: Four Chapters on the Concept of Sovereignty*, G. Schwab (trans.) (Cambridge, MA: MIT Press, 1985), p. 12. See also Agamben's following useful formulation: 'We can define ... the state of exception in Schmitt's theory as the place where the opposition between the norm and its realization reaches its greatest intensity'.

respond adequately to an emergency, urgent decisions need to be taken and therefore norms, and especially legal norms, need to be set aside. Schmitt's move is therefore to situate authority outside of law, in the sovereign who decides the exception, as he puts it at the start of *Political Theology*.[4] The sovereign decision is that which constitutes law, which thus becomes merely an instrument in the hands of the sovereign rather than the warrant for and, indeed, the articulation of state authority. However, the example of colonialism suggests the grave danger of attempting to delimit the reach of the rule of law by taking it to be incapable of dealing with exceptional circumstances that arise as a consequence of emergencies, whether these arise in the colonies, as in the case of Victorian Britain's Empire, or result from terrorist attacks. Instead, I argue, what is required is the protection, minimal though it might turn out to be, of the rule of law against the excesses of executive prerogative to which a Schmittian position on the rule of law leads. Only by holding on to the rule of law and the concomitant notion that the state, if it is to be a liberal and democratic state, needs at all times to act within the limits of legality and thus in accordance with the values upon which it is founded and which the law enshrines, even and especially when it needs to protect those values, can the rule of law and the deep underlying values upon which it is founded be maintained.

The aftermath of the events of 11 September 2001 – the subsequent 'war on terror', including the war in Afghanistan and the invasion of Iraq and various attacks in for instance Bali, Madrid and London – has seen intensive efforts not only to make sense of these events and state responses to them, but also to consider the implications of these responses and formulate possible alternatives to them. What is central to current debates is the question as to the limits of legality: the extent to which this crisis, or indeed other, future crises like it, might or should be dealt with in terms of the rule of law. One crucial factor has, however, received comparatively less attention, namely the relevance of colonialism (and the imperialism that arose from it) for understanding what is happening.[5] Similarly, colonialism and what it can tell us about the limits of

G. Agamben, *State of Exception*, K. Attell (trans.) (Chicago: University of Chicago Press, 2005), p. 36.

[4] *Ibid.*, p. 5.

[5] Both colonialism and imperialism are starting to receive considerably more attention with reference to the current context of the 'war on terror'. For recent contributions to the growing scholarship on the parallels between the Victorian British Empire and the 21st century American one, see the following review essays: J.F. Witt, 'Anglo-American Empire and the Crisis of the Legal Frame (Will the Real British Empire Please Stand Up?)' (2007)

legality is not a central concern in the majority of the essays in the current volume.[6]

In this paper I begin to consider how focusing on colonialism might help us approach current debates on states of emergency and exceptions, and how doing so might provide a perspective according to which some of the central issues might be clarified.[7] These issues involve, in particular, questions concerning the rule of law. As suggested by the passage from K. Sello Duiker's remarkable novel *The Quiet Violence of Dreams* (2001) quoted above, the British colonial experience is one marked by martial law, famously characterised by A.V. Dicey as 'the suspension of ordinary law and the temporary government of a country or parts of it by military tribunals', and said by him to be 'unknown to the law of England'.[8] Dicey of course distinguishes between two different senses in which the term 'martial law' is used: a 'common law right' that functions entirely within the rule of law to repel attack on the state and restore order, and a second kind in which 'military tribunals . . . more or less supersede the jurisdiction of the Courts'.[9] It is this latter kind of martial law which 'is in England utterly unknown to the constitution'.[10] However, Dicey's view is rather optimistic: military tribunals at times did supersede courts, if not in England itself then certainly in its overseas territories: its colonies.

The 'suspension of ordinary law' which Dicey opposes, and which he – perhaps rather prematurely – contends to be unknown to the law of England, is dramatised in the passage from Duiker's novel. The narrator dreams that the leader of a band of soldiers proclaims martial law; soldiers proceed to terrorise the native population and they do so under the authority of the Crown. The passage evokes the lawlessness of that kind of martial law that suspends the common law as well as the terrorising effect this has on the people thus oppressed. Duiker's novel here evokes the brutality of a liberal Empire that, perhaps more often than not, imposed itself

120 *Harvard Law Review* 754; and L. Benton, 'Constitutions and Empires' (2006) 31 *Law & Social Inquiry* 177.

[6] Two notable exceptions are K. Jayasuriya, 'Struggle over Legality in the Midnight Hour' (Chapter 15) and D. Dyzenhaus, 'The Compulsion of Legality' (Chapter 2), this volume.

[7] An emergency is not the same as an exception. I take an emergency to refer to the crisis and the exception as the state of affairs subsequent to it. The emergency would therefore be antecedent to the exception. See O. Gross, 'Chaos and Rules: Should Responses to Violent Crises Always be Constitutional?' (2003) 112 *Yale Law Journal* 1070–1, for a discussion of the distinction between these two terms.

[8] A.V. Dicey, *Introduction to the Study of the Law of the Constitution* (London: MacMillan, 1959), p. 283.

[9] *Ibid.*, pp. 284–5 and 287. [10] *Ibid.*, p. 289.

through sheer force of terror and lawlessness, two terms which my second epigraph, from Hannah Arendt's *The Origin of Totalitarianism*, attempts to connect. Duiker is describing a colonial zone that is totalitarian in its effects, a zone outside the rule of law: an exception.

If it is true that the rule of law did not exist in a recognisably liberal sense in Britain's colonies, nevertheless I argue that the colonial experience did not involve territories that were ever completely lawless, in contemporary parlance legal 'black holes', except possibly at one particular phase of colonialism, namely the moment of conquest.[11] And when the law was suspended by means of martial law to suppress rebellion, the resulting brutality occasioned the fear that the imposition of martial law in a particular colony might spill over to the metropolitan centre and sometimes made such suspension of law deeply controversial. Perhaps the most notable of these controversies is the so-called 'Jamaica affair' which arose when brute force was used by local officials and soldiers under the authority of the governor, Edward Eyre, to suppress an uprising by black Jamaicans in 1865. When word of the governor's actions reached England, a committee was formed to prosecute him, albeit unsuccessfully.[12] What this incident suggests, among other things, is that colonies were not consistently lawless 'zones of indistinction' or states of exception (spaces where law retreats to a minimum).[13] Instead, reconsidering the 'jurisdictional politics' involved in negotiating the relation between the rule of law and exception in colonialism has the potential to shed light on current debates concerning that relation.[14] The present collection of essays may be understood as being engaged in precisely such a jurisdictional politics, that is, as participating in a set of 'conflicts over the preservation, creation, nature, and extent of different legal forums and authorities'.[15] Like various past debates, as often as not in a colonial setting, we are today again considering and reconsidering rival conceptions of the rule of law.

[11] L. Benton, *Law and Colonial Cultures* (Cambridge: Cambridge University Press, 2002), pp. 258–9. For black holes, see J. Steyn, 'Guantanamo Bay: The Legal Black Hole' (2004) 53 *International and Comparative Law Quarterly* 1.

[12] See R. Kostal, *A Jurisprudence of Power* (Oxford: Oxford University Press, 2005). For context and a summary see pp. 12–16.

[13] For the notion of the zone of indistinction, see for example G. Agamben, *Homo Sacer: Sovereign Power and Bare Life*, D. Heller-Roazen (trans.) (Stanford: Stanford University Press, 1998), pp. 19–20. For the connection with colonialism, see pp. 36–8.

[14] See Benton, *Law and Colonial Cultures*, p. 10 for more on 'jurisdictional politics'.

[15] *Ibid.*

II. Extra-legal and legality models

Oren Gross proposes that the best way to protect the rule of law in liberal democracies during an emergency is to invoke extra-legal measures. This proposal takes as its starting point the problem of how the state should respond to exceptional circumstances: whether this should happen within the ambit of the rule of law or outside of it, and what the effect, jurisprudential or otherwise, of either of these choices would be. The violent events to which I referred at the start of this chapter suggest to Gross a number of inadequacies in existing constitutional frameworks for dealing with 'acute national crises'.[16] What he terms the business-as-usual model is naive and rigid; both this model and 'models of accommodation', moreover, threaten contamination of the existing legal system, the 'slippery slope toward excessive governmental infringement on individual rights and liberties while undermining constitutional structures and institutions in the process'.[17] Finally, given the changed circumstances liberal democracies face today, one needs to recognise that the exceptional has become permanent and might no longer readily be distinguished from the normal, while the exception is so urgent as to pose grave danger.

For these reasons, Gross questions both the '*assumption of separation*... our ability to separate emergencies and crises from normalcy'[18] and the '*assumption of constitutionality*... that whatever responses are made to the challenges of a particular exigency, such responses are to be found and limited within the confines of the constitution'.[19] This then leads him, drawing in particular on Locke's theory of the prerogative and Dicey's ideas on *Habeas Corpus* Suspension Acts and Acts of Indemnity, to his proposed solution, namely an extra-legal measures model whereby *ex post* ratification would allow officials to act outside of the law on the grounds of necessity, which would thereby keep emergencies at arm's length from the law, thus preventing contamination which might undermine the legal order.[20]

[16] Oren Gross, 'Chaos and Rules', 1021. [17] *Ibid.*, 1022.
[18] *Ibid.* Also see especially 1070–3. [19] *Ibid.*, at 1022–3.
[20] *Ibid.*, at 1023–4. The most recent statement of the model is O. Gross and F. Ní Aoláin, *Law in Times of Crisis: Emergency Powers in Theory and Practice* (Cambridge: Cambridge University Press, 2006); see Gross, 'Extra-Legality and the Ethic of Political Responsibility' (Chapter 3), this volume, for a summary that addresses objections to the model by arguing that the uncertainty built into it may, if anything, over-deter public officials from acting extra-legally. On the prerogative, see J. Locke, *Two Treatises of Government*, P. Laslett (ed.), (Cambridge: Cambridge University Press, 1988), pp. 374–80. On Suspension Acts and Acts of Indemnity, see Dicey, *Introduction to the Study of the Law of the Constitution*, pp. 224–33.

David Dyzenhaus has serious reservations about Gross's suggested model: Gross, 'despite his awareness of the contours of the debate, finds himself trapped by some of the same assumptions which produce those contours'.[21] Worse, Gross's model is open to abuse: it 'turns out to be highly unstable in theory and the likely result is that in practice his model turns into something distant from, even opposite to, his intentions'.[22] Consequently, Dyzenhaus argues for what he calls a legality model which would deal with emergencies by means of 'imaginative experiments in institutional design' that might involve, in particular, a willingness to loosen 'the grip of a formal doctrine of the separation of powers'.[23]

As both Gross and Dyzenhaus have recognised, and as many of the papers in this collection attest, these questions have particular historical resonance and are in important ways anticipated in the crisis of the Weimar Republic, especially as articulated in Schmitt's ideas on law and exception. Indeed, aside from Locke and Dicey, Schmitt is an important intellectual precursor of Gross, at least in the case of his extra-legal measures model.[24] After all, it was Schmitt who argued forcefully that '[there] exists no norm that is applicable to chaos. For a legal order to make sense, a normal situation must exist'.[25] Schmitt thereby in effect anticipates Gross's proposal to deal with chaotic, unpredictable exigencies outside of the law, though the latter admittedly draws on the former in a qualified way: indeed, to protect the very rule of law Schmitt dismisses.

But the questions are also anticipated in the rather different and quite multifarious settings of colonialism. Gross significantly refers to colonialism as one particularly egregious instance of what he terms 'seepage', whereby attempts to draw clear lines between emergency and normalcy tend to spill over from the 'anomalous zone' of the colony: these measures to contain resistance tend to infiltrate the legal regime of the metropolis over time.[26] There are further reasons why the perspectives lent by a

[21] D. Dyzenhaus, 'The State of Emergency in Legal Theory', in V.V. Ramraj, M. Hor and K. Roach (eds.), *Global Anti-Terrorism Law and Policy* (Cambridge: Cambridge University Press, 2005), pp. 66–7. Dyzenhaus's position is most clearly articulated in Chapter 2 of this volume and in D. Dyzenhaus, *The Constitution of Law* (Cambridge: Cambridge University Press, 2006).

[22] *Ibid.*, p. 67. [23] *Ibid.*

[24] However, it should be noted that Gross is no disciple of Schmitt and, indeed, seeks to distance himself from the latter. See Gross, 'Chaos and Rules', p. 1121. See also O. Gross, 'The Normless and Exceptionless Exception: Carl Schmitt's Theory of Emergency Powers and the "Norm-Exception" Dichotomy' (1999–2000) 21 *Cardozo Law Review* 1825.

[25] Schmitt, *Political Theology*, p. 13.

[26] See Gross and Ní Aoláin, *Law in Times of Crisis*, pp. 181–202; for parallels with Guantánamo, see pp. 202–5.

study of colonialism matter here. In addition to those cited above, I would now like briefly to consider some further factors. In the first instance, we cannot properly understand any of the various attacks and state responses that together constitute the crisis without taking cognisance of the historical fact of colonialism. It is germane that the current perceived threat emanates, largely though of course not exclusively, from the Middle East, which to a significant extent forms the fulcrum of events. The long conflict involving Israel and the Palestinians is itself a consequence of what was an act of colonisation when land settled by Palestinians was occupied by Jews returning from the diaspora.[27] The relation between 'Islam' and 'the West', similarly, cannot be divorced from colonial circumstances: it is the case that both Afghanistan and Iraq were in recent memory British colonies, which strengthens the impression that the invasions of these places are acts of neo-colonial aggression. Another point concerns the controversial detention facilities in Cuba's Guantanámo Bay, the uncertain legal status of which has placed it at the centre of the US's global prison system. Its legal status can be traced back to Cuba's history as a former Spanish colony and to the Spanish-American war that led to Cuba's initial independence, reinforcing the Bush administration's argument that it lies outside the reach of ordinary US law.[28]

What is more, colonialism has had a profound influence on metropolitan law. Dicey's work, for instance, arises from urgent questions concerning the rule of law, martial law and states of emergency in the British Empire. It was decisively affected by notorious events which elicited impassioned public intellectual debate on the rule of law and its limits. These events were a direct consequence of the threat to the rule of law at home in Britain that was perceived to have arisen as a consequence of the actions, already referred to above, of British officials in the colony of Jamaica: these officials openly broke the law in the name of the law.[29] According to Kostal, 'the most explosive feature of this episode, the main reason why it was so vehemently contested and litigated, was that governor Eyre, his senior officers, and their apologists in England, fervently maintained that the suppression had taken place in strict accordance with law. . . . [It] was this contention, this *legal* contention, which had to be impugned and, by

[27] See I. Zertal, *Israel's Holocaust and the Politics of Nationhood*, C. Galai (trans.) (Cambridge: Cambridge University Press, 2005).

[28] D. Gregory, 'The Black Flag: Guantánamo Bay and the Space of the Exception' (2006) 88 *Geografiska Annaler – Series B – Human Geography* 405, especially 410–13.

[29] For the effect of the Jamaica affair on Dicey, see Kostal, *A Jurisprudence of Power*, pp. 456–8. For his brief remarks on the Jamaica affair, see Dicey, *Introduction to the Study of the Law of the Constitution*, pp. 232–3.

best available means, judicially refuted'.[30] As Dyzenhaus points out, in this respect the significance of the episode is that it illustrates what he terms the compulsion of legality, namely 'the compulsion to justify all acts of state as having a legal warrant'.[31] It therefore points to a danger inherent in the politics of the rule of law, which can provide legitimacy to those who claim to act in accordance with it and thus undermine the rule of law itself by means of this very claim.

III. Colonialism and the rule of law

One of the most influential recent accounts of colonialism is that of Partha Chatterjee who, with reference to the British presence in India, proposes that it is characterised by what he terms the *rule of colonial difference.* Of course, colonialism is a highly varied phenomenon – not only were different colonialisms different (for instance, French and British varieties), but colonies within a particular colonialism were treated differently. For instance, the dominions of Canada, Australia, South Africa and New Zealand with substantial white settler populations were treated very differently from 'native' colonies.[32] Indeed, the differentiated treatment of white dominions and other colonies nicely illustrates Chatterjee's position that 'race' was a fundamental factor in colonialism. Drawing on Foucault, Chatterjee points out that 'a persistent theme in colonial discourse until the earlier half of [the twentieth century] was the steadfast refusal to admit the universality of those principles' of modernity which the British supposedly espoused.[33] That is, modern institutions of the liberal democratic state underwritten by British statesmen and their colonial administrators as universally valid and thus in principle applicable to all humans across time and space – institutions such as freedom of speech, the rule of law and democracy itself – were denied consistent applicability in the colonies. Yet it is a striking fact that British colonialism used a liberal discourse of rights and legality to justify itself. Put somewhat crudely, it is because the British viewed themselves as civilised and the 'natives' as uncivilised that they could justify their intervention and its end purpose, namely to 'civilise' the natives: the so-called white man's burden. But, of course, if the colonial

30 Kostal, *A Jurisprudence of Power*, p. 465.

31 Dyzenhaus, Chapter 2, p. 34. For his discussion of how the Jamaica affair illustrates the compulsion of legality, see pp. 48–50.

32 See R.J.C. Young, *Postcolonialism: An Historical Introduction* (Oxford: Blackwell, 2001).

33 P. Chatterjee, *The Nation and its Fragments* (Princeton: Princeton University Press, 1993), p. 16.

project were to succeed it would render itself redundant since, once the natives had been 'civilised', there could be no justification for a colonial presence as the difference between coloniser and colonised would thereby be cancelled. This means that the colonial project is fundamentally contradictory in that it needs to produce the very difference between coloniser and native that it works to cancel. It is Chatterjee's argument that this production of difference involves 'race', which is why one finds a marked process of racialisation in evidence in advanced, late nineteenth-century colonialism, not only in his chosen example (Bengal) but more widely: 'the forms of objectification and normalisation of the colonised had to reproduce, within the framework of a universal knowledge, the truth of the colonial difference. The difference could be marked by many signs ... but of all these signs, race was perhaps the most obvious mark of colonial difference'.[34]

So while colonialism is a liberal project based on universal principles, a set of limitations on these principles is contradictorily built in. The applicability of this project is limited on the basis of race. One of Chatterjee's examples, his discussion of the so-called Ilbert Bill Affair, illustrates how this point pertains to the rule of law. This affair 'brought up most dramatically the question of whether a central claim of the modern state could be allowed to transgress the line of racial division. The claim was that of administering an impersonal, nonarbitrary system of the rule of law'.[35] In this case, Indian judicial officers could not try cases in which Europeans were involved, while no such limitation was imposed on their British counterparts. The viceroy, Ripon, recognised the anomaly and Ilbert, the law member, in 1883 introduced a bill to regularise matters. But public opinion, that is, *white Anglo-Indian* public opinion, was vehemently opposed to the bill, whereupon Ripon retreated and the Bill was withdrawn. Chatterjee comments that what Ripon's '"failure" signalled was the inherent impossibility of completing the project of the modern state without superseding the conditions of colonial rule' and that what the affair illustrates is that 'the colony had to become an exception precisely to vindicate the universal truth of the theory'.[36] In other words, for the liberal ideal of the modern state to be maintained, it required an exception from that ideal: paradoxically, a limitation on the very universality – of suffrage, of freedom of speech, of the rule of law – that is constitutive of the modern state. Colonialism, viewed in this light, displays an inherent

[34] *Ibid.*, p. 20. [35] *Ibid.* [36] *Ibid.*, pp. 21–2.

contradiction in the democratic project of the modern state; to maintain the liberal state (Britain), colonies not only provided material sustenance but functioned on a theoretical level to delimit liberalism and thereby exposed the limitations of that theory.

Similarly, Ranajit Guha, in his powerful argument that colonialism as a system was maintained much more through coercion and sheer force than through persuasion – that it was a 'dominance without hegemony' – points to the limitations of the liberal-democratic 'bourgeois' project and its paradoxical dependence on difference to maintain itself.[37] According to him, 'bourgeois culture hits an insuperable limit in colonialism. None of its noble achievements – Liberalism, Democracy, Liberty, Rule of Law, and so on – can survive the inexorable urge of capital to expand and reproduce itself by means of the politics of extra-territorial, colonial dominance'.[38] That is to say, there is a tension between the expansive character of capital and the universalist character of the 'bourgeois culture' that it constitutes. Capital, to survive, needs to expand: it needs ever more raw materials, labour and new markets. While the concepts Guha enumerates are based on the precepts of universality, it is integral to the universalist character of this culture also to expand to other *territories*; for Guha, colonialism in this sense is an inherent part of the liberal-democratic project. Yet that project at the same time cannot withstand its own expansion: the actual practice of colonialism, by means of which liberalism would expand itself, apparently inevitably fails to meet the criteria of universality it demands.

Some of Guha's most damning judgments pertain to the alleged rule of law in India: for much of its colonial history, the rule of law was 'merely a body of executive orders, decrees, regulations' and 'the execution of the laws, made for the people but not by them, was all too often characterised by double standards – one, until the end of the nineteenth century, for the whites and the other for the natives, and during the remainder of the British rule, one for the administrative elite, British and Indian, and the other for the rest of the population'.[39] Rule of law, it turns out, is merely 'the name given by the common sense of politics to [the] ideology' of law.[40] For Guha there is no rule of law to speak of in colonialism, which thus in principle constitutes a state of exception from the rule of law.

Chatterjee and Guha present not only powerful critiques of colonialism, specifically as regards the rule of law, but thereby present a challenge – and

[37] R. Guha, *Dominance without Hegemony* (Cambridge, MA: Harvard University Press, 1997), p. 71.

[38] *Ibid.*, p. 67. [39] *Ibid.*, pp. 66–7. [40] *Ibid.*

a warning – to contemporary liberal-democratic politics. Their views on the absence of the rule of law implies, in the end, that colonialism constituted a sphere outside the law. One important instance of the idea that colonialism constituted such a lawless space emanates from Schmitt, while the notion of bare life derives from Giorgio Agamben. It is therefore to a consideration of the implication of their work for an understanding of the role of the rule of law in colonialism to which I turn next.

IV. Bare life: colonialism, 'race' and law

In a chapter that is arguably central to her conception of *The Origins of Totalitarianism*, Arendt describes the colonial encounter in terms that clearly anticipate the notion of bare life as adumbrated by Agamben. The colonial scene as she describes it is one strikingly marked by lawlessness. She focuses on Africa in order to consider the 'discoveries' of race and bureaucratisation as devices in the service of imperialism and capitalism and thus traces the late nineteenth-century development and systematisation of these two technologies of political organisation which were to intersect, according to her, just a few decades later in the totalitarianism of the Nazis.[41] Her chapter is divided into three parts, focusing first on the role of the Boers in South Africa in the development of race thinking and its subsequent imperial deployment in Africa; then considering the place of gold in this process; and finally elaborating on bureaucracy as a concomitant of the expansive character of imperialism.

Arendt argues that 'race was the Boers' answer to the overwhelming monstrosity of Africa – a whole continent populated and overpopulated by savages' and says that in South Africa we can see the way in which autochthonous 'savages' were not only marginalised, but indeed rendered invisible, because they were deemed to be so close to nature as to be part of it.[42] In an important passage, Arendt puts this as follows:

[41] Arendt, *The Origins of Totalitarianism*, pp. 185–6.

[42] *Ibid.*, p. 185. Arendt's account of Africa and the role of 'race' in it is not uncontroversial. See S. Dossa, 'Human Status and Politics: Hannah Arendt on the Holocaust' (1980) 13 *Canadian Journal of Political Science/Revue canadienne de science politique* 309; A. Norton, 'Heart of Darkness: Africa and African Americans in the Writings of Hannah Arendt', in B. Honig (ed.), *Feminist Interpretations of Hannah Arendt* (University Park: The University of Pennsylvania Press, 1995), pp. 247–61; N.C. Moruzzi, *Speaking through the Mask: Hannah Arendt and the Politics of Social Identity* (Ithaca: Cornell University Press, 2000), pp. 86–113, 173–4, 180, 182.

> What made them different from other human beings was not at all the color of their skin but the fact that they behaved like a part of nature, that they treated nature as their undisputed master, that they had not created a human world, a human reality, and that therefore nature had remained, in all its majesty, the only overwhelming reality – compared to which they appeared to be phantoms, unreal and ghostlike. They were, as it were, 'natural' human beings who lacked the specifically human character, the specifically human reality, so that when European men massacred them they somehow were not aware that they had committed murder.[43]

The Africans whom the Boers encountered were, to them, part of nature – '"natural" human beings who lacked the specifically human character, the specifically human reality'. This helps explain how 'European men' could find it normal not only to maltreat but, indeed, to massacre, the people they encountered. Consequently, the Boers 'ruled over them in absolute lawlessness . . . living parasitically from their labor'.[44]

Arendt's description of the colonial scene not only demonstrates the rule of colonial difference but also its intersection with the rule of law, limiting as it does the reach of the rule of law and creating supposedly lawless spaces. But this description also anticipates Agamben's evocation of life reduced to bare life or expendable raw material. Drawing on Aristotle, Agamben at the start of *Homo Sacer* distinguishes between *zoē* and *bios*, natural versus cultural life or in Aristotle's terms, animal versus human life. For him, bare life is '[*not*] *simple natural life, but life exposed to death (bare life or sacred life) is the originary political element*'.[45] Bare life is life that is exterminable or disposable: it is life which is deemed to be without value and thereby redundant. For Agamben, the archetype of this bare life is the *Muselmann* in Nazi camps: this is 'the most extreme figure of the camp inhabitant'.[46] But the perspective Arendt brings to bear on colonialism suggests another important instance of such life: that of colonised 'natives'. Arendt's consideration of the colonial scene suggests that 'non-European' lives often were expendable, something which it would be hard to deny.[47] Let me now turn to how it is that bare life and the colony might be connected in the first place, before discussing how Arendt explains the lawless colonial scene with reference to her view concerning the links

[43] Arendt, *The Origins of Totalitarianism*, p. 192.
[44] *Ibid.*, p. 193.
[45] Agamben, *Homo Sacer*, p. 88; his italics.
[46] *Ibid.*, p. 184. Agamben takes this ironic term – it means 'Muslim' – from Primo Levi.
[47] For one instance of this expendability, compare the history of the Belgian Congo. For a popular account, see A. Hochschild, *King Leopold's Ghost* (Boston: Houghton Mifflin, 1999).

between totalitarianism and law. In short, colonialism is conceived by Agamben, following Schmitt, as a zone of exception from the rule of law, an idea that we have seen both Chatterjee and Guha implicitly underwrite in their discussion of the role of the rule of law with reference to the rule of colonial difference.

While Arendt focuses on imperialism and the colonialism that preceded it, Agamben tends to neglect it. He posits but does not develop the idea that the New World constituted a zone beyond the law: an exception from the law. In doing so, he draws on Schmitt's discussion, in his 1950 *Der* Nomos *der Erde*, of the *ius publicum Europaeum* (European public law) which according to Schmitt constituted the old Eurocentric world order. Schmitt's analysis is founded on his understanding of the centrality of spatial ordering, and thus of colonisation, to any order. According to him, 'all subsequent regulations of a written or unwritten kind derive their power from the inner measure of an original, constitutive act of spatial ordering', namely the *nomos*, and this constitutive act is 'established by land-appropriation, the founding of cities, or colonisation'.[48] This then relates to Schmitt's argument concerning the idea of a supranormative and decisionist '*formalization* of traditional notions of just war'.[49] Schmitt's selective reading of Hobbes enables him to argue that such a formalisation tends to disable the possibility of seeing the political enemy 'as morally inferior or even subhuman'.[50] He then develops the point 'that colonial plunder and violence *against* non-European peoples performed a ventilating function for inter-European tension and helped contribute to the "taming" of warfare *on the European continent itself*'.[51] Extra-European, colonial spaces suffered the 'exported' violence previously held in reserve for European wars, which in Schmitt's account had previously been morality-fuelled conflicts based on notions of good and evil that enabled the reduction of the enemy to subhuman status and would lead to the total obliteration of the enemy, including enemy civilians. On this account, subsequent to the formalisation of war in Europe on the basis of legal codes involving sovereignty, the exterminations of war on European soils were reduced, though at the cost of being 'vented' on those outside of Europe who, as racialised, uncivilised beings could therefore be deemed 'subhuman'. Thus: 'What ultimately counts in this formalized

[48] C. Schmitt, *The* Nomos *of the Earth*, G.L. Ulmen (trans.) (New York: Telos, 2006), p. 78.

[49] W.E. Scheuerman, 'International Law as Historical Myth' (2004) 11 *Constellations* 539; his italics throughout.

[50] *Ibid.*, at 539–40. [51] *Ibid.*, at 541.

conception of warfare is whether the entity waging war possesses certain (formal) attributes of state sovereignty, which in practical terms means that Europeans distinguished clearly between highly ritualized inter-European *wars between states* and (far more violent) wars against non-state entities employing force ("barbarian" peoples for example, or pirates)'.[52]

There are problems inherent in Schmitt's account such as his historical oversights concerning atrocities within Europe itself in his nostalgic view of the *jus publicum Europaeum* as well as other causes for the domestication of warfare.[53] Though these problems cast doubt on Schmitt's provocative theory, it should be clear how it relates to Agamben's description of bare life and the idea that colonies might be conceived as constituting spaces beyond the law. To illustrate, Agamben quotes Schmitt's reference to Locke's statement that '[in] the beginning, all the world was America'.[54] He reads this as meaning that Locke associates the New World with the state of nature where everything is possible. Schmitt makes it clear that he thinks the colonies were, quite literally, beyond the law: he makes the connection explicit when he describes the colonial spaces created by amity lines as analogous to his notion of the state of exception.[55] The world, for Agamben as for Schmitt, is historically divided between the West and the rest, Europe and the colonies; the latter were zones 'of free and empty space' where the rule of law did not obtain since the colonised were deemed subhuman.[56]

This characterisation of the colonial world is strongly reminiscent of Arendt's view of totalitarianism, as it is of her description of Africa as a phantom place in which colonialists killed 'natives' without realising the moral significance of their acts. It also suggests Chatterjee's rule of colonial difference, whereby colonial dominance was maintained through processes of racialisation. It certainly suggests one reason why Arendt calls Africa a 'phantom' place: to the colonialists it constituted a space beyond the law and, thereby, something like a state of exception. In such a world, positive law would be displaced by what is claimed to be the timeless essence of law: 'the law of History or the law of Nature', as Arendt puts it in the final chapter of *The Origins of Totalitarianism*.[57] A crucial aspect of her analysis of totalitarianism, as we shall see later, is the idea that the system does not introduce a new totalitarian form of law, nor that it is in any way

[52] *Ibid.*, at 542. [53] *Ibid.*, at 544.
[54] Agamben, *Homo Sacer*, p. 36; Scmitt, *The* Nomos *of the Earth*, p. 97.
[55] On amity lines, see Schmitt, *The* Nomos *of the Earth*, pp. 92–9. [56] *Ibid.*, p. 98.
[57] Arendt, *The Origins of Totalitarianism*, pp. 461–2.

simply lawless, but rather that it is founded on the idea of unmediated access to the essence of law and thereby supposedly entails the mechanical fulfilment of the state of things as they are meant to be. Totalitarianism sees itself as the 'end of history' or the inevitable expression of whatever contingent category in terms of its logic is taken to be natural, such as 'race'. It thus posits itself as truth and justice and is willing to sacrifice any and all principles in order to attain the end point to which it is supposedly driven by its embodiment of law. Thus, for Arendt, in totalitarian societies, and in the colonial societies that we have seen she thinks anticipated them, what we find is not so much a state of lawlessness as a form of hyper-law. However, this results in a severe distortion of the rule of law: from this perspective, a totalitarian society precisely does not give up on the rule of law but deploys it in the service of the larger law that it supposedly embodies.[58]

Agamben's appropriation of Schmitt's notion of the colonial world as constituting an exception, which is how he manages to associate it with bare life in the first place – since bare life, for Agamben, is that which the sovereign exception produces as much as it is produced by that exception – is based on a twofold assumption, both sides of which are problematic. First, Agamben seems to assume that the colonial world in fact did constitute an exception and thereby that it was beyond the law. In other words, he seems to assume, like Guha and arguably Chatterjee, that the rule of law did not obtain in the colonies. This is a problematic assumption, as I will discuss below. The second and perhaps even more problematic assumption concerns the nature of the exception: despite his arguments that the exception constitutes what he repeatedly terms a 'zone of indistinction', to the contrary Agamben's characterisation nonetheless implies that it is possible in some clear way to distinguish between norm and exception, between a situation where the rule of law obtains in some or other clear-cut way and one where this is not the case.[59] In other

[58] This point can be illustrated in the case of the society Arendt is describing, namely colonial South Africa. Indeed, it helps one understand the role of the rule of law in the later manifestation of that colonial society in the form of its successor state: in the case of apartheid, the rule of law was formally upheld, though by means of the highly problematic 'plain-fact' approach. See for example D. Dyzenhaus, *Judging the Judges, Judging Ourselves* (Oxford: Hart, 1998), pp. 16–17.

[59] E.g., see Agamben, *Homo Sacer*, pp. 19, 21, 25 and 37; Agamben, *State of Exception*, p. 26. It should be noted that there are divergent interpretations of Agamben's understanding of the status of law in the exception. On the basis of statements such as that 'the state of exception [is] an emptiness and standstill of the law', Fleur Johns infers that for Agamben the exception 'is juridical in form and effect [yet embodies] an emptiness of law'. Agamben, *State of*

words, Agamben's off-hand characterisation of the colonial world as a world in which the law is suspended tends to downplay the processual, interactive nature of law and the rule of law: the fact that it involves a constant *negotiation* of the limits of the law and thereby of the relation between norm and exception. The point that I shall develop is that it is precisely in such negotiation that space can be opened for action. That is, the dialectic of 'stable determination and responsive change', which is part and parcel of law, enables the possibility of politics.[60] This suggests that we need to consider the sphere of politics as one *through which* to approach the emergency, the exception and the rule of law: a democratic politics is enabled by the rule of law just as it enables the rule of law.

Before elaborating on this crucial point in order to conclude the chapter, let me briefly sketch how Agamben's reading of Schmitt might relate to an understanding of the relationship between colonialism and current debates on states of exception and the rule of law. Following Schmitt, Agamben argues that the sovereign is defined by the decision as to the exception: the moment when the law is suspended is of cardinal importance here. Thus the sovereign *nomos* is 'the constitutive event of law'.[61] The state of exception is not merely outside the rule of the legal structure, that which is excluded from it, but it is that which makes the legal structure possible in the first place. It is thus both outside *and* inside the structure: it is a 'zone of indistinction between outside and inside, chaos and the normal situation'.[62] And it is 'the sovereign decision on the state of exception [which] opens the space in which it is possible to trace borders between inside and outside and in which determinate rules can be assigned to determinate territories'. Given the intricate relationship between the event of law and the exception which delimits it, then, one could understand Agamben's reading of Schmitt to suggest that the *nomos* of the *ius publicum Europaeum* is constituted by that which is excepted from it. In his reading, in other words, the legal order of metropolitan Europe, its

Exception, p. 48; F. Johns, 'Guantánamo Bay and the Annihilation of the Exception' (2005) 16 *European Journal of International Law* 624; also see Oren Gross's insightful discussion of Agamben's use of the *iustitium*, Chapter 3, which tends to confirm this reading. On the other hand, others have read Agamben as suggesting that 'zones of anomie and lawfulness [co-exist] ambiguously in the state of exception'. C. Campbell and I. Connolly, 'Making War on Terror? Global Lessons from Northern Ireland' (2006) 69 *Modern Law Review* 938.

60 P. Fitzpatrick, 'Tears of the Law: Colonial Resistance and Legal Determination', in K. O'Donovan and G.R. Rubin (eds.), *Human Rights and Legal History: Essays in Honour of Brian Simpson* (Oxford: Oxford University Press, 2000), p. 129.

61 Agamben, *Homo Sacer*, p. 36.

62 *Ibid.*, p. 19.

Ordnung, is dependent on the 'taking of land' (*Landesnahme*) which is also a 'taking of the outside' (*Ausnahme*).[63] This *Landesnahme*-as-*Ausnahme* is colonialism-as-exception.

It is important to be clear on the point that for Agamben the state of exception, despite the imbrication of norm and exception, constitutes a 'juridically empty' space.[64] Such a 'juridically empty' space would then historically be constituted by the colonies. It is Agamben's analysis that, starting with World War I:

> [The] constitutive link between the localization and ordering of the old *nomos* was broken and the entire system of the reciprocal limitations and rules of the *ius publicum Europaeum* brought to ruin. [This] has its hidden ground in the sovereign exception. What happened and is still happening before our eyes is that the 'juridically empty' space of the state of exception (in which law is in force in the figure – that is, etymologically, in the *fiction* – of its own dissolution, and in which everything that the sovereign deemed de facto necessary could happen) has transgressed its spatiotemporal boundaries and now, overflowing outside them, is starting to coincide with the normal order, in which everything again becomes possible.[65]

In Agamben's Schmittian understanding, the state of exception obtaining in the New World as a state of nature where everything was possible (and where, as we have seen Arendt note, 'natives' were supposed to be part of nature and therefore expendable as bare life) and which defined Europe and European law, is now as it were before our eyes returning to Euro-America. In other words, the lawlessness or condition beyond the law of the colonies is now no longer limited to the erstwhile colonies but extends back to the metropolis. Presumably this is then how Agamben would read not only the 2005 riots in the Parisian *banlieus* and in French cities more generally, but also 9/11, the Bali, Madrid and London bombings and current fears of terror. In Agamben's reading of Schmitt, the empire is striking back. North Africans, Palestinians and others, who either themselves or whose ancestors come from (erstwhile) colonies as zones beyond the law constituted by European colonial powers are now no longer only on the outside of Euro–America looking in. Agamben thinks that as instances of bare life they would in colonial times have been, in Schmitt's terms, 'outlaw[s] of humanity' so that colonial wars against them could 'thereby

[63] *Ibid.*, p. 19. [64] *Ibid.*, p. 38. See also n. 59. [65] *Ibid.*

be driven to the most extreme inhumanity'.[66] And today they are waging, so the argument would go, an anti-imperial war, though now the Empire is primarily that of the US and what it stands for and the bare life that defines the law is no longer limited to the safely distanced colonies from which labour and raw materials were once, and still are, being extracted.

V. Rule of law or rule of colonial difference?

However, the assumption that colonies constituted zones of exception in which the rule of law did not obtain is problematic. Colonialism, as noted above, is by far too vast and varied an enterprise to make generalisations that will hold across all contexts and both Schmitt's and Agamben's generalisations concerning it as constituting an instance of the exception therefore, in principle, become problematic. As an instance of this complexity, Lauren Benton in her study of legal regimes highlights the fact that 'groups seeking to undermine colonial law often found themselves arguing for broadening, rather than restricting, state jurisdictional claims so that rights recognised under state authority could be extended more widely'.[67] The apparent paradox here is striking: not only did the colonised often find themselves within the rule of law, but often they were, too, arguing to *extend* colonial law so as thereby to resist it more effectively. That is, a 'jurisdictional politics' arose that involved a negotiation of cultural boundaries which would be deployed in the resistance to colonialism. But, at the same time, while the broadening in some contexts of such legal authority therefore included the reach of the law and its extension to the colonised, in other settings those in power would seek to demarcate more clearly jurisdictional boundaries in order thereby to enhance state legal authority. This would sometimes lead to whole ethnic communities being outlawed and defined as 'criminal tribes' outside the law. In yet other contexts, attempts were made to strengthen colonial law by distinguishing it from so-called 'traditional law' which it would, in fact, 're-create in quite distorted forms'.[68]

Benton considers the colonial arena, in its diversity and complexity, to have been one where the colonised had agency and were by no means

[66] C. Schmitt, *Concept of the Political*, George Schwab (trans.) (Chicago: University of Chicago Press, 1996), p. 54.

[67] Benton, *Law and Colonial Cultures*, p. 15.

[68] *Ibid.* See also Benton's illuminating discussion, pp. 167–209, of legal pluralism in the Cape Colony and in early nineteenth-century New South Wales, which illustrate the complexities not only of the rule of law in colonial settings, but also its intersection with 'race'.

merely victims or just instances of bare life. She ends by formulating the crucial conclusion that the processes by means of which the modern colonial (and post-colonial) state came into being, involved a lengthy and convoluted *politics* whereby a diversity of legal systems were transformed, often violently but also often through complex negotiation, into the legal dominance of the colonial state: 'Colonial states did not in an important sense exist *as* states in the early centuries of colonialism. They did not claim or produce a monopoly on legal authority'.[69] It is, therefore, not the case 'that the rule of law [never] came to exist in colonial settings', which is how Benton paraphrases Guha's argument that we have already considered.[70] Rather, she argues that 'the colonial state emerged in part out of a legal politics engaging both colonizers and colonized', which allows her to qualify Guha's thesis by arguing in a much more nuanced way that the rule of law could and did exist in some colonial contexts and that it formed part of the thorough-going imbrication of colonial and indigenous practices: 'Guha is . . . right . . . that nineteenth-century state making was not the product of consensus . . . . But the forms of dominance taken were fashioned out of an interactive politics and not simply the logical extension of conquest'.[71]

This is a useful corrective to an overly simplistic view of the colonial world as a lawless zone of indistinction or space of exception. What Guha, as well as one might add Schmitt and Agamben, seems to be focusing on is one moment of colonialism, namely the moment of conquest when, indeed, brutal violence operated in a context that was lawless.[72] To consider the moment of conquest and its genocidal violence in these terms may be just, but to view late colonialism as characterised by the absence of the rule of law is to overlook the complexities involved in the dialectic between the colonial and the indigenous that resulted in the emergence of the colonial state. And, finally, viewing colonies as states or spaces of exception ruled by lawless violence neglects the role that law itself played in that colonial violence.[73]

[69] *Ibid.*, p. 259. [70] *Ibid.*, p. 255. [71] *Ibid.*, pp. 259–60. [72] *Ibid.*, pp. 258–9.

[73] See Hussain's discussion of the role played by the rule of law in establishing empire: one important justification for colonialism was that it supposedly brought the rule of law to primitive or despotic societies. Also significant is his characterisation of law as one of the instruments of violence in colonial regimes: rather than understanding the colonial world as a lawless vacuum, Hussain shows how law and its imposition forms part of colonial history itself and thereby how it has impacted on contemporary conceptions of the rule of law. N. Hussain, *The Jurisprudence of Emergency: Colonialism and the rule of law* (Ann Arbor: The University of Michigan Press, 2003). See also Gregory, 'The Black Flag: Guantánamo Bay and the Space of the Exception', 409–10.

Nevertheless, Agamben's work remains a timely reminder of the consequences of limiting the rule of law: such limitation does tend to produce what he terms bare life and we have seen this bare life produced in complex ways in Guantánamo Bay, Abu Ghraib, the invasion of Iraq and its current bloody aftermath. These places and these events, Agamben would suggest, reduce people to bare life that may be exterminated. They also thereby illustrate the dangers in defending threats to liberty through illiberal means: it is not even a matter that such defending discredits the liberal system it is meant to defend, but – and this is the real danger – they subvert that system itself. Limiting the rule of law, whether explicitly or by default, for instance in assuming that it cannot deal with emergency situations or needs to be limited so as to protect it from the risk of seepage, already subverts an essential aspect of the rule of law: that, as Dicey puts it, 'the law of the constitution is the result, not the source of the rights of individuals'.[74] The basis of law is constituted by fundamental values and rights; these are and should remain inalienable. To except the rule of law from certain situations is also to except the fundamental values and rights from which that law derives and it is therefore to subvert them.

VI. Conclusion: colonialism and a culture of justification

Paying attention to colonialism in the current debates concerning the limits of legality helps give us a broader view; it encourages us to resist the temptation of limiting the reach of the rule of law. In addition, it alerts us to the tendency of the exception to produce bare life: the rendering expendable of people, in this case, by means of illiberal procedures to protect liberal values. Yet there is also a danger in unreflectively absolutising these liberal-democratic values, as Arendt's work on totalitarianism suggests.

In the final chapter of *The Origins of Totalitarianism*, Arendt is concerned with what she terms 'the fundamental difference between the totalitarian and all other concepts of law'.[75] In claiming to represent justice as a transcendent principle or idea, totalitarianism in fact is claiming not to represent it at all but, rather, to present it in unmediated fashion: 'Totalitarian lawfulness, defying legality and pretending to establish the *direct* reign of justice on earth, executes the law of History or Nature without translating it into standards of right and wrong for individual

[74] Dicey, *Introduction to the Study of the Law of the Constitution*, p. 282.
[75] Arendt, *The Origins of Totalitarianism*, p. 462.

behavior'.[76] That is, 'totalitarian lawfulness' abstracts law and thereby elevates it to 'justice'; law here pretends to be the purity or essence of law, the concept of justice itself rather than its translation or interpretation. Totalitarianism's delusion is that it has a direct line to the transcendent, whether this be God or the master narrative of History or Nature. Totalitarian states tend to claim to have direct access to the Truth and to be the embodiment of True Justice. This is, among other things, what she means by the totalitarian 'identification of man and law'.[77]

Though Arendt has in mind totalitarian systems, in particular Stalinism,[78] we may with proper care extend her ideas to liberal democracies: 'Rights, positive law, constitutional frameworks – all contribute mightily to containing the tendency to treat human beings as raw material. Yet, from Arendt's perspective, liberalism fails to imagine or comprehend the worst, and therefore fails to see that the preservation of rights and procedural safeguards ultimately depends on worldliness'.[79] To treat human beings as raw material is to reduce them to bare life: the rule of law is crucial in containing the tendency so to reduce the arbitrariness and discretion inherent in the rule of men. But liberalism needs to remain vigilant, which is to say worldly; it needs to be actively *political*. Politics is here seen as the realm of the *vita activa*, the active life that engages in the world.[80] Arendt's work suggests that it is precisely when liberalism becomes unreflective, taking itself in an unquestioning way as given and its values as essential that the threat of totalitarianism is at its greatest. To stop the defence of non-tyrannical government from turning such government into tyranny, we need to be conscious that attempts to limit the reach of the rule of law – to see Guantánamo Bay or colonialism as exceptions that do not affect us and the liberal order of politics – are doomed to rebound, paradoxically, in the liberal deployment of tyranny.

Giving up on, or limiting the reach of, the rule of law in dealing with emergencies opens the door to the untenable contradiction that liberty

[76] *Ibid.*, my emphasis. [77] *Ibid.*

[78] But note that Arendt problematically 'makes terror the essence of totalitarian rule in what is now frequently regarded as an empirically unfounded comparison between the everyday life of the ethnic German under the National Socialist regime and the experience of the Soviet citizen under the Stalinist terror'. M. Halberstam, 'Hannah Arendt on the Totalitarian Sublime and Its Promise of Freedom', in S.A. Aschheim (ed.), *Hannah Arendt in Jerusalem* (Berkeley: University of California Press, 2001), p. 106.

[79] D.R. Villa, *Politics, Philosophy, Terror: Essays on the Thought of Hannah Arendt* (Princeton: Princeton University Press, 2000), p. 203.

[80] M. Canovan, 'Introduction', in H. Arendt, *The Human Condition* (Chicago: Chicago University Press, 1998), p. 15.

is sought to be protected through illiberal means such as the rendition of prisoners to countries where torture occurs or suspicionless preventive detention.[81] But even worse, such illiberal means bespeak a serious threat to perhaps one of the most important functions of law in liberal democracies, that is, in societies which are committed to the project of democracy. This threat is to the commitment of such societies to what might be call the justificatory culture of law that is anti-dogmatic and always open to inquiry, to being revisited and reconsidered. To impose the rule of law and believe in its good is, then, not to elevate it to some or other supra-historical or otherwise transcendent good – such as the 'True Justice' of totalitarianism – but precisely to keep questioning what we mean by the rule of law. To stop such interrogation and succumb to dogmatism would in principle open the way to a shift from the rule of law to the rule of men, and thence potentially to totalitarianism, as would an insistence on constituting law from the outside (as Schmitt would), through he who decides the exception. Rather, law in a liberal-democratic setting is best understood as 'self-constituting', since its authority as law fundamentally derives from its being law: it has 'authority over those subject to [its] power because it is wielded through law'.[82] Thus constituting law from the outside or delimiting its reach (which in the end amounts to something similar) is to delimit law in a way that is dangerous, not only for the well-rehearsed reason that it opens the door to discretion and prerogative but most especially since it subverts law's self-constitution.

Like democracy, the rule of law is a project that can in principle never finally arrive, for the political process of actively interrogating, negotiating and reflecting that is constitutive of democracy would end if it were, or were thought, to have arrived. For this reason 'the rule-of-law project' – understood as a legal culture of justification which consists to large measure of what we may call 'law talk', and thus forms part of a 'jurisdictional politics' – is an essential part of the democratic project.[83] Of course the

[81] On these means, and in particular the example of suspicionless preventive detention, see D. Cole, 'The Priority of Morality: The Emergency Constitution's Blind Spot' (2004) 113 *Yale Law Journal* 1753, which responds to B. Ackerman, 'The Emergency Constitution' (2004) 113 *Yale Law Journal* 1029. Also see Ackerman's response to Cole: B. Ackerman, 'This Is Not a War' (2004) 113 *Yale Law Journal* 1871.

[82] Dyzenhaus, Chapter 2, p. 34.

[83] For the rule-of-law project, see especially D. Dyzenhaus, *The Constitution of Law* (Cambridge: Cambridge University Press, 2006); on law as a culture of justification, see D. Dyzenhaus, *Recrafting the Rule of Law* (Oxford: Hart, 1999), pp. 7–10; for law talk and the allied idea of a legal frame, see Witt, 'Anglo-American Empire and the Crisis of the Legal Frame', 781–4 and *passim*.

rule of law is not some miraculous guarantee of freedom and justice. And it is true that certain dangers inhere in the rule of law, of which the foremost may well be the 'compulsion of legality' that characterises jurisdictional politics in liberal democratic states, a force which can serve to accord a 'veneer of legality' and therefore legitimacy to state actions.[84] But such dangers are part and parcel of democratic jurisdictional politics. And this is exactly where current debates on the rule of law and emergencies intersect most productively with questions of empire and colonialism: like those Victorians who defended Governor Eyre's actions in the Jamaica affair, would-be contemporary American imperialists who wish to export liberal values and democracy arguably also insist 'on an imperial exception to the rule of law in the governance of alien peoples'.[85] Such talk of an 'imperial exception' threatens to locate authority outside legality, particularly in the executive (compare the notion of an imperial presidency)[86] and thereby radically to undermine the very values that the (neo-)colonial empire is meant to export. This is a lesson contemporary democracies, especially those with imperial ambitions, whether openly articulated or not, would do well to remember.

[84] Dyzenhaus, Chapter 2, pp. 39 and 33.
[85] Kostal, *A Jurisprudence of Power*, p. 21.
[86] See W.E. Scheuerman, 'Presidentialism and Emergency Government' (Chapter 11), this volume.

15

Struggle over legality in the midnight hour: governing the international state of emergency

KANISHKA JAYASURIYA

I. Introduction

While it is premature to enter a final verdict on the impact of the events of 11 September 2001 on the political and constitutional order of liberal democracies, one point remains clear: the events of 9/11 have ushered in a vigorous and highly contested academic debate on issues relating to the state of emergencies and the rule of law. What is more, this is far from a mere academic debate. Practices such as torture that were once beyond the pale have now become matters of public concern and debate. Indeed, that these items are now on the public agenda is emblematic of the fact that the events of 9/11 have been influential in transforming our thinking about some fundamental constitutional principles and the institutional edifice of liberal democracies.

On this score there is some justification in Bruce Ackerman's provocative view[1] that the attacks of 9/11 have fundamentally altered the frameworks of the laws of war and crime in Western liberal democracies. In fact, Ackerman goes on to provide an innovative proposal to construct a limited term 'emergency regime' which will return to a *status quo ante* at the end of the emergency.[2] This chapter challenges the assumption implicit in Ackerman's work on emergency powers – an assumption shared by David

I am grateful for the comments and suggestions of participants in the workshop associated with this volume, most especially Victor V. Ramraj, Rueban Balasubramaniam and Johan Geertsema.

[1] B. Ackerman, 'The Emergency Constitution' (2004) 113 *Yale Law Journal* 1053–6.

[2] B. Ackerman, *We the People: Foundations* (Boston: Harvard University Press, 1991). In fairness to Ackerman's earlier work on constitutional transformation, it needs to be recognised that his argument was couched in terms of the domestic sources of constitutional change. In 'The Emergency Constitution', however, Ackerman assumes that the emergencies are externally driven events which require a response but leave the constitution itself intact. Yet this is exactly the divide between the external drives and constitutional structure that I contest in this paper.

Dyzenhaus and Oren Gross – that state responses to the events of 9/11 are situated primarily within a horizon of a national emergency. This assumption obscures the fact that the events of 9/11 have ushered in a distinct form of international emergency that reframes jurisdictional practices that have shaped national constitutional formations. In effect, 9/11 is a global state of emergency, the distinctive nature of which is the growth of a new jurisdiction of emergency governance layered on to the domains of national and international law. It produces forms of administrative power and regulation pertaining to acts in both the international and national domains of governance that bends and makes elastic the boundaries between state and non-state actors and civilians and combatants. The rigidity of these boundary distinctions has been crucial in shaping conditions of national citizenship. Consequently, changes in these boundaries will determine the way in which the state deals with its own citizens as well as persons outside its territory. The nub of my argument is that it is the interplay between jurisdictional domains and, in particular, the creation of distinctive legal regime of emergency governance that need to be at the forefront of the analysis of emergency law and politics.

This new international state of emergency in post-colonial international society creates distinctions between legal spaces that lead to the construction of new legal subjects and categories – for example, through new forms of preventive detention and control orders – which establish new legal jurisdictions within national constitutions. Further supplementing and reinforcing these practices of emergency governance is the UN Security Council Resolution 1373 that provides a framework for global administrative law to combat 'terrorism'[3] and establishes a Counter Terrorism Committee (CTC) to monitor and implement the resolution. This new framework requires 'extensive legislative and administrative changes, the resolution imposed a heavy burden on states, with smaller states particularly "overwhelmed". The CTC has not sanctioned states for non-compliance, instead pursuing a cooperative, non-threatening, technical and regulatory approach'.[4] Global emergency governance is primarily directed at reinforcing national legal and administrative rules and underscores the complex interplay between national and international law in crafting a jurisdiction of emergency governance.

[3] See, for example: B. Saul, *Defining Terrorism in International Law* (Oxford: Oxford University Press, 2006).

[4] *Ibid.*, p. 237.

This complex meshing of jurisdictional practices in emergency governance needs to be located on the wider stage of structural changes created by globalisation in national legal and constitutional practices. Just as the globalisation of production transforms the 'national space' on which domestic regulation takes place, the international state of emergency produces equally disruptive effects on the nationally defined jurisdictional practices of liberal constitutionalism. Novel administrative forms of power established through the exercise of emergency powers create new administrative domains 'in' and 'out' of the national state with strikingly similar effects to that produced by various forms of transnational regulatory governance that transcend the national and international divide.[5] In brief, the events of 9/11 as well as economic globalisation, disturb those constitutive jurisdictional practices comprising post World War II constitutional boundaries.[6] It is these same transnational processes that are working towards transforming our taken-for-granted constitutional practices.

Although the international state of emergency is a novel feature of post-colonial international society, it nevertheless has intriguing parallels with metropolitan responses to colonial emergencies within the liberal British Empire, such as that exemplified by the Jamaica affair examined

[5] See, for example: S. Picciotto, 'The Regulatory Criss-Cross: Interaction Between Jurisdictions and the Construction of Global Regulatory Networks', in W. Bratton *et al.*, *International Regulatory Competition and Coordination: Perspective on Economic Regulation in Europe and the United States* (Oxford: Clarendon Press, 1996); A. Slaughter, 'The Real New World Order' (1997) 76 *Foreign Affairs* 183; A. Slaughter, A. Tulumello and S. Wood, 'International Law and International Relations Theory: New Generation of Interdisciplinary Scholarship' (1998) 92 *American Journal of International Law* 367; W. Reinicke, *Global Public Policy* (Washington: Brookings, 1998); K. Jayasuriya, 'Globalization, Law and the Transformation of Sovereignty: The Emergence of Global Regulatory Governance' (1999) 6 *Indiana Journal of Global Legal Studies* 425; K. Jayasuriya, 'Globalisation, Sovereignty and the Rule of Law: From Political to Economic Constitutionalism?' (2001) 8 *Constellations* 442. The key point to note here is not transnational regulation per se but the way in which transnational regulation becomes entrenched within the governing apparatus of policy making.

[6] I say 'post World War II' because World War II and the ensuing Cold War determined a particular form of national and constitutional politics: see P. Bobbitt, *The Shield of Achilles: War, Peace and the Course of History* (New York: Knopf, 2002). But this view relies heavily on the idea that constitutional change is driven by the transformation of military technology and strategic policy. This is not a very satisfactory explanation of the casual process through which external forces impact on domestic constitutional transformations. I have attempted to provide a more politically inclined perspective in K. Jayasuriya, *Reconstituting the Global Liberal Order: Legitimacy and Regulation* (Oxford: Routledge, 2005) which tries to link the global constitutional settlements to the Cold War domestic social settlement. See also J. Suri, *Power and Protest: Global Revolution in the Age of Détente* (Cambridge: Harvard University Press, 2003).

below.[7] In fact, the 'the Anglo American law of empire has remained strikingly similar over the past 150 years, its landmarks remarkably little changed by the winds of time'.[8] However, while the issues between the two 'liberal empires' may not have changed, the political context of the current international state of emergency is very different as it is now within an international society in which established international legal principles are being jettisoned while at the same time liberal constitutional standards are bypassed through legal and administrative regimes of emergency governance. Nevertheless, there is continuity between the Anglo-American empires in this important sense: 'emergencies' unsettled those jurisdictional practices that underpinned national legal and political institutions and gave rise to various forms of jurisdictional politics – a politics centred around settling the competing jurisdictional claims arising from the creation of sites of emergency governance.

In times of political and legal crisis, those jurisdictional practices that shape boundaries and 'spaces' of constitutions are visible in sharp relief as they become subject to contention. This notion of constitutional spatiality is useful in that it captures the way the national frame of constitutional protection has been challenged by the so-called 'war on terror'.[9] Therefore, the response to the events of 9/11 goes to the heart of the nationally

[7] See also the work of N. Hussain, *The Jurisprudence of Emergency: Colonialism and the Rule of Law* (Ann Arbor: University of Michigan Press, 2003), who argues in a somewhat Schmittian fashion that the 'rule of law' depends on its relationship to its absence that is the exception. He argues that this is particularly pertinent in the colonial context where the 'writ of liberty' is in constant tension with the regimes of colonial rule and expansion. The tension between these two forces was crucial to the operation of colonial institutions. This is persuasive but as I argue below it is still a partial account of the law and politics of colonial emergencies. The other side of the question is the jurisdictional fluidity and contestation of the boundaries assigned by colonial authorities. It is the contest over the legal status of individuals under emergency regulation in the colonies, which is an important part of the jurisdictional politics of emergencies. This is a theme forcefully presented by Blinder – who argues for a pre-independence American transatlantic constitution that 'had grown to maturity as part of a conversation about when the laws of England applied and when local laws and practices could diverge because of the people and place. This culture came to revel in the existence and tension of dual authorities, it understood the advantages and disadvantages of having a distant decision maker, and linked constitutional interpretation to the changing substantive concerns of the empire'. M. Blinder, *The Transatlantic Constitution: Colonial Legal Culture and the Empire* (Cambridge, MA: Harvard University Press, 2004), p. 186. It is exactly these forms of juridical tensions and conflicts that characterise the international state of emergency but this is as much within the boundaries of the national constitution as outside of it.

[8] F. Witt, 'Anglo America and the Legal Frame (Will the Real British Empire Please Stand Up)' (2006) 120 *Harvard Law Review* 756.

[9] Jayasuriya, *Reconstituting the Global Liberal Order.*

constituted practices of jurisdictional politics across a range of liberal democracies to the extent that notions such as 'citizenship' are being transformed. In essence, the post-9/11 global emergency has fractured the contingent relationship between territory, national constitution, and citizenship, and this in turn has disrupted jurisdictional practices within and between nations.

In Part II, I analyse how the character of 9/11 as an international emergency has profound consequences for liberal constitutionalism creating a hybrid domain of emergency governance that cuts across and beyond the boundaries of liberal constitutionalism. But this is not an unproblematic process. It generates its own contradictions and tensions and for this reason the paper argues that emergency power be viewed as an instance of jurisdictional politics. In Part III, I explore the form of this jurisdictional politics as a 'struggle over legality'. This struggle over legality brings politics back into the analysis of emergency powers, but it is a politics moulded around competing normative-legal claims.

II. The international state of emergency and jurisdictional politics

We begin the analysis of jurisdictional politics with an examination of what has been termed the 'Schmittian problematic' of the emergency. In his comprehensive survey article on emergency powers, William Scheuerman[10] reminds us that the work of Carl Schmitt implicitly or explicitly continues to be an enduring influence on the debate over liberal constitutionalism and emergency powers. For Schmitt, emergencies remain an unavoidable fact of political life that cannot be dealt with by existing liberal norms and therefore require the exercise of 'pure decision' outside of, but yet within, the legal order. This is mainly because it is the legal order that must identify the actor who is to exercise this executive prerogative. In short, the 'exception is different from anarchy and chaos, order in the juristic sense still prevails even if it is not of the ordinary kind'.[11] The inability of liberalism to justify or sanction emergency powers means that liberal regimes are left with 'non-lawful' ways of dealing with a state of exception. Hence for Schmitt, the 'only apparent recourse available to political actors confronted with a political exception is to act illegitimately

[10] W.E. Scheuerman, 'Emergency Powers and the Rule of Law after 9/11' (2006) 14 *Journal of Political Philosophy* 161.

[11] C. Schmitt, *Political Theology: Four Chapters on the Concept of Sovereignty* (Cambridge: MIT Press, 1985), p. 12.

and hope to pass off such action as legitimate'.[12] Crucially, this Schmittian boundary of law and exception takes place within an assumed set of national boundaries. The national framing of the emergency is an enduring motif in the post-9/11 debate on constitutionalism and emergency powers.

However, the events of 9/11 characterise a novel kind of global emergency that has come under the rubric of the 'war on terror' which is a curious kind of war: it is not amenable to the traditional laws of war which regulate the conduct of conflicts between states. Conversely, the elements of domestic apparatus of law enforcement are being used to hinder or curtail the activities of all those who are engaged in this so-called war on terror. An international state of emergency is one that cuts across jurisdictional boundaries and is potentially not limited in duration or scope. It also involves action against transnational non-state actors, and is often driven by issues of identity. Rather than a direct threat to sovereignty, it is often perceived as an attack not on a particular nation but on a commonly shared set of political values. Consequently, an international emergency consists of the following: (a) political enemies who fall between criminal law and the law of war; and (b) a set of interrelated administrative measures that in effect amount to a specialised system of emergency governance located within the national state but simultaneously national and transnational in scope.

One of the major consequences of the international state of emergency is the criminalisation of international politics through the emergence of a new form of global administrative law against terrorism. In the aftermath of the events of 9/11, the Security Council passed Resolution 1373,[13] which imposed binding obligations on all members of the United Nations to adopt legislative and executive measures to combat terrorism. In fact, the Resolution incorporated instruments such as the Terrorism Financing Convention which do not have universal support within the ambit of this binding resolution.[14] In effect, the Resolution created a form of global administrative law that '. . . requires all member states to review their domestic law and practice to ensure that terrorists cannot finance themselves or find safe havens for adherents or their operatives on these states' territory'.[15] This new global administrative law shapes not only domestic

[12] J. McCormick, *Carl Schmitt's Critique of Liberalism: Against Politics as Technology* (New York: Cambridge University Press, 1997), p. 151.

[13] SC Res. 1373, 28 September 2001, S/RES/1373 (2001).

[14] B. Saul, *Defining Terrorism in International Law* (Oxford: Oxford University Press, 2006).

[15] E. Rosand 'Security Council Resolution 1373, the Counter-Terrorism Committee, and the Fight against Terrorism' (2003) 97 *The American Journal of International Law* 333 at 333.

law but also fundamental constitutional practices. Even as it criminalised terrorism, the UN Security Council failed to provide a consensus as to the definition of terrorism that could be incorporated in the Resolution. Nevertheless, Resolution 1373 provided an opportunity to introduce new measures through national legislation to combat money laundering and create a formal list of alleged terrorist organisations. These measures infringe basic constitutional values and principles, and effectively create a new specialised system of emergency governance.

This system of emergency governance is crucial to understanding the international state of emergency. Specialised systems of emergency governance create separate jurisdictions inside and outside national boundaries to monitor, control and detain those deemed to be a threat to the constitutional order. Indeed Guantánamo, far from being a 'legal black hole', is in fact a site of emergency governance that straddles national and international law, regulated by complex administrative regulations and subject to contestation by multiple authorities. These new spaces of emergency governance in liberal democracies serve to entrench a new supra-national administrative regime of regulating emergencies – various measures under the umbrella of Security Council Resolution 1373[16] but also through bilateral agreements on joint intelligence sharing,[17] the practice of rendition and even regulations on airline passenger data between the EU and the US[18] – thereby cutting across boundaries of national constitutions. Hence, one of the consequences of the post-9/11 global emergency is the creation of a new form of legal and administrative regime whose boundaries are contested by a process of jurisdictional politics.

The concept of 'jurisdictional politics' is borrowed from Lauren Benton's work on the long and contested shift from the legal pluralism of the early modern period to the state-centric law of the colonial period.[19] Benton argues that in the early modern period social actors operating in different legal regimes were able to construct a set of shared understandings

[16] B. Saul, *Defining Terrorism.*

[17] On US and EU intelligence cooperation see K. Archik, 'Europe and Counterterrorism: Strengthening Police and Judicial Cooperation', Congressional Research Service: Library of Congress Report RL 315109 (2006). Available at www.au.of.mil/au/awc/awigate/crs/r131509.pdf.

[18] 'EU, U.S. Clinch Air Passenger Data Deal' *Agence France Presse* (6 October 2006) on racial profiling and air travel. See also M.J. DeGrave, 'Airline Passenger Profiling and the Fourth Amendment: Will CAPPS II Be Cleared for Takeoff?' (2004) 10 *Boston University Journal of Science & Technology Law* 125.

[19] L. Benton, *Law and Colonial Cultures* (New York: Cambridge University Press, 2002).

of importance of law and legal institutions as mediating structures through which goods and information could cross borders. The intersection of these distinct legal jurisdictions is shaped by 'jurisdictional politics' which means '. . . conflicts over the preservation of, creation and nature of and extent of different legal forums and authorities'.[20] Jurisdictional politics provides a useful heuristic framework for analysing how the international state of emergency creates new jurisdictional practices that reach into and beyond national constitutional boundaries.

Jurisdictional politics is at the heart of the response of the US, UK and Australia to the attacks of 9/11. However, it is a response that denies the protection of the law of war to enemy combatants on the basis that it is not a conventional war between states. At the same time, individuals classified as 'enemy combatants' are denied the basic protections of domestic law on the grounds that they are engaged in a broader war on terror. These new legal categories and subjects belong to a specially created system of administrative regulation of 'enemy combatants'. Since 9/11 this system of emergency governance has been developed through the use of administrative regulation as well as legislation such as the Patriot Act in the US, a range of anti-terrorism legislation in the UK and the Anti Terrorism Bill 2005 in Australia. In Australia, for instance, the introduction of preventive detention, control orders, as well as specially designed 'rules of engagement', have, in effect, created a regulatory framework of emergency governance for 'enemy combatants'. The distinctive feature of this emergency governance is not the untrammelled exercise of sovereign decision[21] but the creation and entrenchment of new forms of administrative power and jurisdiction such as those over the treatment of 'enemy combatants'. The creation of these legal subjects and categories produces a trench of emergency governance in domestic and international law.

This point is best illustrated by examining the role of enemy combatants. Such enemy combatants occupy a status that David Caron[22] aptly describes as a legal void created when individuals fall between a 'legal

[20] *Ibid.*, p. 10.

[21] This is the central argument of those such as G. Agamben, *State of Exception* (Chicago: University of Chicago Press, 2005), who suggests these spaces amount to black holes that consists of what he calls 'bare life'. Agamben's 'Schmittian' notion of the camp as a field of bio politics existing outside of law represents a misreading of Schmitt who in *Political Theology* was certainly insistent that exception belongs to the constitutional order.

[22] D. Caron, 'The Rules of War: Emergency Rule Leaves Us Morally Ill At Ease' UC *Berkley News* (15 June 2004). Available at: www.berkeley.edu/news/media/releases/2004/06/15_caron.shtml.

enforcement box' and the 'international war crimes box'. In this sense, enemy combatants – nationally or internationally – fall into a legal black hole between the law of war and the law of crime. Hence, for the US it has been argued that the

> administration ignored both the law of war and constitutional requirements and established a new legal regime for the treatment of enemy combatants, largely in order to conduct interrogations with minimal constraints. The results have been disastrous. 'Guantanamo' has become a symbol throughout the world of U.S. disregard for the rule of law, even though the Afghanistan invasion itself was widely supported as justified and legal, and even though the taking of prisoners is a natural (and humane) consequence of such an invasion.[23]

These sentiments may well be justified, but the idea of a 'legal void' fails to acknowledge that jurisdictions and categories are in effect being created to control enemy combatants. More significantly this notion of a legal void continues to remain within a nationally based model of emergency that fails to recognise crucial boundary issues raised by the post-9/11 global emergency. These boundary issues concern the blurring of the boundary between domestic and transnational; the boundary between 'legitimate' and 'illegitimate' armed conflict; and the boundary between criminal law and political justice. Boundary issues such as these raise fundamental questions as to how this legal black hole transforms the implicit nationally based forms of constitutional jurisdiction. In essence, these new forms of legal practices change the territorial boundaries in which the constitution operates and show how flexible boundaries are increasingly used to deny access to constitutional protection.

The logic of the discussion so far about jurisdictional politics implies that we need to explore more carefully the role of territoriality in the shaping of constitutional regimes. Globalisation or transnationalisation unravels what we might broadly term the 'national space'[24] in which governance takes place. Therefore, the tension both John Ruggie and Charles Maier[25]

[23] K. Marin and J. Onek, '"Enemy Combatants" The Constitution and the Administration's "War on Terror"' (2004) *American Constitution Society for Law and Policy* 19. Available at www.acslaw.org/pdf/enemycombatants.pdf.

[24] See here, for example, the work of H. Lefebvre, *The Production of Space* (Oxford: Blackwell, 1991), which has been instrumental in pointing to the way in which the organisation of capitalist production transforms the perception and representation of those spaces that are central to the understanding of governance.

[25] J. Ruggie, 'Territoriality and Beyond: Problematizing Modernity in International Relations' (1993) 47 *International Organisation* 139; C. Maier, 'Consigning the Twentieth Century to

emphasise between governance and national territorial space may be seen as the defining feature of the emerging new global order.[26] Governance and territoriality are being uncoupled in a way that challenges the traditional 'Westphalian' frame of politics and law. The slow but steady eclipse of this 'Westphalian' frame poses immense difficulties for the traditional antinomies – between legality and legitimacy and between sovereignty and society – that underpinned the 'governmental' model of sovereignty. However, far from being a wholesale displacement of sovereignty, the international state of emergency reflects the emergence of new forms of complex sovereignty.[27] This transformation is best understood in terms of the emerging jurisdictional politics – and more especially a transnational domain of emergency governance – that cuts across the more conventional and national constitutional boundaries.

The adoption of this framework of jurisdictional politics allows us to locate the significance of the post-9/11 international state of emergency in terms of two contending forces, namely, globalisation and national territoriality of legal spaces. One of the few to seriously consider the relationship between territoriality and legal transformation is Kal Raustiala[28] who in his innovative essay analyses what he terms 'legal spatiality'.[29] Legal spatiality, which is intrinsically tied up with conceptions of the Westphalian territorial state, cannot be understood solely through reference to domestic causal factors. Rather, broad shifts in international relations, both economic and political, appear to have influenced legal conceptions of territoriality in the US.[30]

History: Alternative Narratives for the Modern Era' (2000) 105 *American Historical Review* 807. Emergency governance of the kind described in this paper may reflect the unbundling of territoriality from national constitutional boundaries whose multiple boundaries now extend both outside and inside national territorial spaces.

26 C. Maier, 'Consigning the Twentieth Century to History: Alternative Narratives for the Modern Era'.

27 For the notion of 'complex sovereignty' see K. Jayasuriya, *Reconstituting the Global Liberal Order.*

28 K. Raustiala, 'The Evolution of Territoriality: International Relations and American Law', Research Paper No 05–6, University of California, Los Angeles (2003). Available at http://papers.ssrn.com/sol3/papers.cfm?abstract_id=700244.

29 For a discussion of the relationship between geography and law see R. Ford, 'Law's Territory (A History of Jurisdiction)' (1999) 97 *Michigan Law Review* 843. P. Passavant, *No Escape: Freedom of Speech and the Paradox of Rights* (New York: New York University Press, 2002) draws attention to the importance of moral geography in delineating who has constitutional rights.

30 Raustiala, 'The Evolution of Territoriality', 32.

Raustiala identifies the powerful structural forces – such as the very specific form that globalisation has taken in the last decades – which have led to the growing influence of legal extra-territoriality, and he notes that in the long term this legal spatiality waxes and wanes with the political interests of key political actors and institutions. But the problem with this argument is that 'extra-territoriality' may not be all that unique. As Raustiala points out, there is a long history of the US establishing separate extra-territorial jurisdiction in colonial contexts such as in the Philippines or China. In both colonial and contemporary cases, it is not so much extra-territoriality that is reflected but the creation and determination of different jurisdictional domains for the treatment of non-citizens.

Moreover, this reduction of legal spatiality to the mere assertion of 'extra-territoriality' has limits that become evident when we look more closely at constitutional structures. Here, what matters is not so much extra-territoriality, but the drawing of internal and external boundaries that no longer coincide with territorial boundaries. For instance, the treatment of enemy combatants through such legal instruments as control orders in Australia and the UK (to be discussed below) is not really an assertion of extra-territoriality but a redrawing of internal boundaries within nationally defined constitutional structures. Or take, for example, the even more contentious issue of the monitoring and regulation of Muslim citizens in Western Europe, where the policing and monitoring of internal boundaries are of crucial significance.[31]

It is not extra-territoriality per se that distinguishes emergency law in the post-9/11 period, but rather an international state of emergency that regulates international politics as a form of crime control. This crime control approach can be found in the use of rendition by nationally based agencies, such as the CIA, to take people outside the territorial boundaries of the US to prisons where prisoners – including citizens of allied countries – can be denied constitutional protection against torture.[32] In a similar way, domestic law becomes enmeshed in international politics with grave implications for fundamental constitutional protections. For example,

[31] C. Joppke, 'The Retreat of Multiculturalism in the Liberal State: Theory and Policy' (2004) 55 *British Journal of Sociology* 237; M. Mamdani, *Citizen and Subject: Contemporary Africa and the Legacy of Late Colonialism* (Princeton: Princeton University Press, 1996). See also K. Engle, 'Constructing Good Aliens and Good Citizens: Legitimizing the War on Terror(ism)' (2004) 75 *University of Colorado Law Review* 59.

[32] For example, see Report on British complicity in US rendition. I. Cobain and L. Harding, 'UK "breaking law" over CIA secret flights' *The Guardian* (5 December 2005). Available at http://politics.guardian.co.uk/foreignaffairs/story/0,11538,1657737,00.html.

the introduction of financial regulation of charities, in part through the application of the international regulation, shapes fundamental practices such as freedom of association and speech within national constitutions.[33]

In each of these examples, what matters in shaping 'constitutional spatiality' is the way the international state of emergency reframes the internal and external boundaries of the national constitution. For this reason, it is more useful to consider constitutional-spatiality rather than extra-territoriality in terms of the emergence of new jurisdictional domains that weaken the link between territoriality and national constitutional structures. Consider, for example, the way global administrative law on terrorism conflicts with international obligations on human rights. This is underlined by Vivek Kanwar who, in an insightful article, identifies[34] the emerging system of international governance as part of the fragmentation of international law. Fragmentation of this sort is not inconsistent with our argument, but we need to go beyond this to look at the implications of fragmentation for the jurisdictional practices within the national container of liberal constitutionalism.

We need to be clear on one point. What is distinctive about 'constitutional spatiality' in the post-9/11 context is not that external influences have suddenly become more important for constitutional practices – they have always been important – but the fact that new transnational trenches of administrative control are being constructed alongside, and within, existing constitutional practices. To the extent that 'constitutional spatiality' is a product of various jurisdictional practices, it is apparent that these practices have been unsettled as a consequence of the international state of emergency. Hence, the international state of emergency represents a form of jurisdictional politics which is an intrinsic feature of the creation of legal spaces that often requires the use of novel techniques and instruments of administrative power that may create new kinds of legal subjects.

[33] N. Healy, 'The Impact of September 11th on Anti-Money Laundering Efforts and the European Union and Commonwealth Gatekeeper Initiatives' (2002) 36 *International Lawyer* 733–49; A. Hardister, 'Can We Buy Peace on Earth? The Price of Freezing Terrorist Assets in a Post-September 11 World' (2003) 28 *North Carolina Journal of International Law and Commercial Regulation* 605; C. Larose, 'International Money Laundering Abatement and Anti-Terrorism Financing Act of 2001' (2004) 30 *Journal of College and University Law* 417.

[34] V. Kanwar, 'International Emergency Governance: Fragments of a Driverless System' (2004) 7 *Critical Sense* 41. Especially useful in Kanwar's article is the notion of the driverless system of emergency governance.

Boundaries are a recurring motif in this framework of emergency powers. Constitutional boundaries determining who has access to certain legal forums, resources and rights are – to use the apt phrase of Sarat *et al.* – 'constituted and policed'. It is the boundaries themselves that shape the nature of the constitution through boundaries 'that create and effectuate the rule of law through the peculiar artifice of establishing boundaries and policing border'.[35] In periods of constitutional transformation, fluid jurisdictional boundaries create new categories of legal subject, forums and procedures of governance that run through systems of legal and social governance. Hence we need to ask: what determines the politics of boundary making? And here the lens of our jurisdictional political framework is particularly relevant and valuable in that it would enable us to observe the jurisdictional practices which are constantly transformed by individuals and groups seeking to resist, accommodate and contest these practices.

A close parallel to jurisdictional politics can be found in Israel's response to emergency through what Bauruch Kimmerling[36] calls the 'internal control system'. According to this system, constitutional practices in effect create a distinctive zone of regulatory control for Jewish and Arab citizens and individuals in Israel and the occupied territories. What is distinctive about this zonal system[37] is that it produces new forms of constitutional spatiality which in turn create new legal subjects and categories and also define the boundaries of politics. Analogously, colonialism has created a set of jurisdictional politics that led to a constitutional topography which differed from those associated with the more uniform jurisdictional practices of liberal constitutions.[38] Of course, these are only analogies, but they do serve to underline the crucial role of emergency politics in the cartography of new forms of constitutional spatiality.

The importance of emergency powers lies in the fact that it establishes an increasingly complex system of administrative regulation that develops across jurisdictions. As such, various emergency laws – particularly in

[35] A. Sarat, L. Douglas and M. Umphrey (eds.), *The Limits of Law* (Palo Alto: Stanford University Press, 2005).

[36] B. Kimmerling, *The Invention and Decline of Israeliness: State, Society and the Military* (Berkeley: University of California Press, 2001).

[37] It also provides, as Passavant notes, a complex moral geography for constitutional practices: see Passavant, *No Escape*.

[38] See, for example: M. Mamdani, *Citizen and Subject: Contemporary Africa and the Legacy of Late Colonialism* (Princeton: Princeton University Press, 1996); C. Elkins, *Imperial Reckoning: The Untold Story of Britain's Gulag in Kenya* (New York: Henry Holt and Company, 2005); Hussain, *The Jurisprudence of Emergency*.

the US, UK and Australia – reflect the contentious consolidation of the new administrative sphere of emergency politics. These new boundaries and categories of 'enemy combatants' within domestic law extend far beyond criminal law to various areas of domestic governance ranging from immigration control to issues of academic freedom.[39] It amounts to the proliferation of new forms of institutions that regulate the individual within spaces of emergency regulation.

III. The struggle over legality

The exercise of executive power over Guantánamo, the issuing of control orders and the practices of rendition can thus be seen as attempts to create new jurisdictional practices. The significance of the events of 9/11 is that it produced a global emergency that has ruptured the contingent relationship between territory, national constitution and citizenship, thereby creating a regime of emergency governance that disrupts jurisdictional practices within and between nations. Here, it is important to note that emergency governance implies a process of legal classification of specific acts and individuals as enemy combatants rather than the suspension of law within a specific territory. It is a system of emergency governance that runs across and within national boundaries. For this reason it is difficult to imagine the operation of something like Gross's extra-legal model of emergency governance within the context of this global emergency.

Yet, these jurisdictional regimes are contested and resisted through the legal process. The consequent jurisdictional politics will reflect the tensions and contradictions as individuals and groups contest their inclusion and treatment within jurisdictional domains. And this political resistance indicates a failure to create a stable legal configuration of jurisdictional practices. Law and politics might thus be seen as competing explanations of emergency powers but the thrust of the argument here is that law and politics are mutually constitutive. Political claims have to be framed in terms of competing legal understandings of the extent and reach of executive power. Jurisdictional politics is not merely a subterfuge for political struggles. It is this issue that I examine in the section below.

[39] See, for example, B. Doumani, *Academic Freedom After 9/11* (Cambridge: MIT Press, 2006) and J.L. Keith, 'The War on Terrorism Affects the Academy: Principal Post-September 11, 2001 Federal Anti-Terrorism Statutes, Regulations and Policies that Apply to Colleges and Universities' 30 (2004) *Journal of College & University Law* 239–335 for an overview of issues raised by the events of 9/11 for issues of academic freedom.

David Dyzenhaus argues that there is a normative 'compulsion of legality' in rule-of-law states.[40] This compulsion of legality amounts to a shared sense of the fundamental values of the legal order such that 'compulsive' pressures to legality remain grounded in a notion of legality as a shared project among the legislative, executive and judiciary. In this model, the judiciary has an especially prominent role given the fact that the 'constitutional role of judges is to see to it that the fundamental values of the legal order are preserved by whatever means are most appropriate'.[41] On this view, judges must adopt the position – unless explicitly told by the government that the executive is operating outside of the rule of law – that the legislature and the executive share in a common rule-of-law enterprise.

There is considerable merit in this model of legality as a mode of regulating the jurisdictional politics of international emergencies. Nevertheless, the difficulty with this notion of 'compulsion to legality' is its association with a controversial substantive conception of the rule of law. However, as Dyzenhaus in this volume recognises, many of the spaces of legal 'exception' may well be given a 'thin veneer of legality'[42] by either legislative action or judicial validation of various courses of emergency action such as detention without trial. Although the compulsion of legality may lead institutions of legal order to 'cooperate in devising controls on public actors which ensure that their decisions comply with the principle of legality', it can also set in motion a cycle of legality in which 'the content of legality is understood in an ever more formal or empty manner' contrary to the rule-of-law project.[43] This caveat to the compulsion of legality is better understood to mean that in times of crisis and emergency the taken-for-granted assumptions of legality are subject to political contention. Legality, then, is the basis on which contention is organised as both government officials and individual citizens engage in the push and pull of jurisdictional politics.

There is a parallel here with similar conflicts over jurisdictional politics in the British colonial empire. Perhaps the most well-known case in this regard is the so-called 'Jamaica affair' – the subject of recent major work by Kostal[44] – which welled to the surface of public consciousness of the

[40] D. Dyzenhaus, *The Constitution of Law: Legality in a Time of Emergency* (Cambridge: Cambridge University Press, 2006).

[41] *Ibid.*, p. 216.

[42] Dyzenhaus, 'The Compulsion of Legality' (Chapter 2), this volume, p. 56.

[43] *Ibid.*

[44] R. Kostal, *A Jurisprudence of Power: Victorian Empire and the Rule of Law* (Oxford: Oxford University Press, 2005).

deep constitutional and legal dilemmas for a liberal empire created by the use of martial law in colonial jurisdictions. The case arose from the actions taken by Edward Eyre, the Governor of Jamaica, in the brutal suppression of an uprising in the town of Morant Bay and the execution of a prominent coloured leader under the auspices of martial law in 1865. Back in England, these actions provoked a protest against as well as strong showing of support for Eyre's conduct. All this led the formation of the 'Jamaica Committee' whose membership included John Stuart Mill. The intention of the Committee was to persuade the government to establish an investigation into the actions of Eyre and, more importantly, to pursue criminal prosecutions against Eyre.

We use the example of the Jamaica affair for our discussion of jurisdictional politics as a means of constructing our framework of emergency powers as struggle for legality. The comparison allows us to highlight the similarities and differences between the current global emergency and the dispute over the declaration of martial law within the British Empire. In particular, there are several significant features of the legal debate on the Jamaica affair, which are relevant for our analysis of emergency powers. The Jamaica affair as well as the use of emergency powers in the post-9/11 global emergency involve a legal debate about the reach and purpose of extra-territorial constitutional power which is: framed in terms of competing normative-legal claims about the purpose and limits of executive action in peripheries of the empire; concealed in a deeper political struggle for legality and politics; and assumed as an implicit relationship between the colonies and the metropolis as the working of a moral geography law. The next three sections will consider these points in turn.

A. Competing normative-legal claims

The entire debate over the Jamaica affair demonstrates something akin to Dyzenhaus's compulsion of legality. Significantly, both critics and supporters of Eyre's action felt compelled to justify their actions in legal terms, that is, in terms of the limits and boundaries of state power under emergency conditions. In fact, the struggle over legality itself masked a set of important and shared legal consciousness which facilitated the argument over competing legal claims about the justifiability of martial law. And this has a resonance with the current debates about international emergency. But perhaps more importantly, the Jamaica affair highlighted the fact that times of crisis are precisely those times when taken-for-granted assumptions about state power – in this case the legal permissibility of executive action in the colonies – become the subject of legal debate. This is clearly the case with the current global emergency where the taken-for-granted assumptions such as detention without trial and the use of torture become contentious issues. Nevertheless, there is one key difference from the Jamaica affair. In the US, UK and Australia, the main protagonists seeking to challenge and shift taken-for-granted legal assumptions are not those outside the executive but individuals and groups within the executive.

In terms of this broader jurisdictional politics of legality we can identify cases such as *Hamdi* v. *Rumfeld* in the US regarding the definition of enemy combatants as emblematic of a struggle over the legality of newly created jurisdictions of emergency governance and the nature of its relationship to judicial power. The case concerned the legality of the detention of Hamdi, an American citizen whom the government has classified as an 'enemy combatant' for allegedly taking up arms with the Taliban. In fact, the factual grounds for this categorisation as an 'enemy combatant' were only on the basis of a six-page document written by Michael Mobbs to Defence Undersecretary Douglas Feith. Hamdi's father filed a habeas corpus petition on his behalf and the Appeal Court decided that he was entitled only to limited inquiry into his detention under the war powers of the political branches. The plurality of Supreme Court judges in reversing this decision of the Appeal Court argued that 'although Congress authorized the detention of combatants in the narrow circumstances alleged here, due process demands that a citizen held in the United States as an enemy combatant be given a meaningful opportunity to contest the factual basis for that detention before a neutral decision maker'.[45]

The case was primarily framed in terms of separation of powers and not in terms of Hamdi's legal rights.[46] Separation of powers issues are important, but it is equally important to realise that pivotal here is the particular category of 'enemy combatants' which transforms the legal status and identity of the individual even in the case of a US citizen. Pushing individuals into this jurisdiction determines the identity of the legal subject as well as the forum through which the individual's case is decided. Therefore, the 'the enemy designation makes the difference

[45] *Hamdi* v. *Rumsfeld*, 542 U.S. 507 at 507 (2004), *per* Justice Sandra Day O'Connor.

[46] C. Wilke, 'War v Justice: Terrorism Cases, Enemy Combatants and Political Justice in US Courts' (2005) 33 *Politics and Society* 4, 637–99 at 645.

between the treatment that Hamdi was accorded and the treatment that a criminal suspect in the United States is normally accorded'.[47]

It is this legal subject and category of 'enemy combatant' and corresponding narrowing of rights for these subjects that is distinctive in the new domain of transnational emergency regulation. Even while the court upheld the petition, these legal categories themselves were given legitimacy. But this does not mean the boundaries or the rules and procedures for the designation of 'enemy combatants' are fixed. Rather, cases such as *Hamdi* demonstrate the often ambiguous boundaries of the category of 'enemy combatants' as well as the limits of administrative discretion in the treatment of such individuals. For this reason, such cases amount to what may be called 'rules of engagement' between the judiciary and system of emergency governance. In effect, these rules of engagement create a novel form of jurisdictional politics in the wake of the post-9/11 international emergency.

B. The relationship between law and politics

A defining feature about the Jamaica affair was that while remaining as a struggle over legality, this legal debate itself was underpinned by competing political alliances. Hence, as we have argued, political conflict is intrinsic to the struggle for legality. Kostal argues that the paradox of the Jamaica affair is that it stopped being about Jamaica and at the

> end of 1866 the affair had metamorphosed into a dispute over English law and politics. This was the result of agency and circumstance. Under the leadership of Mill the Jamaica Committee redefined the controversy. The Jamaica affair was no longer mainly about the violence done to the hapless black peasantry. It was now mainly about the violence done to the laws of England.[48]

In this regard, Kostal notes that one of the concerns of the Jamaica Committee was that conceding the case might well provide a legal foundation for executive power to be used against political movements in England, such as, for example, those proposing to broaden the franchise.

At issue in various cases such as *Hamdi* and the use of control orders in Australia or the UK is the juridical construction of 'enemy combatants'. But this juridical construction is an intrinsically political process of deciding who is a threat to the political order. The critical issue here is that

[47] *Ibid.*, at 645. [48] Kostal, *A Jurisprudence of Power*, p. 190.

the emerging jurisdictional politics is not merely about the differential treatment of enemy combatants but rather about the very boundaries of the political. Here Kimmerling's work is especially significant because he describes the way in which the 'the state's multiple, yet simultaneously invoked, social and political boundaries'[49] work to define the political status of citizenship and the resulting entitlements to political and civil rights. Emergencies compel liberal empires to invoke these multiple boundaries of citizenship, at the edges of which there is constant conflict and resistance. In this sense, the jurisdictional politics of liberal empires is about the boundaries of the 'political' itself.

But there is another sense in which this struggle over legality is political. Again, the Jamaica affair is instructive because of the intriguing role of the Jamaica Committee itself. Here, struggle over legality depends not on the exemplary actions of the judiciary but rather on the strength of political debate in the public sphere. Yet, what is most striking about the current global emergency is that the public sphere itself is rather muted. Indeed, the pervasive politics of fear[50] in advanced liberal democracies militates against such robust contention. Therefore, it may well be that the burden Dyzenhaus places on the judiciary as the primary agent in the 'compulsion of legality' could be misplaced. The Jamaica affair reveals and the post-9/11 events confirm that the taproots of such a compulsion of legality depend on the existence of a critical public sphere within the liberal democracies.

More broadly, the Jamaica affair highlights the fact that the legal dispute was the site of a political struggle over the nature and purpose of state power. The Jamaica Committee's response to martial law was primarily driven by the fears of the dire effects of martial law on domestic political opposition. There is a similar domestic political logic in the legal claims for expanded executive power that seeks to contest those civil and political rights that have been entrenched in the post-war period. But the crucial difference is that this push to create and expand new forms of executive power emanates from the administration of President George Bush or the British Cabinet. Reinforcing my arguments, Greenhouse[51] has recently pointed out that many of the arguments for military tribunals or commissions in the United States echo numerous political struggles by

49 B. Kimmerling, 'Jurisdiction in an Immigrant Settler Society: the "Jewish and democratic state"' (2002) 35 *Comparative Political Studies* 10, 1119–44 at 1123.

50 Jayasuriya, *Reconstituting the Global Liberal Order.*

51 C. Greenhouse, 'Hegemony and Hidden Transcripts: The Discursive Arts of Neoliberal Legitimation' (2005) 107 *American Anthropologis* 3 at 356–68.

conservative administrations and politicians against civil rights. Indeed, Greenhouse argues that there is a hidden transcript – using the terminology of Scott[52] – which portray 'civilian institutions as forums where efficiency is hindered by rules of procedure crafted to protect civil rights by the advocates these commentators delegitimate (and even caricature) as "liberals"'.[53] The paramount issue here is that legal contests reflect deeper and ongoing political struggles over constitutional narratives of state power.

In this regard, one of the striking elements in the response to the events of 9/11 as compared with the passions aroused by the Jamaica affair is the absence of sustained political movements against such measures as detention without trial or the use of control orders. These differences may, in turn, direct us towards a more fundamental transformation within political liberalism. I have argued elsewhere that in advanced liberal democracies political freedom comes to be understood not in terms of the practices in the public sphere but in terms of the form of threats to common values or a 'way of life'.[54] The significance of articulating political freedom in this way is that the political and legal order is directed towards the subjective affirmation of particular modes of existence and the identification of threats to these forms of life. This is done even at the cost of commitment to formal processes of legality and principles of political equality that underpin this legal order. There is here a significant deviation from, even an implicit hostility to, both legality and universal political principles such as political equality. Political unity is defined in terms of adherence to a common set of values. By challenging the core values of the political system, we endanger the moral basis and legitimacy of a liberal political culture. Political freedom is defined in terms of adherence to a common set of values under attack from an undefined enemy. It is an understanding of liberal freedom which ironically leads to deeply illiberal practices.

C. Risk and moral geography of law

The Jamaica affair brings us to a consideration of the competing geographies of law. Of course, central to the Jamaica affair – even though it was essentially an internal legal debate – was a moral geography of law. Over

[52] J. Scott, *Domination and the Arts of Resistance: Hidden Transcripts* (New Haven: Yale University Press, 1990).

[53] Greenhouse, 'Hegemony and Hidden Transcripts', 363.

[54] Jayasuriya, *Reconstituting the Global Liberal Order.*

and above the essentially legal and political debate, the case was as much about the potential treatment of non-English speaking people within the context of a liberal empire. Indeed for the defenders of Eyre's action, the relationship between legal spaces in the colonies and the metropolis overlapped a moral geography of law, that is, that colonial subjects were not be entrusted with the legal rights held by those in the metropolis. Instead of this moral geography of law, advocates of specialised domains of emergency governance now use the language of risk management so that various groups and individuals are now thought to pose a particular risk to the political order. It is this new model of risk management that for the large part determines the classification of individuals, and acts as threats to the political order. Hence this risk management leads to the framing and construction of political enemies; it is an intrinsically political form of risk management.

A novel element of new detention regimes is the use of preventive detention to control individuals who are considered to be 'at risk' to the political order. 'At risk' here invokes time itself as a factor in justifying the expansion of the administrative power of intelligence and security agencies. It is argued that such agencies are best placed to determine this future 'risk liability'. Not only does this notion of risk embedded in these conceptions limit the oversight of judicial agencies, it also crucially serves to diminish the role of representative assemblies and the contestation and pluralism central to these assemblies. Hence the effect of legal instruments such as the control and preventive detention orders is to create new legal categories and legal spaces that effectively constitute a category of 'political enemies' distinct from the normal criminal law.[55] This definition of the political enemy 'at a minimum suggests the plausibility of relaxed standards. At the extreme, the enemy designation denies the other's legal and moral personality. Public vilification can therefore legitimise infringements and defendants' rights'.[56] Here it is interesting to note some parallels with Schmitt's definition of the 'partisan'[57] where those enemies are outside the law because of their irregular status, their mobility and their territorial attachment. The point is that these 'irregulars' are seen to fall outside the normal laws of war because they do not share with the adversary the law

[55] See Kanwar, 'International Emergency Governance', for an application of this notion of fragmentation to international emergency governance.

[56] Wilke, 'War v Justice', 657.

[57] See, for example, W.E. Scheuerman, 'Carl Schmitt and the Road to Abu Ghraib' (2006) 13 *Constellations* 108.

of war and its traditions. This has certainly become an important element in the treatment of foreign enemy combatants as outside the normal standards of international law.

In this context, the partisan enemy for Schmitt is something that is 'existentially different' and therefore must be fought with all the necessary means at disposal and this means that the enemy is placed beyond the normal laws of war. Hence 'neither law nor independent judgment nor the idea of justiciable offense have a place'.[58] However, the relevant point to be underscored is that these designated enemies are placed within distinctive domains and the construction of these domains shapes the meaning and boundaries of politics. Certainly conservative lawyers such as John Yoo within President Bush's administration wrote a memorandum that became the basis of legal justification of the detention policy.[59] The memo argued that in wartime the President could use any method to deal with enemies. Yoo's description of the enemy and its possible treatment certainly has much in common with Schmitt's views.[60]

But the argument is equally applicable to domestic enemies. Let me illustrate with some recent Australian legislation. Under Australian legislation a preventive detention order authorises Federal Police to take a person into custody for a possible 48 hours. In conjunction with state laws, this period may be extended for a longer period. The New South Wales Terrorism (Police Powers) Act allows detention for up to 14 days. Control orders are issued for the purpose of monitoring, and restricting, the activities of persons who may potentially engage in acts of terror. Breaching the control order is subject to a maximum of five years' imprisonment. Senior members of the Australian Federal Police can request a control order and with the written consent of the Attorney General may apply to the Federal Court or the Federal Magistrates' Court to issue an interim order. A former Australian High Court judge notes that this involvement of the judiciary amounts to an 'attempt to vest Federal Courts with a power that

[58] Wilke, 'War v Justice', 659.

[59] The memorandum is reprinted as 'Memo 4 – Application of Treaties and Laws to al Qaeda and Taliban Detainees' (January 9, 2002) in K.J. Greenberg and J.L. Dratel (eds.), *The Torture Papers: The Road to Abu Ghraib* (New York: Cambridge University Press, 2005), pp. 38–79.

[60] This is a point superbly made by Scott Horton on the Balkanisation blog. Horton argues that for 'Schmitt, the key to successful prosecution of warfare against such a foe is *demonization*. The enemy must be seen as absolute. He must be stripped of all legal rights, of whatever nature. The Executive must be free to use whatever tools he can find to fight and vanquish this foe'. S. Horton, 'The Return of Carl Schmitt' *Balkinization* (7 November 2005). Available at http://balkin.blogspot.com/2005/11/return-of-carl-schmitt.html.

is non-judicial'.[61] Control orders are a form of preventive detention which stands outside the normal criminal and penal law, and, perhaps more significantly, signals a regime of monitoring and supervision of individuals on the basis of the potential risk they pose to the political order.

These new categories of risk remain essentially political and to that extent control orders and preventive detention remain instances of 'political justice'.[62] But this is political in a very curious way. The category of the public or political enemy originates outside the legal system but is then given validity and recognition within the legal system. In the development of these new detention regimes both globally and nationally one sees the growth of new forms of 'ethical' criteria or 'moralism' which are then given recognition within emergent regulatory systems. These new regulatory systems point to the troubling emergence of a form of natural law that is increasingly playing a significant role in domestic and international law. In this regard Kanwar has drawn pointed attention to the deformalisation and fragmentation of international law.[63] To be sure, these new forms of governance are based on notions such as 'risk management' that are only tenuously connected to older notions of natural law. Yet, these practices still depend on practices of risk management that lie outside the formal legal system.[64] In a more significant sense, the corollary of the fragmentation of constitutional spatiality is the emergence of these new incarnations of natural law. These departures from legal formalism are at the very heart of the political equality deliberation and contestation that was – albeit very imperfectly – a part of legal formalism.

IV. Conclusion

The growing scholarly literature on transnational regulation transcends the unhelpful dichotomy between national and transnational. Transnational regulation not only becomes embedded within the governing apparatus of the national state, but is also situated within an interlocking web of

[61] M. McHugh, 'Terrorism Legislation and the Constitution' (2006) 28 *Australian Bar Review* 117.

[62] Wilke, 'War v Justice'.

[63] See Kanwar, 'International Emergency Governance' for an application of this fragmentation argument to international emergency governance. But what this argument needs is more explicit recognition of the nature of the international state of emergency.

[64] Indeed they depend on what Murphy calls technologies of recognition to validate legal claims. T. Murphy, 'Legal Fabrication and the Case of Cultural Property', in A. Pottage and M. Mundy (eds.), *Law, Anthropology and the Constitution of the Social* (Cambridge: Cambridge University Press, 2004).

regulatory governance in advanced capitalist countries. The international state of emergency following the events of 9/11 signals that such a process is occurring within national constitutions where boundaries and borders are being drawn for the differential treatment of individuals. These new boundaries and borders, as argued here, are best cognised as a form of jurisdictional politics: that is, the emergence of a new domain of administrative regulation over those individuals and citizens who are thought to pose a risk to the political order.

But it goes beyond the creation of a new system of regulating international emergencies. New forms of administrative regulation shape what Kimmerling[65] argues the 'very boundaries and meanings of politics'. The emerging jurisdictional politics serves to constitute legal categories of political enemies. In the context of the argument advanced here it is especially important to recognise that these new forms of risk originate outside of the political system and are subsequently given recognition within the legal system. Here, there is shift towards a form of natural law in the international domain through notions such as pre-emptive intervention, as well as within the domestic order through new ideas of political risk. It is these forms of 'moral governance' given recognition through the legal system that may pose the gravest risk to pluralism and contention of liberal politics.

The legal and political debate on emergency laws operates within a 'national container' of constitutional practices. And it is this national territorial framework which is unsettled by the internationalisation of the emergency. It is not only this very 'national container' of constitutional practices that the international state of emergency makes problematic, but also the temporal framework in which legislative and judicial institutions operate. Political leaders such as Blair and Bush have used the argument that the rapid response time needed for response to emergency situations limits the longer time period needed for deliberation by Parliaments.

Even more significantly we see a shift towards a 'risk management' framework that makes notions such as pre-emption – either national or global – an element within risk management systems. For example, control orders that have been used in Australia and the UK are premised not on adjudicating the illegitimate activities of individuals in the past but on managing the future risk that individuals may pose for social order. This internationalisation of the emergency then challenges the temporal

[65] Kimmerling, 'Jurisdiction in an Immigrant Settler Society' at 1119–44.

framework that organises the work of judicial and legislative bodies. As such, this poses the gravest difficulty for both representative politics and notions of the rule of law. However, this is above all a political process; key political actors use these changes to entrench new systems of emergency governance. Nevertheless, these political conflicts take the shape and form of a struggle over legality and it is the unfolding of this legal and political debate that will determine the nature of the emerging jurisdictional regime of emergency powers.

16

Inter arma silent leges? Black hole theories of the laws of war

C.L. LIM

I. Introduction

Let us consider the Gross–Dyzenhaus debate in light of recent controversy over applying the laws of war in the Bush administration's war on terror.[1] David Dyzenhaus argues against having 'black holes', as he calls it, in the law. He criticises Oren Gross,[2] who says that there are certain situations where officialdom may have to step outside the law – such as where an official commits torture under the now-famous 'ticking bomb' scenario. In such cases, the official may later be embraced within the law, through an amnesty, pardon, legislative indemnity and so on.[3] The classic example is the official who might have no choice but to commit torture, even where that violates the law but who leaves her treatment or punishment for society to judge as it sees fit in the aftermath. To be sure, Gross is not saying what, for example, the Bush administration was saying at one point – that officials can torture with legal impunity.[4] To the contrary, Gross argues for his model partly because the law should never create an exception for torture. He argues, counter-intuitively perhaps, that we aid legality – or the law's ability to constrain – by forcing officials to step outside the law.[5]

[1] See D. Dyzenhaus, 'The State of Emergency in Legal Theory' in V.V. Ramraj, M. Hor and K. Roach (eds.), *Global Anti-Terrorism Law and Policy* (Cambridge: Cambridge University Press, 2005), p. 65; O. Gross, 'Stability and Flexibility: A Dicey Business', in Ramraj, Hor and Roach (eds.), *Global Anti-Terrorism Law and Policy*, p. 90.

[2] See, e.g. Dyzenhaus, 'The State of Emergency', in *Global Anti-Terrorism Law and Policy*, p. 65.

[3] See, e.g. Gross, 'Stability and Flexibility', in *Global Anti-Terrorism Law and Policy*, p. 92 for a brief summary of Gross's extra-legal measures model.

[4] Memorandum from J.S. Bybee, Assistant Attorney General, Office of Legal Counsel, to Alberto R. Gonzales, Counsel to the President, (1 August 2002) regarding Standards of Conduct for Interrogation under 18 U.S.C. ss. 2340–2340A ('Bybee Memorandum').

[5] See further, O. Gross, 'Are Torture Warrants Warranted? Pragmatic Absolutism and Official Disobedience' (2004) 88 *Minnesota Law Review* 1481.

Dyzenhaus fears that Gross's extra-legal measures model poses no legal and constitutional constraint upon public officials at all. Once we countenance extra-legal conduct, the law's constraints go straight out the window. Dyzenhaus proposes the need for experimentation with imaginative legal institutions instead for the handling of emergency situations. These institutions would operate within a 'legality model' even where they seek to deal with emergency situations.[6] For him, the 'Legality model ... preserve[s] the assumption of constitutionality in that it insists that the values of the rule of law are not to be compromised'.[7]

Considering the Gross–Dyzenhaus debate in light of recent controversy over the application of the laws of war in the war on terror compels us to reconsider their assumptions about how questions of international legality actually feature in such situations of emergency and to reconsider our broader thoughts about the nature and functions of law in such situations. For example, Gross says that accounting for international legality would influence the conduct of officialdom and this is likely to make officials tailor their actions to the law even where they might feel compelled to step outside domestic legality.[8] On this view, international legality aids domestic legality. Similarly, Dyzenhaus at one juncture ponders international law's absolute prohibition of torture in similar terms.[9] I would like to question this optimistic but unwarranted view about the role which legal rules and standards continue to play in emergencies. I do so by looking at how, at the height of the war on terror, arguing about international humanitarian law became a justification of official atrocity.

II. The 'exceptional' nature of international legal regulation

Using well-known examples from the war on terror, this chapter argues that we need to look more closely at the kinds of controversies that the Dyzenhaus–Gross debate seeks to address – namely, the problem of exceptional legal regulation or the regulation of exceptional situations. We need to look more closely at the kinds of conditions in which a suspension of ordinary legal regulation might occur. Such conditions are not simply empirical – such as the fact that there is a national emergency or that

[6] By 'emergency situation', I take him to mean to include such things as war or other national, civil emergency or indeed some situation of purported military necessity during wartime.
[7] Dyzenhaus, 'The State of Emergency', in *Global Anti-Terrorism Law and Policy*, p. 83.
[8] Gross, 'Stability and Flexibility', in *Global Anti-Terrorism Law and Policy*, p. 104.
[9] Dyzenhaus, 'The State of Emergency', in *Global Anti-Terrorism Law and Policy*, p. 84.

there is in fact a ticking bomb somewhere. They also involve questions of law, albeit of a nature which would infuse social facts with meaning (e.g. whether 'permissible torture' is not, in the end, an oxymoron). Such questions include questions of international legality.

Let us take questions about international legality into the heart of the Gross–Dyzenhaus debate and not treat international legality as something that lies outside of it – to quote Holmes, like some brooding omnipresence in the sky. In short, we would like to see if we can treat international legality in a similar way to how Dyzenhaus and Gross treat domestic legality and how our answers to that question affect our understanding of the debate.

Using the case of terror suspects, I would like to show that neither the extra-legal measures model nor the legality model account for *how we really argue* about international rules, particularly such rules that apply in the kinds of situations which Gross and Dyzenhaus want to talk about. These ways of arguing include the view (1) that applying international law domestically is exceptional, (2) that the laws of war do not apply somehow to terrorists and otherwise non-conventional types of combatants and (3) that applying human rights law in wartime is somehow odd.

I shall focus on the US Supreme Court's ruling in *Hamdan* v. *Rumsfeld*[10] and the Opinion of then Assistant Attorney General Jay S. Bybee.[11] The latter became the United States's policy on torture for two years and sparked controversy when leaked after the events in Abu Ghraib prison. These examples show how the Bush administration had tried to create legal black holes in the laws of war by relying on the three strategies of exclusion mentioned above in the administration's various legal arguments.

III. Hamdan *v.* Rumsfeld

A. The facts

In *Hamdan*, the Supreme Court ruled against the Bush Administration's use of military tribunals for the trial of terror suspects, finding, among other things, that such use violates Common Article 3 of the Geneva Convention.[12] Appellant, Salim Ahmed Hamdan, asserted his rights as an

[10] *Hamdan* v. *Rumsfeld* 548 U.S. (2006); 126 S.Ct. 2749 (2006).

[11] See Bybee Memorandum.

[12] See, e.g. Geneva Convention Relative to the Treatment of Prisoners of War of 12 August 1949, 6 U.S.T. 3316, 75 U.N.T.S. 135. In addition to Common Article 3, which is apparently limited to 'conflicts of a non-international character' (the question here being whether the global war on terrorism is a conflict of a 'non-international character'), there is also

enemy combatant under Article 3 ('non-international armed conflicts'). But the US Court of Appeals ruled that the Geneva Conventions do not apply under US law.[13] Further, even if the Conventions did apply under US law, they might not accord POW rights to members of al Qaeda, which presumably Hamdan, who was Osama bin Laden's driver, was. We will take a brief look at these two issues which reflect three ways by which international legality is commonly swept to the periphery of legal policy and legal-theoretical debate.

B. Applying the Geneva Conventions under US law

One issue that arose in *Hamdan* was whether the Geneva Conventions are binding in domestic law. As the US government had ratified the Geneva Conventions, this question falls to be governed by Chief Justice Marshall's classic ruling in *Foster* v. *Neilson*:[14]

> In the United States... [o]ur Constitution declares a treaty to be the law of the land... equivalent to an act of the legislature, whenever it operates of itself without the aid of any legislative provision. But when the terms of the stipulation import a contract, when either of the parties engages to perform a particular act, the treaty addresses itself to the political, not the judicial department; and the legislature must execute the contract before it can become a rule for the Court.

Do the terms of the Geneva Conventions 'import a contract'? District Judge Robertson had applied Chief Justice Marshall's ruling in support of a finding that the Geneva Conventions are directly applicable in the United States.[15] The D.C. Circuit overruled, but the Supreme Court went on to recognise the applicability of the Geneva Conventions on other grounds. Yet Justice Stevens did so by circumventing a thorny doctrinal issue, ruling that the Uniform Code of Military Justice (hereafter 'UCMJ') incorporates the Geneva Conventions in referring to 'the laws of war'.[16] Among other

the further category of 'protected persons' under Article 4 of the (Fourth) 'Civilians' Convention which affords broad 'catch-all' protection. Article 4 only excludes the nationals of co-belligerents and those of neutrals in their home territory; see Geneva Convention Relative to the Protection of Civilian Persons in Time of War of 12 August 1949, Art. 4, 6 U.S.T. 3517, 3544, 75 U.N.T.S. 287 at 314.

13 344 F. Supp. 2d 152 (D.D.C. 2004), *rev'd*, 415 F.3d 33 (D.C. Cir. 2005).

14 *Foster and Elam* v. *Neilson*, 27 U.S. (2 Pet.) 253 (1829).

15 344 F. Supp. 2d 152 (D.D.C. 2004), *rev'd*, 415 F.3d 33 (D.C. Cir. 2005).

16 U.S. Code, Title 10, c. 47.

things, this raises the question of how far Congressional statute should be interpreted consistently with the Conventions.[17]

I shall not delve into the reasoning of the US Supreme Court beyond that,[18] but will say a little more about Marshall's self-executing treaties doctrine as an illustration of the kinds of doctrinal complexities that are often encountered in dealing with questions of treaty application. The 'default rule' (subject to exceptions) in the Restatement (Third) of Foreign Relations Law appears to be that a treaty is usually considered to be self-executing.[19] This is in a way contrary to the 'default position' which Marshall C.J. took in *Foster*. Subsequent case law has not been much clearer on where the default position lies. Justice Butler in *Asakura* v. *City of Seattle* took the Restatement's default position,[20] but the Fifth Circuit in *U.S.* v. *Postal*[21] and Seventh Circuit in *Frolova* v. *U.S.S.R.* seem to have taken the opposite view – i.e. that the presumption or default rule is against self-executing treaties.[22] Other factors also provide uncertain guidance, such as the importance to be given to the question of whether the treaty provides for private rights. The Second Circuit in *Dreyfus* v. *Fink* seems to have suggested that a private right of action is presumptive evidence of a self-executing treaty.[23] Likewise, with the Southern District of Florida in *U.S.* v. *Noriega*, but there the court also ruled that the Geneva Conventions did not provide for a private right of action.[24] Elsewhere, it has not been so clear that providing for a private right of action is anywhere near conclusive.[25]

So, first, the application of an international legal rule or an international legal treaty right is often treated as something exceptional.

[17] See *The Charming Betsy*, 6 U.S. (2 Cranch.) 64 at 117–18 (1804).

[18] See J. Cerone, 'Status of Detainess in Non-International Armed Conflict and their Protection in the Course of Criminal Proceedings: The Case of *Hamdan* v. *Rumsfeld*' *American Society of International Law Insight* (14 July 2006), online: www.asil.org.

[19] It arguably does so by defining self-executing treaties negatively (i.e. by defining 'non-self-executing' treaties, as opposed to self-executing treaties), see Restatement (Third) of Foreign Relations Law, s. 111(4) (1987).

[20] 265 U.S. 332 (1924).

[21] 589 F.2d 862 (5th Cir. 1979) ('one would expect that in these circumstances the United States would make that intention clear').

[22] 761 F.2d 370 (7th Cir. 1985) ('Treaties . . . if not implemented by appropriate legislation . . . do not provide the basis for a private lawsuit unless they are intended to be self-executing').

[23] 534 F.2d 24, 30 (2d Cir. 1976).

[24] 746 F. Supp. 1506 (S.D. Fla. 1990).

[25] Restatement (Third) of Foreign Relations Law, s. 111(4) (1987) (distinguishing the question from the question of remedies).

C. (Dis-)applying the Geneva Conventions to the Taliban and al Qaeda

Second, the Bush administration also considered that even if the Geneva Conventions were self-executing, they do not grant POW status to the Taliban and al Qaeda.

Some people may consider that this had to do with whether the war against terror was truly a 'war' at all.[26] But this was really a question of US domestic law – whether there may be a need for Congress to declare war under the Constitution's 'Declare War Clause'.[27] The 'war' question is irrelevant under international law, for the following reasons. The Charter outlaws not 'war', but 'the use of force' in Article 2(4) – this is a more capacious concept than war.[28] The Charter permits such use of force only in limited circumstances.[29] Similarly, humanitarian law – e.g. Common Article 2 to the Geneva Conventions – only requires that there be an 'armed conflict' in order to trigger its protection.[30] Moreover, whether a military campaign or armed conflict is justified under the Charter, the *jus in bello* and the Geneva Conventions apply. This includes rules on the way POWs ought to be tried and treated.

The situation today is very different from the past. Previously, protection was confined only to declared wars and so countries simply stopped declaring wars. That created a loophole which the framers of the Geneva Conventions subsequently tried to close. And, today, most of us would like to say that you could hardly imagine a situation where the application of humanitarian law could easily be evaded.

But, according to the Bush administration, fighting terrorism in the twenty-first century somehow still takes us outside the realm of international humanitarian law.[31] This policy had been established by the Reagan

[26] See C.F. Bradley and J.L. Goldsmith, 'Congressional Authorisation and the War on Terrorism' (2005) 118 *Harvard Law Review* 2047.

[27] U.S. Const. Art. I, s. 8 (the 'Declare War Clause').

[28] United Nations Charter, June 26, 1945, 59 Stat. 1031, T.S. No. 993, Art. 2(4).

[29] *Ibid.*, Art. 51 and C. VII.

[30] See, e.g. Geneva Convention Relative to the Treatment of Prisoners of War of 12 August 1949, 6 U.S.T. 3316, 75 U.N.T.S. 135, Art. 2. The relevant clause reads: 'In addition to the provisions which shall be implemented in peacetime, the present Convention shall apply to all cases of declared war or of any other armed conflict which may arise between two or more of the High Contracting Parties, even if the state of war is not recognized by one of them'.

[31] See White House Fact Sheet on Status of Detainees at Guantánamo, Office of the Press Secretary, 7 February 2002. In relation to Common Article 2, the way the Fact Sheet put it was that 'Al-Qaida is not a state party to the Geneva Convention'. The Supreme Court

administration which feared terrorists masquerading as freedom fighters.[32] Thus, when it came to the war on terror, the current Bush administration took the stand that al Qaeda – being a quintessentially terrorist entity – does not satisfy Common Article 2 because that provision only applies to inter-state wars. As for Common Article 3, its reference to 'non-international armed conflicts' does not cover al Qaeda either because the conflict with al Qaeda is 'international' or at least, 'transnational'.[33] Turning to the Taliban, they cross the Article 2 threshold (inter-state war with Afghanistan). However, the Taliban do not satisfy four essential criteria in Article 4.A(2) of the (Third) 'POW' Convention – having a responsible command, having a fixed distinctive sign, carrying arms openly and mounting operations that are conducted in accordance with the laws and customs of war. As a result, or so the administration argued, the Taliban also do not enjoy POW status.[34]

Part of this reasoning depends on saying that if you are going to be treated as a civilian or lawful non-combatant, then you should not act like a combatant and that if you do and you are not part of the military of a state, you would be an unlawful belligerent or illegal combatant. This

in *Hamdan* v. *Rumsfeld* ruled that Common Article 3 of the Geneva Conventions applied nonetheless to such 'conflict[s] not of an international character'; 548 U.S.˙(2006); 126 S.Ct. 2749 (2006). See n.34 below.

32 See President Ronald Reagan, 'Message to the Senate Transmitting a Protocol to the 1949 Geneva Conventions' (29 January 1987), online: Ronald Reagan Presidential Library www.reagan.utexas.edu. Cf. Protocol Additional to the Geneva Conventions of 12 August 1949, and Relating to the Protection of Victims of International Armed Conflicts (Protocol I), 8 June, 1977, Art. 44 and 75, 1125 U.N.T.S. 3 at 7. Part of the criticism of the United States's position has to do with the applicability of Article 75 of Protocol I as a 'catch-all' provision under customary international law; see, e.g. P. Sands, *Lawless World: America and the Making and Breaking of Global Rules* (London: Allen Lane, 2005), p. 150.

33 For the argument that Common Article 3 applies to purely internal conflicts such as civil wars, see, e.g. Senate Committee on the Judiciary, '*Hamdan* v. *Rumsfeld*: Establishing a Constitutional Process', 11 July 2006 (Testimony of Theodore B. Olson). In Mr Olson's words, the recent ruling in *Hamdan* v. *Rumsfeld* 'that Common Article 3 applies to stateless terrorist groups committing sustained international attacks is directly contrary to the official position of the executive branch'. See *Hamdan* v. *Rumsfeld* 548 U.S. (2006); 126 S.Ct. 2749 (2006).

34 Geneva Convention Relative to the Treatment of Prisoners of War, 12 August 1949, 6 U.S.T. 3316, 75 U.N.T.S. 135, Art. 4.A. This presumes that the requirements of Art. 4.A(2) are 'scoped into' Art. 4.A(1). Alternatively, it might be argued that these requirements are (also) part and parcel of customary international law and that as such they apply to, condition and limit the scope of Art. 4.A(1) protection, confining that protection only to such persons who fulfil these requirements. But experts may reasonably disagree about whether it is part of customary international humanitarian law.

final category – of the illegal combatant – is perhaps more a creature of Anglo-American law than one of international humanitarian law.[35]

In sum, the Bush administration argued that fighting al Qaeda and the Taliban falls outside the laws of war. This is the second strategy of exclusion which makes international legality something of an abnormality or curiosity in such debates. At best, international legality is to be considered and then dismissed as if the national authority had all the authority to decide on this question for itself. Part of the problem has to do with the relative absence of formal enforcement mechanisms to compel obedience to international legality as well as the absence of courts of compulsory jurisdiction which may pronounce authoritatively on the law. This absence or lack of centralised courts leads international lawyers to talk about how countries 'auto-interpret' international law. And this is what the Bush administration did. Now to the Bush administration's third exclusionary strategy.

D. Humanitarian law as human rights limitation

1. Historical background

Much of the debate about the treatment of POWs was framed almost exclusively in terms of humanitarian law, seemingly to the exclusion of human rights law. This is not a new problem and it reflects a certain 'legal practitioner viewpoint' about the matter. Going back to the period immediately following World War II, there was some confusion during the drafting of what became the Geneva Conventions about the extent

[35] See further J.C. Yoo, 'The Status of Soldiers and Terrorists under the Geneva Conventions' (2004) *Chinese Journal of International Law* 135 at 137 *et seq.* citing *Ex parte Quirin*, 317 U.S. 1, 30–31 (1942); I. Detter, *The Law of War*, 2nd edn (Cambridge: Cambridge University Press, 2000), p. 148. For a recent restatement of this position, see Senate Committee on the Judiciary, 'Hamdan v. Rumsfeld: Establishing a Constitutional Process', 11 July 2006 (Testimony of Theodore B. Olson). For criticism of this category being unknown to international law, see Sands, *Lawless World*, p. 162, citing an ICRC spokesperson's statement. Likewise, the International Court of Justice, the International Criminal Court and subsequently, the Supreme Court have all rejected the idea that Common Article 3's protection in 'non-international armed conflicts' is limited to non-state combatants who are engaged purely in internal civil war. Instead, the term 'non-international armed conflict' in Common Article 3 extends protection to non-state combatants (i.e. whether they are engaged in a 'domestic' or 'international' conflict). See *Case Concerning Military and Paramilitary Activities in and against Nicaragua* (*Nicaragua v. USA*), 1986 I.C.J. 14 at 25, I.L.M. 1023 at para. 218 (1986); *Prosecutor* v. *Tadic*, Appeal Decision (ICTY, Appeals Chamber, 1995) at para. 67; *Hamdan* v. *Rumsfeld* 548 U.S. (2006); 126 S.Ct. 2749 (2006).

to which international human rights obligations also applied to states in wartime. The problem is historical and conceptual.[36]

I shall do no more than to convey a sense of the historical problem as the subject has been admirably treated elsewhere. Following World War II, war crimes were a feature of the Nuremberg and Tokyo trials, but to extend criminalisation to what the Nazis did outside the actual incidents of inter-state armed conflict, a new category of 'crimes against humanity' was created. This new crime applied to conduct outside the battlefield but which were nonetheless linked to the war itself or at least to the causes of the war.[37] It became a kind of 'half-way house', as Professor Geoffrey Best has described it,[38] between war crimes and human rights violations.

Human rights law was only in its infancy in the 1940s. It was not until 1951 that the first international human rights treaty was finalised and that was confined to the countries of the Council of Europe.[39] In legal theory, the argument was only beginning to take root that international law was a little more than the law which lays down rights and obligations between states, but that it also placed legal obligations on states in respect of the treatment of natural persons. Scholars such as Sir Hersch Lauterpacht were at the forefront of the theories required to make these new legal ideas a part of mainstream international legal thought.[40]

Having said all that, no one seriously questioned that the Geneva Conventions enforced international human rights. But an attempt to make that more explicit in the Conventions failed. The International Committee of the Red Cross (ICRC) had proposed such explicit language to the (Fourth) 'Civilians' Convention[41] but discussions on including such

[36] For the historical part, see Geoffrey Best, *War and Law Since 1945* (Oxford: Clarendon, 1994), p. 67.

[37] For the Bernays Plan, see, e.g. B.F. Smith, *The Road to Nuremberg* (NY: Basic Books, 1981), pp. 48–74. But the tribunal at Nuremberg chose to ignore the Charter's inclusion of acts committed before the war. See Charter annexed to the Four Power Agreement, 8 August 1945; H. Lauterpacht, *International Law and Human Rights* (London: Stevens, 1950), p. 36.

[38] Geoffrey Best, *War and Law*, p. 67.

[39] Convention for the Protection of Human Rights and Fundamental Freedoms, 4 November 1950, 213 U.N.T.S. 222, as amended by Protocols Nos. 3, 5, 8, and 11 (hereafter, 'European Convention').

[40] So far as Lauterpacht was concerned: 'The Charter of the United Nations is a legal document; its language is the language of law, of international law . . . It would therefore appear that to the extent to which the Charter incorporates obligations to respect the fundamental human rights and freedoms it amounts to recognition of individuals as subjects of international law'; Lauterpacht, *International Law and Human Rights*, pp. 34–45.

[41] J. Pictet (ed.), *Commentary on the Geneva Conventions of 12 August 1949* (Geneva: ICRC, 1952), vol. I., p. 20.

language ran aground during the negotiations, leading to the entire removal of the ICRC proposed language.[42]

2. The Bush administration's theory

So, to be fair, the Bush administration was not alone in saying that once humanitarian law was shown not to apply to Taliban and al Qaeda suspects held by the United States, other human rights guarantees would also not apply.[43] The whole debate was also framed almost exclusively in terms of the laws of war, specifically humanitarian law. Viewing the whole matter in terms of the application of the United States's own standards as opposed to international human rights standards is also not that difficult to comprehend. As Professor Louis Henkin has pointed out, in America, 'human rights' are typically viewed to be 'for export only'.[44]

Yet such 'human rights exceptionalism' meant also that once it can be shown that the US Constitution does not apply in Guantánamo,[45] the Geneva Conventions do not apply either; the question concerning the treatment of these suspects falls, therefore, into a kind of black hole of international legality.[46] Notwithstanding that, as far as the Bush administration was concerned, the UCMJ did apply[47] and its guarantees are similar to those to be found in the Geneva Conventions.[48] The effect was

[42] Best, *War and Law*, pp. 70–1. There was also apprehension, as Best explains, on the part of the ICRC in getting caught up in the political controversy in the United Nations regarding 'human rights'.

[43] See H. Krieger, 'A Conflict of Norms: The Relationship between Humanitarian Law and Human Rights Law in the ICRC Customary Law Study' (2006) 11 *Journal of Conflict & Security Law* 265.

[44] L. Henkin, *The Age of Rights* (New York: Columbia University Press, 1990), pp. 74–7.

[45] Cf. *Sale* v. *Haitian Centers Council*, 509 U.S. 155 (1993); cf. T. Meron, 'Extraterritorial Violation of Human Rights by the U.S.' (1994) 9 *American University Journal of International Law and Policy* 213; T. Buergenthal, 'To Respect and Ensure: State Obligations and Permissible Derogations' in L. Henkin (ed.), *The International Bill of Rights: The Covenant on Civil and Political Rights* (New York: Columbia University Press, 1981), pp. 73–7.

[46] Brief for the Respondents in *Rasul et al.* v. *George Bush et al.* and *Al Odah et al.* v. *George Bush et al.* (Nos. 03–334 and 03–343) (Sup. Ct. October 2003).

[47] U.S. Code, Title 10, c. 47.

[48] White House Fact Sheet on Status of Detainees at Guantánamo, Office of the Press Secretary, 7 February 2002. As the Fact Sheet puts it: The detainees will receive much of the treatment normally afforded to POWs by the Third Geneva Convention. 'However, the detainees will not receive some of the specific privileges afforded to POWs, including . . . access to a canteen to purchase food, soap, and tobacco . . . a monthly advance of pay . . . the ability to have and consult personal financial accounts . . . the ability to receive scientific equipment, musical instruments, or sports outfits'.

nonetheless to turn the whole matter into a domestic issue for the United States and this is what concerned even America's friends abroad.

The United States was also not alone in taking the position that where the laws of war apply but do not protect, human rights treaties cannot help where what occurs takes place outside the territories of the country against which the human rights obligation is sought to be placed. The European Court of Human Rights took the same position in the *Bankovic* ruling even if it did not necessarily equate 'jurisdiction' with 'territory'.[49]

Finally, some experts agree that, as a matter of abstract legal principle, human rights law does not always apply where humanitarian law leaves a void. But others would say that human rights law would apply by default in such a case. Yet others say this would be true only where there is no conflict between humanitarian law and human rights law in the first place. There is also the view that there can never be a conflict because humanitarian law is only a more specific form of human rights law.[50] These abstract theories notwithstanding, the fact that humanitarian law was originally meant to have a limited scope of application – namely, where a war or more broadly, an armed conflict occurs – while human rights was meant to apply more widely in peacetime, cannot ignore some important developments in the late twentieth century. In a world where inter-state war had become illegal, low-intensity conflicts and state-sponsored terrorism took over.[51] Post-war humanitarian lawyers who were prescient enough to realise this latest guise which 'war' now took in the era of Cold War conflicts, began to look for ways by which humanitarian law and indeed human rights law too, might be applied to such situations.

It was in that context that the Reagan administration rejected such supplementation of the Geneva Conventions as would (or should) afford legal protection to freedom fighters or terrorists. And it was against this background that the reflex action of the lawyers for the Bush administration was to reject the application of POW protection to al Qaeda and Taliban prisoners. They argued that the law of armed conflict applied to the

[49] (2002) 11 *Butterworths Human Rights Cases* 439. For commentary, see C. Greenwood, 'The Applicability of International Humanitarian Law and the Law of Neutrality to the Kosovo Campaign' (2002) 31 *Israel Yearbook on Human Rights* 111 at 141–3.

[50] For these and other views, see, e.g. Krieger, 'A Conflict of Norms', generally.

[51] See C.L. Lim, 'The Question of a Generic Definition of Terrorism under General International Law', in V.V. Ramraj, M. Hor and K. Roach (eds.), *Global Anti-Terrorism Law and Policy* (Cambridge: Cambridge University Press, 2005), pp. 37 and 38–40.

exclusion of international human rights law,[52] but that the law of armed conflict did not protect such persons. As for the al Qaeda–Taliban link, this was supported by another theory – namely, that the international law rules of state responsibility would make the Taliban (insofar as it was the government of Afghanistan) responsible for the terrorist actions of al Qaeda – this is the now newly emergent rule against harbouring terrorists.[53]

IV. The Bybee Memo and international law exceptionalism

Yet even if all these theories of the Bush administration were accepted (and the US Supreme Court did not accept them), we might think that torture presents an entirely different set of considerations. The degree of overlap between international human rights and humanitarian law may be small in the ultimate analysis – extending only to a shortlist of 'the right to life, the right not to be tortured or otherwise inhumanely treated, the right to trial before sentence, and the right not to be punished for what was not an offence at the time of commission'[54] – but one issue on which such overlap is clearly conceded is torture. Talking about torture, therefore, yields important insights about the limitations of the strategies discussed above. It does so because it is absolutely prohibited internationally.[55]

The Bybee Memo had sought to legalise torture in the war on terror. The Memo was subsequently withdrawn but it remains instructive.[56] It performed all three doctrinal moves above which had led to *Hamdan*. First, that international law does not always apply in domestic law or an even more extreme version of this – that the permissibility of an official act under domestic law is conclusive. Second, that humanitarian law which prohibits the torture and ill treatment of POWs does not protect al Qaeda

[52] Response of the United States of America dated 21 October 2005 to Inquiry of the UNCHR Special Rapporteurs dated 8 August 2005 Pertaining to Detainees at Guantánamo Bay, online: American Society International Law www.asil.org.

[53] See R. Wedgwood, 'The Fall of Saddam Hussein: Security Council Mandates and Preemptive Self-Defense' (2003) 97 *American Journal of International Law* 576.

[54] Geoffrey Best, *War and Law*, p. 69.

[55] Convention against Torture and Other Cruel, Inhuman or Degrading Treatment or Punishment. Adopted; United Nations General Assembly resolution 39/46 of 10 December 1984, U.N. Doc. A/Res/39/46, Art. 2(2) (hereafter, 'Torture Convention'). See also, the International Covenant on Civil and Political Rights, 16 December 1966, S. Treaty Doc. No. 95-2, 999 U.N.T.S. 171, Art. 4(2), 7.

[56] I have benefited greatly from H.H. Koh, 'Can the President be Torturer in Chief?' online: Indiana School of Law www.law.indiana.edu.

and Taliban suspects.[57] Third, that international human rights law does not apply to the torture (in the international sense) of terror suspects. There was also a fourth argument. While torture is a crime under US federal law,[58] human rights law obligations undertaken by the United States, including the Administration's zero tolerance to torture policy, do not apply outside the territories of the United States.[59] This 'extra-territoriality' argument has since been precluded by the 2005 McCain Amendment.[60]

It is against this background that the Bybee Memo has been fiercely criticised. What the Memo says is that officials who commit what is tantamount to torture in the international sense should not be legally accountable. Protest followed its leakage in the aftermath of the revelations of widespread torture in Abu Ghraib prison. According to the Bybee Memo, many such acts of torture would be permissible where the President and lower-level officials act under the President's Commander-in-Chief authority under the US Constitution. The significance of the Commander-in-Chief argument is that it seeks to preclude Congress ever

57 See Bybee Memo at 14 and 16–18 ('Congress enacted the criminal prohibition against torture to implement CAT'; 'Executive branch interpretation of the treaty supports our conclusion that the treaty, and thus Section 2340A, prohibits only the most extreme forms of physical or mental harm'; the 'Executive's interpretation is to be accorded the greatest weight in ascertaining a treaty's intent and meaning'; 'the Bush administration submitted the following understanding'; 'The Senate ratified CAT with this understanding'). Essentially, these show that international treaty law as it applies in the United States is to be applied according to the understanding of the Executive Branch. There is nothing inherently wrong with this view, bearing in mind it has to do, simply, with the reception of international law into domestic law or how the United States views its obligations under the treaty. That it may be entirely wrong about the United States's true treaty obligations is another matter altogether. But *contra* Sands, *Lawless World*, pp. 212–3. As for the second strategy, this is accomplished somewhat differently in two further moves. First, according to the Bybee Memo, 'application of Section 2340A to interrogations undertaken pursuant to the President's Commander-in-Chief powers may be unconstitutional' and that '[f]inally, even if an interrogation method might violate Section 2340A, necessity or self defence could provide justifications that would eliminate any criminal liability', *ibid.* at 46. Second, the prior decision to use Guantánamo was meant precisely to circumvent access to the US federal courts, following *Johnson* v. *Eisentrager* 339 U.S. 763 (1950). This strategy failed; *Rasul et al.* v. *Bush et al.* 542 U.S. 466 (2004). However, the strategy also seems to have been intended to circumvent the United States's obligation to ensure the observance of human rights within its territories, following *Sale* v. *Haitian Centers Council*, 509 U.S. 155 (1993). But see 'U.N: States Must Respect Rights in Territory They Control: U.S. Cannot Deny Rights Protection to Detainees at Guantanamo', online: Human Rights Watch www.hrw.org (citing the Human Rights Committee).

58 18 U.S.C. ss. 2340–2340A (2000).

59 This tracks the ruling in *Sale* v. *Haitian Centers Council*, 509 U.S. 155 (1993). See above n. 45.

60 'McCain Amendment' to Defense Appropriations Act. H.R. 2863 ss. 1002–3.

second-guessing the President and creates a blank cheque for the executive. Suffice to say that the US Constitution would have to trump the US's international law obligations for what the Memo says here to be meaningful.

V. The sphere of international legality

There are a number of ways in which international law enters into the picture here. For example, the 'superior orders' defence is unavailable under international criminal law. It has been unavailable since Nuremberg[61] and the preclusion of such a defence is now recognised in the Rome Statute of the International Criminal Court.[62] The United States is not party to the Rome Convention, but nonetheless remains subject to the Court's jurisdiction in cases where torture is committed in the territory of a state which is party to the Convention.[63] This somewhat undermines the impression that auto-interpretation or national legal policies (be they judicial, legislative or executive) are sufficiently determinative, which they are not.

But more importantly, international law defines torture more widely and makes its prohibition absolute.[64] So the argument that the prohibition ought not to be absolute either assumes the absolute international prohibition of torture to be irrelevant or calls for international law reform. Even the US federal courts have not gone that far. In *Committee on U.S. Citizens* v. *Reagan*, Circuit Judge Abner Mikva put the international prohibition of torture on the same plane as the Constitution and suggested its enforceability by US courts.[65] Likewise, violation of the international prohibition of torture is, in the eyes of the majority of the US Supreme Court, actionable under the Alien Tort Claims Act.[66] So this tracks Gross's point that even if the official can get away from criminal punishment, that

[61] Report of the International Law Commission to the General Assembly on the Principles of International Law Recognised in the Charter of the Nuremberg Tribunal and in the Judgment of the Tribunal, 5 U.N. GAOR, Supp. No. 12, at 11–14, U.N. Doc. A/1316 (1950), Principle IV.

[62] Rome Statute of the International Criminal Court, U.N. Doc. A/CONF.183/9, 17 July 1998, Art. 33. The Rome Statute is nuanced in this regard; cf. Statute of the International Tribunal Art. 7(4), 25 May 1993, 32 I.L.M. 1192 at 1194 (1993).

[63] See Rome Statute of the International Criminal Court, Art. 12.

[64] Convention against Torture and Other Cruel, Inhuman or Degrading Treatment or Punishment. Adopted; United Nations General Assembly resolution 39/46 of 10 December 1984, U.N. Doc. A/Res/39/46, Art. 2(2).

[65] 542 U.S. 692 (2004) at 725.

[66] *Rasul et al.* v. *Bush et al.* 542 U.S. 466 (2004).

official may not get away from a private suit. As is patently the intent of the alien tort statute, it extends to those tortured outside the territories of the United States – e.g. in Guantánamo.

VI. A textured view of international legality

I now want to introduce the picture of international legality which both Dyzenhaus and Gross share, and which, I argue, needs to be modified. According to the Gross–Dyzenhaus view, the absolute international prohibition of torture should be taken as precisely that – an absolute and unchanging international perception of unacceptable conduct. This is accurate enough as it stands. If there is anything which testifies to this common assumption of humanity, it is the twentieth-century emergence and growth of an international human rights movement.[67] For international humanitarian law too, the idea that combatants should not be caused unnecessary suffering and that civilians should not be harmed has had an even longer provenance. As far as torture is concerned, human rights and humanitarian law converge.[68] For international law to now subject this to exception is almost unthinkable. But it misdescribes what actually occurs in practice – not just that virtually all states commit torture, but that some attempt to justify their conduct in distinctly *legal* terms.

Gross and Dyzenhaus recognise the complex answers which the Common Law conception of the rule of law would be called upon to provide in true emergencies. But, strangely, they appear to hold a more sanguine view of international legality. International law prohibits torture, Gross says. He says that this fact tends to support his extra-legal measures model because the *very existence* of international standards makes their violation more risky and therefore less likely to happen but for the most extreme cases where violation might be the outcome only of carefully deliberated choice.

[67] For the history of Amnesty International, for example, see J. Power, *Like Water on Stone: The Story of Amnesty International* (London: Allen Lane, 2001).

[68] See, e.g. the Rome Statute of the International Criminal Court, U.N. Doc. A/CONF.183/9, 17 July 1998, Art. 7(1)(f) which lists torture as a crime against humanity. This mirrors Art. 5(f) for example of the earlier Statute of the International Criminal Tribunal for the Former Yugoslavia; Statute of the International Tribunal Art. 7(4), 25 May 1993, 32 I.L.M. 1192 at 1194 (1993). The difference is that by the time of the Rome Statute, 'peacetime torture' (i.e. absent a nexus with armed conflict) had clearly been accepted as a crime against humanity; see further, Lim, 'Towards a Generic Definition', 55–6.

International law *should* cause the domestic official to track domestic legalities more closely while tracking international law.[69] Painful as it might be to say this, it is not what tends to happen. Similarly, it may be insufficient for Dyzenhaus to suggest that defences to torture tend to be couched as excuses and not justifications – and that torture is basically 'unlegalisable'.[70] The problem lies in their picture of international legality and the following discussion will address four rough ways by which international legality is commonly perceived – flatly rejecting or including international legality and either including or excluding international legality based on a case by case or textured view of the application of international law.

Gross says the international prohibition of torture will generate greater risks for domestic officials and confine their acts to truly extraordinary situations. Yet the Bush administration took a more 'textured', creative and doctrinally *contested* view of international legality. Unlike Dyzenhaus's and Gross's 'flat inclusionary' view of international legality, the Bush administration tried to 'legalise' torture.[71]

Let us also put aside the 'flat exclusionary' argument that torture is not (absolutely) prohibited because one would be hard placed to find this argument actually made. A country or government which takes such an outright exceptionalist view – i.e. a state committed to an open policy of torture – does not exist to the best of my knowledge. Instead, rights violators would typically be expected to deny that torture occurs at all, or more plausibly, although often just as incredibly, to deny official knowledge while admitting that torture by officials could possibly have taken place. These cases are different from the case where the prohibition of torture is rejected outright.[72] The closest example we come to involves the case where extreme forms of punishment or extreme practices may be defended on cultural or religious grounds, but only because they are seen to fall outside the meaning of 'torture' in the first place.[73] This really amounts

[69] See, e.g. Gross, 'Stability and Flexibility', in *Global Anti-Terrorism Law and Policy*, p. 104.

[70] Dyzenhaus, 'The State of Emergency', in *Global Anti-Terrorism Law and Policy*, pp. 84 and 87.

[71] For Dyzenhaus's attempt to reduce this to a legal-doctrinal problem, namely a problem with our doctrines on the domestic application of international law, see D. Dyzenhaus, *The Constitution of Law: Legality in Time of Emergency* (Cambridge: Cambridge University Press, 2006), pp. 190–6.

[72] For a fascinating discussion, see 'The Authority of the United States Executive to Interpret, Articulate or Violate the Norms of International Law' (1986) 80 *American Society of International Law Proceedings* 297, generally.

[73] At the very least it amounts to saying this: 'We don't have to say explicitly that we're in favour of torture. It would not surprise me very much if some administration said: "We do

to the textured (i.e. doctrinally contested and creative) exclusion model, not a flat exclusion model. It is more akin to the Bush Administration's arguments.

Liberal international legal theory postulates a further 'textured inclusionary' model of international legality. International law would be internalised and debated in terms which reflect the substance or strength of the domestic government of individual nations. According to this view, liberal democracies are more likely to internalise international law successfully. This is what a 'textured inclusionist' model of international legality would suggest.[74] At its most extreme, liberal conceptions of international legality become difficult to distinguish from international legality itself.[75] This is not a flat view of international legality – it does not treat international legality as a constant and uniform presence. But it is a controversial view and for good reason. Dyzenhaus, for example, recognises the complexity of the issue – namely, the aspiration to universal legality and the rule of law. He criticises Gross for having wedded himself so closely to a Diceyan model that both Gross and Dicey ultimately appeal to 'substance' not 'law'. This is done, according to Dyzenhaus, 'through the claim that the Extra-Legal Measures Model has a legitimate place if, and only if, as [Gross] says, the community is "worth saving"; a "despotic, authoritarian, and oppressive society is not worth the effort"'.[76] Gross retorts that such a community (i.e. one that is 'worth saving') is 'a condition that ought to underlie any meaningful discussion of emergency powers'.[77]

But that is not how international law works. It is difficult to see how what Gross is saying here is different, for example, from saying that some people might ultimately have the moral authority to torture, but others do not. In saying this, he goes beyond the argument that international law scholarship sometimes embodies a 'fake notion of tolerance' – i.e. that international law is too malleable.[78] At least that viewpoint recognises the complexity of international legality's aim to universal application.[79] What

not accept the notion that there are any human rights unless we have agreed to them by covenant."' *Ibid.*, at 11 (Professor Louis Henkin).

[74] See, e.g. K.W. Abbott, 'International Relations Theory, International Law and the Regime Governing Atrocities in Internal Conflicts' (1999) 93 *American Journal of International Law* 361, for a survey of 'liberal' and other theories of international law.

[75] For such an extreme view, see F.R. Téson, 'International Law', in P. Cane and M. Tushnet (eds.), *The Oxford Handbook of Legal Studies* (Oxford: Oxford University Press, 2003), p. 941.

[76] Dyzenhaus, 'The State of Emergency', in *Global Anti-Terrorism Law and Policy*, p. 71.

[77] Gross, 'Stability and Flexibility', *Global Anti-Terrorism Law and Policy*, p. 106.

[78] See Téson, 'International Law', 947. [79] *Ibid.*, at 946.

Gross seems to be saying turns that on its head – instead of saying torture is unacceptable anywhere, he says torture is acceptable depending on where and who you are (i.e. whether you are a liberal-democratic society). Unless we take the view that liberal democracies tend, by definition, to be true observers of international law or that what is true of liberal democracy is true for international legality, we should take international law more seriously.

So these are some of the difficulties with the flat inclusionary and exclusionary as well as textured inclusionary viewpoints. Let us now turn to a fourth conception – a textured conception of international legality, which might perhaps be described in conventional jurisprudential terms. Consider that H.L.A. Hart criticised the social-scientific insufficiency of having a mere 'external viewpoint' of the law. He argued that a 'critical reflective' viewpoint or recognition of the 'internal aspect of rules' provides a better account of social reality and, crucially, of the idea of having a legal obligation.[80] Contemporary analytical jurisprudence – Dworkinian jurisprudence, to use Dyzenhaus's example – criticises the insufficiency of Hart's viewpoint. Specifically, that neither we nor legal officials would always tend to ascribe the same meaning to what we would call 'the law'. What Hart called the 'internal viewpoint' consists instead of attempts to interpret the law creatively and to contest the law since people talk about the law and legality in different ways and they use different senses of these words.[81] Thinking about international legality in this way also allows us to understand why states tend to contest international legality in preference to admitting international illegality and indeed why many international legal standards are still withheld by states from the compulsory jurisdiction and final adjudicatory authority of international tribunals.

VII. Revisiting the Gross–Dyzenhaus debate

Let us simply concede that it would be better or more accurate to view international legality this way. Oren Gross's official would now have to calculate the odds of whether she might ultimately prevail with an argument not unlike some of the Bush administration's arguments. Our official will

[80] H.L.A. Hart, *The Concept of Law* (Oxford: Clarendon, 1961), p. 86.

[81] See, e.g. R. Dworkin, 'Legal Theory and the Problem of Sense', in R. Gavison (ed.), *Issues in Contemporary Legal Philosophy: The Influence of H.L.A. Hart* (Oxford: Clarendon, 1987), p. 9.

try to develop powerful legal arguments in favour of the conduct which she supports. The aim of these arguments would be to persuade international opinion. International law is only a tool, albeit an important one, in this regard. But our Grossian official takes the risk that her arguments about international legality might fail.

This, more nuanced, picture of the rule of law would tend to affect not just the official's arguments about international legality, but also her arguments about domestic law. For example, our official might be expected to factor in the likelihood of affecting the domestic interpretation of laws through imaginative ways of arguing about international legality. Returning to the example of the war on terror, the State Department led by Secretary of State Colin Powell and the legal secretary, Mr William Howard Taft IV, were in deep disagreement with the Justice and the Defence Departments' view about placing al Qaeda and Taliban suspects under the protection of the POW Convention.[82] This is not difficult to comprehend. The State Department, unlike Justice, has to deal with what other governments think. Similarly, senior military officers know the risks of undermining humanitarian law protections.[83]

All this would at least suggest that the risks to officials who choose to act on the basis of the extra-legal measures model are different depending on whether you are talking about the domestic or the international legal order. The risks domestically may not be so great if one could get away with a technical court room argument, or failing that, appeal to national sentiment. They seem greater on the international plane, where influencing public international opinion is the principal aim and one would be better advised to admit international illegality even, indeed especially, if a domestic official had acted extra-legally under domestic law. The reason for this difference is because the value judgments required of an *ex post facto* ratification of official 'illegal' action will, on the international plane, tend to be informed by values that are not purely within the determination of the legal society or culture in question. Some values, including universal values like the absolute international prohibition of torture, should not be subject to a domestic torture warrant system or *ex ante* institutionally imaginative exception not simply because of the risk of abuse, but also because the *individual* society or legal system may not have the moral and legal authority *internationally* to justify or excuse the individual. This in

[82] For a summary account of these events, see e.g. Sands, *Lawless World*, pp. 154–5.

[83] T. Golden, 'After Terror, a Secret Rewriting of Military Law' *New York Times* (24 October 2004).

fact is one way for Gross to resolve a fundamental tension between his extra-legal measures model which he says is available to liberal democratic societies and his flat view of international legality. Yet flat legality is not the answer – it is a cheat.

Ex post ratification would fare no better, complicated by the need to obtain not only national but also international approval. In those cases where international approval must still be sought, the tendency, as we have seen, is not always to argue internationally as one would nationally. The tendency in anticipation of being charged with an international law violation is to tailor one's arguments within a legality model. One reason is that international law advisers know that even liberal democratic societies are not usually perceived to have sufficient moral resources to argue that they should somehow be exempted from the torture prohibition. So they often search out legal-doctrinal exceptions. They do not usually resort to extra-legal arguments.[84]

What about Dyzenhaus's legality model when viewed through the lenses of textured international legality? Dyzenhaus puts his faith in *ex ante* legislative institutional experimentation during periods of crisis – he gives the example of the United Kingdom Special Immigration Appeals Commission.[85] This at least has the trappings of legality. Yet it is not clear how far that would get you internationally for the same reasons given above. For torture, I suspect that the answer is 'not at all'. Dyzenhaus needs to account more closely for this difference between experimentation under domestic law and under international law.[86]

[84] Cf. Oren Gross's remarks in 'Extra-Legality and the Ethic of Political Responsibility' (Chapter 3), this volume, pp. 75 and 90. The closest case in which, for example, the International Court of Justice has come to a consideration of extra-legal measures is perhaps its highly controversial Advisory Opinion on the *Legality of the Threat or Use of Nuclear Weapons*, (1996) I.C.J. 226. In paragraph 2E of the operative part of the Opinion, the Court ruled (7:7, with the President's casting vote), that: '[I]n view of the current state of international law . . . the Court cannot conclude definitively whether the threat or use of nuclear weapons would be lawful or unlawful in an extreme circumstance of self-defence, in which the very survival of a State would be at stake'. This example comes closest perhaps to our 'ticking bomb' scenario. This finding of a *non liquet* was fiercely criticised in the dissent of the current President of the Court, Dame Rosalyn Higgins. Yet even the existence of a *non liquet*, assuming such a thing is possible in legal theory, is different from saying that one can act extra-legally.

[85] Dyzenhaus, 'The State of Emergency', in *Global Anti-Terrorism Law and Policy*, p. 87.

[86] He probably needs to do more than that if he is also to account for the distinction we have hinted at between curtailments in due process guarantees and allowing torture. I shall say no more of this for now because the foil I have used here, which is his earlier paper against Oren Gross, does not focus on the example of torture.

VIII. Conclusion

The official charged with explaining the policies of her nation – say where a national indemnity is available – is not usually a heroic sort. She does not usually admit that her country is acting extra-legally. 'War' itself 'has become a legal institution'[87] and thus wartime measures are also typically sought to be *justified* in legal terms. This is what observation of actual international law advisory practice teaches us. Official heroism, a strong *motif* in Oren Gross's account, is not only likely to be rare, it lacks feasibility as a strategy of international legal argumentation.

To complicate things, the violating official and the official called upon to explain a nationally authorised indemnity internationally would also tend to be different people. Depending on their functions, they would view international legality differently. The interaction between the positions of these different officials is also likely to be complex in practice.[88] Because the State Department probably knew how hard it would be to make the argument internationally, leaving aside the practical wisdom of the policy, it resisted the position taken by Justice and Defence.

Nations are not in the habit of asking to be excused for torture either. They know they have a slim chance of succeeding if they do. No one tried to justify the wicked events in Abu Ghraib. Yet if they did try, they could hardly be expected to argue that it was justified extra-legal conduct, *even if* domestically there might be an attempt to deny, excuse or justify what happened.[89] Trying to justify or excuse torture on the international plane is more hazardous than trying to do so domestically, be it for a

[87] See D. Kennedy, *Of War and Law* (Princeton: Princeton University Press, 2006).

[88] Added to that complexity is that not only different branches of the Executive, but different institutions (e.g. the judiciary, the legislature and the executive) might have different legal views. In *Hamdan*, the Supreme Court sided with a beleaguered State Department and some senior military figures, as well as what it considered Congress's view to be – indeed the ruling can be read simply as requiring these views to be taken into account more fully – while the minority read Congress the other way and sided with the Justice and Defence Departments and the President; see N.K. Katyal, '*Hamdan* v. *Rumsfeld*: The Legal Academy Goes to Practice' (2006) 120 *Harvard Law Review* 65 at 105–12. Following *Hamdan*, the Executive branch, taking its cue from the Court (which had ruled on the relevance of the treaty on the grounds of the wording of a Congressional statute) took the matter back to Congress for a redraft, *Ibid.*, at 113–16; J. Cerone, 'The Military Commissions Act of 2006: Examining the Relationship between the International Law of Armed Conflict and U.S. Law', *American Society of International Law Insight* (13 November 2006), online: www.asil.org.

[89] Justification or excuse in such circumstances would include official inaction on individual accountability; see Op-Ed, 'No Accountability on Abu Ghraib' *New York Times* (10 September 2004).

liberal democracy or even for what David Dyzenhaus calls a 'well-ordered' society. '[F]lying below the radar' as Oren Gross calls it – e.g. distinguishing creatively between lesser conduct and the threshold set by international law for what amounts to torture – is therefore more interesting than Gross would admit.[90] States generally try to fall within some suitable legal exception,[91] not label their conduct exceptional.[92] Talking about whether a form of conduct amounts to torture or to the lesser analogues of cruel, inhuman or degrading treatment or punishment[93] is therefore more fundamental to his position than it might at first appear. This is because no one says or should be able to get away with saying internationally: 'Well, I come from a good society, so we get to torture'.[94]

Having rejected the flat exclusionary view, we should also reject a mannequin-like version of international legality that takes conformity to international legality for granted – i.e. the flat inclusionary view. It is not that Dyzenhaus and Gross do not recognise that states engage in legal interpretative dispute when seeking to escape international legality. Dyzenhaus, however, would reduce this problem to a problem about legal doctrine; namely, our doctrines on the domestic application of international law.[95] Gross likewise discusses the interpretative 'moves' that

[90] See *Tyrer* v. *United Kingdom*, Judgment of 25 April 1978, (No. 26) 2 E.H.R.R. 1.

[91] Clearly, some kinds of legal exception tend to be more suitable than others, depending on the circumstances. For example, you can be creative about the territorial scope of treaties and try to create a legal black hole in Guantánamo, but once the truth breaks out, you are only remotely likely to succeed, if at all, by arguing that the conduct called into question does not amount to torture. The constraints here have to do with the force of events, not legal arguments.

[92] Not least because the torture prohibition is non-derogable both under international humanitarian and human rights law. But non-derogability does not mean 'unlegalisability' to borrow Dyzenhaus's language. Saying that international humanitarian law applies but does not protect and that human rights law cannot apply in its place is not strictly the same thing as saying that the torture prohibition is derogable.

[93] The European Convention does not use the term 'cruel', a term which is found however in the Torture Convention, for example; Art. 16.

[94] Strategically too, once we accept the view that countries do try and justify their conduct in legal terms, we understand that this sort of bare political argument is fraught with difficulty. Britain did not try and defend Sir Arthur 'Bomber' Harris's wartime actions in such manner despite Britain's mortal peril. For as Churchill himself recognised by March of 1945: 'The destruction of Dresden remains a serious query against the conduct of Allied bombing. I am of the opinion that military objectives must henceforward be more strictly studied in our own interests rather than that of the enemy'; Prime Minister's Personal Telegram, 28 March 1945, Serial No. D. 83/5 (on file). The telegram was redrafted, omitting these reasons and dispatched as Prime Minister's Personal Minute, 1 April 1945, Serial No. D 89/5 (on file). Both are online: The National Archives Learning Curve www.learningcurve.gov.uk.

[95] See, e.g. Dyzenhaus, *The Constitution of Law*, pp. 190–6.

state officials make when claiming a right to derogate from international human rights standards in times of emergency, but his discussion is confined to derogable rights.[96] As we have seen, his discussion of absolute non-derogable rights such as torture, for example, takes a different turn and treats non-derogability, what Dyzenhaus calls 'unlegalisibility' at face value. This lacks legal realism and allows the doctrinal distinction between derogability and non-derogability too much control over what and how we think about emergency legality.

Taking a textured view of international legality should cause us to think about domestic legality differently. We do so by accepting, first, the pervasiveness of international law talk – i.e. as a real part of how we actually argue about emergency legislation, emergency action and official conduct in times of war or other emergency. We should also recognise that state officials often resort to such talk as part of an attempt to justify state conduct and therefore that arguments about emergency legality tend to become bound up with legal strategic considerations. Our normative theories about law in times of crisis must reflect this, more complex, understanding of international legality – an understanding which should be rigorous and realistic, not platitudinal.

[96] See, e.g., O. Gross and F. Ní Aoláin, *Law in Times of Crisis: Emergency Powers in Theory and Practice* (Cambridge: Cambridge University Press, 2006), pp. 257–324.

INDEX